SPC for the Rest of Us

SPC for the Rest of Us

A Personal Path to Statistical Process Control

Hy Pitt

ADDISON-WESLEY PUBLISHING COMPANY, INC.

Reading, Massachusetts • Menlo Park, California • New York
Don Mills, Ontario • Wokingham, England • Amsterdam • Bonn
Sydney • Singapore • Tokyo • Madrid • San Juan
Paris • Seoul • Milan • Mexico City • Taipei

The publisher offers discounts on this book when ordered in quantity for special sales. For more information please contact:

Corporate & Professional Publishing Group
Addison-Wesley Publishing Company
One Jacob Way
Reading, Massachusetts 01867

Library of Congress Cataloging-in-Publication Data

Pitt, Hy.
    SPC for the rest of us : a personal path to statistical process control / Hy Pitt.
        p.   cm.
    Includes bibliographical references and index.
    ISBN 0-201-56366-5
    1. Process control—Statistical methods.   2. Quality control—Statistical methods.   I. Title.
TS156.8.P49   1994
658.5′62′015195—dc20   93-8311
                                                                CIP

Cover design by Simone R. Payment
Cover photo by Alain Choisnet, The Image Bank
Text design by Wilson Graphics & Design (Kenneth J. Wilson)

ISBN 0-201-56366-5
Text printed on recycled and acid-free paper.
1 2 3 4 5 6 7 8 9 10 - CRW - 96959493
First Printing, November 1993

To my dear wife, Jeanne:

Loving thanks for your gentle blend
of patience and push.

CONTENTS

My objectives in writing this book are fivefold:

1. To break down the *barriers* associated with that frightful word, statistics, so that learning is not inhibited.

2. To build a firm *foundation of understanding* of the basic statistical principles behind SPC so that the powerful tools will be used and interpreted correctly.

3. To identify *areas of implementation* so that practical uses are readily evident.

4. To develop *personal skills* in the use and communication of these tools in order to instill self-confidence and credibility.

5. To generate *excitement and enthusiasm* so that the personal, internal forces of motivation for learning are released.

This book has been in the making for at least 15 years, but only in my mind. I finally wrote it because it has become increasingly evident to me that the teaching of statistical quality (or process) control, particularly in industry, has left serious gaps in understanding among practitioners. These gaps suggest the need for dynamic approaches in order to implement statistical process control with understanding and effectiveness. Statistics has been rediscovered as a set of powerful tools that enable us to improve the quality of our products, processes, services, and designs; these ultimately lead to lower costs. Because such an achievement can make any company more competitive in the domestic and international marketplace, everyone is trying to learn about these tools.

Attempts to transfer these tools from the hands (and heads) of people trained in statistics to those not so trained have presented new challenges in pedagogy. Statistics has traditionally been considered a dull and mysterious subject. It doesn't have to be that way. For many years, I have tried to enhance the statistical literacy of my students and readers. This book tries to make fundamental statistical principles clear, understandable, relevant, and exciting so that applications can be made correctly and confidently.

For example, Shewhart control charts, perhaps the single most important statistical tool in process control, are based on relatively simple, but elegant and subtle, concepts. However, one false step in reasoning, and one may reach a wrong conclusion about the process. Statistical concepts and skills can be learned effectively to avert statistical embarrassment.

Computer software is useful for reducing tedious hand calculations, but it may inhibit the critical ability to understand and interpret the statistical principles involved. What the person using statistical methods needs are clear understanding, correct interpretation, proper implementation, and an ability to express results in meaningful language. I see the day coming when artificial intelligence (AI) will be used for process analysis and control in the form of computer programs developed from "expert systems." Those who will use these programs can manage more effectively by understanding the statistical principles behind them.

Because of historical precedent and tradition, this book could have been entitled *SQC for the Rest of Us—A Personal Path to Statistical **Quality** Control.* The practical difference between SQC (statistical quality control) and SPC (statistical process control) may be academic. SQC seems to me to be more broad in scope, encompassing a wide range of activities in which statistical methods can be used, from product design to in-process controls to service after sales. SPC, however, has excited many people, perhaps because it suggests a move upstream from "post-mortem" inspection of the finished product to an intense study of the production process itself, from the specific service afforded customers to the system that created it, where action can be taken to prevent the production of defectives (nonconforming units of product) or ineffective service in the first place. Thus, the association of quality control with finished product inspection is being replaced by the more modern and enlightened idea of initially *preventing* defects (nonconformities) or poor service by process and system design that results in better products and better service. My choice of SPC in the book title is intended to reflect its emphasis on prevention of defects.

Recent developments suggest that continued progress in quality and productivity improvement, especially in manufacturing, can be made by moving even further upstream. Advanced statistical methods are being used to design the product initially to make it robust; that is, resistant to environmental influences that can adversely affect the product. In addition, statistical methods are being used to design manufacturing processes to anticipate and counter expected and measurable sources of variation such as those that occur in raw materials, equipment, people, and environments. Such statistical methods include designed experimentation, which is beyond the scope of this book but which is a logical continuation of this book's contents.

It is important to recognize that the use of statistics is only one component, albeit a critical one, in a total program of quality improvement that touches all disciplines, functions, and responsibilities in any organization. The increasing popularity of Total Quality Management (TQM) reflects this comprehensive emphasis.

The sequence of topics and concepts in this book is somewhat different from the way SPC is usually taught. This sequence, which I have found to be very effective in my courses and seminars, is based on a building-block approach, in which new concepts are dependent on previously established and understood concepts. If ideas and techniques are based on a natural, intuitive rationale, they tend to be logical to the student, thereby enhancing learning, comprehension, retention, and interest. One example is to introduce the normal distribution and its probability characteristics before discussing control charts, simply because the normal curve serves as an important model for many charts. Another example is to make the fundamental distinction between population (process) and sample, together with differences in nomenclature, early in the text. This important distinction not only helps us to learn more advanced statistical techniques, it also enables us to state statistical conclusions with clarity of language and meaning, strengthening the important communication skill.

A word about the exercises that follow most of the chapters: Many of the exercises have been designed to challenge the student's initiative in his or her daily work environment, where implementation of the learned principles and the developed skills is realistically achieved. Some of the chapter exercises derive from one comprehensive statistical data set that gives the reader a chance to develop continuity in problem solutions, from which the learning experience may be appreciably enhanced.*

Hy Pitt
Milwaukee, Wisconsin
June 1993

---

* One of the most effective as well as endearing teachers of undergraduate and graduate mathematics in my experience was the late Professor Cyrus Colton MacDuffee at the University of Wisconsin–Madison. His practice of assigning only one relatively easy problem for homework each class day resulted in dedicated students who quickly developed self-confidence, skills, commitment, and enthusiasm for the subject matter.

ACKNOWLEDGMENTS

The contributions of many people must be acknowledged in all gratitude in the production of this book. Let me start with my wife, Jeanne, whose support and encouragement are always treasured. I am grateful to her for assisting in the reading and editing of the manuscript, a task which she has done so well for all of my writing.

My heartfelt thanks go to my two sons for reading the manuscript and providing many valuable suggestions: Dr. Daniel A. Pitt, manager of multimedia systems at Hewlett-Packard Company, Palo Alto, California, and Dr. Ronald E. Pitt, professor of agricultural and biological engineering at Cornell University, Ithaca, New York.

I owe many, many thanks to the outstanding professional staff in the Corporate and Professional Publishing Group of Addison-Wesley Publishing Company, Reading, Massachusetts: editor Leslie Morgan for her encouragement and direction during the critical early months, editor Jennifer Joss for her guidance during the later months, editorial assistant Danielle DesMarais for her timely correspondence, editor-in-chief John Wait for his overall support, marketing manager Kim Dawley and marketing assistant Tiffany Moore for their imagination, production manager Marty Rabinowitz, senior production coordinator Simone Payment, and product information coordinator Pradeepa Siva for their attention to details, and principal reviewer Mark Kasunic for his superb insight and important suggestions. Their cooperation, ideas, patience, and support were exemplary and helped to improve the manuscript.

A special sense of gratitude goes to the many thousands of my students in the hundreds of courses and seminars conducted on behalf of supportive clients throughout the United States, Canada, Puerto Rico, England, The Netherlands, Belgium, and Italy. Because of their willingness to share their valuable experiences with others, I learned much from them.

Special thanks are extended to the following organizations for their kind permission to reprint certain graphics:

- United Feature Syndicate, Inc., for the delightful cartoon strip of "Peanuts" appearing in Chapter 15.

- Universal Press Syndicate for the incisive cartoon strip of "Calvin and Hobbes" appearing in Chapter 27.

- Automotive Industry Action Group (AIAG) for the flow chart, "Selection Procedure for the Use of the Control Charts Described in This Manual," appearing in Chapter 21 and reprinted from their *Statistical Process Control Manual*, 1991.

- American Society for Testing and Materials (ASTM) for tabular entries appearing in Table 2 of the Appendix, and reprinted from their Manual #7, *Presentation of Data and Control Chart Analysis: 6th Edition*, 1990.

- American Society for Quality Control (ASQC) for the confidence belts appearing as Graph 2 in the Appendix, and reprinted from a typically excellent article by Dr. Lloyd S. Nelson, "Confidence Belts for Small Percentages," published in the *Journal of Quality Technology*, July 1981.

Finally, I thank Dr. W. Edwards Deming for our long-standing personal correspondence and generous sharing of materials that date back to January 1975 and for reawakening American interest in statistical applications toward quality improvements that are part of our lives.

And now, dear Reader, bon voyage!

ABOUT THE AUTHOR

Hy Pitt has been conducting quality-related training programs for more than 30 years. He is recognized internationally for his teaching skills in statistics and for practical implementation of modern techniques. Some of his client companies enthusiastically refer to him as "the best teacher of statistical quality control in the country."

Besides the clients he has served throughout the United States, he has conducted many courses in Europe, England, Canada, and Puerto Rico. He was the director of education and training for the American Society for Quality Control (ASQC), headquartered in Milwaukee, Wisconsin, from 1967 to 1970, during which time he developed the ASQC-Certified Quality Engineer (CQE) examination program. A Fellow of ASQC, he is also an ASQC-certified quality engineer.

Author, teacher, lecturer, and consultant, he is listed in *Who's Who in the Midwest* and in *American Men and Women of Science.* He is a member of many technical and professional societies. His direct industrial employment includes positions as manager of statistical services in quality control for United Fruit Company, Boston, and statistical analyst for Oscar Mayer & Company, Madison, Wisconsin. He formed his company, Pitt Training Associates, Milwaukee, in 1973.

He has B.S. and M.S. degrees in mathematics from the University of Wisconsin–Madison, where he also taught mathematics to undergraduates. He has completed course work and language requirements as a Ph.D. candidate in education and statistics at Wisconsin.

In 1989 he served as a member of the Board of Examiners for the Malcolm Baldrige National Quality Award.

Mr. Pitt served in a U.S. Army Air Force weather squadron during World War II, stationed in British Guiana (now Guyana). Active in community affairs, he enjoys sports, camping, astronomy, antique cars, antiques, and collecting sundry items from calculators to cowbells to glass milk bottles and creamers.

Introduction

CHAPTER 1

Revolutions in Quality, Productivity, and Statistics

Everyone believes in quality. Almost any manager would insist that his or her company is a "quality house." We believe in the importance of quality much as Americans believe in baseball, apple pie, and motherhood. What can be done to convert such belief in quality from premise to practice?

1.1 The Old-Fashioned Sign of a Quality House

If you have ever worked in a manufacturing environment, consider the number of times when shipments of product that contained known defective (nonconforming) units were sent to unwary customers or consumers. The scenario may have gone like this: The department manager, on being informed that quality defects (nonconformities) were present in a lot being prepared for shipment, declared, "Ship it!" The manager's objectives were to manufacture product and to ship it, to keep the lines operating, and to keep the employees busy and productive at all times. The customer was responsible for finding the defects. If the customer did not find defects (or at least did not complain about them), then we must be doing something right. But if the customer found defects and complained about them, then we would defend our reputation and repair or replace the defective units. Now isn't that the sign of a quality house?

A scenario in a service environment can be similar, except that customers may be less inclined to complain when service is questionable. As long as the hospital patient says nothing about the long delay before a nurse responds to a call, management will assume that the organization is doing an excellent job.

3

1.2 The Old-Fashioned Way of Meeting Competition

Today we are faced with challenges that are both demanding and exciting: to build quality products that are consistent, to provide quality services that are dependable, and to sell these goods and services at prices that are affordable and competitive. Most people who manage companies are aware of these demands, and they are also somewhat apprehensive about the direct challenges of competitors whose products are better or services are superior and seem to capture increasingly larger shares of the market.

What do we do about it? It seems obvious to most managers that something must be done about the *cost* of their products and services. The reasoning goes like this: If we can sell our products or offer services for a lower price than our competitors do, by reducing our *costs* to make products or to generate services, then we will have the advantage, enjoy a larger share of the market, and increase our profits.

What about quality, you ask? Everyone knows that improving quality is going to cost money, which will add to the cost of the product, which will make it less attractive in the market place, which will cause us to lose our market share and thereby reduce our profitability. It seems logical, therefore, that worrying about improving quality is out of the question!

I hope most readers will recognize the flaw in this logic. This book should convince you that the opposite is true: Improving quality costs less and increases productivity in the long term.

1.3 Enter Productivity

Let's look at the manufacturing environment as a typically current model of the industrial world. The false reasoning begun in the previous section continues: We can lower unit costs by increasing *productivity*. That is, we must produce more units of product with the same resources that we have now if we wish to remain competitive. Then the cost per unit will go down, and we will regain our advantage in the marketplace. We must, therefore, exhort our workers to produce more by working faster and harder.

This scenario is manifested in the concern for and attention to productivity. Let us measure the number of units produced per hour of labor and strive to increase this ratio. This is what many companies try to do in order to become more competitive.

1.4 Enter Quality and Ostrich Management

Unfortunately, the flaw in the reasoning that says we must increase productivity to remain competitive now becomes aggravated because the typical measure of productivity does not take *quality* into consideration. What good is it to increase productivity, measured by the simple ratio of number of units produced (total output) to some convenient base, if, say, 20% of the units produced and shipped are defective in some way? Whatever temporary advantage we may have gained in increased sales can be wiped out by the ostrich costs associated with the manufacture and shipment of defective goods. We call them "ostrich costs" generated by ostrich management because we tend to ignore those costs of poor quality by burying our heads in the sand. What are the costs and effects of ostrich management?

To start with, we produce both good and bad units of product, with the hope that the number of bad units produced is small. Good and bad products cost the same to manufacture. That is, the accounting cost to manufacture a bad unit is the same as that for a good unit because the same costs are involved to operate. They include the usual costs of raw materials, labor, overhead, equipment, utilities, interest, and depreciation. But cost-accounting methods do not usually differentiate between good and bad levels of product quality.

However, *additional* costs are associated with the production of units of product that are defective in some way. They include scrap, rework, repair, downtime, customer returns, replacements, customer complaints, claims, warranty costs, liability, and more. You could probably think of several other kinds of additional costs associated with bad units of product.

All of these defective units must be *subtracted* from the typical productivity formula if that formula is to be realistic and is to serve as a management guide to profitability. We must measure productivity realistically by finding the ratio of *good-quality* product manufactured to the number of labor hours involved (or some other suitable base). In short,

> Wrong productivity formula = Total output/labor hours.
> Right productivity formula = Total output of good product/labor hours.

We must talk about productivity and quality as if they are two connected and dependent entities. There must be a more effective way of increasing true productivity than simply exhorting workers to work faster and harder.

1.5 The Solution

The answer to increasing true productivity is deceptively simple: *Produce only good product!* Now this sounds as if we are back to baseball, apple pie, and motherhood. But what would happen if we could stop producing bad product and produce only good product?

1. The true measure of *productivity ratio* that reflects good quality would rise.

2. The *cost of manufacture* per unit of product would go down because there would be little or no hidden internal costs due to defective product, such as scrap, rework, repair, and so on.

3. The *quality level* of product in the marketplace would automatically improve.

4. If most of the savings in manufacturing cost were passed on to our customers, our product's *market price* would become more competitive.

5. *Market share* would tend to rise if quality is a dominant factor.

6. *Profitability* would increase.

To produce good product consistently, we need to understand the process much, much better. What is there about the process that causes it to produce bad product in the first place? Why does the process behave the way it does? These are very important questions that must be answered if we are to exercise true process control and improvement. They must be answered in an objective way, with facts scientifically established, by careful testing of conjectures, personal opinions, and hypotheses.

We need, in short, better knowledge of the way the process behaves. We need a sense of dedication to pursue the study of the process until we understand it, can identify its idiosyncrasies, and can control it. We need to persevere, and we need to be patient. And we need one more human characteristic: *courage.*

It takes courage to refuse to ship product that you know is defective. It takes courage to stop a line or machine because of a quality problem that arises. It takes courage to converge on a problem that discredits a product or service and to attack the problem with many resources in order to find and remove the cause—and to do it now! It takes courage to make it right the first time and not later when you "have more time." It takes courage to practice the *prevention* of quality defects, which may require a long-term view of the operation, rather than to fight fires that may result in only short-term relief. *This human trait, courage, may well be the most important attribute we need in trying to achieve our quality goals.*

1.6 Enter Statistical Methods and Japan

Statistical methods happen to be the ticket that admits us to the hall of solutions to quality problems. Statistics are the means by which we can understand the process, determine why it behaves the way it does, control it so that the manufacture of defects can be stopped at will, and improve it.

It is safe to say that a worldwide revolution is occurring that places the quality of goods and services at the focus of industrial activity. The revolution started in Japan after World War II. Devastated by war, having little in the way of natural raw resources, owning a notorious reputation for poor quality of products, and being dependent for survival on its finished goods in a developing international marketplace, Japan chose the improvement of quality as its national goal for economic survival. It was a conscious policy mutually agreed on by the leaders of industry, government, academia, and finance, a union of national resources not yet seen in the Western world (United States, Canada, South America, and Western Europe).

As part of the postwar efforts of the United States to support rehabilitation and recovery in Japan, several U.S. experts were sent to help the Japanese change their attitudes about quality and management, learn new skills in manufacture, and acquire know-how in the application of statistical quality control methods. Among these experts were Dr. W. Edwards Deming, a lecturer on statistics and management, and Dr. Joseph M. Juran, a management consultant.

Now, more than a generation later, the world is noting the effects of Japan's dramatic industrial revolution. To say that Japanese products are a formidable force in the international marketplace today is to understate their impact on our lives. When, in 1980, it became known nationally through a television program[1] that the devastating effect of better Japanese products on the U.S. economy had as its driving force the use of statistical methods, American industrial leaders paid attention. The typically American response was to focus first on the specific technique that had a proven track record (statistical quality control), then later develop a comprehensive system needed to achieve the desired result (total quality management).

Considerable attention was paid to Deming, the person principally responsible for teaching the statistical skills to the Japanese that led to that astounding track record. An ironic situation then developed: Americans began sending people to Japan to find out what it was that they, the Americans, had taught the Japanese!

Those same statistical techniques had been taught in the United States during and since World War II. But they had achieved only a modest degree of acceptance for several reasons:

1. The direct responsibility for quality was confined to quality-control personnel and their inspection function and had not yet been considered to be one that was shared by everyone.

2. Management had not yet accepted accountability for quality.

3. Quality improvement was not considered to be a dynamic ongoing activity.

4. Statistical quality-control methods were considered too technical for most people.

---

[1] *If Japan Can, Why Can't We?* by NBC. It featured Dr. Deming.

As a result, very few disciplines and activities outside of the typical quality-control department were introduced to statistics. Managers, particularly top managers, remained isolated from them.

While acceptance and implementation of statistical quality-control methods were only modestly successful in the Western world, Japanese industries became highly competitive and eminently successful. By the late 1970s, many American industries felt the pinch. Among them were the steel, automobile, and electronics industries, and their dependent satellites.

Other aspects of improved skills and knowledge in Japan became evident. New management techniques evolved. Employee involvement and participation were conspicuous and impressive. Americans began to sense that an entirely new way of running a business was emerging and must be explored. The old ways simply were not standing up to the fierce new competition presented by the people of Japan as well as by the people of West Germany, South Korea, Taiwan, and Hong Kong, to name a few.

It was evident that the United States could not wait for the dust to settle. Too many industries and companies were losing their market share and were in danger of being destroyed. With typical American spirit and enterprise, many companies faced the industrial threat head-on. They embraced the new technical know-how, statistical quality control, with determination and commitment. Many companies stopped making fatalistic excuses that the Japanese succeeded because of their homogeneous population, because of their unique culture, or because of strong government and financial support.

The Western world had to play "catch-up ball." But while this was going on, foreign competitors, including some Japanese companies, were moving even farther ahead with new techniques in the use of statistics for product and process improvement. Designed experiments, for example, were rapidly becoming a way of industrial life in several Japanese companies, especially through the popularization of the so-called "Taguchi methods."[2] The concepts of designed experiments have been known and practiced in the Western world for many years, but their practice has been generally confined to personnel highly trained in the use of statistics. In Japan, many people, particularly engineers who have learned statistical methods, routinely design and conduct experiments aimed at improving product performance.

Is the history of Japan's industrial quality dominance being repeated? Will Japan's current advantage manifest itself in another surprise come the next generation? Will there be any closing of the quality gap between East and West? That remains to be seen.

---

[2] Dr. Genichi Taguchi, a Japanese engineer, approached experimental design from an engineer's point of view. His methods, although apparently effective in practice, evoke controversy among some professional statisticians who challenge certain deficiencies in statistical rigor.

1.7 Summary

Most of us will agree that quality is one of the most important ingredients for economic survival today. An untoward emphasis on productivity and the use of an invalid measure detract from the true impact of good quality on productivity, on market share, and on profitability. Good-quality product and bad-quality product cost the same to make, but there are many additional costs, some hidden, associated with bad-quality product. The answer is to stop making bad product and to start making only good product by learning how a process behaves and why it behaves that way. Statistical methods help us to understand and interpret process behavior. We also need dedication, perseverance, and courage to close the quality gap between the successes of the East and failures of the West. That gap still prevails, and its future status remains to be seen.

1.8 Putting It into Practice

1. Examine some of the written policies of your organization to see if quality is a part of those policies. Is there a specific quality policy endorsed by top management? Is an emphasis on quality confined only to manufactured product or a marketed service, or is it broad in scope and does it cover all operations of your organization, including administrative services, sales, purchasing, research and development, engineering, maintenance, distribution, marketing, customer service and satisfaction, and human resources?

2. Collect some cost data from your organization covering the past three months that express the cost of "bad" quality. These may include costs of scrap, rework, downgrading, downtime due to poor quality, product returns and recalls, and customer complaints. Express these costs as a percentage of total sales for the same period. Are you surprised at the magnitude of the amount? Did you find it difficult to obtain cost data? What proportion of these costs, do you believe, are recoverable? Develop a strategy for recovering some of these costs. (This exercise can lead to a more formal quality-cost program.)

Whenever you set out to do something,
something else must be done first.
—Murphy's Law

CHAPTER 2

First, Some Major Management Chores

anagers are the people usually responsible for management of the resources of time, money, goods, equipment, and people.[1] Collectively, managers are referred to as *management* and typically can include the board chairman, the president, the other officers of the company, department heads, general managers, plant managers, general foremen, foremen, and first-line supervisors. Traditionally, management is stratified into three layers: top or upper management, middle management, and lower management. The structure of each layer is usually unique to every organization.

In recent times, an individual employee may also be viewed as a manager if that person is empowered to make decisions that affect time, materials, quality, costs, and other resources. Such an enlightened approach has broad implications of responsibilities, rewards, career satisfaction, and personal growth that are not discussed here.

Before SPC can be properly implemented and made an essential part of ongoing process improvement, three things are required of management: (1) management support, (2) management consistency, and (3) management involvement, all of which are discussed further.

---

[1] The reader is encouraged to look into the Malcolm Baldrige National Quality Award, a public law managed by the National Institute of Standards and Technology, U.S. Department of Commerce. It is a prestigious program that has been in operation since 1988. It recognizes U.S. businesses that have attained quality excellence. Applicants must address a set of examination items within each of seven major categories, the first of which is management leadership in creating and sustaining a quality culture.

2.1 Management Support

First, management must *support* the priority of quality and quality improvement in all areas and disciplines in the organization, as well as the effort to incorporate SPC methods into the operating system. This support must manifest itself in several ways: by spoken word, by written word, by attitude, and by deeds. A company quality policy in writing, for example, signed by top management and distributed to all employees (and possibly also to suppliers and customers), is an excellent start.

Expressions of support, by whatever medium is chosen, must be genuinely sincere. Any program ostensibly supported by top management is doomed to failure if management provides only lip service.

2.2 Management Consistency

Second, management must be *consistent* in that support. If quality is given top priority one day, but becomes second in importance to getting product shipped the next day, then we can expect a general deterioration in quality to follow. When management breaks its own rules without explanation or justification, it has no right to expect others to follow those rules. Under these conditions, in effect, there are no rules. Supporting SPC and being consistent in that support are necessary but still not sufficient.

2.3 Management Involvement

Third, management must be *involved* in the implementation of SPC. This means that management must learn about SPC, become familiar with its principles, direct its applications, and be a part of decisions that are made from the results of SPC use. SPC is not a set of tools to be relegated only to hourly workers because those tools seem to be relatively simple. Indeed, the principles underlying SPC are not that simple; they are elegant yet subtle, practical yet theoretical, simple yet complicated.

Development of the skills inherent in SPC methods—in statistical methods, generally—can become useful to all disciplines and employee levels in any organization.

2.4 Summary

The successful implementation of SPC depends on management's support, consistency, and involvement.

2.5 Putting It into Practice

Evaluate the management of your company or organization on the basis of the three criteria listed in this chapter: support, consistency, and involvement in quality improvement. If any criterion is not being satisfied, discuss the matter with your superior, subordinate, or peer to see what strategy can be developed to satisfy all criteria.

CHAPTER 3

What Is SPC?

SPC stands for *statistical process control*. It is a collection of tools, mostly statistical, which help us to understand what is going on in any process that generates products, services, or information. It helps us to attain insight into the inherent behavior of those processes. Understanding how a process behaves enables us to find the reasons why it behaves that way, enables us to exercise control over that process, and serves also to assist in the redesign and improvement of the process.

Some of these tools are only graphical in nature. All of the tools in this chapter are characterized by some sort of visual diagrammatic representation. A graph or diagram, however, does not necessarily imply that some statistical method was involved. For example, a flow chart, as shown in Figure 3.1, does not depend on statistical data for its creation. Indeed, some companies view SPC as *any means* by which a process can be improved, statistical or otherwise, as long as some graphical method is involved.[1]

The important thing, however, is that we move away from pet theories, personal conjectures, favorite hypotheses, and unsubstantiated hunches to some *objective* procedure that requires the collection, summarization, analysis, and interpretation of information.

3.1 The Tools Of SPC

There are at least nine "tools" of SPC to bring to your attention. Very few companies, in my experience, use all nine tools routinely. It is practical to say, therefore, that you are using SPC even if you are not using all nine tools.

---

[1] It might be considered statistically naive to treat any graphical method as statistical in nature and thus justified to be included in the domain of *statistical* process control. But the good news is that SPC *always* includes some genuinely statistical methods.

Nevertheless, some of these tools, as we shall see, are more correctly identified with the statistical discipline of SPC than others.

The nine tools of SPC, for which more detailed descriptions follow, include:

1. Flow charts

2. Run charts

3. Pareto charts and analysis

4. Cause-and-effect diagrams

5. Frequency histograms

6. Control charts

7. Process capability studies

8. Acceptance sampling plans

9. Scatter diagrams.

3.2 Flow Charts

A *flow chart* is a diagram that shows the progress of work or the flow of materials or information through a sequence of operations. An excellent first step in studying a process for the purpose of finding ways to improve it is to draw a flow chart of its functions. Flow charts are very useful, for example, in studying a manufacturing process because they provide an overall view of the process, enabling us to grasp the process plan. At the same time, we can detect any gaps in the process; that is, there may be some steps or functions that everyone had assumed were in place but were actually not present. We can also detect steps or functions that are overlapping, where two or more departments may be performing the same function unknowingly. Such duplication of effort, of course, can be wasteful, and it is beneficial to be aware of it.

It is a good idea for people who are discussing ways to improve a particular process to draw a flow chart of the process as they see it. But expect to see some differences of opinion. You may even have to observe the process firsthand to get the facts.

Flow charts are not considered to be statistical tools. Figure 3.1 is a flow chart[2] of a strategy for process improvement that shows the important relationship between control charts and process capability studies, two tools described later in this chapter and in more detail in Chapters 18 through 23. Figure 3-1 also appears as Figure 23-4 in Chapter 23.

---

[2] Adapted from an article by H. Pitt, "A Modern Strategy for Process Improvement," *Quality Progress,* ASQC, Milwaukee, May 1985, pp. 22–28.

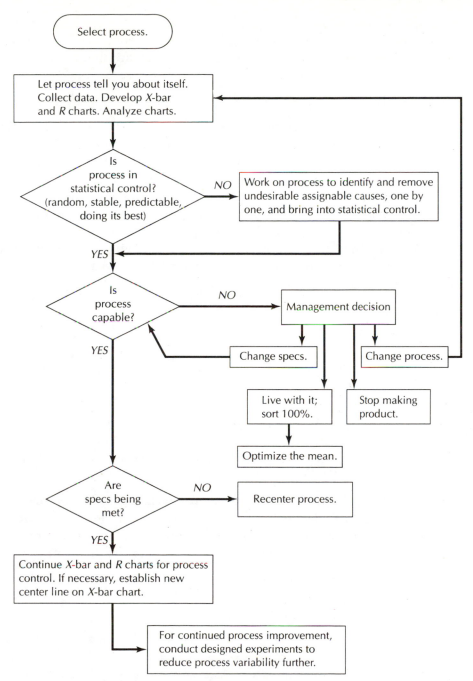

Figure 3.1. Flow chart of strategy for process improvement.

Can you improve on the strategy depicted by this flow chart? Your answer would depend upon your background experience and your understanding of the relationship between control charts and process capability studies.

3.3 Run Charts

A *run chart* is a charting of sample results, usually one sample reading at a time, in chronological sequence. The purpose is to detect any long-term trends or unusual patterns with respect to time. This is often a useful first step in the statistical analysis of a process. It is easy and simple to do, and it sometimes reveals some unexpected process behavior characteristics. Since run charts require the collection of data, they are considered to be statistical tools.

In Figure 3.2 we see the results of weighing only one package a day of a packaged food product for 20 consecutive days. Although we would not expect to see this picture for all packaged food products, what does this result suggest to you? Does it warrant investigation?

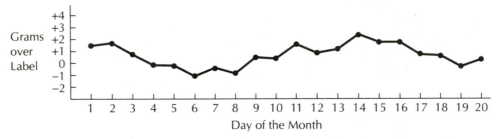

Figure 3.2. Run chart of net weights beyond label weight. Sample size: one package per day.

The chart suggests that the weights follow a cyclical pattern. Investigation is certainly warranted to determine the cause, because the low points would be associated with underweight packages, while the high points would represent excessive weights that result in greater cost. The objective is to maintain consistency in package weights.

3.4 Pareto Chart and Analysis

This analysis involves the so-called *Pareto principle,*[3] which states that not all of the causes that are responsible for some phenomenon occur with the same frequency or with the same impact. In fact, only a relatively few of the causes,

---

[3] As enunciated by J. M. Juran.

among many, may be largely responsible for the phenomenon. Therefore, affecting only those relatively few causes can significantly influence the phenomenon in question.

For example, products may have numerous defects (nonconformities), but the defects occur with varying frequency, and only a few of them account for most of the defects present. Another example: The machines operating on a production floor do not all exhibit the same amount of downtime; a few of the machines usually account for most of the downtime. Another example: Only a few of the many customer accounts are responsible for most of the sales.

When our resources for solving problems are limited (as they usually are), and the problems to be solved are too numerous (as they usually are), then some criterion must be used to select those problems to work on that will have the most beneficial effect if they could be solved. Those selected problems become "the vital few versus the trivial many,"[4] a phrase that has come to be associated with the Pareto principle.

A Pareto analysis can be considered a statistical tool because data are collected, and these data are usually presented in chart form with the causes depicted in rank order. Figure 3.3 presents a *Pareto chart* of the relative frequency of occurrence of 10 defects identified by letters A through J. Note that of the 10 defects shown, three of them (A, B, and C) account for about 75% of all the defects found (examine the cumulative-percent graph portion of Figure 3.3). Thus, if our objective is to reduce the average number of defects per unit of product, then we should harness our limited resources and attack defects A, B, and C. If we can achieve a substantial reduction of these three defects, the final result will be a substantial reduction in the average number of defects per unit of product.

On the other hand, attacking defects according to frequency of occurrence may not be in the best interest of the company. Defects usually occur with different degrees of seriousness to the customer or to the producer. Some other criterion of measure, therefore, may be more meaningful for the company, such as *costs* of the defects. If we can identify the monetary losses attributable to each defect, then we can draw another Pareto chart, ranking the defects according to annual losses associated with them. Thus another dimension to defects may be examined.

We can well expect that the first three defects associated with the higher losses to the company are probably different from those associated with frequency of occurrence. For example, it may be that defect E, which accounted for only 6% of all defects found, may be responsible for 40% of all monetary losses

---

[4] Popularized by J. M. Juran.

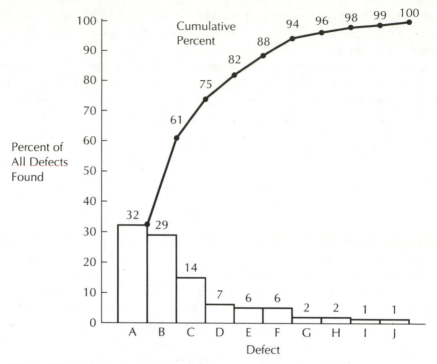

Figure 3.3. Pareto chart of defect frequency of occurrence.

because of the serious nature of defect E. In this case it makes good sense to focus our limited resources on defect E. If we could solve the problems associated with defect E and eliminate or substantially reduce its occurrence, we will have saved the company a great deal of money.

We can even examine other practical dimensions of importance in trying to decide where to allocate our limited resources in order to get the greatest return for our efforts. Other dimensions can include the amount of *invested money* needed to solve the problems and the amount of *time* needed to solve the problems.[5]

Application of the Pareto principle to analysis of process problems has become a useful tool for developing a practical strategy to get the maximum return from limited resources.

---

[5] See, for example, H. Pitt, "Pareto Revisited," *Quality Progress*, ASQC, Milwaukee, March 1974, pp. 29–30. In this article, a Pareto index is developed that incorporates four criteria for deciding which defects to attack.

3.5 Cause-and-Effect Diagram

This is a technique that is somewhat like *brainstorming*. When a group gets together to discuss a particular problem, the participants are encouraged, without intimidation or embarrassment, to suggest factors involved in the problem and their possible causes. The ideas proposed are graphically drawn in a *cause-and-effect diagram*. It is sometimes called an *Ishikawa diagram* after the person who developed it,[6] and sometimes a *fishbone diagram* because of its suggested shape. Major factors appear diagrammatically as lines (or big bones) emanating from a major straight line (spine) that represents the problem at hand. Possible causes related to the major factors are connected to those factors, and the entire sketch takes on the appearance of a fishbone.

A cause-and-effect diagram can reveal important relationships among the various possible causes, providing additional insight into the problem. The possible causes then must be investigated, usually by test and experimentation, to confirm or deny the suggested causes of the problem at hand.

Cause-and-effect diagrams are not statistical in nature; yet they are often included in SPC programs because of the assistance and insight they provide in helping to solve problems. In addition, the development of cause-and-effect diagrams associated with specific problems encourages employee participation at all levels, tapping the hidden resources of knowledge and experience that any organization holds.

Figure 3.4 is a cause-and-effect diagram that identifies some of the factors that can contribute to (or inhibit) quality improvement. In this example, six major factors (big bones) have been identified: (1) people, (2) materials, (3) management (often not mentioned), (4) equipment, (5) measurements, and (6) environment. Management is identified as one of the possible major factors because certain management responsibilites, identified by the smaller branches shown in the figure, can influence quality improvement.

For each of these major factors, some associated secondary factors (smaller bones) may be identified, such as design, maintenance, and capability connected with the equipment factor. The diagram can be expanded further to include other factors (even smaller bones) associated with each of these secondary factors.

The major factors (big bones) selected are specific to the problem (the effect) being investigated. For example, if the problem is an inefficient gas furnace, some of the major factors or possible causes that are associated with the effect

---

[6] Dr. Kaoru Ishikawa, a Japanese pioneer in quality control methods, invented the cause-and-effect diagram technique in 1943. See his popular book, *Guide to Quality Control*, 2nd revised English edition, published by Asian Productivity Organization, Tokyo, 1982. Available from UNIPUB/Kraus, New York, 1986.

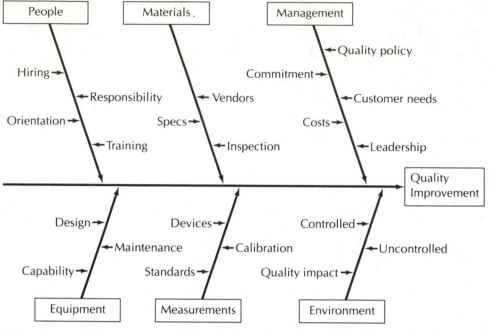

Figure 3.4. Cause-and-effect (or fishbone or Ishikawa) diagram.

might include the gas lines, the thermostat, the electric blower, and the meter, to name just a few. What additional factors (bones) would you include in Figure 3.4?

3.6 Frequency Histogram

The *frequency histogram* is a fundamental statistical tool of SPC. It is an effective way of summarizing process data graphically that, without calculations, can illustrate three basic characteristics of the data:

- A sense of the magnitude of the *mean* (or average)

- A sense of the *variability* in the data

- Some idea of the possible *pattern of variation*, which can be useful to make predictions about the process that generated these data.

In addition, we can see quickly whether or not the process is meeting specifications.

Frequency histograms are easy to generate by hand, as we shall see in Chapter 6. Although many practitioners like to use computers to generate his-

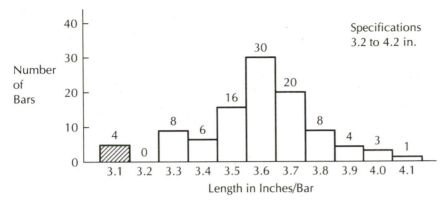

Figure 3.5. Frequency histogram of lengths of 100 steel bars (in inches).

tograms, because of the belief that such work is manually tedious, we shall see that hand-generated histograms have certain advantages in clarity and presentation.

Figure 3.5 is a histogram representing the frequency distribution of the different measurements of a sample of 100 lengths of bar stock. We can see that four of the 100 readings are outside the specification limits of 3.2 to 4.2 inches. Is this good, bad, or to be expected? The answer to this question depends on one's attitude toward specifications. If you believe that a *certain amount* beyond the specification limits is permissible, then the histogram does not exhibit any problems. If you believe that *no units of product* should exceed specification limits under any circumstances, then the histogram tells us that a problem does indeed exist. In either case, it is our basic attitude toward specifications as a governing device that determines our response to such histograms.

Additional insight into a problem can often be gained by plotting the data in a times series or chronological sequence, such as in a run chart, in addition to the histogram. The behavior of the sample data in a time series may reveal certain patterns that may provide a clue as to the source of any problems that the time series may exhibit.

3.7 Control Charts

Control charts, particularly Shewhart control charts,[7] are the one statistical tool that is completely identified with SPC. It can be truly stated that *if you do not use*

---

[7] Dr. Walter A. Shewhart, the inventor of control charts, was a member of the technical staff of Bell Telephone Laboratories. See his classic book, *Economic Control of Quality of Manufactured Product*, D. Van Nostrand Company, New York, 1931. Although out of print for many years, reprints (1980) can be obtained from the American Society for Quality Control, 611 E. Wisconsin Avenue, Milwaukee, Wisconsin 53201.

control charts in your process, you are not using SPC. Conversely, *if you use only control charts in your process, you are using SPC but not effectively.* We must understand the principles that underlie control charts and develop the proper skills for their implementation, but we should also learn to use the other tools as well in order to gain more insight into process behavior.

A collection of important basic statistical concepts exists that should be understood and mastered even before control charts are introduced to you. These concepts are covered in Part Two of this book. When you have a firm foundation of these statistical concepts, the subtle as well as the practical aspects of control charts will become more apparent, and the chances that you will use control charts properly with satisfying insight will be enhanced.

Too many companies have been unsuccessful in their attempts to use control charts at some time during the past 35 years or so. One of the reasons is that control charts were once thought to be a highly technical and little understood tool that belonged only to the quality control or quality assurance technical staff. The charts took on an exclusive statistical mystique with their own language, symbols, and formulas. As a result, many control chart programs tended to degenerate into meaningless record-keeping exercises.

In more recent times, fortunately, interest in control charts has been renewed because management has come to recognize that this powerful statistical tool has had dramatic impact in improving products, processes, and quality, while reducing costs of manufacture, thereby making companies, especially like those in Japan, much more competitive. At the same time, however, control charts are considered by some companies to be the exclusive tool of people on the production floor, a tool that tells a machine operator, for example, when to adjust the machine and when not to adjust the machine. This limited application of a control chart, we shall learn, misses its true mission.

Computer software has been developed in recent years to do the charting for us, to save time, to assure accuracy, and to take the drudgery out of the necessary calculations. This is all well and good, except that this simplistic treatment of control charts has been an obstacle to their effective use and interpretation. In fact, when control chart theory is adequately grasped, when control charts are treated as a true management tool and implemented with good understanding and knowledge at all levels in a company, then the full impact of their statistical power will be realized and appreciated.

We will see in Chapters 18 through 22 that control charts give us insight into the *statistical* behavior of processes. For example, a process that is said to be in *statistical control* is behaving in a random fashion (devoid of unusual influences); it is stable; it is predictable; and it is doing its best. Notice that nothing is said about the process meeting specifications. Here we have a situation in which the *language* of control charts plays a vital role in our ability to use them correctly.

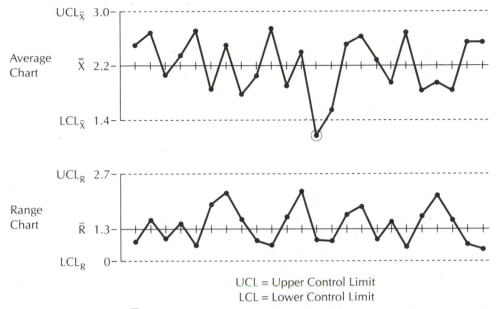

Figure 3.6. Average ($\overline{X}$) and range (R) control charts for package net weights in pounds (subgroup sample size = 5 packages).

Figure 3.6 shows a typical pair of control charts, one for sample means (or averages) and one for sample ranges for weights of a packaged product. Each of the plotted points represents the average and range of five readings. The correct interpretation of these charts is that the ranges are *in statistical control*, but the averages are *out of statistical control*. What can you say about the process meeting specifications? Answer: Nothing, because the process knows nothing about specifications.

3.8 Process Capability Studies

To determine if a process (or machine) is capable of meeting the specifications, it is necessary to run a *process capability study*. This is a statistical exercise conducted under certain controlled conditions. The capability of a process is usually reflected in the *inherent variability* that the process exhibits. The knowledge of whether or not a process has this inherent ability to meet specifications is so vital in any process improvement program that process capability studies are, like control charts, considered to be an essential statistical tool for SPC.

In Chapter 23 we study in detail the conditions for conducting such a study. Please note that this subject is discussed *after* control charts are introduced. The reason for this sequence is that, unknown to too many quality practitioners, the

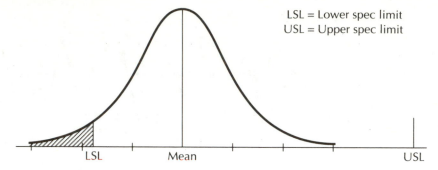

Figure 3.7. Normal curve process model showing specification limits.

capability of a process cannot be determined until the process has been brought into statistical control, and the control chart is used to determine the latter status. It is of special interest to note also that, when we find that a process is *not* capable of meeting specifications, management must enter the discussion and exercise its decision-making responsibility in selecting alternative directions.

The *frequency histogram* and an appropriate *probability model*, when the process is in statistical control, are the statistical tools used for expressing graphically the capability of a process. Figure 3.7 is a probability model (the *normal curve*) used in a typical situation. If this model is the correct one for the process, is this process capable?

The answer to the question just posed is yes, this process *is potentially capable*, despite the fact that a portion of the process exceeds the lower specification limit. The reason is that the total variability of the process, as measured by the total spread of the curve at the base, is less than the total spread of the specifications— that is, the tolerance—which you can measure easily from Figure 3.7. If the process could be recentered so that its mean is near the midpoint between the specification limits, the process will then meet the specifications. Thus, the important statistical considerations in determining process capability consist of three parts: the state of statistical control, its variability, and its centering.

3.9 Acceptance Sampling Plans

For many years quality control was directly associated with whether or not a production or shipment lot of items was acceptable. That determination was made by inspecting *every item* in the lot. This is known as *100% inspection*. Because of the fallible nature of human beings, particularly in their visual senses, power of concentration, and level of fatigue, this type of inspection was not always dependable. We have all encountered situations that revealed differences among inspectors. Even the same inspector was not always consistent with himself or herself.

Eventually the practice of taking *samples* from a lot received our attention. But then even more uncertainty arose about the inspection results and the decision on the lot. The problem of uncertainty seemed compounded by the fact that *samples can vary*.

One could decide to reject the lot, and the lot might turn out to be acceptable after all. That is not a correct decision and is known as a *Type I error*. On the other hand, it is possible to decide to accept the lot, and the lot might turn out to be unacceptable. That is not a correct decision either and is known as a *Type II error*.

These kinds of wrong decisions are always possible when samples are taken. The situation, in short, seems hopeless when you take samples (and as we saw above, the situation can be equally hopeless if one inspects 100% of the lot). Because such sampling plans can be evaluated by means of probability and statistics, the situation is still *hopeless, but not serious!*

We can examine any sampling plan and its decision rule, and we can determine the probability of making these two kinds of wrong decisions. This puts us in the position of being able to evaluate a sampling plan *before we use it*. We can tell in advance what the risks are of making the two possible types of wrong decisions and therefore judge the adequacy of the sampling plan in terms of the economic consequences of being wrong.

The behavior of a sampling plan can be summarized graphically by an *operating characteristic curve* (or simply an *OC curve*), which identifies the probability of accepting lots with varying levels of quality, usually described in terms of percent defective (or percent nonconforming). Since the determination of the probabilities is a statistical exercise, acceptance sampling plans are appropriately considered to be a statistical tool of SPC.[8]

A typical sampling plan and decision rule might read like this:

Take a random sample of 50 units from the lot.
If we find two or fewer defective units in the sample of 50, accept the lot.
If we find three or more defective units in the sample of 50, do not accept the lot.

This complete description of a sampling plan can be conveniently condensed into two short equations as follows:

$n = 50$ (size of random sample)
$c = 2$ (acceptance number).

These two elements completely describe the sampling plan.

The OC curve for such a plan would look like Figure 3.8. If you were to use this plan, what is the probability of accepting lots that have 4.0% defective units?

---

[8] See Chapter 4 for additional comments on acceptance sampling plans.

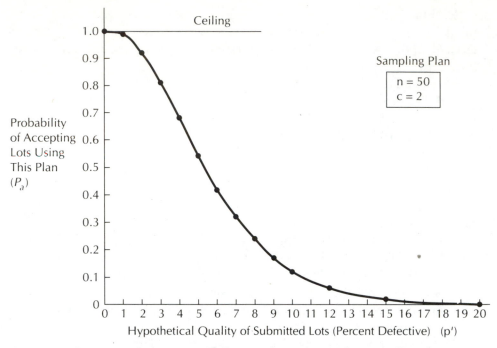

Figure 3.8. Operating characteristic (OC) curve for an acceptance sampling plan.

To read the OC curve in order to answer this question, enter the graph at the base at the hypothetical level of quality, 4% defective. Go straight up until you intersect the curve. At that point move horizontally to the left until you intersect the vertical scale, and read the answer.

The answer is about 0.67. The conclusion is stated as follows: If lots of 4% defective were submitted to this sampling plan, the plan would accept about two-thirds of them and reject about one-third of them. Whether or not this plan is a suitable one is determined by the probability and economic consequences of making a wrong decision. Thus some agreement must be reached first as to what constitutes a "good" lot and what constitutes a "bad" lot in terms of percent defective. Then the OC curve can be read for the probability of rejecting a good lot (distance from the curve to the ceiling) and the probability of accepting a bad lot (distance from the base to the curve).

The important rule to follow is this: *Always determine the OC curve for any sampling plan used*. Otherwise you are sampling in the dark.

3.10 Scatter Diagrams

Another useful statistical tool for SPC, one that helps to discover *associations* or *relationships* between variables, is the *scatter diagram*. By plotting one variable

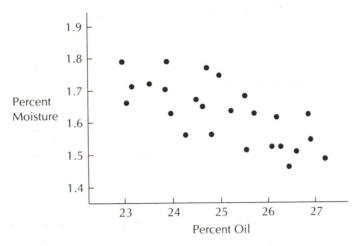

Figure 3.9. Scatter diagram.

against another, we often begin to see things that were not obvious before. The scatter diagram as used in SPC work does not usually go beyond the graphic representation of the data. The analysis is strictly visual. When more sophisticated statistical analysis is applied to these data, however, we can determine a line or curve that "best fits" the data for prediction purposes. We can then calculate certain useful statistics, such as the regression coefficients, the correlation coefficient, and the standard error of estimate.[9]

A real danger associated with the use of scatter diagrams is the possibility of concluding unjustifiably that one of the variables is responsible for causing the other variable. The causal relationship, if any exists at all between the variables, is not established by the scatter diagram; investigative work, including testing and experimentation, is required to determine if any causal relationship exists.[10] However, finding an association between the variables by means of the scatter diagram can give us a *prediction* tool that can be very practical, even though both of the variables may have been "caused" by a common but unknown third variable.

For example, Figure 3.9 is a scatter diagram of data involving the moisture and oil content of a certain processed food based on 25 samples taken from a process. Each point represents two laboratory analyses made from a single sample: percent oil and percent moisture. Is there an association between the

---

[9] These statistical measures are beyond the scope of this book. One would have to consult with a statistician or quality engineer, or explore a statistics textbook, to calculate and interpret the statistical concepts mentioned here.

[10] Consider, for example, the notoriously virtuous claims of the American Tobacco Institute that simply because there is an association does not prove that smoking cigarettes causes lung cancer. Other data, of course, are ignored.

two variables? If percent oil is increased, what can we expect in the behavior of percent moisture? Can one of the variables be predicted from the other? Which one?

Let us answer the questions. Yes, there does seem to be an association between percent oil and percent moisture. *On the average,* as percent oil increases, percent moisture decreases. We can predict percent moisture from percent oil, or we can predict percent oil from percent moisture.

A line of prediction, called a *regression line,* can be drawn to predict one variable from another. But prediction can be tricky, as those who try to predict the scholastic performance of individual students can testify. The reason is that the phenomenon of variability must be taken into account. Hence, a measure of the variability of prediction must be made in order to assess the validity of the prediction result. That measure is part of the study of regression and correlation, which is beyond the scope of this book.

3.11 Additional Comments

Other tools may be included under the heading of SPC. Among these are control charts that are different from the usual Shewhart charts, such as the CuSum chart, the median chart, the moving average and range charts, and others. Other statistical or even nonstatistical tools not listed in this chapter may be included.

Despite the large number of tools that have been associated with SPC programs aimed at both process control and process improvement, we can safely say that only three of them are universally recognized as SPC tools:

1. Frequency histograms

2. Shewhart control charts

3. Process capability studies.

The single most important of these is the Shewhart control charts.

Because of the great need to understand and use these most fundamental SPC tools properly, we will focus our attention on these three tools.

3.12 Summary

SPC stands for *statistical process control* and consists of a collection of statistical and nonstatistical tools used for obtaining vital information about a process, maintaining control over that process, and improving that process and its output. The process may be manufacturing or service-oriented.

SPC tools include, among others, the following:

1. Flow charts

2. Run charts

3. Pareto charts and analysis

4. Cause-and-effect diagrams

5. Frequency histograms

6. Control charts

7. Process capability studies

8. Acceptance sampling plans

9. Scatter diagrams.

Flow charts and cause-and-effect diagrams are not considered to be statistical tools; the others are. Frequency histograms, control charts, and process capability studies are recognized as fundamental SPC tools. Control charts, however, are the one tool completely identified with any SPC program; without control charts one does *not* have an SPC program.

3.13 Putting It into Practice

1. Select a department in your organization with which you are reasonably familiar. Ask a cooperative colleague in that department to draw a flow chart of the basic procedure in that department, such as the flow of materials, components, parts, information, or service segments. You do the same *independently*. Compare the two flow charts. If you find serious discrepancies, resolve them with your colleague first and, if necessary, with the department head.

2. Draw a run chart on some important measurable characteristic (such as length, height, width, thickness, weight, etc.) by taking one sample every hour or every shift or every day for about 25 readings. Is any unexpected pattern emerging? If so, get a couple of opinions as to the cause.

3. Work with your personnel department to determine the frequency of the reasons for absenteeism. Draw a Pareto chart of those reasons. Show your work to the head of the personnel department and discuss what can be done to reduce significantly the total number of absenteeisms.

You don't have to explain something you haven't said.

—Anonymous

CHAPTER 4

What About Acceptance Sampling Plans?

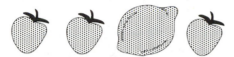

Although acceptance sampling plans are considered by some people to be part of SPC, such plans are not covered in this book (see Chapter 3, Section 3.9). One reason is that acceptance sampling is adequately covered in many other books.[1] Another reason is that acceptance sampling is receiving relatively less attention these days.

4.1 Acceptance Sampling Plans In Perspective

For many years statistical quality control has emphasized the *product*, whether it was in a raw material form or in finished product form. The focus, therefore, was on the acceptance or rejection (nonacceptance) of the product. It was natural, as well as necessary, that statistical sampling procedures should be developed and refined for making decisions of acceptance or rejection of product lots.

A comprehensive probability and sampling science has evolved. The determination of an operating characteristic (OC) curve (see Figure 3.8), which describes how any sampling plan behaves in terms of probability of accepting lots of specific levels of quality, enables us to evaluate the sampling plan's risks of making wrong decisions. Many kinds of acceptance sampling plans and procedures have been published.[2] These plans are still widely used today. But an

---

[1] See, for example, E. L. Grant and R. S. Leavenworth, *Statistical Quality Control*, 6th ed., Part Two, McGraw-Hill Book Company, New York, 1988.

[2] Perhaps the most widely used statistical document in the world is *Military Standard 105 (Sampling Procedures and Tables for Inspection by Attributes)*, originally published by the U.S. Department of Defense and now known as *American National Standard ANSI/ASQC Standard Z1.4-1981*. A similar set of plans for variables, once called *Military Standard 414*, is now known as *American National Standard ANSI/ASQC Z1.9-1980*.

aspect of these plans that tends to disturb some quality practitioners is that their use places the emphasis on product, materials, or components already produced—*after* the fact. At that point, it is too late to change the inherent quality of a lot.

More recently, however, there has been a shift in emphasis. Our attention is increasingly being directed toward the *process* itself, where the practice of *prevention* of quality defects (nonconformities) can be better effected. In short, we are moving upstream in our diligent efforts toward product and process improvement.

It is apparent, however, that the practice of making decisions on lots, based on samples, will continue for a long time to come. Formal acceptance sampling plans will most likely continue to play an important part in many quality programs. Therefore, the need to understand these plans and to become familiar with their probability characteristics is clear. This topic, however, is omitted from this book in order to enhance our emphasis on *prevention* of quality problems, an approach that offers stronger long-term benefits.

4.1 Summary

Acceptance sampling plans focus on product already produced when it is too late to take corrective action on quality defects. We wish to emphasize the prevention of quality problems, and this means directing resources toward the process itself. However, acceptance sampling plans will probably remain in use for a long time.

CHAPTER 5

Who's Afraid of Statistics, Anyway?

You say that you were never good in math or statistics and that you're not a statistician and could never hope to be one? You say that numbers fluster and confuse you and that all of those weird symbols and formulas frighten you? You say that it embarrasses you to present numerical data to anyone? You say that the concepts of statistics are too difficult for you because you can't think that way? You say that if you ever needed statistical work done, you would hire a professional statistician because they're only $1.10 a dozen?[1]

Well, you can stop right there and throw away your excuses and alibis! Numbers don't have to confuse you. Symbols and formulas don't have to frighten you. You can present numerical data as well as anyone can. The concepts of statistics are simple enough for anyone to understand, and you can learn to do statistical work yourself.

Why is all of this possible? Because *you are a statistician*! That is right. You are a statistician because *you think statistically*. The only difference between you and the professional statistician is that the latter person is able to formalize the way of thinking that is common to both of you.

5.1 Statistical Thinking in a Cup of Coffee

For example, suppose that you pick up a cup of coffee. You might add some cream or sugar (or substitutes thereof) and stir the contents. Next, you take a sip, and at that moment you make a decision—*an unconscious one*—to drink or not drink the rest of the coffee. Usually the decision is to drink the coffee. What

---

[1] Increased cost due to inflation.

happens here is that you usually make this decision without any deliberation, contemplation, meditation, or rumination. The entire process of reaching a decision is quite natural and quite effortless.

What you have demonstrated is *statistical thinking*. That first sip is called a *sample*. The rest of the coffee in the cup can be called the *process*, or, more generically in the statistical sense, a *population*.[2] In short, you conducted a statistical exercise that exhibited all of the components of statistical logic and procedure: defining a process, taking a sample, observing the results, following some rules, and reaching a decision. Because of that, you can consider yourself a statistician in the technical and procedural sense.

5.2 What Is Albert Really Like?

Now suppose that you are introduced to Albert for the first time, someone you have never met before. You and he engage in a nonspirited conversation that lasts only a few minutes. During that time you observe him, listen to him, and try to remember his name. At the end of that brief period you find yourself compelled to come to a conclusion as to what kind of a person Albert is. You realize, of course, that you have at least two choices in your judgment of Albert: He is either a fine person, or he is a scoundrel.[3] You find yourself choosing one on the basis of what you see and hear.

Is your judgment fair? Is it right to judge a human being so definitively on the basis of a brief exposure to that person? Probably not. Perhaps the only reliable way in which to determine what kind of a person Albert really is would be to live with him from the moment he is born, go through all of his experiences in life with him and observe how he behaves, until he dies. Because this is obviously an impractical alternative, you may never have the luxury of knowing the truth about Albert!

Yet we do not hesitate to make judgments about other people in this restrictive way. The statistical fact is that your perception of Albert was based on a small *sample* of his life—namely, your brief acquaintance. The sample, indeed, was infinitesimally small; yet this did not deter you. Albert's entire makeup as an individual constitutes the *process* or *population*.

What you engaged in was a genuine statistical experience that contains, once again, the essential logical elements: the process (or population), the sample, the procedure, and the inductive reasoning (from the specific to the general). You went through this experience quite naturally, without strain, thought, or premeditation. *And you don't consider yourself a statistician?*

---

[2] This statistical term and others will be defined more formally in Chapter 7.

[3] The choice of descriptive language and the range of possible impressions are up to you, of course.

5.3 Our Statistical Objective

Simply stated, our objective in industry is to find the *truth* about the real world. More specifically, we wish to determine why an industrial process behaves the way it does, why it produces defective goods or services, and what is needed to achieve improvement. The search for truth, despite impressive advances in modern technology, is still one of the grandest and most rewarding of all human experiences.

Statistically speaking, the real world can be called the *population*. We usually hear the real world described as the *process*, or the *lot*, or the *shipment*, or the *pallet load*, or the *delivery*, or *production*, etc. The observation that we make or the information that we collect is called the *sample*. Based on the results that we observe from the sample, we make a *decision*. The sample merely provides us with information or facts, and those facts usually take the form of *data*.

Having some data at hand does not mean that we can make correct decisions automatically about the population or process. A sizable gap usually exists between the data and the decision, especially the *correct* decision that reveals the truth about the real world. This is where the powerful statistical methods come in, to fill this gap.

We can express these relationships with a diagram (Figure 5.1). When we make an observation of the real world, we *infer* something about it based on the sample we took. This *inference* is expressed in the form of a decision.

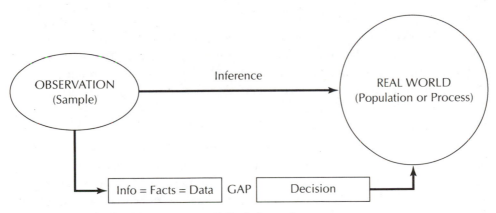

Figure 5.1. Relationships among statistical elements.

Note that the decision is directed to the population on the right-hand side of the Figure 5.1 diagram. *It is very important to note that the decision applies to the population and not to the sample.* Recognition of this principle will help us to word our decisions appropriately. We do not make decisions about the sample; the sample merely provides us with information that, when combined with rules of some sort, results in a decision about the population.

Having data in hand does not automatically enable us to ascertain the truth about a population or process. Hand several people a set of the same data and then observe the different interpretations and conclusions that will be expressed, most of which reflect personal theories and assumptions. Our objective, however, is to find the truth.

5.4 Where Is the Truth at a Meeting?

When a meeting is held among several people representing different departments or disciplines, for the purpose of discussing some problem, several different opinions (often conflicting ones) may be expressed as to what the true cause of the problem is. Each of the opinions may have genuine merit, but which one is the truth, if any?

To find the truth, each opinion must be put to the test of objective data collection and statistical analysis. With an open mind and dependable statistical tools in our hands, we can improve our batting average in making correct decisions.

5.5 Summary

You can consider yourself a statistician because you, like everyone else, think statistically. You rely on samples, often very small ones, to make judgments about populations (or processes). The samples may not always be valid or adequate, but nevertheless we respond to them. Our objective is to find the truth about the real world. Samples provide information, usually in the form of data, and if we apply statistical analysis to the sample data, we can often improve the correctness of the decision that we reach.

5.6 Putting It into Practice

The next time you contemplate going to a movie, determine how you made a decision to go or not to go. Did the movie involve an actor or actress whom you had previously seen? Did you see an advertisement? Did you see or hear a review of the film? Did a friend or spouse influence your decision? When you do come to a decision, identify the several elements in your experience: the process, the sample, the procedure, and the decision or conclusion. Determine if the evidence used was valid.

PART TWO

Basic Statistical Concepts

I hear, and I forget;
I see, and I remember;
I do, and I understand.
—Chinese proverb

CHAPTER 6

A First Look at Data:
The Frequency Histogram

8_{49.2} 𝕴𝕲*37***1**

Suppose someone handed you a sheet filled with data, such as in Table 6.1. What can these data[1] tell you? What can you conclude? Not very much. The sheet is a mass of numbers without apparent order or pattern. If, somehow, we could convert the data into some sort of picture or graphic summary, the visual impression would, without doubt, help to convey whatever it is that the data may be trying to tell us. Furthermore, the imagery would help us to retain the message in our minds.

6.1 Working With Data

The data that we will work with consist of measurements of screw-cap torques, in inch-pounds, made on 100 filled plastic jars taken throughout one production day consisting of two shifts. The jars are one gallon in size and contain a syrup concentrate used by restaurants and institutions. Cap torque is the twisting force needed to open the jar. Specification limits for cap torque are 15 to 25 inch-pounds, with a target (average) of 20.0 inch-pounds. The 100 jars are a *sample* from the day's production. Each (horizontal) row of Table 6.1 consists of five jars obtained at about the same time during the production run. Groups of five jars at a time, therefore, are taken approximately every 50 minutes, or ten times a shift. The sequence of sampling begins at the first (top) row and ends at the last (bottom) row.

---

[1] The word *data* is often treated erroneously as a singular noun. In fact, however, the word is plural and requires a plural verb or modifier. The singular form of data is *datum*.

Table 6.1. Screw-Cap Torques, 100 Plastic Jars, in Inch-Pounds; Sample from One Day's Production

21	21	19	20	24
23	20	26	21	23
21	23	17	21	19
21	22	25	24	20
17	18	20	20	20
18	15	20	21	20
23	23	23	18	22
23	20	14	21	20
25	24	24	19	19
21	21	25	15	19
15	21	19	20	21
17	15	16	20	19
13	17	17	19	17
22	20	18	21	16
17	21	18	21	21
17	20	21	19	21
19	21	22	17	20
21	18	20	23	22
19	26	20	24	28
26	26	25	26	24

Before we do any calculating with the sample data, let us see if a *picture* of some sort can give us some idea of important characteristics that would be of interest. The average cap torque would seem to be important. The percent of torques that are outside of specifications would also seem to be important, and that bit of information would be related to the amount of variability that is present. Can a graphic analysis provide us with this information? The answer is yes and then some.

First, we wish to get some idea of the *total spread* of all the data; that is, the difference between the smallest and largest readings. Locate and circle the smallest and largest readings on the data sheet of Table 6.1. Then subtract the smallest from the largest. You should get:

    Largest reading: 28 in.-lbs.
    Smallest reading: 13 in.-lbs.
    Total spread: 15 in.-lbs.

The total spread is 15 inch-pounds. Second, we wish to divide (or group) this total spread into *intervals* or *cells*. Grouping the data into intervals will enable us to draw a picture, called a *frequency histogram* (or simply *histogram*), that will help us see a pattern of variation if one exists. This is accomplished by *tallying* (counting) the data by intervals.

6.2 Number of Intervals

The number of intervals to be used is not fixed or automatically determined. Generally a simple rule of thumb is used: *anywhere from 6 to 20 intervals,* depending on the amount of data that we have.[2] If there are too few intervals, we may not be able to see the underlying pattern of variation, but the same can be said if there are too many intervals (see Figure 6.1). For small amounts of data, fewer intervals are needed than for large amounts of data. Thus it is a matter of trial and error to determine the number of intervals that will best describe the data. With about 50 to 200 readings or measurements available, *about 10 intervals* will usually give us a good picture of the distribution of data.[3]

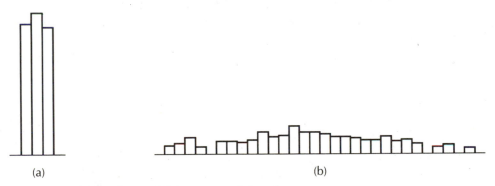

(a)   (b)

Figure 6.1. (a) Too few and (b) too many intervals.

We could tally the number of times (*frequency*) that each of the 16 possible *different* readings occurred in our data, readings from 13 to 28 inch-pounds

---

[2] Authors vary in their choice of number of intervals. See, for example,

    (a) E. R. Ott, *Process Quality Control*, McGraw-Hill Book Company, New York, 1975, p. 8: *13 to 20.*

    (b) I.W. Burr, *Elementary Statistical Quality Control*, Marcel Dekker, New York, 1979, p. 10: *8 to 12.*

    (c) J. D. Braverman, *Fundamentals of Statistical Quality Control*, Reston Publishing Company, Reston, Virginia, 1981, p. 17: *at least 5 to at most about 20.*

[3] You may find that some authors recommend specific numbers of intervals for specific numbers of readings or measurements, even providing a formula for that purpose. All of these efforts should be considered as guidelines only. This writer's experience with mountains of data from many varied industries has resulted in "about 10 intervals" as a very practical guide that is also easy to remember. For a table of specific numbers of intervals, see Kaoru Ishikawa, *Guide to Quality Control*, 2nd revised English edition, available from UNIPUB/Kraus, New York, 1986, p. 9, Table 2.3.

inclusive. A disadvantage of tallying the readings in this way is that we may end up with too many intervals; but an advantage is that we can determine exactly the number of jars in our sample that fell outside or inside specification limits. For our data here, you should find that two jars are outside the lower specification limit of 15, while six jars are outside the upper specification limit of 25. If the number of possible different readings is small, say 6 to 10, it is usually not helpful to group the readings together to form intervals, because one may end up with too few intervals. Any guideline that you use is just that: a guideline.

6.3 Choosing Interval Size

All intervals should be of the same size or width. Suppose that we take the total spread of 15 inch-pounds and divide it by 10. Then each *interval size* or *cell width* would be 1.5 inch-pounds, which is not a convenient interval size, because the original data are reported in whole numbers, not in tenths. Therefore, another rule of thumb is to *select intervals that correspond to the original data in number of decimal places.*

It seems reasonable, therefore, to round 1.5 to 2 for interval size. To include the smallest reading of 13, the first interval can be either 12–13 or 13–14. Suppose that we start with 12–13 for the first interval. The *cell limits* of the first interval are 12 and 13. Then the next interval is 14–15, and the next one is 16–17, etc. The complete list of intervals that covers the total spread of the data would look like this:

> 12–13
> 14–15
> 16–17
> 18–19
> 20–21
> 22–23
> 24–25
> 26–27
> 28–29

Thus we end up with nine intervals, which is "about" ten intervals, adequate for our data. Note here that the interval size of 2 in.-lbs. is not determined by the difference between the cell limits in any interval. *The interval size is determined by the difference between any two corresponding successive cell limits.* For example, the difference between the lower limit of the first interval, 12, and the lower limit of the second interval, 14, is 2, identifying the interval size. Similarly, the difference between the upper limit of the first interval, 13, and the upper limit of the second interval, 15, is also 2. This procedure for determining interval size applies to any two successive intervals.

6.4 Intervals Based on Specifications

Still another criterion that can be used to determine the limits of the intervals involves the specifications for the characteristic being studied. Since the specifications for cap torque are 15 to 25 in.-lbs., it would seem desirable to make 15 the *lower* limit of a particular interval. Then all readings *below* 15 would fall exclusively in intervals below that figure, making it easy to determine the exact number and percentage of readings outside the lower specification limit for the sample data.

Similarly, it would seem desirable to make 25 the *upper* limit of a particular interval. Then all readings above 25 would fall exclusively in intervals *above* that figure, making it easy to determine the exact number and percentage of readings outside the upper specification limit for the sample data.

Unfortunately, both desires often cannot be satisfied simultaneously. In the preceding example, the lower specification limit of 15 is contained in the interval 14–15, which also includes readings that are outside the specification limit. This makes it difficult to distinguish, for that interval, those readings that are within specifications from those that are outside specifications. But in the case of the upper specification limit of 25, it is contained in the interval 24–25, all of whose readings are within the specification limits. Frequently, therefore, the criterion of specification limits, among other criteria that are used, results in compromises in determining the intervals to be chosen. If the lower specification limit had been 14 instead of 15, then all readings in the interval 14–15 would also have been within specifications.[4]

6.5 Tallying the Data

Now we face the task of tallying the data to see how many readings fall in each of the nine intervals. It may be instructive to start by describing one method that is *not* usually recommended:

> Look over the data in Table 6.1, and count the number of readings that fall in the first interval, 12–13; then look over the data to count the number of readings that fall in the next interval, 14–15; and so on until you have looked over the data nine times to account for all nine intervals. This method is slow and may result in many errors in tallying, to say nothing of the tediousness of having to scan through the set of data many times.

A better method is to *tally each reading, one at a time*, making a *tally mark* beside the interval in which the reading falls. A tally mark can consist of a short vertical

---

[4] One does not change the specifications to 14 to 25 in.-lbs., for example, merely to accommodate statistical convenience!

line, such as I. As tally marks accumulate for each interval, it is helpful to make every fifth tally a *diagonal line,* such as /, across the previous four tally marks so that the tally marks appear in groups of five, such as ⍰. This will make it easy for you to count all of the tally marks when you have completed the tallying.

Prepare a worksheet with a column for the intervals and, next to it, a broad column for the tally marks, as shown in Figure 6.2. Label the column headings. When you have completed the tally of all 100 readings, your final tally result should look like the worksheet on Figure 6.2. What you see in Figure 6.2 with the tally marks is almost what the final histogram will look like, except that the histogram is turned 90 degrees. Be sure to leave room on the right side of your worksheet for several more columns of information that we will need for summarizing the data.

The next step is to identify another column on the worksheet. This column is labeled *f* for *frequency.* Count the interval tallies, and record the results as shown in Figure 6.3. If you add up all the frequencies for the nine intervals, they should total 100, the total sample size. You are now ready to draw the *frequency histogram.*

Interval	Tally
12–13	I
14–15	⍰
16–17	⍰ ⍰ I
18–19	⍰ ⍰ ⍰ II
20–21	⍰ ⍰ ⍰ ⍰ ⍰ ⍰ ⍰ II
22–23	⍰ ⍰ III
24–25	⍰ ⍰
26–27	⍰
28–29	I

Figure 6.2. Tally of the data by interval.

Interval	Tally	*f*
12–13	I	1
14–15	⍰	5
16–17	⍰ ⍰ I	11
18–19	⍰ ⍰ ⍰ II	17
20–21	⍰ ⍰ ⍰ ⍰ ⍰ ⍰ ⍰ II	37
22–23	⍰ ⍰ III	13
24–25	⍰ ⍰	10
26–27	⍰	5
28–29	I	1
	Totals	100

Figure 6.3. Showing a column for frequencies by interval.

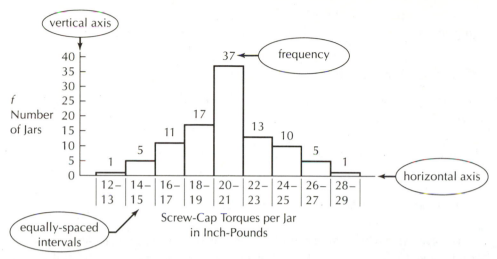

Figure 6.4. Frequency histogram.

6.6 Drawing the Frequency Histogram

Draw a *horizontal axis* as a baseline and a *vertical axis* to the left (see Figure 6.4). Identify the horizontal axis as "Screw-Cap Torques per Jar in Inch-Pounds." Divide the horizontal axis into nine equally spaced intervals, and identify them as we have done previously: 12–13, 14–15, 16–17, etc. You should include *every* interval to account for the entire spread of the data, even those intervals for which there may be no readings. Omitting any interval for which there are no readings will badly distort the final picture and may result in misinterpretations of the histogram.

Identify the vertical axis as *f* for "Frequency." Although frequency is a correct identification for the vertical axis, it is not really complete. It is better to identify the vertical axis as "Number of Jars." The scale of the vertical axis must start at 0 (zero) where the two axes meet. Many people leave that number out, but it is a legitimate number and ought to be shown. Note now that the highest frequency for an interval is 37 for the interval 20–21. Therefore, the vertical scale can go up to 40. Then divide the vertical scale between 0 and 40 in any convenient manner, in 10s (tens) or 5s (fives) or integers (ones).

Next, for each interval on the horizontal axis, draw a *rectangle* upward from the horizontal axis whose *height corresponds to the number of readings in the interval* as read from the vertical scale. There should be no gaps between rectangles; they should touch each other with a common border between adjoining rectangles.[5]

---

[5] If you separate the rectangles from each other, leaving gaps between them, you will then have a *bar graph,* which is more useful for *attribute* data. The data in our example are considered to be *variable* data and imply a continuous scale of measurements, although in whole numbers.

Your frequency histogram should now look like Figure 6.4. The various components of the histogram are identified for clarity.

6.7 What Does the Histogram Say?

The histogram can tell us three things without our having to perform any calculations:

1. Approximately what the *average* is

2. A sense of the *variability* of the data

3. Some idea of the *pattern of variation*.

The *average* can be seen to be in the neighborhood of 20 to 21 in.-lbs.; we shall soon be able to calculate it. Although we know what the total spread of the data is, from 13 to 28 in.-lbs., the histogram shows how the data are distributed between these two readings. This gives us a sense of the *variability* in the data, but we shall soon be able to express the variability in a more precise way. The *pattern* of variation is not quite as evident except to one with an experienced eye in working with data, but it does appear that at least some symmetry is apparent. We will look at patterns of variation in more detail later and learn that they are important in helping us to make predictions about the process.

6.8 Using the Histogram as a Communications Tool

The histogram can be an impressive supplement to any oral or written report. It is a visual summary of the data that conveys vital information that almost anyone, even those with little or no experience in dealing with data, can easily and quickly grasp.

If you have a meeting among your colleagues concerning a problem that is under study and discussion, you will certainly hear many ideas offered to explain the cause of the problem. Those people, however, who back up their statements with objective data and graphic summaries, such as the histogram, are the ones to whom more serious attention will likely be given.

A histogram that summarizes graphically some relevant data can be photocopied and distributed to all people present at a meeting. Before that is done, however, the histogram should be as complete a document as possible. It should contain basic information that will preclude the need to answer embarrassing questions about its background, such as "How big a sample did you get?" or "What period of time do the data cover?" In short, the histogram document should be self-contained.

Some basic information that might be included on the histogram document includes the following:

1. The *product* and its *characteristic*

2. *Unit of measurement* (Never leave this out, even if you believe that everyone present knows what it is.)

3. *Plant* or *organization* involved

4. *Time period* covered

5. *Shift* (if it is relevant)

6. *Production line* (if it is relevant)

7. *Machine* (if it is relevant)

8. *Operator* (if it is relevant)

9. *Total sample size.* (Note that in Figure 6.4 the number of readings for each interval is also shown at the top of each rectangle.)

10. *Specifications* and *target* for the characteristic under study

11. *Source* of the data (quality assurance, engineering, etc.)

12. *Artist* who prepared the histogram and *date* prepared.

Sometimes other bits of information are desirable, such as how the sample was obtained and how the characteristic was measured or tested. In any event, there is usually enough room on the histogram document sheet to include all of the relevant information as concisely as possible. Inclusion of this basic information will show that you have thought about your data and have anticipated important (and possibly embarrassing) questions. Being prepared is half the credibility; the rest is in the data.

6.9 Showing Readings Outside Specifications

Another suggestion is in order concerning specifications. The specifications for cap torque are 15 to 25 inch-pounds. If there are any readings in the sample data that are outside of the specifications, it is helpful to indicate this on the histogram by *shading, coloring,* or *marking in some way* those rectangles or portions of rectangles that are outside the specifications. The reader can then tell at a glance the approximate percentage of readings that are outside specifications. If this were done for our histogram in Figure 6.4, the picture would look like Figure 6.5:

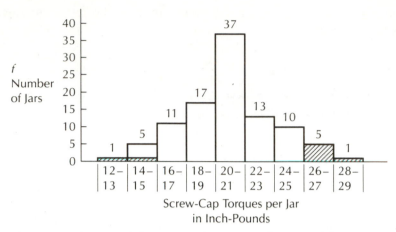

Figure 6.5. Frequency histogram showing readings outside specification limits.

We know from our initial scan of the data that the one reading in the first interval (12–13) is actually 13 in.-lbs., out of specs. One reading in the next interval (14–15) is 14 in.-lbs., also out of specs. All six readings in the last two intervals are obviously out of specs. Therefore, the first rectangle and the last two rectangles are completely shaded, but only a portion of the second rectangle is shaded. It is an acceptable practice to shade only a portion of a rectangle, but notice that the partial shading of the second rectangle (interval 14–15) occupies a certain *height* of the rectangle instead of a *width*, because height reflects frequency.[6]

For the moment set aside your worksheet until some basic statistical concepts are discussed in the next few chapters. Then some final calculations with these data will be made in Chapter 14 that express more specifically the important characteristics of average, variability, and predictions about the process.

6.10 Summary

A set of data can be summarized graphically using the frequency histogram. The data are grouped into intervals, the number of which can run from 6 to 20, depending on how much data are available. A practical guideline is to use about 10 intervals. Listing the intervals, tallying the data, and placing the tally marks next to the appropriate interval enable us to draw a histogram easily. The histogram is drawn with rectangles whose heights correspond to the number of

---

[6] Some practitioners, however, prefer to shade a proportionate width in order to give the impression that the base scale is a continuous measurement scale, something like a ruler.

readings in each interval. We can then observe, without calculations, what the approximate average is, how much variability there is, and some notion of the pattern of variation. Shading those rectangles that are outside the specification limits helps to estimate quickly the percentage of nonconformities. The histogram becomes an effective and self-contained communications tool for conveying statistical information provided that relevant background information is also shown on the document sheet containing the histogram.

6.11 Putting It into Practice

1. Samples of four packages of a popular snack food are taken every 30 to 45 minutes from the end of a packaging line before the package is closed and sealed. The sampled product is analyzed for fat content, in percent, on a machine on the production floor that provides a quick and reliable analysis. The specifications for the product are 11.4% ± 0.3% fat; that is, the target is 11.4%, and the specification limits are 11.1% and 11.7%. The data are arranged in groups of four, each group taken at about the same time:

11.2	11.2	11.8	11.4
11.4	11.3	11.3	11.4
11.4	11.9	11.3	11.4
11.8	11.5	11.7	11.7
11.4	11.5	11.5	11.3
11.4	11.5	11.6	11.6
11.5	11.6	11.4	11.4
11.4	11.5	11.5	11.6
11.5	11.6	11.6	11.6
11.2	11.5	11.3	11.5
11.3	11.3	11.4	11.5
11.7	11.6	11.3	11.5
11.4	11.4	11.2	11.4
11.5	11.4	11.0	11.7
11.8	11.4	11.7	11.6
11.3	11.4	11.4	11.5
11.4	11.3	11.5	11.4
11.5	11.4	11.4	11.5
11.4	11.5	11.7	11.3
11.4	11.5	11.5	11.4

Prepare a frequency histogram from these data. Answer the following questions:

(a) What is a reasonable interval size?

(b) What is your guess as to what the average of the sample data is?

(c) Is the process on target?

(d) What percentage of the samples are outside specification limits?

(e) How would you evaluate this process?

2. Collect from 60 to 100 readings on some important characteristic of one of your products that is under study or discussion. Prepare a frequency histogram according to procedures described in this chapter. Be sure to include relevant background information. Make copies and distribute them to those involved in the study or discussion. What did you learn? Were you able to answer all questions asked? What was the impact on your colleagues? If there is a statistician in your group, discuss the results with him or her.

Answers to Problem 1

(a) The interval size is 0.1%. The overall spread is $11.9 - 11.0 = 0.9\%$. Dividing this by 10 gives us 0.09%, and rounding this to a convenient number gives us 0.1% for interval size. But this is also the measurement unit for percent fat, which is recorded to the nearest 0.1%. Therefore, the "intervals" consist of the readings to 0.1%:

    11.0
    11.1
    11.2
    11.3
    etc.

(b) The histogram shows that the sample average is a little higher than 11.4% fat.

(c) We do not know for sure. If the samples were taken according to standard operating procedures (SOP) written in some manual, then we would conclude that the process is reasonably close to target.

(d) Five out of the 80 readings are outside spec limits. This represents 6% outside specs for the sample taken.

(e) This is not a good process. The histogram shows that there is too much variability in the process. The cause or causes for the excessive variability may be due to the inherent variability in the process or due to some outside disturbing factors that tend to increase the natural variability. In either event, the process must be studied carefully.

CHAPTER 7

Population (Process) Versus Sample—Nomenclature

One of the most important concepts in understanding statistical methods is to distinguish between a *population* and a *sample*. The ability to make this distinction will help to assure you that you have a clear notion of the items or data that you are studying, that you will be using the right language in expressing conclusions, and that you will be using the correct formula in certain instances.

7.1 Definition of Population

Population: A group of similar items about which we wish to make a decision.

The statistical interpretation of *population* is not necessarily about groups of people. Interpretations that you may be familiar with almost daily include *process, lot, batch, shipment, delivery, pallet load*, etc. In SPC, as in other applications of statistical methods, our conclusions are generally directed to the population and not to the sample.

An additional statement helps to describe population more clearly: *A population is usually described in terms of space (meaning location) and time.*

Some examples of populations follow:

1. Packaged 1-lb. baked white bread produced during the past week in plant A. We might be interested in their true average weight.

2. One make of automobile, this year's model SX, that was sold during the past month at dealers east of the Mississippi River. We might be interested in the car-to-car variability in miles-per-gallon fuel usage.

3. Cancelled bank checks processed through a particular branch during a three-month period. We might be interested in the percentage that are overdrawn.

Notice that the elements of *space* and *time* are present in all of these descriptions. When conducting any kind of statistical study, it is essential that the population under study be clearly defined and described at the outset.

7.2 Definition of Sample

Sample: A portion of the population.

The definition does not identify the size of the sample. It could be anywhere from one item (a sample of *one*) to the entire population, process, or lot (a *100% sample*).

7.3 True Information About a Population

The only sure way of obtaining the *truth* about a population is to measure, check, test, or inspect *every item* in the population. This important principle must be kept in mind as you explore the techniques of SPC. But 100% sampling can be time-consuming, costly, and even ineffective if we depend, for example, on human visual inspection. Samples are often the only efficient way to obtain information about a population.

Consider, for example, a lot that consists of thousands of stored fireworks devices, such as firecrackers, rockets, etc., that are exploded during festive celebrations. If management insisted on knowing the *true* percentage of defective fireworks in the lot—those that will not explode properly—there is only one way of getting that information: Ignite every one. Those that do not explode or explode improperly are the defective ones; those that do explode properly are the good ones.

If every device is ignited, the true information about the percentage of defective fireworks in the lot will be available, but the entire lot will have been destroyed and none will be left to sell. Is management willing to pay this price for the absolute truth? Hardly. A sample is the practical answer to this dilemma. (If research resources and time were available, one might develop innovative testing methods that are nondestructive and cost-effective.)

Information obtained from samples, however, may not necessarily tell the truth about the population. Information can vary from one sample group to another sample group. In short, there is *variability* in sample information. The best statement that we can make, therefore, is that the information from a sample is an *estimate* of the truth in the population. If you keep this limitation in mind when reporting sample results and do not assert that the sample results *are* the truth, you will show that you respect the uncertainty in sample data.

When making a statistical study about a population (process, lot, etc.), we invariably depend on samples to provide us with information. The purpose of such a study is to be able to make some definitive statement about the population involved. Any conclusion, decision, or judgment that derives from sample results, therefore, must be carefully worded in a way that directs it to the population under study. Good statistical habits require some expertise in language control; the skill is almost a form of art. We will see examples of this later.

7.4 Nomenclature for Population and Sample

The distinction that we try to make between population and sample is so important that we use different symbols or nomenclature to distinguish between the two concepts. Table 7.1 contains the more frequently used statistical characteristics and their distinguishing nomenclature.

Table 7.1. Nomenclature: Population Versus Sample

Characteristic	Population	Sample	Relationship
Number of Items	N	n	
Mean (average)	μ	$\overline{X}$	$\overline{X}$ is an estimate of μ
Variance	σ^2	S^2	S^2 is an estimate of σ^2
Standard deviation	σ	S	S is an estimate of σ
Proportion	π or p'	p	p is an estimate of p'
Correlation	ρ	r	r is an estimate of ρ

7.5 Parameters and Statistics

Parameters: The characteristics of the population.

Parameters are treated as *constants* for a defined population. For example, the true average weight of a specified lot of packaged snack foods is some particular unknown number. We take samples in order to get some idea (an estimate) of the magnitude of that unknown number.

As shown in Table 7.1, we generally use Greek letters to designate parameters of a population:

- μ is the Greek lowercase letter *mu* for the mean

- σ is the Greek lowercase letter *sigma* for the standard deviation, a measure of variability

- π is the Greek lowercase letter *pi* for the proportion of some attribute of interest

- ρ is the Greek lowercase letter *rho* for the correlation coefficient.

Because the Greek letter π is commonly identified with the constant 3.14159 . . . , which relates various parts of a circle, we tend to break the rule here of using Greek letters and assign the symbol p' (pronounced *p-prime*) for the true proportion in a population.

Sample statistics (or simply **statistics**): The characteristics of the sample.

Sample statistics are treated as *variables* because they tend to vary from sample to sample. When one selects samples of, say, 10 items at a time from a process, the averages of groups of 10 items will undoubtedly vary. This is where difficulty arises in trying to determine what the true average of the entire process is.

This is also where theoretical statistics enters to help us determine how much variability exists in those sample averages and how large a sample we need to collect to get a good grasp of the true process average.

7.6 Statements of Estimates

The relationships in the last column of Table 7.1 are statements that we should become accustomed to writing. They will prevent us from making false statements that sample results are the true population results. We suggest a more compact way of writing these statements:

$$\overline{X} = \text{Est. of } \mu$$
$$S^2 = \text{Est. of } \sigma^2$$
$$S = \text{Est. of } \sigma$$
$$p = \text{Est. of } p'$$
$$r = \text{Est. of } \rho$$

Some statisticians identify a sample estimate of a population characteristic by placing a "hat" above the symbol for the population parameter. Thus $\hat{\mu}$ (pronounced *mu hat*) designates an estimate of μ. Therefore $\overline{X} = \hat{\mu}$. This can be somewhat confusing because the symbol with the hat is not that different at a glance from the symbol without a hat, particularly when the type size is small. In addition, using the hatted symbol does not reinforce the idea that the sample result is, indeed, an *estimate* of the population parameter. Therefore, this author prefers to express the relationships between population parameters and their sample estimates with short words that help to make the relationships more clear. In statistical work we should expend a little more effort to achieve clarity of communication.

7.7 Summary

The distinction between the statistical concepts of *population* and *sample* is necessary to make clear statements of conclusions. Use of the correct nomenclature helps to reinforce that distinction. A *population* is a group of similar items about which we wish to make a decision. A process, lot, batch, shipment, delivery, and pallet-load are examples of populations. A population is usually described in terms of space (meaning location) and time. A *sample* is a portion of a population. Characteristics of a population are called *parameters*; they are constants for a defined population. Characteristics of a sample are called *sample statistics* or, simply, *statistics*; they are variables. Symbols for parameters are usually Greek letters. Sample statistics are estimates of population parameters; short statements to that effect help to clarify and emphasize this relationship.

The only trouble with a sure thing
is the uncertainty.

—Anonymous

Kinds of Samples and How to Sample

Since obtaining a sample is so necessary in gaining some knowledge about a population, *how* you get the sample is extremely important. Because practically all of the information about a population, process, or lot depends on the sample, our concern and attention should be consciously directed to the manner in which the sample is obtained. Sampling ought not to be treated as casually as it sometimes is.

Let us consider in detail two of the most important kinds of samples that are used in industrial applications: *random* samples and *stratified* samples.

8.1 Random Samples

Random sample: A sample for which every item in the population has an equal chance of being selected.

Practically every statistical method used today assumes that a random sample has been obtained from the population, process, or lot. The random sample assumption forms the basis for accurately predicting the behavior of the statistical method being used. From a strictly theoretical point of view, unless you have obtained a genuine random sample, your conclusions about the population might be suspect.

In practice, getting a genuine random sample is not always easy. Constraints due to time, personnel, complexity of method, and difficulty of access to the items in the population often dictate the method of sampling. A common practice, in industrial and other applications, is to compromise somewhat on how the sample is obtained. Every effort should be made, however, within practical constraints of time and cost, to obtain a truly random sample before any compromise method is considered. A good compromise that essentially satisfies the requirements for randomness in a practical way can be a satisfactory approach. A poor compromise that blatantly ignores requirements can lead to misleading, and perhaps costly, decisions. When in doubt, consult a statistician.

8.2 A Nonindustrial Example

The need for random samples is elegantly illustrated in public lotteries that several states in the U.S. conduct daily. People who contemplate buying lottery tickets in these states must be totally convinced that they have just as good a chance of losing as anyone else; otherwise they would not participate.[1] Therefore, the state lottery commissions feel obligated to demonstrate visually to the public that the winning numbers (and, hence, the losing numbers) are determined by chance; that is, at random.

You can understand now why the procedure by which winning lottery numbers are selected is often shown live on television. The winning numbers are actually random numbers. A popular method for generating winning (random) numbers is to exhibit see-through plastic containers, each of which contains 10 ping-pong balls numbered from 0 through 9. Three containers are used in order to obtain a three-digit random number for the winning number. The balls are stirred by air movement, and one of them is randomly blown to the top of the container when a hatch is opened.

This visual demonstration can easily persuade any trusting viewer and potential lottery participant that a random process is actually in operation. However, for the process to be truly random, the ping-pong balls would have to be identical in size and weight; this is a hidden assumption about the sampling process you see, an assumption that is rarely challenged.

If you are inclined to take the time to tally, you can observe the number of times that each of the 10 digits represented by the ping-pong balls comes up over some extended period of time, such as several months. If a random process is actually in operation, then *each of the 10 digits should occur approximately an equal number of times.*[2] If you find a significant discrepancy in the frequencies of occurrence, such as one or two numbers appearing unusually fewer or unusually more times than the other numbers, then you have a reasonable basis for being suspi-

---

[1] One might as well consider the probability of *losing,* rather than winning, because that is, by far, the more common experience.

[2] A statistical test, the chi-squared test of goodness of fit, can be applied to such data to see if the assumption of randomness has been violated. See, for example, S. S. Shapiro, *How to Test Normality and Other Distributional Assumptions,* Vol. 3 (revised ed.), Quality Press, American Society for Quality Control, Milwaukee, 1990.

cious about the method being used. A nonrandom cause, therefore, is in operation, and we might call it an *assignable* or *special* cause. Your first thought, undoubtedly, would be the presence of some hanky-panky.

8.3 An Industrial Example

You wish to determine the average net weight of boxes of detergent produced during a run of some 450 boxes on one line during a shift. The boxes are stored in a single location. The population would be defined as the number of filled boxes produced on one line during a specific shift on a certain day in a specific plant.

To determine the net weight of a box, you would need to cut open the cardboard box (thereby making it unfit for reuse) and empty and weigh the contents on a scale. An alternative method for finding out the net weight is to get the gross weight of a box, empty the contents, weigh the empty box and subtract that weight (called the *tare* weight) from the gross weight. To save some time, it might be reasonable to get the weights of just a few of the empty boxes (a sample), calculate their average weight, and use that figure as an average tare weight to be applied to all of the boxes in the lot. If, however, the empty-box weights vary considerably, the procedure of using an average tare weight would not be satisfactory.

If you decide, in all probability, that it is too time-consuming and too costly to weigh every box in the 450-box lot, then you need to collect a random sample. How large a sample should you get? There are statistical methods for determining sample size that consider the discrepancies and risks that one can accept.[3] But you decide, because of the time, labor, and cost involved, to get a random sample of 10 boxes.

One way to obtain a random sample is to identify each of the 450 boxes in some way, write down each box identification on a piece of paper, place all of the pieces of paper in some container, mix them thoroughly, and finally select 10 pieces of paper without looking at the container of papers. That would be, indeed, a genuine and valid random sample. But, admittedly, it would also be an awkward, clumsy, and time-consuming method.

The method can be streamlined considerably by using a *table of random numbers*.[4] Each of the 450 boxes is assigned a number running consecutively from 1 to 450. Then reference is made to a table of computer-generated random

---

[3] See, for example, G. G. Brush, *How to Choose the Proper Sample Size*, Vol. 12, Quality Press, American Society for Quality Control, Milwaukee, 1988.

[4] See, for example, The Rand Corporation, *A Million Random Digits with 100,000 Normal Deviates*, The Free Press, Glencoe, Illinois, 1955.

Table 8.1. Table of Random Numbers

9777	5872	8521	5314	3203	3697
2686	4363	5129	5153	3800	9091
1842	5709	0145	8173	0791	7965
6245	2560	4341	4870	1426	8743
5784	0696	6619	4257	8549	8721
1448	6835	0048	4346	8105	0323
6091	4886	2898	8271	3721	2162
3608	8756	0933	9337	4021	9134
1689	8544	4051	8808	1206	5312
6885	1129	2357	6945	7732	3859
0383	8383	0850	4876	9770	4903
3624	2804	7766	2005	7201	4693
6340	3450	7569	9554	1182	5399
4174	7163	3669	8660	6154	0334
8855	2021	1857	9344	8423	8865
2729	5247	8580	9528	1517	3514
5810	5979	6347	7843	9938	9046
8236	4036	5221	6379	9812	5680
0666	1069	5903	3636	1673	5369
9641	1424	3371	0237	4690	7579
4759	6202	3897	4394	2881	2093
0726	6099	8402	3998	8948	0704
3008	6523	4751	5635	0962	2904
9097	5912	6678	5600	3551	4640
9821	8686	0438	6271	6882	1180

numbers, a portion of which is shown in Table 8.1. This table displays random digits in groups of four, although groups can be combined or separated in any way you wish. The spacing after every five rows has no significance; it merely aids our reading.

Since the size of the population in our example, 450, contains three digits, we will need groups of three digits from the table. Let us use the first three digits in any group of four that we consider.

Next we need a starting point in the table and a decision as to which direction we will move from this starting point. The starting point, the first group of four, can be determined by blindly pointing to a spot on the page of random numbers. Suppose it happens to be the seventh row from the top and third column of numbers from the left (starting group 2898). Suppose we decide to move downward from there and then to the right and upward if we reach the bottom of the page. It makes no difference in which direction we move from our starting point as long as it is decided in advance; the numbers on the page, after all, are numbers generated at random.

Finally, we select those groups of four whose first three digits are anywhere between 1 and 450 inclusive, corresponding to the boxes in the lot. The first 10 different groups of three digits between 1 and 450 inclusive constitute our random sample of 10 boxes.

In Table 8.1 our starting group is 2898 in the seventh row and third column. The first three digits, 289, are less than 451 and therefore correspond to a box with that assigned number. That is the first box in our sample.

Going down the third column from 2898, we select the next nine groups in which the first three digits fall between 1 and 450 inclusive and are different from each other. Any group of four whose first three digits exceed 450 is ignored. If a three-digit number has already been included in our sample, we ignore it and continue. See if you can verify that our random sample of 10 boxes consists of those numbered as follows:

289	366
093	185
405	337
235	389
085	043

The next step is find and pull those boxes with these assigned numbers from the lot, a procedure that usually entails some physical effort and care.

Those with some experience in using random numbers in this way to select a random sample usually complain that it was sometimes necessary to fetch a sample from the center of the lot where it was most difficult and inconvenient to reach the box or boxes. This is especially true of those people who must sample from pallet loads of product. "It's my tough luck that some of the boxes had to come from the middle of the pallet!" You should exhibit some compassion for people with the responsibility for sampling, but you must insist, nevertheless, that random sampling be done in this way.

Because inconvenience and time become factors to contend with, it is not uncommon for some people to be tempted to deviate from the strict random number approach and to select a sample that is more convenient. If, for example, a pallet of product is involved and temptation is not resisted, the boxes (or units of product) on the *top* and *sides* will be selected for the sample because they are easy to get to. This corruption of the random sampling procedure has a hidden and unexpressed assumption underlying it; namely, every box on the pallet has the same external forces acting on it regardless of its position on the pallet. This is an incorrect assumption. Boxes on the top and sides are more exposed to physical damage than other boxes as the pallet is transported around a busy production floor.

If you are convinced that all product on a pallet is equally exposed to environmental conditions of handling, transport, and ambient exposure, then some compromise in the sampling method may be permitted. But, be careful! One can carry this license to an extreme and sample only from the top, where the product is most accessible. Pallets are usually loaded in the order in which product is produced, with first-produced product on the bottom of the pallet, and last-produced product on the top. If you are looking for certain attributes, such as defects, they may not occur at random but come in "bunches." If so, sampling only from the top of a pallet will result in either a falsely high reading or a falsely low reading of the incidence of those defects. Compromises in sampling methods, although commonplace, can be self-defeating.

8.4 Random Numbers Elsewhere

Admittedly, the use of tables of random numbers can be bothersome at times. A more convenient way of getting random numbers is to use a hand-held scientific calculator that generates random numbers. This feature precludes the need to carry around pages of random numbers. Many scientific calculators today generate three-digit random numbers, which may appear to be a serious limitation when the population or lot size numbers in the thousands. But in this case two consecutive sets of three-digit numbers can be combined to form a six-digit random number, enough to take care of very large lots.

8.5 Stratified Samples

Another important kind of sample that, in some cases, is more appropriate than a random sample is a *stratified sample*.

> *Stratified sample:* A sample that has the same proportion of an attribute that can affect the result as is contained in the population or lot.

The sample is called stratified because the attribute or attributes represent a stratification or layering of the population.

For example, suppose that we wish to estimate the average height of a group of 200 people, and we wish to use a sample of 10 people. We could, of course, select a genuine random sample. We notice, however, that the group of 200 people in this population consists of 70% men (140) and 30% women (60). In general (meaning on the average), men are taller than women. This natural physical difference can bias the result obtained from a purely *random* sample. In a random sample of 10 people, all 10 *could* be men. This would tend to give us a random sample whose average is biased on the high side. Similarly, it is possible that, in a random sample of 10 people, all 10 *could* be women. This would tend to give us a random sample whose average is biased on the low side. Clearly, some pitfalls exist in taking a random sample in this case.

In selecting a stratified sample, we select the 10 people in the sample in the same proportion of men and women as there is in the population. Therefore, we would select seven men and three women for our stratified sample.

The seven men for our sample would be selected *at random* from the 140 men in the population. The three women for our sample would be selected *at random* from the 60 women in the population. Thus, even in the case of a stratified sample, we cannot avoid entirely the need to get a random sample at some stage of sampling.

8.6 Foibles of Stratified Sampling

Arranging the population into strata means classifying or grading into clearly defined groups or layers that could have different effects on the result being evaluated. The designers of the sampling scheme must be sure to account for all *relevant* layers or groups. For example, in considering a population of people around the country who are voting in a popular election, a stratified sample makes sense. Such a sample could be stratified by sex, race, religion, economic status, urban or rural residency, civilian or military, political party, region of the country, etc. A stratified sample can also provide valuable information about the different voting characteristics of each *stratum* or layer.

Leaving out a key layer inadvertently can be devastating and embarrassing. Examples abound where this has occurred during elections. A classic example is the presidential election of 1948, when President Harry S Truman campaigned against Governor Thomas E. Dewey from New York. A prestigious newspaper, *The Chicago Tribune*, used telephone directories to survey thousands of people across the country. The newspaper was careful in obtaining a stratified sample by the categories listed earlier.

When it was completed, the survey showed that Dewey would win by a substantial majority, and the *Tribune* published its survey findings, before all the votes were cast, in an historic headline, "Dewey Defeats Truman." When the votes were all counted, the result was the opposite! Truman defeated Dewey. A photograph of Truman holding up a copy of the ill-fated issue of the *Tribune* has become a classic. Even Walter Mondale, hoping for the same surprise result, held up that same issue when he ran for president against Ronald Reagan during the election campaign of 1984.

What was wrong with the survey? Simply put, some important layers in the stratified sample were unaccounted for. They included people who did not have telephones (a substantial number in 1948) and people who had telephones but were not listed in any telephone directories (not uncommon in the rural communities). It was a stratified sample that was not thoroughly thought out. Similar cases have occurred since then, including a primary election in Wisconsin when absentee ballots were omitted as a stratum, and the prematurely predicted results were overturned when all of the ballots were counted.

Stratified samples taken from pallets of product are typical of such samples in industry. Samples may be taken from the top layers, the middle layers, and the bottom layers of a pallet. This is not a random sample; it is a stratified sample. As long as the one who designates such sampling procedures assumes that layers on a pallet represent some definitive classification, then it is a valid method. But it must be remembered that the samples obtained *within each layer* should be obtained as a *random* sample from the respective layer.

8.7 "Representative" Samples

Representative sample is a common expression used for sampling, but it is incorrect and misleading. It implies that such a sample truly represents the population or lot from which it was drawn and therefore contains information that precisely coincides with that in the population. Nothing could be further from the truth. The mean (average) obtained from a "representative" sample is not the true mean of the population; one could bet money on it.

What does "representative" sample suggest, then? It suggests how the sample is to be obtained. Several U.S. government agencies use this expression. For example, Military Standard 105D,[5] perhaps the most widely used statistical document in the world, says:

> 7.2 REPRESENTATIVE SAMPLING. When appropriate, the number of units in the sample shall be selected in proportion to the size of sublots or subbatches, or parts of the lot or batch, identified by some rational criterion. When representative sampling is used, the units from each part of the lot or batch shall be selected at random.

[5] "Sampling Procedures and Tables for Inspection By Attributes," U.S. Department of Defense, Washington, DC, 1963.

The U.S. Food and Drug Administration (FDA), in its Current Good Manufacturing Practice (GMP) for human and veterinary drugs, describes a representative sample as follows:

> "Representative sample" means a sample that consists of a number of units drawn at random from each part of a lot or batch to assure that the sample accurately represents the lot or batch.[6]

It is quite clear from the two government examples that a so-called representative sample is really a stratified sample and should be designated as such. Otherwise, more accuracy and validity will be attributed to it than it deserves, especially when the phrase "accurately represents" is included.

Other examples can be found where "representative sample" implies a random sample. There is only one truly accurate and representative sample, and that is the 100% sample, meaning the entire population. The phrase "representative sample" should be discarded from our vocabulary because of its deceptive implication. The samples should be called random or stratified.

Other kinds of samples occur in industry, but almost all of them are variations of random or stratified samples. More elaborate sampling methods can be found in surveys of human population, econometric studies, and social and psychological studies.

8.8 Sampling for Additional Information

Many factors influence an industrial process or business enterprise and are reflected in the statistical information that one collects. Your knowledge and intuition, based on experience with a process, as to what factors influence the statistical information, can be put to good use. When a process is studied to gain additional objective insight into why the process behaves the way it does, that knowledge and intuition become the basis for the collection of relevant statistical data.

For example, suppose one is interested in the average thickness and variability of a finished machined part being produced on four manufacturing lines over three shifts. Suppose that the finished parts from each line are collected into four separate bins on each shift, each bin representing a line's production. In a final stage the parts from the three shifts are combined into a common storage area for ultimate shipment to customers.

If random samples are taken from the common storage area, the results should be an adequate estimate of the overall average thickness and variability being produced. If either the overall average thickness or variability is not satisfying

---

[6] *Federal Register*, Vol. 41, No. 31, February 13, 1976.

the requirements (specifications) for this part, a special study would probably have to be conducted to determine the possible causes. The statistical tools that one might use include control charts and process capability studies (see Part Three). To go a step further, if it is company policy to *improve the process continually*, then the special study could become a routine part of the production process. In short, the process would be *continually* studied to find ways of improving it.

Improving a process means to reduce its variability. Therefore the causes of variation would have to be studied. In our example, you can sense that whatever overall variability one finds in the final combined storeroom, that variability is caused by at least two important factors: differences among the four lines and differences among the three shifts. There may be other factors, such as the raw material that is used, the condition of the machining equipment, the skill and supervision status of the personnel, the measuring instruments, the intervals of time, the ambient environmental conditions that prevail, the process steps, and perhaps others.

It would seem logical, therefore, to modify the simple random sampling procedure originally suggested and at least get some information about the effects of differences among the shifts and differences among the lines. This can be done without much additional effort. The results would simply be summarized and, better yet, graphed according to line and shift.

Thus the sampling would have to be conducted upstream; that is, at the end of each line and during each shift. Do you recognize this method of sampling as a form of stratified sampling? Assembling the data in this fashion will help to determine if there are important effects on thickness due to shift or to line. Of course, any data thus collected would have to be properly identified by shift and line.

There is, unquestionably, a certain discretion as to how samples are to be collected and how data are to be summarized. One's knowledge and experience become useful factors in investigative work of this kind.

8.9 Summary

Since the sample is the important source of information about a population (process or lot), how we get a sample is vital. A *random* sample is one for which every item in the population has an equal chance of being selected. It is unbiased, without prejudice. A random number table is an objective way of obtaining a random sample, although it may not be an easy way. Scientific calculators are useful for generating random numbers. If certain groups, strata, or layers in a population could bias the results of a strictly random sample, then a *stratified* sample is more appropriate. Such a sample is divided into strata or layers in the same proportion that they exist in the population. Getting either a random sample or a stratified sample requires care in planning and execution. So-called representative samples are a misnomer; they are basically random samples or stratified samples and should be designated accordingly. Sampling that identifies certain possible factors that can affect the results, such as line and shift, is a useful approach in investigative work.

50% of the game is 90% mental.

—Yogi Berra,
former baseball manager

CHAPTER 9

Some Rules of Probability

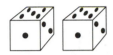

The theory of probability is comprehensive, fairly elaborate, and certainly interesting. It is used extensively to estimate the likelihood of events that can occur and is useful in many practical situations, such as the probability of rain or the probability that a sampling plan will accept a product lot. We need not explore the theory in great detail.[1]

Some of the basic rules (also called *laws*) of probability will be helpful to us in interpreting SPC tools, particularly control charts, and these will be the subject of interest in this chapter. We do need, however, to start with some fundamental concepts that form the basis for these rules of interest.

9.1 Definition of Probability

Consider some event, such as the occurrence of a particular defect on a unit of product. We can designate the event as E. The probability of the occurrence of event E can be written as $P(E)$.

The *probability of event* E can be defined from a simple fraction in equation form,

$$P(E) = \frac{\text{Number of ways event } E \text{ can occur}}{\text{Total number of possible outcomes}}. \tag{9.1}$$

---

[1] Probability topics that include, for example, sample spaces, combinations and permutations, conditional probabilities, Venn diagrams, tree diagrams, Bayes's theorem, and probability distributions other than the normal distribution are beyond the objectives of this book and may be found in standard textbooks.

Probability values are never negative; nor are they greater than one. Probability can be expressed in three different ways:

1. As a fraction, such as 1/20

2. As a decimal proportion, such as 0.05

3. As a percentage, such as 5%.

Equation (9.1) is the *classical definition of probability*. It is also a theoretical probability, because it can be calculated without verification from an actual experiment or test.

9.2 Coins, Assumptions, and Models

A simple example of using Eq. (9.1) involves a coin. Without tossing a coin or even having a coin in your possession, you can determine the theoretical probability of getting a head when you toss a coin. Of course, your answer will be 1/2. In terms of using Eq. (9.1), there is only one way to get a head (the numerator), and there are two possible outcomes (the denominator).

The reason that you were able to come up with the answer of 1/2—a theoretical answer—is that you made certain *assumptions* concerning the coin, no doubt without even expressing them. Those assumptions included:

1. The coin has a head and a tail (the two possible outcomes).

2. The coin will not land on its edge.

3. The coin is balanced, meaning that the amount of metal or alloy in the sculpture (called *bas-relief*) on the face of the coin is the same on either side. (Do you believe that this is true?)

4. The coin was tossed in a random fashion; that is, there was no bias or cheating in the toss.

From these assumptions almost anyone would say that the probability of getting a head is 1/2. That is,

$$P(\text{Heads}) = 1/2 \text{ (or 0.5, or 50\%).} \tag{9.2}$$

Equation (9.2) is called a *model* for the coin, a theoretical prediction of the anticipated behavior of the coin *in the long run*. Like any model, it has some assumptions behind it, expressed or not expressed, such as those listed earlier.

9.3 Proving Validity of the Model

What is truly interesting (as if it has been only mildly interesting so far) is that *you can never prove that this model is correct*! Consider this: If you tossed this coin 10 times, you would not always get exactly five heads and five tails every time that you tossed it 10 times. Indeed, the percentage of heads (or tails) could vary considerably from 50% during any group of 10 tosses, even if the model is valid. If you tossed it 100 times, you would not always get exactly 50 heads and 50 tails every time that you tossed it 100 times, even if the model is valid; but we would expect the occurrence of a head (or tail) to be somewhat closer to 50%. If you tossed it 1,000,000 times, you would not always get exactly 500,000 heads and 500,000 tails every time that you tossed it 1,000,000 times, even if the model is valid; but we would expect the occurrence of a head (or tail) to be even closer to 50%.

We can never get *exactly* 50% heads and 50% tails in an extended series of tosses; but the more that we toss the coin, the closer our results will be to 50/50. Our intuition tells us, therefore, that the only way that we can *prove* that the model of $P(\text{Heads}) = 1/2$ is correct is to toss the coin an *infinite number of times*. Obviously we cannot do this with the limited amount of leisure time that we have available. Therefore, we can never prove that the model is correct by tossing any coin.

The best that we can hope for is to be able to tell (detect, that is) when at least one of the four assumptions has been violated. If the coin is not honest—if both sides, for example, are heads—then tossing the coin a limited number of times will yield only heads, a series of events that is certainly unlikely *if the model were true*. If we use one of the rules of probability discussed later, then we can calculate the probability that such a series of *unlikely* events can occur. If the probability turns out to be unusually small, then it consitutes valid evidence for rejecting the model.

9.4 Empirical Probability

If you were asked to determine the probability of getting certain high-impact plastic parts whose lengths are outside of specifications at the time of manufacture, you really have no basis for calculating a theoretical probability. It would not seem to be possible to be aware of all possible outcomes. You would have to consider the properties of the raw material used, the characteristics of the cutting machine, the fallibilites of the machine operator as a human being, the peculiarities of the measuring instruments used, and the idiosyncracies of the weather and other environmental conditions and their effect on everything.[2]

---

[2] An alternative approach is to conduct a statistical process capability study; see Chapter 23.

What you can do, of course, is take a sample of parts, measure their lengths, determine the proportion that are outside of specifications, and report that result. But do you have the *truth* as to the actual proportion outside specifications in the entire process? Not at all. What you have is an *estimate* of the truth.

The proportion found in the sample is called an *empirical probability* because it is based on observation, not on theory. It should be obvious that the empirical probability can change as you collect more samples and more data.

9.5 Rule 1: Rule of Complementation

If only two possible events can occur, then the sum of the two individual probabilities will be equal to one. In short, the events represent the totality of what can happen.

Examples of such events:

1. The product works properly, or the product fails.

2. The product meets the specification, or it does not.

3. It will rain, or it will not.

4. The restaurant service is satisfactory, or it is not.

The second event in each case is the *antithesis* or opposite of the first event. If we call the first event *E*, then the second event is called *Not E*. Therefore, Rule 1 would be expressed as follows:

$$P(E) + P(Not\ E) = 1. \tag{9.3}$$

Using the first example above, we can state that

$$P(\text{Product works}) + P(\text{Product fails}) = 1.$$

It sometimes happens that one of these probabilities is easier to calculate than the other. Since we have a simple equation, we can express the probability of one event in terms of the other. That is,

$$P(\text{Product works}) = 1 - P(\text{Product fails}),$$

and so if we knew the probability of product failure, then we could determine the probability that the product works.

Rule 1 can easily be extended to situations in which more than two events can happen. For example, if a product can be classified OK or Not OK, the classification Not OK might be further divided into Scrap and Rework. Thus,

$$P(\text{OK}) + P(\text{Scrap}) + P(\text{Rework}) = 1.$$

The three possible events would constitute the totality of the events that can happen to the product as far as we are concerned.

9.6 Rule 2: Addition of Probabilities for Mutually Exclusive Events

If two events E and F are mutually exclusive (that is, they cannot occur together), then

$$P(E \text{ or } F) = P(E) + P(F). \tag{9.4}$$

This rule can best be described by example. If we had a six-faced die, such as one used in a game of craps, then the probability of getting, say, a three or four in one throw of the die would be determined as follows:

$$P(3 \text{ or } 4) = P(3) + P(4).$$

The events, faces 3 and 4 on a die, are mutually exclusive, because they cannot come up together when the die is thrown. If we make the usual assumptions about the die being honest, perfectly balanced, and thrown in a random fashion, then the probability of getting a 3 is 1/6, and the probability of getting a 4 is also 1/6. Thus the probability of getting a 3 or 4 is

$$P(3 \text{ or } 4) = 1/6 + 1/6 = 2/6 = 1/3.$$

Rule 1 (complementation) is a special case of Rule 2 (addition), in that *all* of the mutually exclusive events are considered. For example, the product works properly *or* it does not.

One way to remember Rule 2 is to associate the *or* condition with *addition* of the individual probabilities.

9.7 Rule 3: Multiplication of Probabilities for Independent Events

If two events E and F are independent (that is, the occurrence of one event does not affect the occurrence of the other event), then

$$P(E \text{ and } F) = P(E) \times P(F). \tag{9.5}$$

If we had a coin in one hand and a six-sided die in the other hand, and we tossed the coin and threw the die at the same time, the results would be independent of each other. What we get on the die is not affected by what we get on the coin, and vice versa. Using Rule 3, we can calculate, for example, the probability of getting a tail on the coin *and* a 5 on the die:

$$P(\text{tail on coin } and \text{ 5 on die}) = P(\text{tail on coin}) \times P(\text{5 on die})$$
$$= 1/2 \times 1/6$$
$$= 1/12.$$

Of course, all of the assumptions previously listed regarding the coin and the die are considered to be valid and in effect.

One way to remember Rule 3 is to associate the *and* condition with *multiplication* of the individual probabilities.

Going back to our coin-tossing discussion, suppose that we start off with a coin that is not honest—say both sides are heads. Tossing this coin will yield only heads, of course. How many times will we have to toss it before we conclude that the model, $P(\text{Heads}) = 1/2$, does not apply to this coin and, therefore, at least one of the assumptions has been violated? The answer: When the probability of occurrence is very small or highly unlikely. If we apply Rule 3 to tossing a coin that is supposed to be honest, then the probabilities of various outcomes are as follows:

$$P(\text{2 heads in a row}) = 0.5 \times 0.5 = (0.5)^2 = 0.25,$$
$$P(\text{3 heads in a row}) = (0.5)^3 = 0.125,$$
$$P(\text{4 heads in a row}) = (0.5)^4 = 0.0625,$$
$$P(\text{5 heads in a row}) = (0.5)^5 = 0.03125,$$
$$P(\text{6 heads in a row}) = (0.5)^6 = 0.015625,$$
$$P(\text{7 heads in a row}) = (0.5)^7 = 0.0078125.$$

When the probability gets very small, we still have two possible decision choices: (1) the coin is all right, and we obtained one of the rare occurrences or (2) the model for the coin has been discredited because at least one of the assumptions has been violated. Where would you put your money? Surely we should not have to toss this coin more than seven times to establish evidence "beyond a reasonable doubt" that the assumed model is wrong. Probabilities of less than 0.01 (or 1%) are considered small, and so we should have concluded, after only seven consecutive heads, that the coin is not honest. Our chance of being wrong in that conclusion is 0.0078125, which is small indeed. Does that tell you where to put your money?

In actual class demonstrations by the author using a *two-headed coin*, many students are not convinced that seven heads in a row are quite conclusive evidence that the model is wrong, and they will insist on stronger evidence and more tosses (and therefore more heads in a row), sometimes beyond 15 tosses! (They always demand to see both sides of the coin, but that is like knowing what the population is like before you sample from it.) Their attitudes change, however, when they learn the rules of probability. Thus we often cannot directly confirm a probability model, but we can find evidence, beyond a reasonable doubt, that the model is wrong, if the model is actually wrong.

9.8 The Courtroom Analogy to Process Quality

The situation with the coin is analogous to that in our courts of law. A defendant is presumed to be innocent at the outset. The plaintiff must come up with *convincing* evidence that discredits the assumption of innocence—that is, evidence "beyond a reasonable doubt"—before the jury or the judge will declare the defendant to be guilty. If the evidence is not convincing, then the defendant is declared to be "not guilty," meaning that the evidence was not substantial and that the presumption of innocence has not been discredited. Strictly speaking, the defendant has to do nothing, but we know that the defendant must come up with his or her own evidence of innocence because evidence can be contrived (indeed, by both sides).

Proving that a production process is yielding acceptable product involves the same sort of reasoning. In a high-volume operation where it might not be possible or practical to inspect or test every unit of product, you may not be able to *prove* that a lot is acceptable. But a sample of product can provide evidence that the lot is unacceptable if the negative results from the sample have a very small probability of occurrence when the lot is supposedly satisfactory. What we consider as very small probability is determined by the risk we wish to take of being wrong when we say that the lot is unacceptable. That risk is the same as that "beyond a reasonable doubt" maxim expressed in a courtroom situation.

The risk of being wrong has business and economic consequences that are associated with it, such as having to sort product 100% or recalling a lot. If you have *no evidence* that a process is producing unsatisfactory product, what do you do? Generally, nothing. You leave the process alone. You are expected, however, to take corrective action if you have any convincing evidence that the process is unsatisfactory. The evidence must be convincing to you. As you will see in Part Three where we use some SPC tools, convincing evidence is determined by its probability of occurrence when the process is assumed to be satisfactory (innocent).

9.9 A Real-Life Example of Multiplying Probabilities (Rule 3)

Rule 3 has appropriate application when it comes to interpreting control charts, but let us consider an example that is closer, at present, to our daily lives. An important application of Rule 3 involves products or systems with components whose performance can be considered independent of other components.

For example, consider an automobile that has four new tires. If the probability of each tire operating 30,000 miles without significant delays due to a flat is 0.85 (based on studies made by the manufacturer), what is the probability of *all four tires* operating 30,000 miles without delays due to a flat? Let us designate the tires as A, B, C, D. Then, assuming that the four tires will perform independently of each other, the probability of all four tires operating without a flat is

P(A *and* B *and* C *and* D operating 30,000 miles without a flat)
= P(A with no flat) $\times$ P(B with no flat) $\times$ P(C with no flat) $\times$ P(D with no flat)
= 0.85 $\times$ 0.85 $\times$ 0.85 $\times$ 0.85
= 0.52200625 = about 52%.

This is not a very high *system* probability,[3] considering the inconvenience, delay, and cost of fixing a flat tire. One obvious way to increase the probability of the system working properly (traveling 30,000 miles without serious delays due to a flat tire) is to *improve the quality of the tires* so that they are less susceptible to flats. If the quality were improved so that the individual probabilities increase to 0.95, then the system probability would become $(0.95)^4$ or about 81%, a substantial improvement, although still not as high as we would like it to be.

Must the improvement in tire quality entail much added cost? Perhaps, but not necessarily so. If there were some additional cost involved, such as better quality raw materials used, then the added cost would have to be weighed against greater customer satisfaction (*customer delight* is an even more desirable goal), increased market share, and profit improvement. It is possible that the improved quality can be achieved without significant added cost by some minor change in the way tires are built (such as better control of the curing process), by some modest cost in operator training (substantial human skill is involved in most tire building), or by an improved blend of raw materials (perhaps improving the accuracy of weighing materials that constitute a batch).

---

[3] This expression is equivalent to *system reliability*, which is the probability that the system will operate successfully (defined) under certain stated conditions for a specified period of time or cycle or distance.

If process or product improvement is pursued with vigor and enthusiasm, and improvement goes on continually, then all corners of the business enterprise will benefit from the rewards that assuredly follow.

9.10 Redundancy or Backup System

Quality practitioners who contribute to product design might be involved in *redundancy* to enhance product performance. This involves a *backup* in case a component in the product fails. Redundancy is typical in the design and construction of space vehicles, especially those that are manned. The dramatic improvement in probability of a redundant system working properly must be weighed against the cost of adding another component and the additional space and weight required.

In the case of our tire example, redundancy is achieved by including a *spare tire* in the vehicle. The spare tire enables us to increase the probability of traveling 30,000 miles without undue delay as a result of flat tires. An emergency brake can also be considered a redundancy feature enabling one to stop the car if the regular brakes fail for any reason.

9.11 Calculations for a Simple Redundant System

Let us consider a simple example to see what happens to a system probability when redundancy is introduced. Suppose that the system consists of only two parts, A and B, that operate independently and are backups to each other. Only one of these parts needs to work in order for the system to work properly, and each of these parts has a success probability[4] of 0.85. If one part fails, the other can take over the function. Graphically the situation would look like that shown in Figure 9.1. The system in Figure 9.1 will work under any of the following conditions:

1. If A fails and B works

2. If B fails and A works

3. If A and B both work.

It should be obvious that the system will fail only if *both* parts fail. What, then, is the probability that the *system* will work?

---

[4] The backup parts do not necessarily have to have the same probability of working properly.

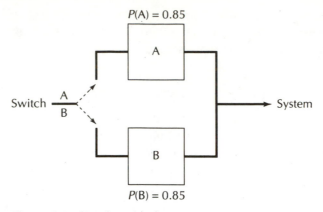

Figure 9.1. Simple redundant system.

If we could calculate directly the probabilities for each of these three condi-tions occurring, then all we would have to do is apply Rule 2 and *add* the individual probabilities in order to find the probability that the system will work, since the three conditions are mutually exclusive. Do you recognize the *or* situa-tion that this problem represents?

Let us calculate the probabilities directly. The probability of each part work-ing properly is 0.85. Then the probability of Part A failing, using Rule 1, is

$$P(\text{A fails}) = 1 - P(\text{A works})$$
$$= 1 - 0.85$$
$$= 0.15.$$

Similarly,

$$P(\text{B fails}) = 0.15.$$

Now calculate the probability of each of the separate conditions under which the system will work:

Condition *1:* $P(\text{A fails } and \text{ B works})$ $= P(\text{A fails}) \times P(\text{B works})$
$= 0.15 \times 0.85$
$= 0.1275.$
Condition *2:* $P(\text{B fails } and \text{ A works})$ $= $ same as Condition 1
$= 0.1275.$
Condition *3:* $P(\text{A works } and \text{ B works}) = P(\text{A works}) \times P(\text{B works})$
$= 0.85 \times 0.85$
$= 0.7225.$

Notice that we used both Rule 1 (complementation) and Rule 3 (multiplication for independent events). Since the system will work if any one of the above conditions prevails, then, by means of Rule 2,

$$\text{System probability} = P(\text{Condition 1 } or \text{ Condition 2 } or \text{ Condition 3}$$
$$\text{prevails})$$
$$= 0.1275 + 0.1275 + 0.7225$$
$$= 0.9775 = \text{about } 98\%.$$

Thus we have a dramatic improvement in performance when redundancy is introduced into the system.

In some cases an easier method is to calculate the system probability indirectly by starting with the fundamental Rule 1:

$$P(\text{System works}) + P(\text{System fails}) = 1.$$

Now express the desired probability in terms of the other probability:

$$P(\text{System works}) = 1 - P(\text{System fails}).$$

It may be easier to calculate the probability that the system *fails* in this example. The system will fail if *both parts* fail. Thus we must calculate the probability that Part A *and* Part B will both fail, using Rule 3:

$$P(\text{A } and \text{ B fail}) = P(\text{A fails}) \times P(\text{B fails})$$
$$= 0.15 \times 0.15$$
$$= 0.0225, \text{ the probability that the system fails.}$$

We are to calculate, however, the probability that the system works. Using Rule 1 again:

$$P(\text{System works}) = 1 - P(\text{System fails})$$
$$= 1 - 0.0225$$
$$= 0.9775 = \text{about } 98\% \text{ (same result as before).}$$

Again, this represents a tremendous improvement in performance of the system, achieved as a result of introducing redundancy into the system. If you are interested in probability approaches of this sort, it is recommended that you study the field of *reliability engineering*.[5]

---

[5] See, for example, P. D. T. O'Connor, *Practical Reliability Engineering*, 2nd ed., Quality Press, American Society for Quality Control, Milwaukee, 1985.

It was assumed that the device that *switches* from one part to another works perfectly without failure. In more complicated problems the reliability of the switch is included in the system reliability calculation.

9.12 Summary

The classical definition of probability is a theoretical probability that has behind it assumptions often not expressed. *Theoretical* probability represents a model for the defined process. An *empirical* probability uses actual observational data and therefore is an estimate, subject to variation and uncertainty. Three basic rules of probability were introduced:

Rule 1: Complementation

Rule 2: Addition of Probabilities for Mutually Exclusive Events (the OR situation)

Rule 3: Multiplication of Probabilities for Independent Events (the AND situation)

Examples of all three rules were given. When a system can be represented by a model, certain assumptions accompany that model. The model usually cannot be proved to be correct; but samples can be used as evidence that the model is incorrect, with the risk of being wrong expressed as a probability. A process can be treated as "innocent" if there is no evidence or insufficient evidence to discredit it. But a sample from the process can contradict the assumption of innocence if the probability of the sample result is sufficiently small. Probabilities of less than 0.01 (or 1%) are considered sufficient evidence. An analogy is made to a court of law. Redundancy of components in a system results in substantial improvement in the system probability of performing successfully (also called reliability).

9.13 Putting It into Practice

1. Determine the theoretical probability of some performance aspect of a component designed by your research or engineering department (such as the shelf life of a food product, or a computer key making firm contact when depressed 100,000 times). Get basic information from people in that department. Note the assumptions made.

2. Determine the empirical probability of an important defect that can occur on one of your products or in service performance. With actual data, do this for two different periods of time to show that this probability varies.

3. Select a component, product, system, or service with which you are acquainted. Make a statement that describes the probability of success, incorporating the four elements of reliability (*Hint:* It can be done.):

   (a) Probability

   (b) Definition of successful performance

   (c) Conditions under which performance is defined

   (d) Time period, number of cycles, or distance.

CHAPTER 10

Measures of Central Tendency: Mean, Median, Mode

When data are summarized, it is natural to think that some number is central to the data in the sense that all of the data seem to cluster around this particular number. It is almost as if this one central number were to be treated as "representative" of the data.

In this chapter we consider three such numbers, all of which play a part in SPC. We examine their unique properties and learn how to calculate them. To be sure, other such measures of central tendency are available, but these three will engage our attention.

10.1 The Mean

The *mean* is the most popular measure in SPC work and in statistical work in general. Its complete technical expression is *arithmetic mean*. Its more common expression is *average*. The words *mean* and *average* are often used interchangeably.

In industrial applications the mean is important because it is used in determining costs. The average length for a machined part can be used to determine the total cost of material usage in manufacturing. The average amount of material used in making a part is reflected in the market price charged. The average fill in a food package can be converted to the total cost of product "giveaway," the amount that exceeds the label weight.

Mean: The sum of all the readings divided by how many readings there are.

We could express this formula using words as follows:

$$\text{Mean} = \frac{\text{Sum of all the readings}}{\text{Number of readings}}.$$

It would not be practical to use all of these words every time the mean is described, and so we use some convenient symbolic notation and a formula that are easy to learn and efficiently compact.

We have different notation for the mean depending on whether we are talking about the mean of a *population* or the mean of a *sample*:

$$\text{Population mean: } \mu = \frac{\Sigma X}{N} \tag{10.1}$$

The symbol Σ is the capital Greek letter, *sigma*, and represents the operation of *summation*. One would read it as "sum what follows." What follows the summation symbol in Eq. (10.1) is the letter X, which is used to represent the data collectively. The letter N is the total number of readings in the population, and the Greek letter μ, or *mu*, represents the mean of the population.[1]

$$\text{Sample mean: } \overline{X} = \frac{\Sigma X}{n} \tag{10.2}$$

Although the nomenclature is different, the formula is the same for both the population mean and the sample mean. That is, the method for calculating the mean is the same: the sum of all the readings (in the sample or population) divided by the number of readings (in the sample or population).

You may find Eqs. (10.1) and (10.2) written in textbooks in more elaborate fashion. Equation (10.2), for example, may be seen written as

$$\overline{X} = \frac{\sum_{i=1}^{n} X_i}{n}$$

which is read "the sum of the X_i readings from $i = 1$ to $i = n$, all divided by n." The small notations above and below the summation sign Σ are called the *limits of the summation*. The numerator says that each of the readings in the sample is assigned the letter X with a numerical subscript and we are to add them: $X_1 + X_2 + X_3 + \ldots + X_n$. We omit the small notations in Eqs. (10.1) and (10.2) and still understand what the formula says.

---

[1] Refer to Table 7.1 in Chapter 7 to refresh your memory concerning nomenclature that distinguishes between population and sample.

10.2 Properties of the Mean

There are two important properties of the mean:

1. The mean has the same unit of measure as the original data.

It may be too obvious to mention this property, but it should be stated, neverthe-less. If the original data, for example, are in centimeters, then the mean is also reported in centimeters. The unit of measure should always be included when reporting the mean.

2. The mean is affected by extreme values.

Readings that are far from the rest of the data tend to pull the mean in their direction. For example, consider the five readings 6, 8, 2, 4, 17 inches. They add up to 37, and the mean is 37 divided by 5, or 7.4 inches. The first four readings are fairly close to each other and have an average of 5.0 inches. The last reading, 17 inches, is much larger than the rest of the data and pulls the overall average upward to 7.4 inches. It is true, however, that *all* readings affect the mean, but the extreme readings have a more noticeable effect.

When a mean is calculated, the number of decimal places in the answer may be numerous, and the practitioner is often in a dilemma as to how many decimal places should be included in the rounded answer. It is not true that reporting many decimal places somehow enhances the accuracy of the answer. A recom-mended practice for rounding the answer is to *report the mean to one more decimal place than the original data.* [2]

The justification for this practice lies in the fact that the mean has the prop-erty of falling between the numbers in the original data, something like falling between the chairs or between the planks. For example, the mean of two whole numbers (integers) such as 3 and 4 ounces is 3.5 ounces. The original data are in whole ounces, but the mean is in tenths of an ounce—that is, to one decimal place. By using one more decimal place in expressing the mean than the original data have, we are indicating that the mean can, indeed, fall between original numbers in the data set. It is assumed in this discussion that all of the readings in the original data set have been recorded initially to the same number of decimal places.

---

[2] Some people laughingly refer to this practice as "Pitt's rule," although the author does not lay claim to inventing it. It just makes good sense, and it is promoted vigorously. Another source that promotes this rule is Kaoru Ishikawa, *Guide to Quality Control,* 2nd revised ed., Asian Productivity Organization, 1982, Tokyo, pp. 67–68.

Another example: A sample of seven steel pins was collected, and their diameters were measured and recorded to the nearest thousandth of a millimeter, with the following results:

20.885 mm
20.862
20.893
20.857
20.878
20.860
20.877

The sum is 146.112 mm. The mean, 146.112 divided by 7, calculates to 20.87314286 mm (on a 10-digit calculator).

What do you report for the mean? Since the original data are in *three* decimal places (thousandths of a millimeter), the mean is reported to *four* decimal places (ten-thousandths of a millimeter). The mean is therefore reported as

$$\overline{X} = 20.8731 \text{ mm.}$$

Remember that this is a sample result; it is an estimate of the population mean. It is even appropriate to write

$$\overline{X} = 20.8731 \text{ mm} = \text{Est. of } \mu$$

to remind yourself and others that the sample mean is not the truth but an estimate of the truth, which is the unknown population mean. Reporting the mean to four decimal places does *not* imply that the original measurements were made to four decimal places; it merely reflects the fact that the mean, unlike the original data, does calculate to more than three decimal places. You will find that the practice of adding one more decimal place to the reported mean is useful, appropriate, easy to remember, and consistent.

10.3 The Matter of Rounding

Surprisingly, very few books on statistics directly address the practice of rounding numbers. One can surmise what the preferred method is for rounding by studying carefully an author's examples and exercises. Many people seem to employ some systematic procedure for rounding, perhaps learned in high school or grade school, and this is appropriate as long as it is used consistently. Others seem to be uncertain as to how to proceed.

A useful guide for rounding in statistical work today is to *round the final calculated answer, not the interim calculations that lead up to the final answer.* Hand calculators and computers, by their very nature, retain all of the decimal-place figures within their built-in capacity while computation is going on, and all or most of the figures appear in the final calculated answer. The statistical practitioner, therefore, needs to round only the final answer. The advent of hand calculators and personal computers, which may give a final answer to many digits and decimal places—often many more than are actually necessary—has aggravated the dilemma for both beginning and advanced statistical practitioners, and so we need some rules or guides.

Rounding final answers involves eliminating some of the digits. Two methods will be introduced here, and you are advised to choose one of them:

> **Method 1:** If the digits to be eliminated start with **0 through 4,** the preceding digit is left unchanged. If the digits to be eliminated start with **5 through 9,** the preceding digit is rounded up to the next number.

For example, if original data have been recorded to one decimal place, and you wish to report the mean to two decimal places, the calculated answer may appear as 8 to 10 digits in a calculator display. Let us see how Method 1 is applied.

If the first digit to be eliminated is **0 followed by all zeros,** there is no change in the final rounded result:

2.460000000 becomes 2.46.

If the first digit to be eliminated is **0 followed by numbers not all zeros,** or if the first digit to be eliminated is **1 through 4,** the final rounded result is *smaller* than the calculated answer:

2.460000001 becomes 2.46,

2.461933789 becomes 2.46,

2.462395618 becomes 2.46,

2.463209836 becomes 2.46,

2.464572846 becomes 2.46.

If the first digit to be eliminated is **5 through 9,** the final rounded result is *larger* than the calculated answer:

2.465000000 becomes 2.47,

2.465209301 becomes 2.47,

2.466309875 becomes 2.47,

2.467093763 becomes 2.47,

2.468429367 becomes 2.47,

2.469374823 becomes 2.47.

When the digit to be eliminated is **exactly 5** (that is, 5 followed by all zeros), this rounding method presents a certain bias. Regardless of what the preceding digit is, anywhere from 0 through 9, the rounded number will always be larger than the calculated answer.

There is a slight bias in using Method 1 because there seem to be more possibilities for a larger rounded result than for a smaller one. But that claim is applicable only to the situation where the number to be eliminated is exactly 5 and where there are many such numbers in the data set. Such a situation is highly unlikely, except when a device provides a digital readout and the last digit displayed is either 0 or 5. Remember that this discussion is limited to rounding the *final calculated answer* and not to a set of data. The purported bias, therefore, is usually not significant, noticeable, or serious when dealing with real data.

Another method is used by some professional statisticians and authors because it tends to avoid the alleged rounding bias noted in the previous method:

> **Method 2:** If the digits to be eliminated start with **0 through 4,** the preceding digit is left unchanged. If the digits to be eliminated start with **5 followed by digits not all zero,** or start with **6 through 9,** the preceding digit is rounded up to the next number. If the digit to be eliminated is **exactly 5** (followed by all zeros) and the preceding digit is **even,** it is left unchanged; if the preceding digit is **odd,** it is rounded up to the next even number.

For example,

2.455000000 becomes 2.46,

2.455209301 becomes 2.46,

2.464572846 becomes 2.46,

2.465000000 becomes 2.46,

2.465209301 becomes 2.47,

2.466309875 becomes 2.47,

2.475000000 becomes 2.48.

Admittedly, any rounding method used is an arbitrary one. Whichever method you choose, use it consistently. The author's choice over the years has been Method 1 with no noticeable side effects.

10.4 Calculating the Mean: Ungrouped and Grouped Data

You would think that nothing more needs to be said with regard to calculating a mean: we all understand how to do it. One situation, however, deserves some discussion: *ungrouped* versus *grouped* data.

Suppose we had 10 readings in centimeters:

$$\underline{X}$$

9 cm
7
8
9
8
7
8
9
8
$\underline{7}$

$$\Sigma X = 80 \text{ cm.} \tag{10.3}$$

This set of data is said to be *ungrouped* in the sense that the numbers are in a single column, much like hanging them on a string. The letter X at the head of the column of data represents all of the data collectively. To calculate the mean we obtain

$$\overline{X} = 80/10 = 8.0 \text{ cm.}$$

Notice that the mean is reported to one decimal place when the original data are in integers and that the decimal digit is shown *even if it is 0*. The number 0 is meaningful; it does not signify "nothing."

Do we treat these data as a population or as a sample? Since we have chosen to call the mean $\overline{X}$ instead of μ, this is our way of saying that these data are to be treated as a sample from some defined population.

When the data are arranged in *grouped* form, we list the *different readings* (column labeled X) in the data and then show the *number of times* (column labeled f for *frequency*) that each reading occurs. We now have two columns:

$\underline{X}$	$\underline{f}$
7	3
8	4
9	3

$$\tag{10.4}$$

The layout in (10.4) actually involves ten numbers, not six as it may appear. The layout is read as follows: "We have 3 sevens, 4 eights, and 3 nines." That's a total of 10 numbers. In fact, if we add the frequency column, we will get the total sample size. Thus we have

$$\Sigma f = n. \tag{10.5}$$

To calculate the *mean of grouped data*, we must multiply the two columns together in Eq. (10.4), creating a third column, which is labeled fX (or sometimes Xf). The third column is called either "f times X" or "X times f":

X	f	fX
7	3	21
8	4	32
9	3	27
Totals	10	80

$$\tag{10.6}$$

The mean is the sum of the third column (fX) divided by the sum of the second column (f). Thus, for *grouped data*, the formula for the mean is

$$\overline{X} = \frac{\Sigma fX}{\Sigma f}$$
$$= \frac{80}{10}$$
$$= 8.0 \text{ cm}, \tag{10.7}$$

the same result as before for ungrouped data. Note that in (10.6) the column labeled X is not added up because such a total is meaningless.

When different readings tend to repeat in a set of data, grouping them can save you much time and work. At the same time the data are arranged in a format that enables you to draw a frequency histogram (see Chapter 6).

10.5 The Median

Median: The middle value in a set of data.

It is a word that you have seen, undoubtedly many times, on highway signs warning the motorist not to cross the "median strip" that separates opposing streams of traffic. Later we shall see that a very easy-to-use control chart is the *median chart.*

The important property of a median is that *there is the same number of readings larger than the median as there are readings smaller than the median* in the set of data.

To find the median, the data must first be arranged in order of magnitude, either from smallest to largest or from largest to smallest. The reading (or two readings in certain situations) that is in the middle is the median. For example, suppose that we have five readings arranged from smallest to largest:

24, 36, 57, 84, 98.

The middle value, 57, is the median.

If the number of readings is *odd*, as in the preceding example, there is only one middle value, and it is the median. If the number of readings is *even*, however, there are actually *two* middle values. In this case the median is traditionally obtained by simply averaging the two middle values.

Suppose, for example, that we include a sixth number, 150, to the set above:

24, 36, 57, 84, 98, 150.

The two middle values are 57 and 84. Their mean is 141 divided by 2, or 70.5. The median, therefore is 70.5. Note that there are three readings above 70.5 and also three readings below 70.5, exhibiting the property of the median.

10.6 The Mode

Mode: The most frequent value.

The third measure of central tendency is the *mode. It is the reading that occurs most frequently in a set of data.*

For example, for the set of 10 readings arranged in grouped form in (10.4), the mode is 8. For the frequency histogram of screw-cap torques shown earlier in Figure 6.4, the mode is the *interval* 20–21 in.-lbs.

Figure 6.4 is an example of a *unimodal* histogram, meaning that it has only one mode. Histograms that exhibit two modes are called *bimodal* and are not uncommon. Typically, they describe two populations, such as two shifts, two production lines, two machines, or two operators producing at different means (or levels).

A histogram should present a clear picture of two populations before one concludes that there are two modes. Little ups and downs on a histogram do not necessarily indicate that there is more than one mode. Figure 10.1 depicts a clearly bimodal distribution.

When it appears evident that two separate populations are being depicted and that there are, indeed, two modes present, the modes usually do not occur

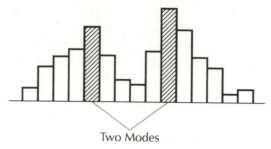

Figure 10.1. Bimodal distribution.

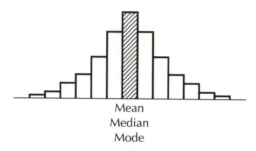

Figure 10.2. Symmetrical distribution with
mean = median = mode.

at the same frequencies. The mode with the higher frequency can be called the *primary mode,* and the mode with the lower frequency can be called the *secondary mode.*

When the mean, median, and mode all have the same value, the histogram (or distribution) is said to be *symmetrical,* as shown in Figure 10.2.

10.7 Summary

The three measures of central tendency of principal interest in SPC are the *mean, median,* and *mode.*

The *mean* is the most widely used among the three and is commonly called *average.* It is calculated by simply adding up all of the readings and dividing by the number of readings. The mean of a population is designated μ, and the mean of a sample is designated $\overline{X}$; $\overline{X}$ is an estimate of μ. The mean has two interesting properties:

1. It takes the same unit of measure as the original data.

2. It is affected by extreme values.

A good practice is to report the final answer to one more decimal place than the original data.

Two methods for rounding data, especially the mean, were discussed. Whichever method the reader chooses should be used consistently.

Data can be arranged in ungrouped or grouped form. Grouped data require one column for the different readings that occur in the set of data, called X, and another column for frequencies, called f, at which the different readings occur. When the mean is to be calculated from grouped data, still another column is needed, called fX, which represents the product of each different reading by its frequency of occurrence.

The *median* is the middle value. An equal number of readings falls above the median and below the median. When an odd number of readings is examined, there is only one middle value, and it is the median. When an even number of readings is examined, there are two middle values, and the average of them is the median for the data.

The *mode* is the reading with the highest frequency. A histogram with one mode is called unimodal; a histogram with two distinct modes is called bimodal. When the mean, median, and mode all have the same value, the distribution (histogram) is symmetrical.

10.8 Putting It into Practice

1. Five people in a department have the following annual salaries:

   $25,000, $25,500, $26,000, $26,500, $67,000.

   The last salary is that of the department manager.

   (a) What is the mean salary?

   (b) What is the median salary?

   (c) Which is more representative of the data, and why?

2. Take a small survey in your department to determine what methods are used by your associates for rounding data, particularly averages. What will you do about the different methods that you will likely find?

3. If your company manufactures a consumer product, measure some quality characteristic of importance from two different shifts or lines or periods of times. Collect from 60 to 80 readings, and draw one frequency histogram for the combined data. Keep the identity of the two sets of data intact. Is the distribution unimodal or bimodal? If it is distinctly bimodal, investigate the

situation to find the specific reason or reasons for bimodality, and determine what corrective action is needed; then see to it that corrective action is taken. Follow up in a few days to determine if the corrective action that was taken was effective.

Answers to Problem 1:

(a) $34,000.00

(b) $26,000

(c) It depends on the purpose of using a measure of central tendency. The mean can be used for budgeting the salary costs for the department. The median can be used to depict the distribution of personnel around that value since an equal number of people have salaries above the median and below it.

CHAPTER 11

Measures of Variability: Range, Standard Deviation

You've been buying the same brand of corn flakes for a long time, generally enjoying its light brown color, its crispy intact flakes, and its flavor. A new box is opened, and you find that some flakes have been burned black, several flakes are broken into small pieces and even into a fine powder, and there is a slight, perceptible off-flavor when eaten with milk. Although you have been accustomed to seeing some variability in quality and appearance, it is obvious that "they have gone too far this time." You are surprised and lament that "the quality is really bad." *What will you do about it?* You have some alternatives:

1. Return the box to the store, and ask for a refund or replacement.

2. Write to the producer.

3. Do both of the above.

4. Stop buying that brand without informing anyone, but be sure to let your friends know about your unhappy experience.

5. Continue to buy that brand, and shrug off the experience.

If you chose alternative 4, the most likely response, the producer may be in trouble, unaware of the problem in the marketplace.

11.1 Associating Variability with Quality

Whether we realize it or not, uniformity (lack of variability) is equated with quality. We, as consumers, do not like too much variation in our products or services; it causes us to lose confidence; it causes us to lose a sense of security because we cannot predict how the product will perform or how the service will be rendered. If our expectations of satisfactory performance of products or services are satisfied, then we tend to become loyal customers and consumers and purchase the products or services repeatedly. The product and service *are* what we *perceive* them to be.

Variability is not only the key to the *control* of quality; it is also the key to *improvement* in quality. Our efforts should always be directed at reducing the variability of key quality characteristics. Reduced variability is not only its own reward; it also justifies savings in material, time, and labor. Reduced variability means more consistent performance and therefore enhances confidence in the product or service expectation and perception. Reduced variability means parts that fit better, more uniform response to changing environmental conditions, more consistent service, and fewer surprises for the customer and consumer. Car owners who are convinced that they have bought a "lemon" are experiencing excessive variability. Consumers who find that a food package contains much less than the printed label weight or count are experiencing excessive variability. Patrons of restaurants who find that the table service can be excellent on one visit and deplorable on another visit are experiencing excessive variability.

11.2 The Rewards for Reducing Variability

The rewards for reducing variability are enormous, providing benefits to both the producer and customer. Consistently good service in a restaurant can make customers loyal patrons for many years. Reduced variability in packaged-food weight can justify a slight reduction in *average* fill, which, for high-volume items, can result in millions of dollars saved annually and still provide protection against underweight packages. Reduced variability in manufactured hardgoods means less scrap and rework.

The new focus today is on reducing variability. Unfortunately, a machine operator does not have a toggle switch on the equipment labeled "More Variability" and "Less Variability." Reducing variability is an elusive pot at the end of the rainbow, requiring great knowledge about processes, enlightened management leadership, elaborate technical skills, fairly sophisticated statistical methods, patience and perseverance, and a dramatic change in our way of thinking about processes.

11.3 Why Variability?

Why do products and their characteristics vary? After all, every responsible manufacturer tries to maintain identical conditions of production. Yet frequency histograms of measurable characteristics always exhibit some variability.

Several major factors contribute to the variability that we see or measure. These factors can be remembered mnemonically by identifying them with the letter *M*:

1. *Materials:* We know that raw materials exhibit variation, whether they are natural or produced by some supplier. We sample and inspect lots of incoming materials because we know there will be variability, not only from lot to lot, but also within lots.

2. *Machines:* We see that there is variability in performance among pieces of equipment, even so-called identical pieces of equipment. The capability of machines varies. Downtime due to machine malfunction varies from machine to machine.

3. *Men* (generically, *People*): All of us differ from each other in some way, especially in the ways that we use our variable skills. These differences also contribute to the variability of products and services that we offer, despite our attempts to provide uniform training to employees.

4. *Methods:* These are the ways that materials, machines, and people are configured to produce goods and services. Two plants with the same product mix and the same equipment do not perform equally. That is one major reason why companies with multiplant operations are inclined to compare the performances of their plants.

5. *Measurements:* Some of the variability that you see is due to the measurement tools and measurement techniques used. This source of variability is getting increasing attention.

6. *Environment* (unfortunately, no M-synonym unless we deliberately misspell it as *emvironment*): Typical environmental characteristics include the surroundings, physical conditions, circumstances (such as air, water, and noise pollutants), and influences—including weather—that affect processes, products, people, and services. Some efforts can be made to control these conditions, such as sealing a bearing against dirt or installing air conditioning. As the movement to improve quality is directed more upstream from the product to the process that makes it, we can expect that movement to continue upstream even further so that the product and the process are designed to be *robust;* that is, able to withstand the vagaries of environment, equipment, materials, people, and other conditions that tend to increase process variability.

7. *Management:* Without question we must include management and management practices because they play a part in the variability that we experience

in our products, processes, and services. After all, management must make the mundane, commonplace decisions, such as what quality level to put into the marketplace, what process methods to use, what capital equipment to buy, what materials to purchase and from whom, what kind of people to hire and how to train them.

11.4 The Average Is Not Enough

By now you should be aware of the fact that the mean, or average, does not tell the entire story of product performance. As a simple example, suppose that we had three columns of data, all with the same mean of 10.0:

A	B	C
8	0	−10
9	5	0
10	10	10
11	15	20
12	20	30
$\overline{X} = 10.0$	10.0	10.0

As we move from left to right, you can see that the variability in each column increases. The mean of 10.0, the same for all columns, does not tell the whole story.

11.5 The Range

A logical and simple measure of the variability in each column is the *range*, designated R. In column A, for example, some people would say that the range is 8 to 12. Statistically, however, *range is defined as the difference between the largest reading and the smallest reading.* It is calculated by simply subtracting the smallest number from the largest number in a group. We can write the formula for the range as

$$\text{Range} = R = (\text{Largest number}) - (\text{Smallest number}). \tag{11.1}$$

The ranges for the columns in our example, then, are

A	B	C
$R = 4$	20	40.

We can see that, indeed, the range increases as we go from left to right, confirming the increase in variability that we observed casually. An important characteristic of the range to remember is that *the range is never negative,* even if all of the numbers in the group are negative.[1]

The range is a very useful measure of variability as long as the group for which the range is being determined is small. Samples of five or even smaller are often used for variables control charts (discussed in Chapters 18 through 22). Ranges are usually not calculated for sample groups of more than, say, 15 readings.[2]

Thus we have a need for a more universal measure of variability, and that need is satisfied by the *standard deviation.*

11.6 The Standard Deviation

The concept of standard deviation as a measure of variability is becoming more widely referred to in quality improvement programs that involve statistical process control. The standard deviation has always been important in statistical quality control, in statistically designed experiments, and in statistical applications generally.

Dozens of informal surveys in classes conducted by the author indicate that many more people in industry today have heard of standard deviation than was true just a few years ago. However, only a relatively small percentage of them (no more than 25%) use standard deviation in their work on a regular basis. The same surveys indicate that a much smaller percentage (less than 5%) understand what standard deviation really is.[3]

The reasons why standard deviation seems to be little understood are not surprising. It has often been taught strictly as an unchallenged formula where one is exhorted to plug in the numbers and grind out an answer. It has taken on a mystique of its own whose authority and validity are not to be questioned. It has also been quite tedious to calculate; but with the advent of electronic calculators and personal computers, the calculation of the standard deviation is no longer a fearful exercise.

---

[1] This characteristic is the result of the number and arithmetic system that we have learned to use successfully in our daily affairs, in business, and in science. For example, for the numbers -10, -22, and -35, the smallest number is -35 (not -10), and the largest number is -10 (not -35). Using Eq. (11.1), the range is $(-10) - (-35) = -10 + 35 = 25$, a positive number.

[2] Beyond groups of 15, the range loses its efficiency in reflecting the overall variability because the probability increases, as the sample size increases, of catching an extreme value or outlier, thereby inflating the variability in the group.

[3] See the author's paper, "Standard Deviation, Plain and Simple," presented at the 42nd Annual Quality Congress of the American Society for Quality Control, May 9–11, 1988, Dallas, Texas, and published in the Congress transactions, pp. 771–778.

The underlying difficulty of understanding standard deviation—to say nothing of trying to explain it to someone—still remains and, too often, results in confusion, misuse, and misinterpretation. It does not have to be that way. We now develop the concept of standard deviation in a series of meaningful stages that call on your inherent common sense and intuitive logic.

11.7 Stage 1: A Feeling for Variability Using "Deviations"

We start by comparing two histograms in Figure 11.1, both drawn to the *same scale*. The histogram of Figure 11.1(a) appears to have more variability than the one in Figure 11.1(b), but the overall range or spread of each is not the determining clue that we use. We judge the variability by *using the mean as a reference point and measuring how far the readings are from the mean* for each histogram. The distances of the individual readings from the mean are called *deviations from the mean*, or simply *deviations* for short.[4]

It should be clear that the deviations of the individual readings, *on the average*, for the histogram in Figure 11.1(a) are greater than the deviations of individual readings, *on the average*, for the histogram in Figure 11.1(b). This is why we say that histogram (a) has more variability than histogram (b). Take another look at Figure 11.1 so that the concept of *distance from the mean*, or *deviation*, of the individual readings is meaningful and clear.

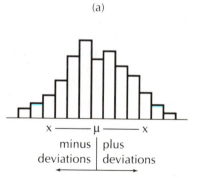
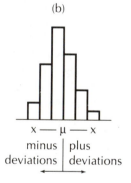

Figure 11.1. Comparing variabilities.

---

[4] Alternative measures of variability occasionally are suggested in the literature. A recent one, for example, suggests the "pairwise differences" as an alternative to the standard deviation, in which the mean, or any other location of the distribution, is *not* used as a reference point. See, for example, Peter M. Heffernan, "New Measures of Spread and a Simpler Formula for the Normal Distribution," *The American Statistician,* May 1988, Vol. 42, No. 2, pages 100–102. Although there may be certain advantages cited for this newer measure of variability, it is doubtful that it will replace the standard deviation in the foreseeable future.

With this pictorial concept in mind, we are ready for a technical definition for standard deviation:

Standard deviation: A kind of average deviation from the mean.

This is a strange way to write a technical definition! The reason for the use of nontechnical language will become more apparent when we see how standard deviation evolves as an acceptable measure of variability.

11.8 Stage 2: An Exercise with Some Numbers

Let us now try to obtain a numerical measure of standard deviation. For the sake of illustration, we start with five simple numbers. Although you may choose any five numbers, we will work with 7, 2, 6, 1, 3, and let ounces be their unit of measure. These data will be treated as a *population* for the moment.

Arrange the numbers in a column, designate them collectively as X, add them up, and calculate their mean as in Figure 11.2. Note that calling the mean μ is consistent with the declaration that these data are to be treated as a population and not as a sample.

		Original Data
		X
		7 oz
		2
		6
		1
		3
Sum:	$\Sigma X =$	19 oz
Mean:	$\mu =$	3.8 oz

Figure 11.2. Original data.

11.9 Stage 3: The Sum of the Deviations from the Mean Is . . .

Next, we wish to find out how far each of these numbers is away from the mean; that is, to find *the deviation of each number*. We calculate[5] the deviation by subtracting the mean μ from each of the numbers X. In short, we calculate the difference $(X - \mu)$. Then add up the deviations and calculate their mean as in Figure 11.3.

---

[5] The deviations are calculated like distances between two cities on a road map. If we know how far away two cities on the same route are from our starting point, the distance between them is determined by subtracting one distance (the nearer one) from the other distance.

Original Data X	Deviations $(X - \mu)$	
7 oz	+3.2 oz	
2	−1.8	
6	+2.2	
1	−2.8	
3	−0.8	
	+5.4	(Sum of positive deviations)
	−5.4	(Sum of negative deviations)
Sum: 19 oz	0.0 oz	
Mean: 3.8 oz	0.00 oz	

Figure 11.3. Deviations from the mean.

When a column of figures consists of signed numbers—that is, both positive and negative numbers—an easy and efficient way to add up the numbers is to add the positive and negative numbers separately as shown in Figure 11.3.

The deviations add up to *zero*! This result may appear to be a coincidence or an error, but it is neither. *The sum of the deviations from the mean will always add up to zero.* It is true no matter what numbers you start with or how many there are, as long as the mean is calculated to enough decimal places. *Therefore, the mean of the deviations will also be zero.* Try it yourself with any set of data.

What we are observing here is a unique property of the mean. One way to understand this "quirk" is to consider the mean as behaving like the *center of gravity* on which the deviations will balance (sum to zero) (see Figure 11.1 again). All of the positive deviations are precisely cancelled by the negative deviations. Therefore, using simply the deviations from the mean as they stand is no way to get a measure of variability. We must do something about those negative numbers that cancel the positive numbers.

11.10 Stage 4: The Absolute Deviations

One thing that we can do is simply ignore the negative signs and treat each deviation as if it were a positive number. In other words we can behave as if we do not care whether the original number X is to the right of, or greater than, the mean (positive deviation) or to the left of, or smaller than, the mean (negative deviation). We may simply wish to know the *absolute value of the deviation*. The absolute value of an expression is designated by drawing small vertical lines around it, $|X - \mu|$. We add up the absolute deviations and calculate their mean as shown in Figure 11.4.

The mean of the absolute deviations, 2.16 oz, sometimes designated MAD, is a calculable measure of variability. It has, however, some problems in use.

	Original Data X	Deviations $(X - \mu)$	Absolute Deviations $\|X - \mu\|$
	7 oz	+3.2 oz	**+3.2 oz**
	2	−1.8	**+1.8**
	6	+2.2	**+2.2**
	1	−2.8	**+2.8**
	3	−0.8	**+0.8**
Sum:	19 oz	0.0 oz	**10.8 oz**
Mean:	3.8 oz	0.00 oz	**2.16 oz**

Figure 11.4. Absolute deviations.

First, absolute expressions tend to be difficult to manipulate algebraically, especially in subsequent statistical analyses. Second, we have some difficulty in assigning a physical meaning to this value as it relates to the original data. As a consequence, the mean of the absolute deviations is rarely used by practicing statisticians as a meaningful or useful measure of variability. So our dilemma remains with us on how to deal with the negative signs of the deviations from the mean.

11.11 Stage 5: The Squared Deviations and the Variance

Is there any other way that we can get rid of those negative signs? There assuredly is: *Square the deviations*. We should recall (from high school algebra) that squaring a negative number results in a positive number. This gives us another column of numbers to work with, called the *squared deviations*. We add the squared deviations and calculate their mean in Figure 11.5.

	Original Data X	Deviations $(X - \mu)$	Absolute Deviations $\|X - \mu\|$	Squared Deviations $(X - \mu)^2$
	7 oz	+3.2 oz	+3.2 oz	**+10.24 oz²**
	2	−1.8	+1.8	**+3.24**
	6	+2.2	+2.2	**+4.84**
	1	−2.8	+2.8	**+7.84**
	3	−0.8	+0.8	**+0.64**
Sum:	19 oz	0.0 oz	10.8 oz	**26.80 oz²**
Mean:	3.8 oz	0.00 oz	2.16 oz	**5.360 oz²**

Figure 11.5. Squared deviations.

The last mean calculated in Figure 11.5, 5.360 oz², is the mean of the squared deviations. It is officially designated the *variance*. It is easy to work with mathematically, and it plays an important part in many statistical applications such as estimation techniques, hypothesis testing, and analysis of experimental data. But it has some problems, too. First, it is an inflated value when compared with the absolute deviations. Note that, in Figure 11.5, except for the last number in our data set, the squared deviations are considerably larger than the absolute deviations. Second, it has a strange unit of measure, *ounces squared*, which has no physical meaning. In short, we lost our original unit of measure, ounces, when we squared the deviations.

Is there a sensible way of bringing the mean of the squared deviations "back into the ballpark" and at the same time retrieve our original unit of measure, ounces? Yes, there is.

11.12 Stage 6. The Happy Last Step

You may have guessed what the last step should be: *Take the square root of that last mean (the variance).* This operation will (sort of) undo the squaring of the deviations that we performed in Stage 5. It will also recover our original unit of measure, ounces. Our result, carried to the 10-digit limit of a calculator, is

$$\sqrt{5.360} = 2.315167381 \text{ oz.} \tag{11.2}$$

What you have just obtained in Eq. (11.2) is the *standard deviation, σ (sigma)*.

11.13 Review of the Stages Leading to Standard Deviation

Let us review carefully the steps that we have taken that led quite logically to the standard deviation:

1. First, we started with a set of data X consisting of N numbers.

2. Next, we added them up and calculated their mean μ.

3. Next, we calculated the deviations from the mean $(X - \mu)$ in order to get a measure of variability using the mean as a logical reference point. We observed, however, that these deviations from the mean added up to zero (always); the positive deviations are precisely cancelled by the negative deviations.

4. Next, after considering and rejecting the absolute values to get rid of the negative signs, we squared the deviations as a way of removing the negative signs, obtaining $(X - \mu)^2$.

5. Next, we added up the squared deviations and calculated their mean, called the *variance (sigma squared)*,

$$\sigma^2 = \frac{\Sigma(X - \mu)^2}{N},$$

(11.3)

which was seen to be inflated in value that changed our original unit of measure.

6. Finally, we took the square root of the variance in order to retrieve the original unit of measure and to deflate it as well, giving it the magnitude of the original deviations. This gave us the *standard deviation (sigma)*,

$$\sigma = \sqrt{\frac{\Sigma(X - \mu)^2}{N}}.$$

(11.4)

Equation (11.4) is the definition formula for the population standard deviation.

11.14 Characteristics of the Standard Deviation

The standard deviation has some of the same characteristics as the mean:

1. It has the same unit of measure as the original data.

2. It is affected by extreme values, which tend to enlarge the standard deviation.

3. When reporting the standard deviation, it should be rounded to one more decimal place than the original data.

It may surprise you that the standard deviation, a measure of variability, has the same characteristics as the mean, a measure of central tendency. The reason is that the standard deviation is a kind of mean itself.[6] When we developed the standard deviation, recall that in Stage 5 we calculated the *mean* of the squared deviations before we took the square root.

It is appropriate and highly recommended, when working with data, to summarize the results of our calculations so that the final answers are conspicuously visible from the myriad of numbers, calculations, equations, and formulas that led up to the final answers. Accordingly, for the data in our exercise,

$\mu = 3.8$ oz
$\sigma = 2.3$ oz.

Note that *both* the mean and the standard deviation are reported to the same unit of measure and to the same number of decimal places (one more than the original

---

[6] Recall that, in Section 11.7, we defined the standard deviation as a "kind of" average deviation from the mean.

data), a practice that is easy to remember and has statistical validity. Note also that the standard deviation is somewhat similar in magnitude to the mean of the absolute deviations, 2.16 oz, which is usually the case.

As a method for remembering the definition formula [Eq. (11.4)] for the population standard deviation, some people memorize the convenient phrase, *Root-Mean-Squared-Deviation*, or its acronym, *RMSD*. Either one expresses the order (in reverse) in which we performed the operations:

1. We calculated the *deviations* (D) from the mean.

2. We *squared* (S) the deviations.

3. We calculated the *mean* (M) of the squared deviations.

4. We took the square *root* (R) of the last result.

Such a mnemonic device can hardly substitute for a clear understanding of how the standard deviation is evolved as a logical measure of variability.

11.15 The Sample Standard Deviation

Equation (11.4) is the definition formula for the *population* (or process) standard deviation, since the data in Figure 11.2 were originally identified as population data. When the data, however, are sample data, any standard deviation calculated from them is an *estimate* of the population standard deviation. The definition formula and nomenclature are changed to

$$S = \sqrt{\frac{\Sigma(X - \overline{X})^2}{n - 1}}.$$

(11.5)

Equation (11.5) is the definition formula for the sample standard deviation.

The three important differences between Formula (11.5) for *sample* standard deviation and Formula (11.4) for *population* standard deviation are as follows:

1. We call it S instead of σ. Similarly, the sample variance is written S^2 instead of σ^2.

2. We use $\overline{X}$ instead of μ because we usually do not know the true population mean.

3. We divide by $n - 1$ instead of by N.

Remember that $\overline{X}$ is an estimate of μ, that S is an estimate of σ, and that S^2 is an estimate of σ^2.

11.16 Why Divide by $n - 1$?

A perceptive and natural question that many people ask is "Why do we divide by $n - 1$ instead of by n?" A lengthy technical explanation, not necessary here, involves such concepts as *unbiased estimates* and *degrees of freedom*.[7] An adequate explanation is the following: If we were to divide by n, the calculated sample standard deviation would tend to underestimate the standard deviation in the population. This would be especially true if the sample size is very small. Dividing by $n - 1$, a smaller number than n, represents an adjustment to improve the estimate. Note that $n - 1$ is the denominator of a fraction; the smaller the denominator, the larger the fraction. Therefore, the smaller the sample size, the larger the adjustment effect of $n - 1$.

For example, if we had considered the five numbers in our exercise (Figure 11.2) as a sample instead of the population, we would have divided by 4 instead of by 5 when calculating the sample standard deviation, S. We, then, would have obtained.

$$S = \sqrt{\frac{26.80}{4}} = \sqrt{6.7} = 2.588435821 = 2.6 \text{ oz.}$$

This result is somewhat larger than the 2.3 oz we would have reported when the data are treated as the population, and that is to be expected when the denominator in a fraction is made smaller. As the sample size gets larger and larger, however, the use of $n - 1$ instead of n has less and less impact on the fraction. Some practitioners divide by n when the sample size is at least 30, but it is good advice to stick with $n - 1$ consistently to remind yourself that you are dealing with sample data. Since almost all of the statistical work that we encounter in industry and elsewhere involves sample data, using $n - 1$ should become routine.

11.17 Do Calculators and Computers Discriminate?

Scientific hand-held calculators usually distinguish between the sample standard deviation (dividing by $n - 1$) and the population standard deviation (dividing by N). The nomenclature that is used to distinguish between the two may vary from one calculator brand to another. You can be sure, however, that the formulas used to perform the calculation differ between sample and population and reflect the difference in denominators of the definition formulas of Eqs. (11.4) and (11.5).

When computer software is used to calculate the standard deviation, it is not always clear which formula the program uses; that is, it is not always clear

---

[7] For an explanation of these concepts, see any good statistics book, such as A. J. Duncan, *Quality Control and Industrial Statistics*, 5th ed., Richard D. Irwin, Homewood, Illinois, 1986.

whether the program is treating the data as a sample or as a population. It is the responsibility of the user, therefore, to determine which standard deviation, sample or population, is actually programmed so that the appropriate interpretation of the result can be made. If the population formula happens to be the one that is programmed, and the data are actually from a sample, especially a small one, then the calculated result may badly underestimate the true variability in the process under study. One may be misled into concluding that the variability in the process is satisfactory or acceptable, and the opposite may be true.

11.18 1–2–3: A Simple Computer Test for Standard Deviation

If the documentation for the computer software does not describe the formula for standard deviation (which would indicate whether the data are being treated as a sample or as a population), then a simple test using just a few numbers should reveal the program's direction. Enter any three *consecutive* integers, such as 1, 2, 3. You should get the following results when the computer printout reports standard deviation:

1. If the answer is 1, the program is treating the data as a *sample;* that is, $S = 1$.

2. If the answer is 0.816496581, the program is treating the data as a *population;* that is, $\sigma = 0.816496581$ (before rounding).

11.19 Summary

As consumers and customers we equate uniformity and consistency—that is, lack of variability—with quality, because a product that performs consistently (well) enhances our ability to predict its performance, and this provides us with confidence concerning the product. Variability is not only the key to the control of quality; it is the key to the improvement of quality. Variability is affected by materials, machines, people, methods of manufacture, measurement methods, environment, and management practices.

A simple measure of variability is the range, designated R, which is the difference between the largest and smallest numbers in a group. The range is never negative. It is easily understood, but it is appropriate for small sample sizes of, say, 15 or fewer readings.

A more universal measure of variability is the standard deviation. The importance and use of the standard deviation are increasing as the focus on variability and its effects becomes more widely appreciated. Yet standard deviation is little understood by the great majority of quality practitioners and other users.

Standard deviation for a set of data is a kind of average deviation (or distance) around the mean of the data. The concept can be grasped from a series of arithmetic stages from which the definition formula for population standard deviation, σ, logically emerges. The key limitation in its development is that the sum of the deviations from the mean is always zero. We end up with the squared deviations from the mean, the average of which is the variance, σ^2. Since the variance is an inflated value that also changes the unit of measure, the square root of the variance, known as the standard deviation, σ, is the final, logical result. The standard deviation has three of the same characteristics as the mean.

The sample standard deviation, S, is an estimate of the population standard deviation, σ. The population standard deviation formula contains N in the denominator, while the sample standard deviation formula contains $n - 1$ in the denominator. The reason for using $n - 1$ in the denominator is to make the sample standard deviation a better estimate of the population standard deviation. One should be aware of how calculators and computers distinguish between sample standard deviation and population standard deviation. A simple 1–2–3 test can be used to determine which standard deviation, sample or population, is programmed in a computer.

11.20 Putting It into Practice

1. The following set of measurement data is in centimeters.

    12.1, 15.6, 9.8, 12.8, 15.2, 17.4, 13.0, 16.6, 15.4, 11.7

    (a) Calculate the sum and the mean.

    (b) Calculate the deviations from the mean, and verify that their sum is zero.

    (c) Calculate the squares of the deviations and then their sum.

    (d) Calculate standard deviations, first treating the data as a population and then as a sample. How would you report the results?

2. If your department reports standard deviation as a measure of variability, examine three different kinds of statistical reports coming out of your department, and determine if the unit of measure is being reported for standard deviation. How many decimal places are being reported? Determine which standard deviation is being reported, sample or population. If you find discrepancies, correct them by discussing the problem with the originators of the reports.

3. If you use statistical computer software, use the simple 1–2–3 test described in this chapter to determine if the programmed standard deviation is that for a population or for a sample. If necessary, question the specialists in the data

processing office of your organization. If the distinction is not recorded in computer printouts or if it is not known, find out why and do something about it.

Answers to Problem 1

(a) Sum = 139.6 cm; mean = 13.96 cm.

(b) The deviations from the mean are −1.86, +1.64, −4.16, −1.16, +1.24, +3.44, −0.96, +2.64, +1.44, −2.26. Sum of deviations = +10.40 −10.40 = 0.

(c) $\Sigma(X - \text{mean})^2 = 53.2440$.

(d) $\sigma = \sqrt{53.2440 \div 10} = 2.307466143$; report 2.31 cm.
$S = \sqrt{53.2440 \div 9} = 2.432282878$; report 2.43 cm.

*I am ashamed to tell you
to how many figures I carried these calculations,
having no other business at the time.*

—Sir Isaac Newton

CHAPTER 12

Calculating Formulas for
Sample Standard Deviation *S*

3.1 SPC USA **4 1 5 9 . . .**

In Chapter 11 we learned about standard deviation as a measure of variability and how the formula for it was logically derived. We also learned that there was one definition formula for standard deviation if the data were a population and a slightly different definition formula if the data were a sample. Now the question that we must address is this: In the real world of industrial operations, manufacturing, engineering, and research, will the data that we deal with be for a population or for a sample?

Almost everyone should agree that we work with *sample* data almost all of the time, certainly much more frequently than with population data. It is not at all a common practice, in high-volume manufacturing processes typical today, to measure every item produced by the process. It is usually prohibitive in cost and may not be physically or practically possible, especially if the item must be destroyed (as in a laboratory test). Therefore, the definition formula for the sample *S* will be our basic formula for standard deviation:

$$S = \sqrt{\frac{\Sigma(X - \overline{X})^2}{n - 1}}. \tag{12.1}$$

12.1 Problems Associated with the Definition Formula

If you worked the first exercise at the end of Chapter 11, you may agree that the direct use of this formula by calculating the squared deviations from the mean is not exactly the easiest task in the world. First you have to calculate the mean; then subtract the mean from each of the original readings to get the deviation from the mean; then square each of the deviations from the mean; then add up the squared deviations; then divide the sum by either N or $n - 1$; and finally take the square root.

In some cases (perhaps many) the sample mean could run into many decimal positions. For example, suppose that the calculated sample mean turns out to be 1.166666666 . . . , an unending decimal resulting from dividing 7 by 6. Should you round the sample mean first to very few decimal places before you subtract it from each of the readings? Or should you use the sample mean intact as calculated with all of its decimal positions (within the limits of your calculator or computer)?

It would be statistically correct to retain all of the decimal positions when you subtract the sample mean from the readings *in order for the sum of the deviations to become exactly zero*. If the aim of your calculations is to calculate the standard deviation as accurately as the collected data will permit, then only the *final answer* for standard deviation should be rounded, not any of the figures obtained *during* the calculations.

If you decide, however, to round the sample mean before you subtract it from every reading, then each deviation from the mean $(X - \overline{X})$ is in error by some slight amount, and these errors tend to accumulate as you go through all of the readings in your sample. In fact, in this situation, the sum of the deviations will likely not turn out to be exactly zero.

Another rounding error can occur when you divide the numerator by the denominator in the definition formula (12.1), giving you the variance, and then decide to round the variance before taking the square root. Finally, after taking the square root, you would round the answer using some rule or guideline, such as those discussed in Chapter 10. Thus, in actual use, the definition formula (12.1) for the sample standard deviation contains three opportunities for rounding error in its separate steps during calculation.

12.2 Calculating Formulas for S for Ungrouped Data

We will introduce here, in formulas (12.2) and (12.3), two very popular alternative formulas for S that are actually easier to use for calculations, although they appear to be more complicated.[1] They are *algebraically equivalent* to each other and to the definition formula (12.1).

The first alternative, formula (12.2), involves fewer possibilities for rounding errors and is preferred by the author. The second alternative, formula (12.3), is

---

[1] It is quite easy to derive these formulas from the definition formula (12.1), and it is also easy to derive these formulas from each other, since they are all algebraically equivalent, but we shall not do it here. Readers truly interested in their derivation can do it themselves by expanding the definition formula—that is, expanding the expression $\Sigma(X - \overline{X})^2$—or by examining a formal statistics textbook.

widely used in designed experiments where the data are analyzed by the analysis of variance (ANOVA). There are other formulas for calculating S, but these two are the most popular:

$$S = \sqrt{\frac{n(\Sigma X^2) - (\Sigma X)^2}{n(n-1)}}, \tag{12.2}$$

$$S = \sqrt{\frac{\Sigma X^2 - \dfrac{(\Sigma X)^2}{n}}{n-1}}. \tag{12.3}$$

To use these efficient formulas for S, we need three quantities to substitute in them:

1. The sample size n

2. The sum of the original readings ΣX

3. The sum of the squares of the readings ΣX^2.

The formulas in Eqs. (12.2) and (12.3) are for *ungrouped* data. Let us practice using these formulas before discussing *grouped* data.

12.3 Use of the Calculating Formulas

Recall the 10 readings in centimeters that we used in Chapter 10, layout (10.3), to calculate the mean for both ungrouped and grouped data. Consider these 10 numbers again as a sample from some defined population. We now calculate their squares in Figure 12.1 so that we can substitute the column totals directly into the calculation formulas.

Original Data X	Squares X^2
9 cm	81 cm²
7	49
8	64
9	81
8	64
7	49
8	64
9	81
8	64
7	49
$\Sigma X = 80$ cm	$\Sigma X^2 = 646$ cm²

Figure 12.1. Original ungrouped data and their squares.

We have the three figures needed (including $n = 10$) to substitute in the calculating formulas for sample standard deviation. First, formula (12.2):

$$S = \sqrt{\frac{10(646) - (80)^2}{10(9)}} = \sqrt{\frac{6460 - 6400}{90}} = \sqrt{\frac{60}{90}}$$

$$= \sqrt{0.666666666 \ldots} = 0.816496580 = 0.8 \text{ cm.}$$

Now, formula (12.3):

$$S = \sqrt{\frac{646 - \frac{(80)^2}{10}}{9}} = \sqrt{\frac{646 - 640}{9}} = \sqrt{\frac{6}{9}}$$

$$= \sqrt{0.666666666 \ldots} = 0.816496580 = 0.8 \text{ cm.}$$

The results are the same. If we had calculated the sum of the squared deviations from the mean $\Sigma(X - \overline{X})^2$ and substituted it into the definition formula (12.1), the result would also be the same. (Can you verify this?)

This example shows the equivalence of the three formulas for sample standard deviation. The three formulas for S may not always produce identical answers if any rounding is done in the middle of the calculations. Formula (12.2) involves only the sum and the sum of squares in the numerator where rounding should *not* take place and is, therefore, least susceptible to rounding errors.[2]

---

[2] The author has seen practitioners start with data in hundredths (two decimal places), such as 1.23, 1.41, 1.39, etc., and then *round* the squares of these numbers to hundredths (two decimal places). This is not a correct procedure at all; it compounds rounding errors. The squares of such data should contain four decimal places, and all of them should be retained for subsequent substitution into the formulas.

X	*f*	*fX*	*fX*²
7	3	21	147
8	4	32	256
9	3	27	243
Column Totals:	$\Sigma f = 10$	$\Sigma fX = 80$	$\Sigma fX^2 = 646$

Figure 12.2. Grouped data and their squares.

12.4 Calculation Formulas for *S* for Grouped Data

When the data in Figure 12.1 are grouped, we will have a column labeled *f* for *frequency*. Refer back to layout (10.6) in Chapter 10 where the mean of our data in grouped form was calculated. We multiplied each reading *X* by its frequency *f*, creating another column labeled *fX* (read *f times X*).

To calculate the standard deviation, we need another column that involves squares of the original data *X*² multiplied by their frequency *f*. The new column, therefore, will be labeled *fX*² (read *f times X-squared*) as shown in Figure 12.2. Notice that the column totals are the same as those in Figure 12.1. Also note that the sum of the frequencies is the total sample size, 10; that is, $\Sigma f = n$. There are two ways to obtain the figures in the last column, *fX*²:

1. Square the figure in the *X* column and multiply the result by the figure in the *f* column. This is the more difficult method.

2. Multiply the figure in the *fX* column by the figure in the *X* column. This is the easier method.

Calculating formulas (12.2) and (12.3) for the sample standard deviation are modified slightly to accommodate the frequencies involving grouped data. Wherever there is an *X*, insert the frequency letter *f* in front of it. *Thus, the two calculating formulas for grouped data become:*

$$S = \sqrt{\frac{n(\Sigma fX^2) - (\Sigma fX)^2}{n(n-1)}} \tag{12.4}$$

$$S = \sqrt{\frac{\Sigma fX^2 - \dfrac{(\Sigma fX)^2}{n}}{n-1}} \tag{12.5}$$

Substituting the results of Figure 12.2 into either formula (12.4) or (12.5) will yield the same results as those obtained for ungrouped data.

12.5 A Reminder Concerning Estimates

When you calculate $\overline{X}$, the sample mean, remember that it is not the true mean of the population (or process) but an estimate of it. That is,

$$\overline{X} = \text{Est. of } \mu. \tag{12.6}$$

Similarly, when you calculate S, the sample standard deviation, it is not the true standard deviation of the population (or process) but an estimate of it. That is,

$$S = \text{Est. of } \sigma. \tag{12.7}$$

Reminding yourself of these limitations of the results of your calculations is not a sign of statistical weakness; it is a sign of respect that you have for the uncertainty in your sample data. It will also prevent you from making claims that are unjustified and unproven by the sample data at hand; namely, that the true mean is the calculated $\overline{X}$ or that the true standard deviation is the calculated S.

12.6 Applications of the Sample Standard Deviation

The sample standard deviation has many applications in industry, science, and research. It is used to estimate *variability*, not only for characteristics that are measurable, but also for characteristics that are attributes, such as proportions, number of defectives (nonconformances), and number of defects (nonconformities). We shall see these applications when we discuss control charts in Part Three.

It is used to calculate *confidence intervals* for parameters of a population, such as the true mean, the true variance, the true standard deviation, and the true proportion. The intervals have limits within which the parameter of a process lies with a given level of confidence (probability).

It is used for *testing hypotheses* regarding parameters of a population. It is used to make *comparisons,* such as the difference in performance between an established method and a new method.

Perhaps the widest use of standard deviation in industrial and other applications is in *predicting* the percentage of units that meet (or do not meet) certain criteria, such as specifications or targets. Such applications frequently involve determining the area under the so-called normal curve (Chapter 16). Process capability studies are other examples of this application (Chapter 23).

The importance of standard deviation cannot be overemphasized, which leads us to the need to understand this statistical concept much better now than we have in the past, and much better in the future than we do now. We will study some of the applications of standard deviation in Part Three.

12.7 Summary

Most of our work in industry and in other disciplines involves sample data. Therefore the definition formula for the sample standard deviation S is the basic formula to use. Some problems are associated with this formula, which involve rounding the results and complexity in calculations. Several alternative versions of the definition formula are available; all are algebraically equivalent and serve our purpose better in terms of ease of calculation and minimization of rounding errors. We concentrated on two of them. They require only the sample size, the sum of the readings, and the sum of the squares of the readings, all easy to obtain. Slight modifications of the formulas to incorporate frequencies will accommodate grouped data. The practitioner must be constantly reminded that the sample mean is an estimate of the population mean, and the sample standard deviation is an estimate of the population standard deviation. The sample standard deviation has many applications: to estimate process variability, to determine confidence intervals, to test hypotheses, to make comparisons, and to determine areas under the normal curve.

12.8 Putting It into Practice

1. Use the five numbers from Chapter 11 that were used to demonstrate how the standard deviation is evolved,

   7, 2, 6, 1, 3.

   Treat them as a sample from some defined population, and calculate the standard deviation S using *both* alternative calculating formulas (12.2) and (12.3) introduced in this chapter.

2. Collect some sample data, say, $n = 25$, that are recorded to two decimal places (in hundredths). Calculate the sample standard deviation S *twice* using one of the calculating formula versions that require the sum of squares: formula (12.2) or (12.3). The first time, when you square the readings, retain the four decimal places. The second time, round the squared readings to two decimal places. Do you find any difference between the two calculated results before rounding the final answer? Do you find any difference when you round the final answer for reporting?

3. Collect at least two different brands of scientific calculators. Do the calculators differentiate between population and sample standard deviation? Examine their user manuals to find out which version of the sample standard deviation formulas is programmed. Are the versions different? If they are

different, enter the data from Problem 2, and see if the calculated sample standard deviations are different. If the results are different, make a decision as to which calculator, if any, you would prefer to use.

Answers to Problem 1

$\Sigma X = 19$; $\Sigma X^2 = 99$.

$S = 2.588435821 = 2.6$ oz after rounding.

Same result for both formulas.

You propound a complicated mathematical problem. Give me a slate and half an hour's time, and I can produce a wrong answer.

—George B. Shaw

CHAPTER 13

Estimating Process Standard Deviation from Ranges

Having gone through Chapter 12, you may have experienced a certain amount of anxiety in dealing with elaborate formulas for the standard deviation and the painstaking care you must exercise in substituting numbers correctly into those formulas. Take heart. There is relief for us in the many calculators and computers available that make calculating the standard deviation a snap. In addition, however, there is a quick, easy, and popular way of estimating the population standard deviation *by the use of the mean of several ranges,* or *average range,* provided that certain steps and precautions are taken.

Perhaps the apparent complexity of the standard deviation formulas has contributed to the sparse understanding of this concept of variability that seems to be so widespread.

13.1 Steps in the Use of the Average Range to Estimate σ

Six short, simple steps must be followed when using ranges to estimate the population standard deviation:

1. The sample data are assumed to be arranged in *random order.* (This requirement really means that the process is assumed to be *in statistical control,* explained in the next section.)

2. Group the data into smaller groups, called *subgroups,* each with the same number of readings.

3. Calculate the *range, R,* for each of the subgroups. You will then have as many ranges as there are subgroups.

4. Calculate the *average range,* $\overline{R}$ (read *R-bar*), by adding up the ranges and dividing by the number of ranges.

5. Obtain a special factor, d_2 (read *d-sub-two*), from a suitable table, such as Table 2 in the Appendix at the back of the book. This factor depends on the number of readings that are contained in each subgroup; that is, subgroup size.

6. Divide $\overline{R}$ by d_2 (read *R-bar over d-sub-two*) to obtain an estimate of the population standard deviation:

$$\overline{R}/d_2 = \text{Est. of } \sigma. \qquad\qquad (13.1)$$

13.2 Caution Regarding the Use of $\overline{R}/d_2$

Equation (13.1) is certainly much simpler and easier to use than any of the calculating formulas for S that were introduced in Chapter 12, and for that reason it is widely used by many quality practitioners.[1] It is also widely misused and misinterpreted as well. Please pay special attention to the following warning:

> Equation (13.1) may be used to estimate the process standard deviation *only* if the process is in statistical control.

The phrase "in statistical control" means that the process is:

1. Behaving in a random fashion

2. Stable

3. Predictable.

When these conditions exist, the process is said to be in statistical control and doing its best in its present configuration. This desirable status of the process can be described in several ways. The forces that drive the process are

---

[1] We will find in Chapter 19 that this formula for estimating the population standard deviation plays a very important part in determining the control limits for the control chart for averages.

common to every output of the process, what Deming refers to as *common causes*. Any variability observed in the process reflects chance, random, unspecific causes and not undesirable *assignable causes* that cause the variability to increase unexpectedly.

The net result is a process that is stable in its behavior and therefore predictable in its performance. This is the essence of statistical control. How do we determine if the process is in statistical control? We use control charts that are *properly interpreted*. Control charts are introduced formally in Part Three after some additional important statistical concepts have been presented.

13.3 An Illustration of the Importance of the Caution

Suppose that samples of three valves are taken every 2 hours from a process that makes small fluid valves. The characteristic being measured is pressure needed to open the valves, and the unit of measure is pounds per square inch (psi). The foreman has obtained readings over one shift as shown in Table 13.1.

Table 13.1. Fluid Valve Data in psi

8 A.M.	10 A.M.	12 Noon	2 P.M.
37	142	66	94
33	144	61	96
35	145	60	99

The shift ends at 2:30 P.M., at which time the foreman, Bill, calls in a quality engineer, Jack, and asks him, "Can you give me an idea of what the standard deviation has been during my shift?" It seems that the foreman had taken a course or two on SPC and was at least acquainted with the concept of standard deviation. He continues, "Here are the results of our sampling during the shift," and he shows the data of Table 13.1 to Jack.

Jack looks at the data and immediately thinks of $\overline{R}/d_2$ as a quick way of getting the standard deviation. He tells Bill, "Just wait a minute, Bill, and I'll have your answer for you." Jack proceeds to determine the range for each subgroup of three taken at each sampling and gets the results shown in Table 13.2 (which you can verify).

Table 13.2. Ranges of the Subgroups (psi)

8 A.M.	10 A.M.	12 Noon	2 P.M.
4	3	6	5

He sums the ranges to get

$$\Sigma R = 18 \text{ psi.}$$

Then he divides that sum by four to get the average range:

$$\overline{R} = 18/4 = 4.5 \text{ psi.}$$

Next, he obtains the appropriate value of the special factor d_2 from Table 2 in the Appendix for sample subgroups of three:

$$d_2 = 1.693.$$

Finally, he divides $\overline{R}$ by d_2 to get his final estimate for the process standard deviation:

$$\overline{R}/d_2 = 4.5/1.693 = 2.658003544 = 2.7 \text{ psi.} \tag{13.2}$$

It has taken Jack only about a minute to do the calculation, and he proudly brings his results to Bill, the foreman. Bill looks at the final figure and shakes his head: "Something is wrong here. This figure seems much too small. I called you in because we had an unusually high number of valves not meeting specs during this shift due to excessive variability. You can see that big pile of rejects there in the storage bin."

Jack says, "Well, perhaps I made an arithmetic error. Let me check my calculations again." He does that and comes back a moment later. "Everything looks OK, Bill. The calculations are correct." Bill merely shakes his head with a mixed expression of bewilderment and doubt.

13.4 Who Is Right, Who Is Wrong, and Why?

An examination of the data in Table 13.1 shows that, without any calculations, the *sample averages* vary considerably from 8 A.M. to 2 P.M. This is a clue that the data are not in random order, in which case the first requirement listed in Section 13.1 for the use of $\overline{R}/d_2$ as an estimate of the process standard deviation has been violated.

If the data had been in random order, the 12 observations would be distributed more uniformly among the four sampling times. We would then expect to get more variability *within* each of the four subgroups, each subgroup containing perhaps a low reading, a middle-sized reading, and a high reading. Each sample of three valves would be tantamount to a random sample of three from the entire process. In this case the *averages* at the four sampling times would be of the *same order of magnitude;* that is, the sample averages would be similar in size. When this occurs, the process is said to be in statistical control.

Since the process does not appear to be in statistical control, because the data are not randomly distributed, then $\overline{R}/d_2$ would tend to *underestimate* the overall variability in the process. The important caution emphasized in Section 13.2 was not heeded.

If one were to calculate the sample standard deviation S using all 12 readings in the example, we would get a better measure of the actual overall variability in the process. You should verify that

$$S = 42.4185494 = 42.4 \text{ psi.} \tag{13.3}$$

Since S is many times larger than $\overline{R}/d_2 = 2.7$ psi shown in Eq. (13.2), it is very clear that $\overline{R}/d_2$ badly underestimated the process variability.

Thus it appears that Bill, the foreman, was correct in his suspicion of excessive variability. Jack, the quality engineer, was wrong to use the quick and easy formula without checking first to see if the process was in statistical control (behaving in a random fashion). Without being challenged by the foreman, the quality engineer would have concluded incorrectly that he had a very good process (very little variability) when, in fact, it was terrible (much variability). This example points out the danger of knowing just a little bit about SPC and ignoring the assumptions and conditions that underlie its tools.[2]

13.5 The Two Estimates, S and $\overline{R}/d_2$

We now have two separate and independent sample statistics, S and $\overline{R}/d_2$, for estimating the population standard deviation σ. *If the process were in statistical control, the two estimates would be similar in size, in which case either sample statistic could be used to estimate the process standard deviation.*

Notice that, in calculating S, all of the data are used, whereas $\overline{R}/d_2$ uses only part of the data; namely, the largest and smallest number in each sample subgroup. In the author's experience, many practitioners consider only S as an estimate of the process standard deviation. But we cannot call S an estimate of σ without also calling $\overline{R}/d_2$ an estimate of σ.

To address the correct identification, relationship, and nomenclature, complete statements should be written:

$$S = \text{Est. of } \sigma \tag{13.4}$$
$$\overline{R}/d_2 = \text{Est. of } \sigma \tag{13.5}$$

---

[2] Jack, the quality engineer, was not fired. He was given additional training in statistical methods that he put to good use as he moved up the corporate ladder.

Equations (13.4) and (13.5) must not be misconstrued. Because they represent two independent ways of estimating the same thing, σ, it does not follow that the estimates are equal to each other. It is wrong, therefore, to state that

$$S = \overline{R}/d_2. \qquad\qquad \textbf{This is incorrect!}$$

Another error is to equate the true population standard deviation, which is usually unknown, with an estimate obtained from sample data. It is wrong, therefore, to state that

$$S = \sigma \qquad\qquad \textbf{This is incorrect!}$$

or that

$$\overline{R}/d_2 = \sigma. \qquad\qquad \textbf{This is incorrect!}$$

13.6 Two Kinds of Variability

The $\overline{R}/d_2$ term represents only *one* kind of variability: the variability *within* subgroups. You might consider the readings in each subgroup as samples from a single batch in a process; then $\overline{R}/d_2$ measures only the variability within batches.

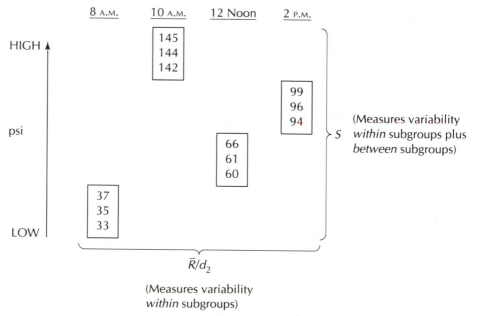

Figure 13.1. Variability within and among subgroups (not to scale).

S, using all of the data, measures the total variability and includes *two* kinds of variability: the variability *within* subgroups (or within batches) plus the variability *between* subgroups (or between batches).

A semigraphical representation of the valve pressure data of Table 13.1, shown in Figure 13.1, may help in understanding the difference between S and $\overline{R}/d_2$. The 12 readings are shown in a roughly approximate vertical scale of psi. You can see that the subgroups differ considerably in average psi, indicating much more variability between subgroups than within subgroups.

13.7 Interpreting the Difference Between S and $\overline{R}/d_2$

The variability between subgroups in Figure 13.1 appears to be quite substantial. Thus the portion of S that represents the variability between subgroups would also be substantial, and $\overline{R}/d_2$ would be *significantly smaller* than S as we saw in Eqs. (13.2) and (13.3). This situation represents a process that is not in statistical control.

If there were very little variability between subgroups (that is, between subgroup averages), then that portion of S that represents the variability *between* subgroups would be relatively small compared to the variability *within* subgroups, and both S and $\overline{R}/d_2$ would be of the same order of magnitude (same ballpark). In this case the process would be considered to be in statistical control.

In dealing with actual sample data from a process that is *not* in statistical control, $\overline{R}/d_2$ would tend to be smaller than S, and the difference would be considered significant. If the process *is* in statistical control, $\overline{R}/d_2$ may turn out to be smaller or could even be somewhat larger than S, but the difference in either case would not be considered significant.

A cursory comparison between $\overline{R}/d_2$ and S may not be sufficient to come to the correct conclusion as to whether or not the process is in statistical control. The definitive SPC tool used to determine if the process is or is not in statistical control is the *control chart*. Thus, in analyzing sample data from a process, it would not be necessary to calculate both S and $\overline{R}/d_2$ to determine if the process is in statistical control; control charts for average and range would be used for that purpose. Since the data would already be arranged in subgoups, $\overline{R}/d_2$ would be readily available.

Some practitioners, however, calculate $\overline{R}/d_2$ and use it as the only estimate of the process variability without the benefit of a control chart analysis. This can be a dangerous procedure. If the process happens to be out of statistical control, $\overline{R}/d_2$ may badly underestimate the process variability, as we saw in the example in this chapter, leading one to conclude that the process variability is much smaller than it actually is.

13.8 Summary

The average range formula is another way of estimating the process standard deviation:

$$\overline{R}/d_2 = \text{Est. of } \sigma.$$

It is much easier to use than any of the formulas for S and is very popular among practitioners for that reason. Data must be grouped into subgroups and the range calculated for each subgroup; the factor d_2, which depends on the size of a subgroup, is obtained from Table 2 in the Appendix. Note this caution, however, in its use: If this formula is to be used to estimate the process variability, the process must be shown to be in statistical control (random, stable, predictable, essentially doing its best). The control chart would be used to determine statistical control.

We now have two formulas for independently estimating the process standard deviation, $\overline{R}/d_2$ and S. Formula $\overline{R}/d_2$ measures only the variability within subgroups; S measures the variability within subgroups plus the variability between subgroups (actually, subgroup averages). When the process is in statistical control, $\overline{R}/d_2$ is not significantly different from S; in fact, it may be somewhat smaller or even somewhat larger, but not significantly so. If the process is not in statistical control, $\overline{R}/d_2$ will be significantly smaller than S. The only sure way to determine if a process is in statistical control is by the use of a control chart.

13.9 Putting It into Practice

1. Refer to Table 6.1 in Chapter 6 containing screw-cap torques on a sample of 100 plastic jars. There are 20 subgroups (rows) of five readings each.

    (a) Calculate the range for each subgroup by row, calculate the average range $\overline{R}$, and estimate the process standard deviation using the formula $\overline{R}/d_2$.

    (b) Estimate with a calculator or computer the process standard deviation using a formula for S. Do you think these two estimates of σ are significantly different from each other?

    (c) Calculate the sample average $\overline{X}$ for each subgroup by row, and plot the 20 sample averages as a run chart.

    (d) What is your initial judgment as to whether or not this process is in statistical control?

2. What procedures, criteria, definitions, or statistical methods are employed in your organization to determine if a process is "in statistical control" or "out of statistical control." Is this the phrase that is used, or is it some other phrase, such as "in control" or "out of control?" Make a note of it for future discussion.

3. If you have access to quality control or quality assurance data, determine if $\overline{R}/d_2$ is being used to estimate a process standard deviation. If it is being used, was there any attempt to determine, first, if the process was in statistical control? Was S used instead? Discuss the matter with the QC/QA person in charge.

Answers to Problem 1

(a) $\Sigma R = 113$; $\overline{R} = 113/20 = 5.65$ in.-lbs.
$\overline{R}/d_2 = 5.65/2.326 = 2.429062769 = 2.4$ in.-lbs. = Est. of σ.

(b) $S = 2.955477708 = 3.0$ in.-lbs. = Est. of σ.
$\overline{R}/d_2$ *looks* significantly smaller than S.

(c) The subgroup averages go from 16.6 to 25.4 in.-lbs. Well, the points do not *look* as if they are bouncing around in a random fashion. At least a couple of points *seem* to be far different from the rest.

(d) The process may not be in statistical control, but frankly *I'm not sure.* I guess we'll have to develop a control chart, using these data, for a correct interpretation. I'll wait until we get to Part Three.

C H A P T E R   1 4

Coding and Decoding Data

🐦 = 1

🐇 = 2

🐑 = 3

The coding of information for various reasons has been a popular practice of human beings for thousands of years. It ranges from the hieroglyphics of ancient Egyptians, as a method of writing, to the sophisticated data transformations of today. As children we probably toyed with the coding of words and letters in order to generate secret messages for our friends.

The coding of data is a common practice. We seem to do it quite naturally as we manipulate numbers in order to simplify our work.

The purpose of *statistical* coding is to convert data, which may appear initially in complicated form, to a simpler form that will ease the burden of calculations as well as speed up those operations.

If you are currently using computers routinely to accept, compute, and summarize data in their original form, however complicated the raw data may be, you may skip this chapter and proceed to Chapter 15. If, however, your data-handling practices are not completely dominated by computers, and you frequently work with raw data either manually or with hand calculators, then this chapter may be of some benefit to you.[1]

The need to understand coding and decoding is especially great when analysis of data involves not only the simple mean but also the more complicated standard deviation (see Chapter 11).

---

* In "Simplifying Data," *Quality* magazine, Hitchcock Publishing, November 1991, p. 31.

[1] For a provocative and convincing discussion of the value of hand calculations, see H. J. Khamis, "Manual Computations—A Tool for Reinforcing Concepts and Techniques," *The American Statistician*, American Statistical Association, November 1991, Vol. 45, No. 4, pp. 294–299.

14.1 Coding and Decoding by Intuition

Suppose that certain measurements in centimeters resulted in the following set of original sample data:

Original Data

104 cm
106
102
101
108

If you were asked to calculate the *mean*, you might be inclined to add up only the unit digits (4, 6, 2, 1, 8), calculate their mean, and then add 100 to get the mean of the original data:

Unit Digits

4 cm
6
2
1
<u>8</u>

Sum of unit digits =   21
Mean of unit digits =   4.2 cm
Mean of original data =   104.2 cm

You can easily verify that 104.2 cm is the mean of the original data using all of the digits in the original data. Certainly the unit digits were simpler, easier, and faster to work with than the original data. Using unit digits here is a simple example of coding the data.

Usually we have little intuitive difficulty in coding data in order to simplify the calculation of the *mean*. Generally, we seem to be able to tell what effect our coding will have on the mean, enabling us to adjust (decode) our calculated answer accordingly.

14.2 Coding and Decoding Formulas

The original data were coded by the use of some sort of coding formula, which is often intuitive and not explicitly stated. As a matter of good procedure, practice, and habit, *always write down the coding formula when coding data*. After all of the calculations are performed with the coded data, then we must do something to express the result in terms of the original data; that is, to *decode* the data properly into the format and magnitude of the original data. Having the coding formula in front of you will help to perform the decoding process correctly.

In our example it should be obvious that we *subtracted 100 from each of the numbers in our original data set* in order to change those numbers into their coded form. Thus the *coding formula* would be written

$$\text{Coded Data} = \text{Original Data} - 100. \qquad (14.1)$$

Formula (14.1) describes specifically how we coded the original data. Solving this simple equation algebraically for "Original data," by adding 100 to each side, gives us

$$\text{Original Data} = \text{Coded Data} + 100, \qquad (14.2)$$

and we can use this expression to change back any of the coded numbers into the original numbers simply by adding 100.

To show how the mean of the coded data is related to the mean of the original data, we can take the *mean* of both sides of Eq. (14.2). This gives us

$$
\begin{aligned}
\text{Mean of Original Data} &= \text{Mean of Coded Data} + \text{Mean of 100} \\
&= 4.2 + 100 \qquad (14.3)\\
&= 104.2 \text{ cm,}
\end{aligned}
$$

which confirms our final answer. Formula (14.3) is the *decoding formula for the mean* in our example. It can be written more simply as

$$\text{Original Mean} = \text{Coded Mean} + 100. \qquad (14.4)$$

Coding and decoding for the *mean* usually present little difficulty. But coding and decoding the *standard deviation* present a different problem. We cannot be quite sure what effect our coding will have on the standard deviation. Therefore, we must develop a set of coding rules and formulas which describe the ways in which coding can be accomplished and determine the effect of the coding on *both* the mean and standard deviation. Then we must establish the decoding rules and formulas so that we can express the results in terms of the mean and standard deviation of the original data.

The coding of data is particularly useful when using one of the calculating formulas for sample standard deviation. Recall in Chapter 12 that in calculating the standard deviation, the *squares* of the data are needed. Without coding, we would have to square each of the original numbers in our example in Section 14.1, ending up with fairly large numbers:

Original Data	*Squares*
104 cm	10,816 cm²
106	11,236
102	10,404
101	10,201
108	11,664

Of course, all of this work can be relatively simple with the use of a scientific (statistical) calculator that will calculate standard deviation for you. You would be inclined to enter the data as they appear in their original form. Even then, however, the coding of the original data to a simpler form could be quite useful *if you were aware of the effect of coding on the mean and standard deviation.*

14.3 A Convenient Table of Formulas for Coding and Decoding

Table 14.1 provides some popular methods for coding data and the related coding and decoding formulas, which should be easy to follow. The coding and decoding methods and formulas are in word form for easy reading. Choosing the constants to use in the coding formulas depends on the format, magnitude, and grouping of the original data. Let us study examples of coding Methods II, III, and V.

14.4 Using Table 14.1: Subtracting a Constant (Method II)

Consider again our example in which 100 is a constant to be subtracted from the original data. Then the *coding formula* is written simply as

$$\text{Coded} = \text{Original} - 100. \tag{14.5}$$

The mean and standard deviation of the coded data are calculated, giving us the *coded mean* and *coded standard deviation.* Now we wish to decode those results in order to get the mean and standard deviation of the original data. Referring to Table 14.1, Method II, the *decoding formulas* are

$$\text{Original Mean} = \text{Coded Mean} + 100 \tag{14.6}$$
$$\text{Original Std. Dev.} = \text{Coded Std. Dev.} \tag{14.7}$$

Note that the decoding formula (14.6) for the mean involves using the constant, 100, in the *opposite arithmetic operation*: addition instead of subtraction. This principle reflects the fact that, in decoding for the mean, we are merely solving the coding formula of Eq. (14.5) algebraically for "Original."

Decoding formula (14.7) identifies another very important and useful principle that can be observed from Table 14.1:

Table 14.1. Formulas for Coding and Decoding Data

Coding Method	Coding Formulas Coded =	Decoding Formulas for Original Mean =	Decoding Formulas for Original Std. Dev. =
I. Add a Constant, C	Original + C	Coded Mean − C	Coded Std. Dev.
II. Subtract a Constant, C	Original − C	Coded Mean + C	Coded Std. Dev.
III. Divide by a Constant, D	Original / D	Coded Mean × D	Coded Std. Dev. × D
IV. Multiply by a Constant, M	Original × M	Coded Mean / M	Coded Std. Dev. / M
V. Combination of above	$\dfrac{\text{Original} - C}{D}$	(Coded Mean × D) + C	Coded Std. Dev. × D

Notes:

1. A good rule for coding grouped data is to use the Mode as the first constant (to subtract) and the Interval Size as the second constant (to divide by):

$$\text{Coded} = \frac{\text{Original} - \text{Mode}}{\text{Interval Size}}$$

This formula converts the original grouped data to signed integers, coded data with the smallest numbers:

$$-3, \ -2, \ -1, \ 0, \ +1, \ +2, \ +3, \text{ etc.}$$

2. If only positive numbers are desired, do not subtract the Mode as the first constant, but subtract the smallest of the original data (or smallest Midpoint). The coded data become positive integers:

$$0, \ 1, \ 2, \ 3, \text{ etc.}$$

3. If the data are grouped by intervals for which Midpoints are determined, replace Original in the formula by Midpoint. The Mode is that Midpoint with the highest frequency.

Subtracting a constant from data (or adding a constant to data) has no effect on the standard deviation.

Subtracting or adding a constant to the original data has the effect of moving the entire distribution of data, intact, down the linear scale (for subtraction of a constant) or up the linear scale (for additon of a constant). Thus every reading is moved the same amount, resulting in no change in the variability or in the shape of the distribution. A simple coding mechanism like subtracting a constant from the original data can save you much effort and time even if you use a calculator.

In the example of sample data used at the beginning of this chapter, you can easily verify that the sample standard deviation S of the original five readings in centimeters, 104, 106, 102, 101, 108, is $S = 2.9$ cm. If 100 is subtracted from these data, the standard deviation of the coded data, 4, 6, 2, 1, 8, is the same: $S = 2.9$ cm.

Adding a constant (Method I) can be treated as a form of *subtracting* a constant. For example, to add 100 is the same as subtracting (-100), and the Method II formulas for coding and decoding apply.

14.5 Using Table 14.1: Dividing by a Constant (Method III)

Suppose that the original data are divided by a constant, say, 5. Then the *coding formula* is

$$\text{Coded} = \frac{\text{Original}}{5}. \tag{14.8}$$

The mean and standard deviation of the coded data are calculated, and now we wish to decode. Referring to Table 14.1, Method III, the *decoding formulas* are

$$\text{Original Mean} = \text{Coded Mean} \times 5 \tag{14.9}$$

$$\text{Original Std. Dev.} = \text{Coded Std. Dev.} \times 5. \tag{14.10}$$

We see here that the decoding procedure is the same for both the mean and the standard deviation; namely, multiplying the coded results by the selected constant, 5. Note again that the arithmetic operation in decoding is the opposite from that used in the coding formula: multiplication instead of division.

Multiplying by a constant (Method IV) can be treated as a form of *dividing by* a constant. For example, to multiply by 5 is the same as dividing by 1/5, and the Method III rules for coding and decoding apply.

14.6 Using Table 14.1: Combination Involving Two Constants (Method V)

Using two constants for coding can often reduce the original data to such simple numbers that subsequent calculations with the coded results can almost be performed with just fingers and toes. In this section we discuss the formulas of Method V in a little more detail.

Suppose that a first constant, say, 100, is subtracted from the original data, and the result is then divided by a second constant, say, 5. Then the *coding formula* is

$$\text{Coded} = \frac{\text{Original} - 100}{5}. \tag{14.11}$$

The mean and the standard deviation of the coded data are calculated, and now we wish to decode. Referring to Table 14.1, Method V, the *decoding formulas* are

$$\text{Original Mean} = (\text{Coded Mean} \times 5) + 100 \tag{14.12}$$

$$\text{Original Std. Dev.} = \text{Coded Std. Dev.} \times 5. \tag{14.13}$$

Note that, in decoding the mean in formula (14.12), the arithmetic operations are the opposite from those used in coding, formula (14.11), and that the constants are involved in reverse order. Note also, in decoding the standard deviation in formula (14.13), that the first constant, 100, which was subtracted from the original data, is not involved, because subtracting a constant (or adding a constant) has no effect on the *variability* of the data, a worthwhile principle noted earlier.

In the next several sections we work with some data in a form that will put Method V to good use.

14.7 Return to Screw-Cap Torque Data: Concept of Midpoints

We are now ready to complete the calculations for the screw-cap torque data of Table 6.1 (Chapter 6) by considering the data in grouped form as was shown in Figure 6.2. Since the data are grouped into *intervals*, it is not possible to multiply the frequency *f* by an interval for the purpose of calculating the mean and subsequently the standard deviation. For example, how can you multiply the interval, 14–15, by its frequency, 5? You can't.

We shall have to *replace each interval with a single number* that "represents" the data in the interval. The most logical number to use is the *midpoint of the interval*.

Interval	Tally	f	Midpoint
12–13	I	1	12.5
14–15	IIII	5	14.5
16–17	IIII IIII I	11	16.5
18–19	IIII IIII IIII II	17	18.5
20–21	IIII IIII IIII IIII IIII IIII IIII II	37	20.5
22–23	IIII IIII III	13	22.5
24–25	IIII IIII	10	24.5
26–27	IIII	5	26.5
28–29	I	1	28.5
Totals		100	

Figure 14.1. Showing a column for midpoints.

The midpoint of any interval is determined by calculating the mean of the two interval limits. Thus the midpoint of the first interval, 12–13, is

$$\text{Midpoint of interval } 12\text{–}13 = \frac{12 + 13}{2} = 12.5.$$

The midpoints of all the intervals are shown in Figure 14.1.

14.8 A Little Bad News About Midpoints

All of the data in each interval in Figure 14.1 are presumed to have the indicated midpoint as their actual mean. This is not really true. For example, the interval 12–13 has only one reading in it, and that reading is 13 in.-lbs. But the midpoint used to represent that interval is 12.5 in.-lbs., obviously incorrect because it is slightly too low. Similarly, the interval 28–29 has only one reading in it, and that reading is 28 in.-lbs. The midpoint used to represent that interval is 28.5 in.-lbs., which is slightly too high.

Most likely, all of the midpoints are in error by some small amount, not really being the exact mean of the data in the respective intervals. We simply expect and hope that the midpoint errors will somehow erase each other—that is, cancel each other out—throughout the set of data, which they will probably not do completely. This discussion leads us to the following observation of importance:

> **We can expect that the mean and standard deviation calculated from the midpoints of intervals will usually be slightly different from a correct calculation obtained by directly entering all individual readings into a calculator or computer.**

This is the penalty that we pay for the convenience of grouping the data into intervals so that we can easily draw a histogram and calculate the mean and standard deviation conveniently from midpoints.[2] We will determine later the amount of error in the mean and standard deviation calculated from the midpoints by entering all 100 original numbers into a calculator, one at a time, for a direct calculation.

The difference between any two consecutive midpoints is also equal to the interval size, namely, 2.0 in.-lbs. This is consistent with the interval size determined by finding the difference between any two consecutive corresponding interval limits.

Convince yourself that there are actually *100 midpoint values,* not the 9 that appear in Figure 14.1. For example, there is *one* 12.5, there are *five* 14.5s, there are *eleven* 16.5s, etc.

14.9 Screw-Cap Torque Data: Coding the Midpoints

From this point on, if we wish to calculate the mean and standard deviation from the midpoints, we will have to treat the midpoints as if they are the original data and do all of our calculations with them. Thus, to find the *mean of the midpoints,* we would have to multiply each midpoint by its corresponding frequency. To find the *standard deviation of the midpoints,* we would have to multiply that result again by the corresponding midpoint. (Remember that we need *squares* of the readings in order to calculate the standard deviation.) Note that, if we perform the calculations using the actual midpoints, the numbers we will have to work with may become quite large and unwieldy, increasing the chance of arithmetic error and also taking more time.

For example, refer only to interval 20–21 in Figure 14.1. We would have to multiply the frequency, 37, by the midpoint, 20.5, and then multiply that result by 20.5 again. The end product just for this interval alone would be 15,549.25.

A way out of this dilemma is to *code the midpoints* in a special way. A good suggestion for coding is contained in the notes at the bottom of Table 14.1, where two special constants, the mode and interval size, are used for coding. According to this note, the suggested *coding formula* using these two constants is

$$\text{Coded} = \frac{\text{Original} - \text{Mode}}{\text{Interval Size}}.$$

Take the mode as the first constant and the interval size as the second constant. This will *result in coded data that are as small as they can possibly be, consisting only of signed integers.*

---

[2] This is another example of the principle that "there is no Santa Claus in statistics."

Interval	Tally	f	Midpoint	Coded X
12–13	l ·	1	12.5	−4
14–15	l卌	5	14.5	−3
16–17	l卌 l卌 l	11	16.5	−2
18–19	l卌 l卌 l卌 ll	17	18.5	−1
20–21	l卌 l卌 l卌 l卌 l卌 l卌 l卌 ll	37	20.5	0
22–23	l卌 l卌 lll	13	22.5	+1
24–25	l卌 l卌	10	24.5	+2
26–27	l卌	5	26.5	+3
28–29	l	1	28.5	+4
Totals		100		

Figure 14.2. Showing a column for coded midpoints X.

In this application of coding, the midpoints are treated as original data, the midpoint with the highest frequency is the mode, namely, 20.5, and the interval size is 2.0. If we call any new coded midpoint "Coded X," then our *coding formula* for the midpoints becomes

$$\text{Coded } X = \frac{\text{Midpoint} - 20.5}{2.0}. \tag{14.14}$$

Thus we can code every midpoint by simply substituting each midpoint into coding formula (14.14). For example, the midpoint, 24.5, will become

$$\text{Coded } X = \frac{24.5 - 20.5}{2.0} = \frac{4.0}{2.0} = +2.$$

Similarly, every midpoint will be coded in this way. We can then add another column of coded X values to Figure 14.1 to obtain Figure 14.2. Remember that there are actually *100* coded X values, not the 9 that appear in Figure 14.2. For example, there is *one* −4, there are *five* −3s, there are *eleven* −2s, etc.

14.10 So You Don't Like Negative Numbers?

Some readers, at this point, may hesitate to do any calculations because of the presence of negative numbers. To avoid negative numbers in the coded X column, the coding formula can be modified by using the *smallest midpoint*, namely, 12.5, instead of the mode, as the constant to subtract from the midpoints. Thus the coding formula would become

$$\text{Coded } X = \frac{\text{Midpoint} - 12.5}{2.0}. \tag{14.15}$$

The coded X values would now become 0, 1, 2, 3, 4, 5, 6, 7, 8, consisting of no negative numbers at all.

As usual, a slight penalty must be paid for the personal convenience, preference, and comfort of having no negative coded numbers with which to work. First, consider interval 20–21 with the highest frequency, 37. We will have to multiply by 37 in order to get fX and fX^2 for that interval; when we used the mode as the first constant, its coded X value became zero so that its fX and fX^2 also became zero. Second, the coded X values would go up to 8 for the last interval, 28–29; when we used the mode as the first constant, the absolute values of the coded X readings were no larger than 4 (from -4 to $+4$) as shown in Figure 14.2. Thus, in avoiding negative coded numbers, calculations usually result in larger numbers, including larger column totals.

14.11 Screw-Cap Torque Data: Preparing to Calculate the Mean and Standard Deviation

At this stage we are ready to do the calculations using the coded X values on the screw-cap torque data of Figure 14.2. Our strategy is to calculate the mean and standard deviation of the 100 coded X values and then decode the results to obtain the mean and standard deviation of the 100 midpoints. This will require, first, that we multiply the X column by the f column (in order to calculate the mean). Then we will have to multiply the latter result by X again (in order to calculate the standard deviation).[3] We will therefore need two more columns, fX and fX^2, as shown in Figure 14.3. Note in Figure 14.3 that some column totals have been entered:

$$\Sigma f = n = 100$$
$$\Sigma fX = -6$$
$$\Sigma fX^2 = 236$$

These column totals will be used in our calculations. Note also that no column totals have been entered for the columns labeled "Midpoint" and "Coded X" because such totals are meaningless. It would be worthwhile to recall coding formula (14.14) that we used for the midpoints before we proceed with the calculations:

$$\text{Coded } X = \frac{\text{Midpoint} - 20.5}{2.0}.$$

---

[3] The reader may wish to review Chapter 10 (calculating sample mean) and Chapter 12 (calculating sample standard deviation).

Interval	Tally	f	Midpoint	Coded X	fX	fX²
12–13	I	1	12.5	−4	−4	16
14–15	l︎H︎I	5	14.5	−3	−15	45
16–17	l︎H︎I l︎H︎I I	11	16.5	−2	−22	44
18–19	l︎H︎I l︎H︎I l︎H︎I II	17	18.5	−1	−17	17
20–21	l︎H︎I l︎H︎I l︎H︎I l︎H︎I l︎H︎I l︎H︎I l︎H︎I II	37	20.5	0	0	0
22–23	l︎H︎I l︎H︎I III	13	22.5	+1	+13	13
24–25	l︎H︎I l︎H︎I	10	24.5	+2	+20	40
26–27	l︎H︎I	5	26.5	+3	+15	45
28–29	I	1	28.5	+4	+4	16
	Totals	100	-----	-----	−58	236
					+52	
					−6	

Figure 14.3. Showing columns for fX and fX^2.

14.12 Calculating the Sample Mean

We first calculate the *mean of the coded data:*

$$\text{Mean of Coded } X = \frac{\Sigma fX}{\Sigma f} = \frac{-6}{100} = -0.06$$

Referring to Method V in Table 14.1, we decode this result to find the *mean of the midpoints:*

$$
\begin{aligned}
\text{Mean of Midpoints} &= [(\text{Mean of coded } X) \times 2] + 20.5 \\
&= (-0.06 \times 2) + 20.5 \\
&= -0.12 + 20.5 \qquad\qquad (14.16) \\
&= 20.38 \text{ in.-lbs.} \\
&= 20.4 \text{ in.-lbs.}
\end{aligned}
$$

For reporting purposes we round the final calculated result, 20.38 in.-lbs., to one more decimal place than the original data, which are in whole inch-pounds. No rounding should be performed during the middle of the calculations; only the final answer is rounded.

14.13 Calculating the Sample Standard Deviation

Since we are dealing with sample data, we must calculate the sample standard deviation S. We will use calculating formula (12.2) for grouped data from Chapter 12:

$$S = \sqrt{\frac{n(\Sigma fX^2) - (\Sigma fX)^2}{n(n-1)}}.$$

We first calculate the *standard deviation of the coded data:*

$$S \text{ (Coded)} = \sqrt{\frac{100(236) - (-6)^2}{100(99)}} = \sqrt{\frac{23600 - 36}{9900}} = \sqrt{\frac{23564}{9900}}$$

$$= \sqrt{2.38020202} = 1.542790336.$$

Again referring to Method V in Table 14.1, we decode this result to find the *standard deviation of the midpoints:*

$$\begin{aligned}
\text{Std. Dev. of Midpoints} &= \text{Coded Std. Dev.} \times 2 \\
&= 1.542790336 \times 2 \\
&= 3.085580672 \\
&= 3.1 \text{ in.-lbs.}
\end{aligned} \tag{14.17}$$

14.14 Summary of Results

It is a wise procedure to summarize the final results at the end of the calculations so that the results are conspicuous:

$$\text{Mean } (\overline{X}) \text{ of Midpoints} = 20.4 \text{ in.-lbs.} \tag{14.18}$$

$$\text{Std. Dev. } (S) \text{ of Midpoints} = 3.1 \text{ in.-lbs.} \tag{14.19}$$

Reinforcing again the idea that we are dealing with sample results that are estimates of the process parameters, we should remember that the results of Eqs. (14.18) and (14.19) are not the population or process mean and standard deviation, respectively. In fact, we should write

$$\overline{X} = 20.4 \text{ in.-lbs.} = \text{Est. of } \mu \tag{14.20}$$

$$S = 3.1 \text{ in.-lbs.} = \text{Est. of } \sigma \tag{14.21}$$

14.15 Comparing Midpoint Results with Direct Calculation

Recall that the midpoints were not the exact means of the readings in the respective intervals. How much of an error did we introduce in calculating the mean and standard deviation for the set of data by using midpoints?

To find out, let us calculate the mean $\overline{X}$ and the standard deviation S of the 100 *original* readings in Table 6.1 (Chapter 6) by entering them into a calculator or computer directly, one by one. These would be considered the correct calculations for the sample mean and sample standard deviation. The correctly calculated results, which can be verified patiently by the reader, are:

$$\overline{X} = 20.45 \qquad = 20.5 \text{ in.-lbs.} \qquad (14.22)$$

$$S = 2.955477708 = 3.0 \text{ in.-lbs.} \qquad (14.23)$$

The corresponding results using midpoints were 20.4 and 3.1, respectively, as shown in Eqs. (14.18) and (14.19). As anticipated, the midpoint results are not exactly the same as the direct-calculation results of Eqs. (14.22) and (14.23), but they are quite close.[4] It is very doubtful that the difference is great enough to preclude the convenient use of midpoints and coding. Certainly it would not affect or alter any decision or conclusion about the process.

Although a sample size of 100 is not really very large in some applications, think about wrestling with a set of readings that number in the several hundreds or even thousands. We would look very diligently for any method that would ease the burden of summarizing the data, such as grouping the data into intervals, determining the midpoints, and coding. When we think of large amounts of data, ultimately we consider the use of computers for processing the data. In either case, data input scheduling could become a logistics problem. It might be desirable to spread the input operation over time, or to enter data periodically, in order to minimize fatigue and attendant errors. Automated measurement and data collection, or automated data acquisition, would appear to be the ultimate solution.[5]

14.16 Summary

If calculations are performed manually and data are in a complicated form, it might be desirable to code the data into a simpler form to ease and speed up calculations and to reduce the incidence of arithmetic errors. Most of us practice coding in some way, especially in calculating the mean, but generally do it intuitively without formally expressing the coding formula used. Any coding formula used should be written down so that the method for decoding back to the original data becomes clear.

---

[4] If we had used another method of rounding, involving even or odd numbers preceding a 5, then the directly calculated mean of 20.45 would have been rounded to 20.4 in.-lbs., making the reported result the same as the reported midpoint mean. Refer to Chapter 10 for a discussion of rounding methods.

[5] The use of computers is discussed in Chapter 25.

The effect of coding on the standard deviation is not as intuitively understood, and we need some formal rules and formulas. Two important and useful observations emerged: Subtracting or adding a constant to data has no effect on the standard deviation; multiplying or dividing the data by a constant also multiplies or divides the standard deviation by the constant.

A table was introduced that identified several popular coding and decoding formulas for both the mean and the standard deviation. In particular, when data are grouped into intervals, midpoints are used and coded. A formula for coding the midpoints that subtracts the mode and then divides by the interval size results in signed integers, a simple data form that works with the smallest numbers.

Grouping the data into intervals and using midpoints to represent the data do not necessarily result in the absolutely correct sample mean and standard deviation of the original data. However, the sacrifice in accuracy is usually minimal and greatly simplifies the calculations. When the mean and standard deviation of screw-cap torque data of Chapter 6 were calculated, using midpoints and coding, the results were very close to the direct (and correct) calculations obtained by entering every reading into a calculator.

14.17 Putting It into Practice

1. The following data were collected in late 1987. They are the weights, in grams (gm), of a sample of 60 molded plastic jars used for packaging bulk aspirin-type tablets. Weight is important because it is correlated with wall strength and material cost. Each sample group consists of five jars obtained approximately every two hours from a molding machine.

Sample Group

1	44.86 gm	44.65	44.98	44.55	44.77
2	44.84	45.00	45.06	44.58	44.93
3	44.71	44.58	44.84	45.10	44.53
4	44.67	45.06	45.00	45.07	45.10
5	45.08	44.73	45.31	45.12	44.97
6	45.05	45.22	45.29	45.16	44.84
7	45.26	45.04	45.36	45.17	44.83
8	45.23	44.63	44.84	44.83	45.02
9	44.98	44.75	44.78	44.68	44.83
10	44.98	45.16	45.39	45.11	45.23
11	44.27	44.85	45.18	44.85	45.34
12	45.22	45.37	45.18	45.00	44.76

(a) Group the data into intervals. What is a reasonable interval size?

(b) Determine the midpoints for the intervals, code the midpoints, and calculate the sample mean and sample standard deviation from the coded data. What is the coding formula used? What are the mean and standard deviation after decoding?

(c) What are the correct sample mean and sample standard deviation obtained from a direct calculation obtained by entering the 60 individual weights, one by one, into a calculator or computer? Any appreciable difference from the results using midpoints?

2. Present the data in Problem 1 to two of your colleagues. Ask them how they would go about calculating the mean (first without using a calculator or computer) and specifically if they would try to code the data in some way first before calculating. If a calculator or computer is used, compare the *reported results* for both mean and standard deviation with those obtained in Problem 1.

3. Examine data contained in a recent report from the quality assurance, engineering, or R&D department that includes the mean of the data (and possibly also the standard deviation). Was any coding performed on the data to facilitate the calculation? If not, would you recommend it? If you do recommend coding, discuss it with the author of the report.

Answers to Problem 1

(a) First interval is 44.20–44.29, second interval is 44.30–44.39, etc. Interval size is 0.10 gm.

(b)   Coded $X = \dfrac{\text{Midpoint} - 44.845}{0.10}$.

After decoding, midpoint results are, after rounding,

$$\overline{X} = 44.960 \text{ gm}, \qquad S = 0.248 \text{ gm}.$$

(c) Direct calculation results are, after rounding,

$$\overline{X} = 44.963 \text{ gm}, \qquad S = 0.245 \text{ gm}.$$

No appreciable difference results from using midpoints.

PART THREE

Key SPC Tools

Public Opinion Survey: For whom the bell-shaped curve polls.
—Suggested by *Chance* magazine*

CHAPTER 15

The Normal Distribution: Serving as a Process Model

The so-called *normal distribution[1] is a mathematical function (or formula) that is used to describe the random behavior of a measurable (variable) characteristic in a population or process.* We use it in SPC to make predictions about processes, which we will do later in this chapter.

The mathematical function is depicted by a graphical curve that is sometimes referred to as the *bell curve* or *bell-shaped curve* because of its similarity in appearance to a bell. It is also referred to as the *Gaussian curve* in honor of Carl Friedrich Gauss (1777–1855), the brilliant mathematician (and astronomer and physicist) whose work on the least-squares method led to the mathematical formulation of the distribution of errors, namely, the normal distribution.

There is no intended difference between the terms *distribution* and *curve*. Distribution suggests how the observations or readings are "distributed" according to the measurement scale used, while curve refers to the graphical result.

15.1 A Model for All Reasons

Figure 15.1 shows a typical normal distribution. It serves as a *model* to describe many phenomena. In industry, generally speaking, it can be used to describe at least 90% (in some industries, even more) of all measurable characteristics, such

---

* Vol. 1, No. 3, 1988, Springer-Verlag.

[1] The "opposite" of a normal distribution is not called an abnormal distribution. The description *normal* was made in 1893 by Englishman, Karl Pearson (1857–1936), often called the "founder of the science of statistics." He also introduced the term *standard deviation* and the symbol σ in 1894.

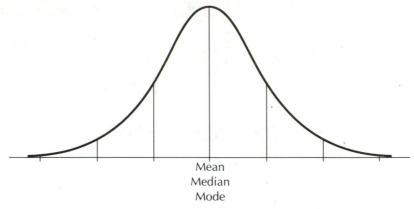

Mean
Median
Mode

Figure 15.1. The normal curve.

as length, width, height, thickness, weight, hardness, other physical characteristics, many chemical characteristics, many electrical and electronic characteristics, and many biological characteristics.

The normal distribution is used in economics, sociology, physics, astronomy, engineering, psychology, education, geology, chemistry, biology, meteorology, politics, and in many other physical and social sciences. In fact, virtually every discipline uses the normal distribution to describe some phenomenon or to predict some characteristic.

The normal distribution is an important model in SPC (see Chapter 3) for a particular reason. The normal distribution is the theoretical basis for the development of control charts, the principal tool of SPC. *One cannot understand control charts adequately without knowing something about the normal curve, serving both as a model and as a predictive tool.* That is why the normal distribution is discussed at this point in this book, before control charts are introduced.

15.2 Three Characteristics of the Normal Curve

If you examine Figure 15.1 carefully, you will note that the normal curve exhibits these characteristics:

1. *Symmetry:* A vertical line drawn through the middle bisects the curve into two parts that are mirror images of each other. Because of the symmetry, the mean, median, and mode have the same reading.

2. *A bell shape:* Indeed the curve does have the appearance of a bell, clustered in the middle and tapering off at both ends.

3. *Smoothness:* The technical term for this characteristic is that it is *continuous.* There are no bumps or steps or gaps, as one would expect to find in a frequency histogram drawn from real sample data. Even if measurements were taken in smaller units, say in ten-thousandths of an inch instead of thousandths of an inch, it would only increase the number of intervals in the frequency histogram, and we would still have bumps, steps, and gaps in the histogram (see Chapter 6). The normal curve does not end, as Figure 15.1 suggests. Theoretically, the curve continues on in both directions, getting closer and closer to the baseline, but never reaching it except at *minus infinity* and at *plus infinity.*

In fact, *you will never see a true normal curve obtained from actual data!* The normal curve is a *theoretical model* for a population or process, whereas when you collect data from a process, those data are invariably *sample* data, from which you can draw a histogram that will not exhibit the characteristics of being simultaneously symmetrical, bell-shaped, and smooth.

15.3 Peppermint Patty Invokes the "Curve" for Salvation

The normal curve has played a part in the academic lives of most of us, and it still continues to do so for many students today. Such a situation can best be described as unfortunate from a statistical point of view.

Do you remember that, when your teacher, instructor, or professor alerted you to an upcoming quiz or exam, he or she may have explained that the quiz would be graded "according to the 'curve'?" The curve referred to is the normal curve. Such a quasi-statistical practice means that, even if everyone in the class had mastered the material, someone was going to get the lowest grade (an F?), which is depicted by the *left tail* of the curve. Even if everyone in the class did poorly, someone was going to get the top grade (an A?), which is depicted by the *right tail* of the curve. Neither result makes sense. Indeed, it is conceivable that everyone in the class could receive the same numerical score, but the percentage of As, Bs, Cs, etc., would be predetermined by the instructor.[2]

The reason that the practice of using the normal curve to grade a class is inappropriate is that this practice violates a very important statistical principle:

---

[2] The idea is not new. In a *Milwaukee Journal* newspaper article of August 19, 1982, Benjamin S. Bloom, a professor of education at the University of Chicago, stated that the deepest flaw in the American educational system is the notion that a third of all students will fail or achieve only minimal results, a third will do moderately well, and a third will master everything the teacher teaches. "It reduces the aspirations of both teachers and students; it reduces motivation for learning in students; and it systematically destroys the ego and self-concept of a sizable group of students."

We must distinguish between a *population* and a *sample* (see Chapter 7). The normal curve is a model for a population, not for a sample. A school class, usually quite finite in size, is actually a sample from a much larger population of similar students. If you argue that the class *is* the population, then the distribution of actual scores is the true distribution, not subject to predictions about other student classes; it may very well be considerably different from a normal distribution.

You may use the sample to get some idea of what the population is like, but you may not ascribe properties of the population to a specific set of sample data because samples vary.

To assign population properties to a sample is to use statistics backwards. See Figure 15.2 for an excellent example, as described in a "Peanuts" cartoon, of the consequences of misusing statistics. (Peppermint Patty, musing over the possibilities, has the right idea.)

As an additional example of the futility of using the normal curve to grade students in a school classroom or in any other environment, let us consider the

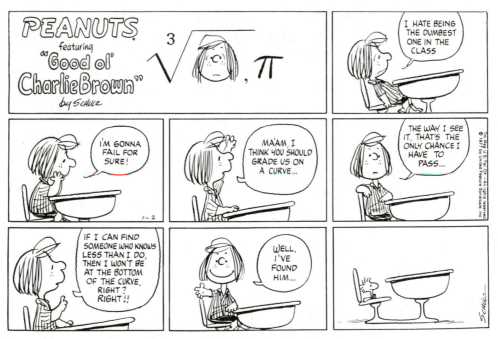

Figure 15.2 Peppermint Patty invokes the "curve" for salvation.

general practice of grading people for performance achievements in industry as a basis for a merit system of rewards (and punishments). Dr. W. Edwards Deming, in a television interview[3] on October 26, 1991, responded to a question, among others, by the moderator concerning what changes companies should make to become more competitive. His answer:

> They [should] stop ranking people, abolish the merit system, so-called system, actually destroying our people. They [should] stop ranking plants, divisions, teams. They [should] stop acting on the last data point. Take action on any outcome that's ruinous.
>
> What's damaging is the forced distribution. For example, only 20% "A", 30% "B", 30% C, 20% "D", forced into a distribution. That's wrong. That's confusion. That's producing artificial scarcity. There's no scarcity of good people, no scarcity of good pupils.
>
> I do not grade my students; how could I? A grade is a label, it's a prediction that somebody will do well, or do badly. He's labeled for life, branded. He carries that brand the rest of his life. Why do it? Why produce artificial scarcity, when there is no scarcity? It's not playing games, business is not playing games. Business is prediction; it requires knowledge. . . .

15.4 The Point of Inflection

Another interesting property of the normal curve has to do with its curvature. If you start at the top of the curve, as if you were on a mountain ski slope, the curvature going down is *convex*. At some point the curvature changes to *concave*. The point at which the curvature changes is called *the point of inflection*. Now draw a vertical line from the point of inflection down to the baseline. *That point on the baseline is exactly one standard deviation away from the mean*!

Because of the symmetry of the normal curve, the point of inflection on the other side of the curve is also exactly one standard deviation on the base scale away from the mean. If a normal curve is drawn carefully to scale, one could estimate the magnitude of the standard deviation by using the point of inflection, drawing a vertical line to the base, and measuring the distance from the mean on the base scale (see Figure 15.3).

---

[3] Deming was identified as a "quality expert" on a public television program, "American Interests," Program No. 1105, "Managing for the 21st Century," air date October 26, 1991. The moderator was Morton Kondracke. Quotation of Deming taken from page 3 of the program's official transcript provided by News Transcripts, Inc., 1333 H Street, NW, Suite 500, Washington, DC, 20005; (202) 682-9050.

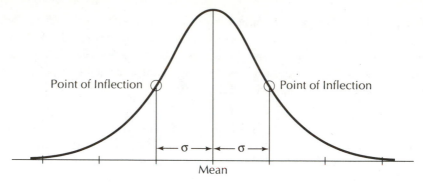

Figure 15.3. Normal curve showing points of inflection and their relation to the standard deviation.

15.5 Areas Under the Normal Curve

If the normal curve is to be used to represent a population or process, then the *proportionate area* under the curve in a given interval coincides with the percentage of individuals in the population or the process that falls within the interval.

Thus, the total area under the normal curve is considered to be 100%, accounting for all units in the population. Because of the symmetry of the curve, half of the total area is to the right of the mean and half of the total area is to the left of the mean. In practical terms we can say that half of the product in the process will have measurements greater than the mean, and half of the product in the process will have measurements smaller than the mean *if the normal curve is the correct model for that process.*

Consider screw-cap torques for plastic bottles introduced in Chapter 6, Table 6.1. Suppose that the total process (that is, population) from which the sample of 100 bottles came, had the following true mean and true standard deviation:

$\mu = 20.5$ in.-lbs.
$\sigma = 2.9$ in.-lbs.

The true process mean and standard deviation can be obtained, of course, by measuring every unit of product produced. If that is not practical, an examination of some past data may give us a good idea of what the true values are, provided that the process is considered stable. Under the latter condition, however, we still must treat the results as *estimates*, but very good ones.

If we can assume that a normal curve is a reasonable model that will represent the population of screw-cap torques, then we can draw a normal curve and identify the *one, two, and three standard deviation* points on the base as shown in

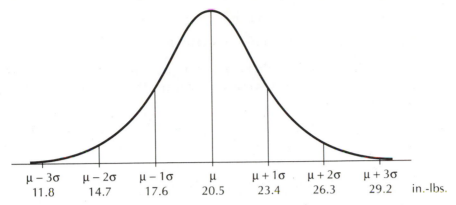

Figure 15.4. Normal curve representing population of screw-cap torques.

Figure 15.4. We now have a graphical representation of the population of screw-cap torques. The unit of measurement on the base is in inch-pounds. We are now in a position to make some predictions about the process.

15.6 Area Between Plus/Minus One Standard Deviation

Let us look at the area under the curve between the two points on the base scale that are one standard deviation away from the mean, 17.6 in.-lbs. and 23.4 in.-lbs.; that is, between $\mu - 1\sigma$ and $\mu + 1\sigma$. That area is a *fixed percentage of the total area under the normal curve: 68.26%*. That area, as a percentage of the total area under the curve, is true for *any* normal curve, regardless of what the mean and standard deviation are and regardless of what the unit of measure is. In short,

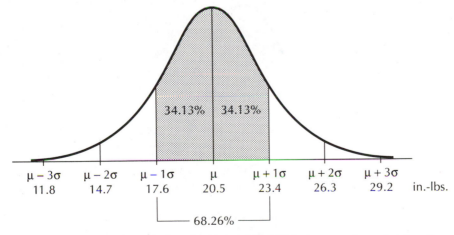

Figure 15.5. Normal curve showing area of 68.26% between −1σ and +1σ of the mean.

$$\mu \pm 1\sigma \text{ corresponds to an area that is 68.26\% of the total.} \qquad (15.1)$$

We can translate Statement 15.1 into a powerful predictive statement:

If the normal curve is the right model for this process, 68.26% of all the plastic bottles should have screw-cap torques that run between 17.6 in.-lbs. and 23.4 in.-lbs.

Because of symmetry, half of the percentage (34.13%) is below the mean, and half is above the mean (see Figure 15.5).

15.7 Area Between Plus/Minus Two Standard Deviations

Now let us move one more standard deviation to the left, bringing us to 14.7 in.-lbs., and one more standard deviation to the right, bringing us to 26.3 in.-lbs. We will look at the area under the curve between these two points; that is, between $\mu - 2\sigma$ and $\mu + 2\sigma$. That area is a *fixed percentage of the total area under the normal curve: 95.44%*. That area, as a percentage of the total area under the curve, is true for *any* normal curve, regardless of what the mean and standard deviation are and regardless of what the unit of measure is. In short,

$$\mu \pm 2\sigma \text{ corresponds to an area that is 95.44\% of the total.} \qquad (15.2)$$

We can translate Statement 15.2 into a powerful predictive statement:

If the normal curve is the right model for this process, 95.44% of all the plastic bottles should have screw-cap torques that run between 14.7 in.-lbs. and 26.3 in.-lbs.

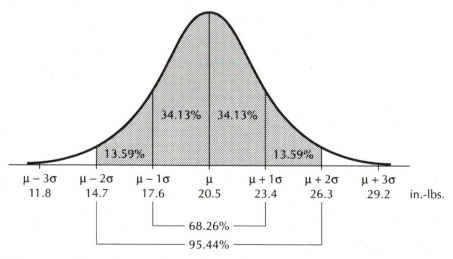

Figure 15.6. Normal curve showing area of 95.44% between -2σ and $+2\sigma$ of the mean.

The curve shows that 13.59% fall between one and two standard deviations on each side of the mean (see Figure 15.6).

15.8 Area Between Plus/Minus Three Standard Deviations

Next, let us move one more standard deviation to the left, bringing us to 11.8 in.-lbs., and one more standard deviation to the right, bringing us to 29.2 in.-lbs. We will look at the area under the curve between these two points; that is, between $\mu - 3\sigma$ and $\mu + 3\sigma$. That area is a *fixed percentage of the total area under the normal curve: 99.73%*. That area, as a percentage of the total area under the curve, is true for *any* normal curve, regardless of what the mean and standard deviation are and regardless of what the unit of measure is. In short,

$\mu \pm 3\sigma$ **corresponds to an area that is 99.73% of the total.**   (15.3)

We can translate Statement 15.3 into a powerful predictive statement:

If the normal curve is the right model for this process, 99.73% of all the plastic bottles should have screw-cap torques that run between 11.8 in.-lbs. and 29.2 in.-lbs.

See Figure 15.7, which also summarizes the results we have obtained so far for areas that are one, two, and three standard deviations away from the mean.

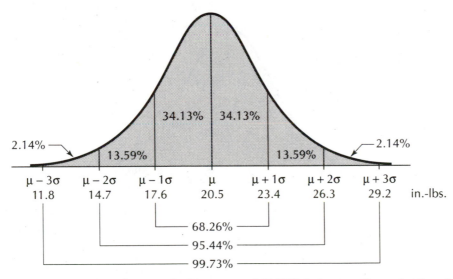

Figure 15.7. Normal curve showing area of 99.73% between -3σ and $+3\sigma$ of the mean.

15.9 Area Outside of Three Standard Deviations

If you were to add up the individual areas shown in Figure 15.7, you would find that they add up to 99.72%, not 99.73%. The reason for the apparent discrepancy is due to rounding of the individual areas. If the individual areas had been reported to one more decimal place, to 1/1000 of a percent, then they would have added up to 99.73% exactly.

It is obvious that the 99.73% area shown in Figure 15.7 is not 100%. There is a 0.27% area remaining beyond the three-standard-deviation points. That remaining area, as a percentage of the total area under the curve, is true for *any* normal curve, regardless of what the mean and standard deviation are and regardless of what the unit of measure is. In short,

Area outside of $\mu \pm 3\sigma$ is 0.27% of the total.   **(15.4)**

Because the normal curve is symmetrical, half of that remaining area is in the left tail and half is in the right tail. That would calculate to 0.135% in each remaining tail area (see Figure 15.8).

If we convert the remaining tail-area percentages to their decimal-fraction form, that would leave 0.00135 of the total area remaining in each of the two tails. We can translate Statement 15.4 into a powerful predictive statement:

If the normal curve is the right model for this process, about one out of a thousand plastic bottles should have screw-cap torques less than 11.8 in.-lbs., and about one out of a thousand plastic bottles should have screw-cap torques greater than 29.2 in.-lbs.

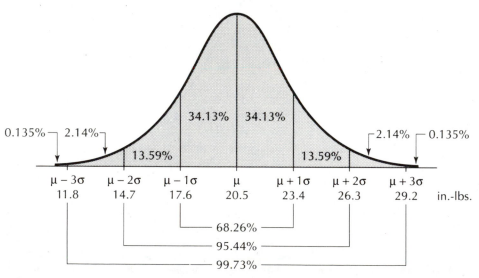

Figure 15.8. Normal curve accounting for 100% of the total area.

So we should not be surprised to find an occasional bottle—about two or three out of a thousand—whose screw-cap torque is outside the three-standard-deviation points. This prediction, like the previous three predictions made, assumes that the normal curve is the appropriate model for the population of screw-cap torques.

15.10 How to Test for Normality: The Eyeball Approach

All of the percentages described in the preceding sections are correct only if the population really does follow a normal distribution. Here we will consider a rather casual, but practical, test that helps to determine whether the normal distribution is appropriate to describe a population or process. More sophisticated tests of a strict statistical nature will be discussed later.

When you are studying a process (whether it is in manufacturing, development, service, or other area of activity), for the purpose of trying to determine its basic behavior characteristics so that you can improve it, you must collect some data in the form of (random) samples taken from the process. If the data are variable in nature—that is, measurable—the drawing of a frequency histogram would be the logical next step.

If the model that represents the process happens to be a normal distribution, the histogram should be reasonably symmetrical and reasonably bell-shaped in appearance. The histogram will form the basis for our *eyeball test for normality:*

> **If a histogram based on sample data is "reasonably symmetrical" and "reasonably bell-shaped," it is acceptable to use a normal curve as the model for the population or process. The normal curve is given the same mean and standard deviation as the histogram (see Problem 1 at end of this chapter).**

Admittedly, this quick and easy test does not constitute any *proof* that the normal curve is the true model for the process. In fact, other models may also work. It is not possible to prove that a particular model is the correct one without measuring every unit in the entire process; if you were to do that, you would not have to conjecture or guess as to what the true process model is.

The true model may be somewhat, or even considerably, different from a normal distribution, and still a random sample of 100 observations may form a histogram that is "reasonably symmetrical" and "reasonably bell-shaped." But if the sample size is "reasonably large," say, at least 50 observations, and if the observations have been obtained in a "reasonably random" manner, and if the frequency histogram formed from them is "reasonably symmetrical" and "reasonably bell-shaped," then a normal curve should provide "reasonably accurate" predictions about the process. The predictive accuracy achieved with the eyeball approach should be adequate for making most practical decisions about the process.

As an example, consider the histogram shown in Figure 6.4 (Chapter 6) for 100 screw-cap torques. Is this histogram "reasonably symmetrical"? The answer is yes. Is this histogram "reasonably bell-shaped"? The answer is yes. Therefore let us use the normal curve as a model for the population of screw-cap torques. The normal curve drawn for this process would have the same mean and standard deviation as those for the sample data, namely,

$$\overline{X} = 20.5 \text{ in.-lbs.} = \text{Est. of } \mu,$$
$$S = 3.0 \text{ in.-lbs.} = \text{Est. of } \sigma.$$

Under what circumstances would you *not* use the normal curve to represent a population or process? Answer: When the frequency histogram is "quite different" from a symmetrical and bell-shaped distribution. For example, look at a histogram that is *skewed* (not symmetrical) as shown in Figure 15.9. If we were

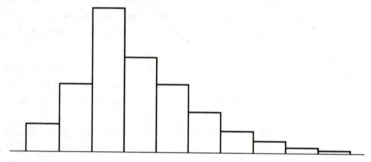

Figure 15.9 Frequency histogram that is skewed to the right.

to use a normal curve to represent the population from which this histogram came, our predictions about that population would likely be very inaccurate. In this situation we have some alternative choices to using the normal curve:

1. Use a probability model that is different from the normal model, such as a Poisson model or one of the family of Weibull curves or some other mathematical model generated by a computer. The advice here is to *see an experienced statistician* for help.

2. Transform the data mathematically in a way that will generate a normal curve. For example, one might take the logarithm of the data, or their reciprocal, or some trigonometric function. The advice here is to *see an experienced statistician* for help.

3. Use a cute trick of some sort. For example, break up the histogram into portions of two separate normal distribution models that have a mean that co-

incides with the mode of the histogram but with different standard deviations for both tails. (The author has used this device successfully.) The advice here is to *see an experienced statistician* for help.

4. Study the process to see if the histogram is skewed due to some quirk in the process that has distorted the sample data in some way. Perhaps the process is not in statistical control as a result of some "assignable" or "special" cause that should not be present. Perhaps the true model for the process, when it *is* in statistical control, is the normal curve (see Chapter 20). The advice here is to *see an experienced quality engineer or statistician* for help.

The eyeball approach suggested in this section will serve its practical purpose in most situations in the real world. It does encourage you to develop a frequency histogram from real data. *Using the normal curve blindly without first looking at a histogram drawn from actual data can result in costly and embarrassing predictions.*

15.11 How to Test for Normality: The Statistical Approach

Several methods are available to statisticians to test for normality that are much more exact than the eyeball approach introduced in the last section. As more process predictions are based on the assumption of a normal distribution, and the importance of testing for normality becomes more recognized, newer statistical methods will undoubtedly be developed for that purpose. Those most well known today include the following:

1. *Chi-square test of goodness of fit:* For each interval (or class) of data for which a frequency has been observed, a theoretical frequency can be calculated based on the population model that is assumed. In particular, if the normal curve is the assumed model, the theoretical frequencies can be calculated using the mean and standard deviation of the sample data. The differences between the observed and theoretical frequencies can be converted to a *chi-squared* statistic whose accumulated value is compared to a probability table. If the total chi-square exceeds a tabled value based on some selected probability of being exceeded, then we can conclude that the sample data could not have come from a normal distribution. Such a conclusion would have the selected probability of being wrong. However, if the total chi-square does not exceed the tabled value, then we have no evidence to discredit the assumption of a normal distribution and can behave, if we wish, as if the underlying distribution is normal. (A formal statistics textbook or a professional statistician should be consulted.)

2. *Normal probability paper (probability plotting):* Graph paper is available, with special scales, on which points derived from the sample data are plotted. If the plotted points "appear" to fall on a straight line, then a normal curve can be presumed for the population or process, in which case the paper provides a convenient way for estimating certain statistics, such as the mean, the standard deviation, and the percentage outside (or inside) of specs. Note that *this method is also an eyeball approach,* because you have to decide whether or not the points lie "reasonably" on a straight line. Since the decision of linearity is usually subjective, two people looking at the same plot might come to different conclusions. Normal probability paper is popular among quality practitioners who conduct process capability studies (discussed in Chapter 23). It must be remembered, however, that the fundamental purpose of normal probablility paper is to see if a normal distribution is a reasonable model for the process. To use normal probability paper primarily to estimate the mean, the standard deviation, and the percentage outside specs—without determining if the normal distribution is a reasonable model or if the process is in statistical control—is an inappropriate use of this graphic statistical tool.

3. *Independence of mean and variance:* If the underlying population distribution is normal, sample means and sample variances will be independent of each other. Various methods are available for testing the independence.

4. *Measures of non-normality—Skewness and Kurtosis:* The departure of a distribution from symmetry can be measured by the *coefficient* of skewness, γ_1. The flatness of the curve or heaviness in the tails of the distribution can be measured by the *coefficient of kurtosis,* γ_2. For a normal distribution, $\gamma_1 = 0$ and $\gamma_2 = 3$. (See a formal statistics textbook for an explanation of these concepts.)

5. *Other methods:* A comprehensive collection is contained in S. S. Shapiro, "How to Test Normality and Other Distributional Assumptions," Vol. 3, revised ed., *The ASQC Basic References in Quality Control: Statistical Techniques,* 1990. See also L. S. Nelson, "A Simple Test for Normality," *Journal of Quality Technology,* 1981, Vol. 13, No. 1, pp. 76–77. (Both publications are from the American Society for Quality Control, 611 E. Wisconsin Avenue, P.O. Box 3005, Milwaukee, WI 53201-3005.)

The assumption of normality must not be taken lightly or blindly. Collect data and, at the least, draw a frequency histogram from them. Only after you are reasonably convinced that the normal curve is a suitable model for the population or process, can you make predictions from the normal curve, which is what we will do in the next chapter.

15.12 Summary

The normal distribution or curve is a widely used mathematical model that describes random behavior of populations or processes in industry, science, and other fields. It has three main characteristics: symmetry, a bell shape, and smoothness (continuous). It is a theoretical model with two parameters, mean and standard deviation. The proportionate area under the normal curve in a given interval coincides with the proportion of units in the population falling within that interval. The mean and standard deviation from sample data are usually used to draw a normal curve to represent a population.

The area between ± one standard deviation from the mean is 68.26% of the total area; the area between ± two standard deviations from the mean is 95.44% of the total area; the area between ± three standard deviations of the mean is 99.73% of the total area. The area outside of three standard deviations on either side of the mean is 0.135%, or about one out of a thousand. These percentages are fixed for all normal curves, regardless of the unit of measure or magnitude of the parameters. The total area under the curve is 100%.

A useful test for normality involves determining from a histogram drawn from sample data if the histogram is "reasonably symmetrical" and "reasonably bell-shaped." More sophisticated statistical tests are available. One should not assume blindly that the normal curve represents a process; a histogram should be looked at first.

15.13 Putting It into Practice

1. Examine the following histograms prepared from sample data from different processes and decide if the normal curve is a suitable model for the process.

   (a) Moisture content of reams of paper:

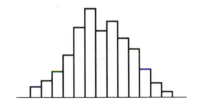

(b) Weights of one brand of candy bars from a day's production:

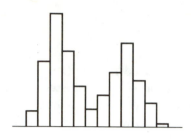

(c) Plating thickness of a finished metal part:

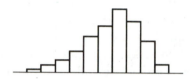

2. Collect a sample (as random as you can) of 50 to 100 measurable observations from your department, plant, line, shift, or service function. Draw a histogram from those data, and decide if a normal curve is a reasonable model for the process or population from which those data came.

Answers to Problem 1

(a) The histogram is reasonably symmetrical and reasonably bell-shaped. We can use a normal curve as a model for this process, and it will be given the same mean and standard deviation as the histogram.

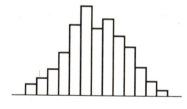

(b) A normal curve will not be a suitable model for this process. It does appear, however, that there are two distinct populations involved, each operating at a different mean or level. It also appears that each of the two separate populations could be represented by a normal curve. (Subsequent investigation revealed that the two populations were actually the two shifts in operation that day. When the data were collected, it was fortunate that the shift was identified. The very obvious difference between the two shifts was a valuable piece of information that, after further investigation, led to the reason for the difference between the two shifts: improper calibration of the cutting equipment.)

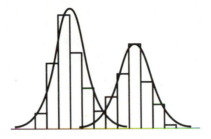

(c) A normal curve will not be a suitable model for this process. The histogram is skewed to the left. Skewed distributions are not uncommon in plating operations.

To prophesy is very difficult,
especially with regard to the future.

—Chinese proverb

CHAPTER 16

Predicting for Variables with the Normal Curve

The characteristics of the normal curve are so well known, and the use of the normal curve as a model for a population or process is so widespread, that we are encouraged to become familiar with it as a popular and reliable tool for making predictions. This chapter will confine itself to measurable characteristics that can be represented by a continuous scale, such as length, width, depth, height, weight, and chemical composition.

16.1 Kinds of Predictions

Several events about a population, process, or product can be predicted when the normal curve is used as a model. Among them are the following:

1. What percent is below the lower specification limit?

2. What percent is above the upper specification limit?

3. What total percent will meet the (two-sided) specification limits?

4. What total percent will not meet the (two-sided) specification limits?

5. What process average will result in, say, 2% of the product being underweight (that is, below the label weight)?

6. (Variations of 1 and 2) What percent of product will exceed the upper limit for moisture content? The lower limit for fat content? For protein content? For industrial grades of 90 and over?

16.2 Is the Normal Curve the Right Process Model?

Before using the normal curve in making predictions, one must be reasonably certain that the normal curve is appropriate as a model for the process. We saw in Chapter 15 that there are several ways to determine the appropriateness of the normal curve as a model.

One suggested method is to draw a histogram from random-sample data and subjectively judge if two criteria are met:

1. Is the histogram reasonably symmetrical?

2. Is the histogram reasonably bell-shaped?

If both criteria are satisfied, the recommendation was made to go ahead and use the normal curve as a model, using the same mean and standard deviation as provided by the sample data. This so-called "eyeball test" seems to serve adequately in the practical world. More sophisticated statistical methods were also mentioned in Chapter 15.

It is imperative that *some* test for normality be applied to the data. To use the normal curve blindly without any test for normality is statistically irresponsible and can be economically dangerous.

If a process characteristic actually follows a model far different from that of a normal curve, such as a severely skewed distribution, and the normal curve is used instead to represent the process behavior, any predictions that are made can be very much in error. The prediction result can be far off the mark, possibly resulting in the wrong business decisions being made with the attendant embarrassment and cost.

For example, suppose one predicts from a normal curve model, whose adequacy has *not* been tested, that fewer than 1% of the units of product will be outside specifications, and in reality it turns out that more than 10% are outside specifications because the normal curve is not the right model. Such a situation can prove to be not only embarrassing but financially costly. Product shipped under the false assumption of less than 1% outside specifications can seriously jeopardize a business relationship between supplier and customer. The underlying principle being described here bears emphasizing:

Do not use the normal curve as a process model without first looking at a histogram and applying a test for normality.

If the normal curve does not appear to be the right model, it may be necessary to consult a professional statistician for assistance in selecting another model, either visually or by computer, or in transforming the data mathematically.

16.3 Areas Under the Normal Curve

The ability to make reasonable predictions about processes that can be represented by a normal curve depends on *determining the area under portions of the curve*. For example, if the mean of a process is 12.5 mm, the standard deviation is 0.8 mm, and the lower specification limit (LSL) is 10.5 mm, that portion of the normal curve area that is less than (below) 10.5 mm is the proportion (or percentage) of the total area that is outside the lower specification limit. Recall that the total area under the curve is 100%, representing the entire process or population. The proportion outside the LSL can also be treated as a *probability* of product falling below the LSL. In Figure 16.1, the shaded area in question is in the left tail.

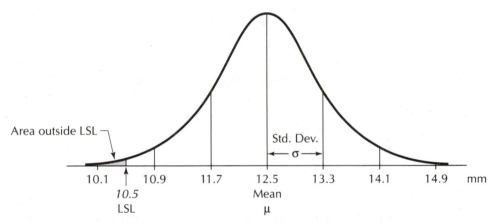

Figure 16.1. Area outside (below) lower specification limit.

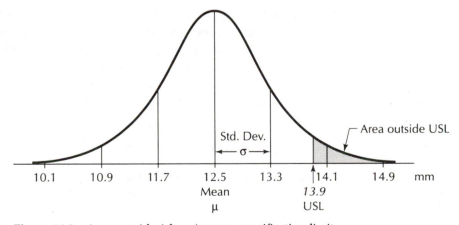

Figure 16.2. Area outside (above) upper specification limit.

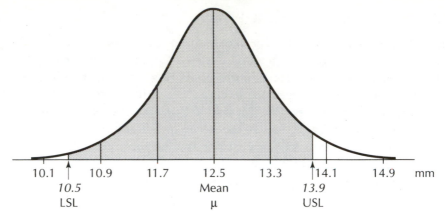

Figure 16.3. Area inside (within) specifications limit.

Without performing any calculations, we can see from Figure 16.1 that the proportion outside the LSL will be relatively small. This suggests, and rightly so, that drawing a picture (using graphics) is a very useful tool for conveying information quickly and effectively.

Similarly, the proportion that will exceed the upper specification limit (USL) of 13.9 mm is shown in Figure 16.2 as the shaded area in the right tail.

Finally, the proportion that will *meet* specifications is represented by the shaded area between the two specification limits as shown in Figure 16.3.

The calculation method usually used to determine the area under any curve, whether the area is beyond a specific base value (such as the upper specification limit) or between two specific base values (such as between the lower and upper specification limits), requires a functional or mathematical formula for the curve and the use of integral calculus. Furthermore, the calculation of areas under a normal curve representing a particular process involves the use of the mean, the standard deviation, and the unit of measure for the process. Each process would have its unique normal curve, and each calculation of area would be unique to that process, making such calculations tedious. Fortunately, we will not have to do it that way, because there is an easier way, as explained in the next section.

16.4 The Standard Normal Curve Using Z Values

The complicated method for determining areas under a normal curve, described in the previous section, seems prohibitive. There is an easier way to make these calculations.

In Figure 16.4, the original base scale of the normal curve, in millimeters (mm), can be replaced by so-called Z *values*, which do not represent any unit of

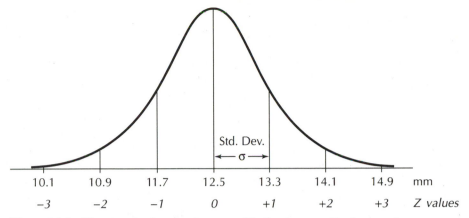

Figure 16.4. The standard normal curve with Z values on the base scale.

measure. Such a normal curve is called the *standard* (or *standardized*) *normal curve.* Then all that we would need is a one-time calculated table of areas under the standard normal curve using the Z values, and the table would be applicable to all situations where the normal curve is used as the appropriate model.

For every reading or measurement in millimeters, there is a corresponding Z value. For each of the millimeter readings shown in Figure 16.4, the corresponding Z value is the number of standard deviations that the original reading is away from the mean. Thus we can state a formal definition for Z:

The corresponding Z value for any point on the base scale is the number of standard deviations that the point is away from the mean.

The Z values can be positive or negative, depending on whether the point in question is greater than (above) the mean or less than (below) the mean, respectively. Some examples:

- The point 14.1 mm is two standard deviations to the right of the mean, and its corresponding Z value is +2.

- The point 10.1 mm is three standard deviations to the left of the mean, and its corresponding Z value is −3.

- The point 11.3 mm is halfway between 10.9 and 11.7 mm and therefore has a corresponding Z value of −1.5.

- The mean of 12.5 mm has a corresponding Z value of zero.

We can calculate the corresponding Z value for any point on the base scale by using the following formula, expressed in words:

$$Z \text{ value for any point} = \frac{\text{Point} - \text{Mean}}{\text{Standard Deviation}} \qquad (16.1)$$

Expressed algebraically, formula (16.1) for any point X can be written

$$Z_X = \frac{X - \mu}{\sigma}. \qquad (16.2)$$

The Z value is considered standardized because it has no units of measure, regardless of what unit of measure the original observations had. For example, if $(X - \mu)$ is in millimeters, then the denominator, σ, is also in millimeters, and their ratio in formula (16.2) is no longer in millimeters. You might recognize the fact that formula (16.2) is equivalent to *coding data* using two constants: The first constant, μ, is subtracted from the original data, X, and then the difference, $(X - \mu)$, is divided by a second constant, σ. See Chapter 14 to review coding procedures.

16.5 Table of Areas Under the Standard Normal Curve

Since the unit of measure has been standardized and, therefore, does not require separate area calculations involving integral calculus, areas under the normal curve can be determined for the standardized Z values resulting in only one table applicable to all normal curve models.

Please refer to Table 1 in the Appendix, "Areas Under the Standard Normal Curve." To use this table, first calculate the Z value that corresponds to any point under study, using formula (16.2), to *two decimal places* (hundredths). In Table 1 locate the first decimal figure (tenths) for the calculated Z in the first column, and the second decimal figure (hundredths) in one of the column headings. The intersection in the body of the table gives a specific area under the normal curve as a decimal proportion of the total area. According to the normal curve sketch shown at the top of the table, the area provided by the table is *in the right-tail portion if Z is positive, or in the left-tail portion if Z is negative.* This sketch is reproduced here as Figure 16.5(a).

Note that the Z values in the table appear to be all positive. We know, however, that Z can take on negative values when the point in question, such as a lower specification limit, is to the left of (below) the mean. Because the normal curve is *symmetrical* around the mean, the area provided by the table will be in the *left tail* when Z is negative.

To summarize these comments:

For positive values of Z, the table provides areas in the *right tail*.
For negative values of Z, the table provides areas in the *left tail*.

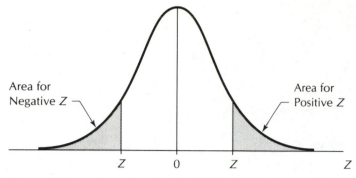

Figure 16.5(a). Areas described in Table 1 of the Appendix.

Keeping the preceding discussion in mind, Table 1 of the Appendix does not need to show negative values of Z, and the table can be printed compactly, making it a convenient reference tool.

At the bottom of Table 1 some values of Z are provided that correspond to commonly used areas in a tail portion of the normal curve:

For tail area $= 0.1000$, $Z = 1.282$

For tail area $= 0.0500$, $Z = 1.645$

For tail area $= 0.0250$, $Z = 1.960$

For tail area $= 0.0100$, $Z = 2.327$

For tail area $= 0.0050$, $Z = 2.576$

For tail area $= 0.0010$, $Z = 3.090$.

Remember that Z is positive if the area in question is in the right tail, negative if the area is in the left tail.

16.6 Use of Other Tables

Table 1 of the Appendix gives only a tail area under the normal curve. Tables have been published that give areas under other portions of the normal curve. We shall see that, regardless of which portion of the normal curve is provided by any table, other area portions of the curve can easily be determined by simple arithmetic.

Some tables may provide areas *from the point in question to minus infinity;* that is, the area to the left of any point in question, as shown in Figure 16.5(b). In this case the table usually consists of two pages, one for negative values of Z (when the point is below the mean) and one for positive values of Z (when the point is

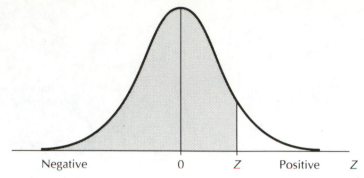

Figure 16.5(b). Area from Z to negative infinity.

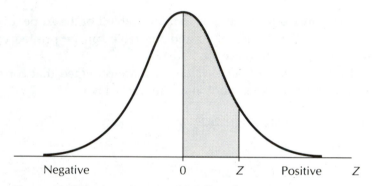

Figure 16.5(c). Area from positive Z to the mean.

above the mean). For example, see Grant and Leavenworth.[1] Other tables may provide the area *from the point in question to the mean for only positive values of Z*, as shown in Figure 16.5(c). For example, see Snedecor and Cochran.[2]

Regardless of which area portion under the normal curve any table provides, it is easy to determine the specific area that you are looking for *as long as you know which area portion is provided by the table*. For example, suppose that $Z = -1.96$, and you wish to determine the area to the left of this point (that is, in the left-tail area) using Table 1 in the Appendix. This table is represented by Figure 16.5(a). Because the normal curve is symmetrical around the mean where $Z = 0$, the area in the table giving the right-tail area (0.0250) is the same for the left-tail area.

[1] E. L. Grant and R. S. Leavenworth, *Statistical Quality Control*, 6th ed., McGraw-Hill, New York, 1988, Table A, pp. 666–667. Care must be taken in reading the column headings that correspond to the second decimal position for Z (that is, hundredths). The column headings for negative values of Z are in reverse order from the headings for positive values of Z. The order, however, is correct in terms of the area increasing from minus infinity to the particular Z value.

[2] G. W. Snedecor and W. G. Cochran, *Statistical Methods*, 7th ed., The Iowa State University Press, Ames, Iowa, 1982, Table 3, p. 468.

Suppose that you use a table represented by Figure 16.5(b). The area to the left of $Z = -1.96$ would be provided by the table directly (0.0250) because the table includes negative values of Z.

Suppose that you use a table represented by Figure 16.5(c). Again, because of the symmetry of the normal curve, the area to the right of the shaded area is the same as the area to the left of $Z = -1.96$. The table would show the shaded area to be 0.4750, and it would be necessary simply to subtract that area from 0.5000 to obtain the tail area of 0.0250.

A desirable feature of any published statistical table that provides areas under a curve is to include a graphic or drawing of the curve showing, by shading, the specific area provided by the table. If a table does not graphically identify the portion of the curve for which the area is provided, a good suggestion is to sketch it in at the top of the table.

16.7 Practice in Reading Table 1 of the Appendix

Confirm your ability to read this important table. Try the following exercises. The correct answers follow.

1. If $Z = -1.25$, area in the left tail is _____.

2. If $Z = +2.68$, area in the right tail is _____.

3. If $Z = -1.96$, area to the right is _____.

4. If $Z = +0.56$, area to the mean is _____.

5. If the right-tail area is 0.0392, the corresponding Z value is _____.

6. If the left-tail area is 0.2643, the corresponding Z value is _____.

Answers:

1. 0.1057

2. 0.0037

3. $1.0000 - 0.0250 = 0.9750$

4. $0.5000 - 0.2877 = 0.2123$

5. $Z = +1.76$

6. $Z = -0.63$

We now introduce the step-by-step procedures for determining the area under the normal curve and then go through an exercise.

16.8 Steps in Calculating Areas Under the Normal Curve

Being able to determine the area under the normal curve, and therefore make predictions about a process, can be one of the most useful skills that a quality practitioner can acquire. Table 16.1 shows 10 steps in calculating the area under the normal curve.

The first six of the steps concentrate on graphics before any calculations are actually performed. A major task in solving problems is to *communicate* effectively to others the definition of the problem, the methods used, and the results. In working on statistical problems, you should try to provide some graphic illustration of the problem and its data. Presenting arithmetic calculations alone, regard-

Table 16.1. Steps in Calculating Areas Under the Normal Curve

1. Verify from a histogram that the normal curve is an acceptable process model: reasonably symmetrical and reasonably bell-shaped.

2. Draw a normal curve (as best as you can). It need not be perfect.

3. Identify the base unit of measurement.

4. Identify the following seven points on the base (using the sample mean and sample standard deviation). The points should all be equally distant from each other.

   • The mean

   • Plus and minus (±) one-standard-deviation point

   • Plus and minus (±) two-standard-deviation points

   • Plus and minus (±) three-standard-deviation points

   (You now have a graphic model of the process in original units of measurement.)

5. Identify the point in question on the base.

6. Identify the area in question under the curve.

7. Calculate the corresponding Z value for the point in question.

8. Refer to a table of areas under the standard normal curve. Know which portion of the curve the area in the table designates.

9. Enter the table with the calculated value for Z, and read the given area in decimal proportion. If necessary, translate into the area in question.

10. Report the area in percent (rounded).

less of how simple you may think them to be, can be intimidating to some people and can reduce the impact of the presentation. *One picture is worth a thousand figures* (see Chapter 26).

16.9 Walk-Through Exercise

Let us work through a problem together following the steps in Table 16.1. Sample packages of a 15-ounce snack-food product were taken periodically throughout a day until 100 packages were obtained by the end of the day. The packages were all weighed to the nearest one-hundredth of an ounce by weighing the gross package and subtracting an average tare weight, thus resulting in a net-content weight. The sample average and standard deviation for the net contents were as follows:

$$\overline{X} = 15.12 \text{ oz.}$$
$$S = 0.07 \text{ oz.} \tag{16.3}$$

The problem: Estimate the percentage of packages that will be underweight in the process; that is, less than the label weight of 15 ounces.

Step 1: A frequency histogram formed from the sample data was reasonably symmetrical and reasonably bell-shaped, allowing the use of a normal curve as a process model.

Steps 2 through 6: Identify the unit of measurement, the seven points on the base, and the point and area in question (see Figure 16.6).

Step 7: Calculate Z that corresponds to 15.00 oz. We can see from Figure 16.6 that it will be negative and somewhere between −1 and −2.

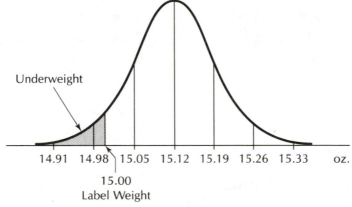

Figure 16.6. Model of the process showing point and area in question.

$$Z_{15.00} = \frac{15.00 - 15.12}{0.07} = \frac{-0.12}{0.07} = -1.71 \qquad (16.4)$$

Steps 8 and 9: Tabular entry in Table 1 of the Appendix gives area as 0.0436.

Step 10: Percentage of packages underweight is 4.36%.

Wait! This problem is not yet completed. Read the following section.

16.10 Introducing a Key Statistical Word: "About"

Step 10, the concluding statement in the previous exercise, is not properly worded. It implies that the percentage of underweight packages can be predicted *to the nearest one-hundredth of one percent.* This is a very unlikely level of accuracy of prediction when one considers that there were many uncertainties in this exercise: Two process characteristics were *estimated* and one giant *assumption* was made.

The process mean μ and the process standard deviation σ were *estimated* by the results in Eqs. (16.3), using $\overline{X}$ and S respectively. In addition, because the parameters of the process, μ and σ, are estimated, even the value of Z in Eq. (16.4) is an *estimate* of the number of standard deviations that the point in question, 15.00 ounces, is away from the true and unknown process mean, μ. Finally, it was *assumed* that a normal curve is the correct process model.

These expressions of uncertainty should alert us to the need to use great care in reporting the results. Any tabular entry, such as those in Table 1, are not the absolute truth that permits one to report the result to the nearest one-hundredth of one percent with stubborn conviction. It is strongly recommended, therefore, that the conclusion in Step 10 be stated as follows:

The percentage of underweight packages is *about* 4%.

There should be no hesitancy in using the word "about" (or, if you prefer, "approximately") or in reporting the percentage underweight to the nearest whole percent. It shows that we are dealing with, and respect, the uncertainty inherent in sample data. Furthermore, expressing the result in this conservative manner will have no effect on how we will behave toward the process or on whatever action is taken. In fact, the result can even be expressed as "about 5%" without changing the action taken.

16.11 Use of Hand Calculators for the Normal Curve Area

Currently, several brands and models of scientific (statistical) calculators provide areas under selected portions of the standard normal curve.

Usually dual-function keys give areas in three different portions of the normal curve, corresponding to those shown in Figures 16.5(a), (b), and (c). Once the specific portion is selected, the area appears in the display in decimal form, sometimes to as many as six decimal places.

Calculators that contain this information are easy to use, very convenient, and relatively inexpensive. They replace published tables, such as Table 1 in the Appendix.

Many computer software programs also provide normal curve areas. Always check the operator's manual for either computer or calculator instructions (see Chapter 25).

16.12 Shortcut Methods for Approximating Areas Under the Normal Curve

Over the years several methods have been proposed that preclude the use of either tables or calculators by using simple shortcut methods, some of which can be memorized. These methods enable one to make quick approximations of areas under the normal curve without the use of notes.

For example, one approximation method proposed by Arvind K. Shah[3] exhibits the desirable features of being easy to remember, has "computational simplicity," and shows "relatively small error." The approximate area under the standard normal curve *from zero to a point Z* in absolute positive value is given by the following formulas:

If Z is between 0 and 2.2, inclusive, use area formula $Z(4.4 - Z)/10$.

If Z is between 2.2 and 2.6, use area 0.49.

If Z is greater than or equal to 2.6, use area 0.50.

The maximum absolute error using these approximations was found to be 0.0052, or about 1/2%. Shah's description of the need for a simple approximation method is of interest:

> Over the past few years, I have been called to serve as an expert witness in several court cases involving statistical application. In some of these court cases, as an expert witness I was not permitted to carry anything on the witness stand and was asked some statistical questions and given very little time to respond. In such situations, I needed areas under the standard normal curve several times and was forced to "estimate" these rather quickly. None of the approximation formulas

[3] A. K. Shah, "A Simpler Approximation for Areas Under the Standard Normal Curve," *The American Statistician*, American Statistical Association, Alexandria, Virginia, February 1985, Vol. 39, No. 1, p. 80.

presented in the literature is suitable under such circumstances. This motivated me to work on developing a simple approximation formula suitable for instances in which tables and/or calculators are not available or not permitted.

16.13 Summary

This chapter confines the use of a normal distribution to representing measurements that vary on a continuous scale. Before the techniques in this chapter are applied to normal curves, one should confirm first that the normal curve is a reasonably appropriate model for a population or process. A test for normality, either casual or based on statistical procedures, should be applied to sets of data, particularly a histogram, before assuming that the normal curve model is correct.

Predictions about processes that can be represented by a normal curve include determining the percentage that do or do not meet specifications. Making predictions involves determining areas under portions of the normal curve, the total area corresponding to 100%, the entire process. Although integral calculus is the mathematical tool used for calculating areas under a curve, standardizing the normal curve enables us to use one table of areas for all normally distributed processes, regardless of the unit of measurement or magnitude of the observations. The actual measurement scale is replaced by Z values, the number of standard deviations away from the mean. The formula for converting any observation X to its correponding Z value is given by

$$Z_X = \frac{X - \mu}{\sigma}.$$

The Z values have no unit of measurement; hence, the term *standardized*. The corresponding Z value for any point may be positive or negative (or zero), depending on which side of the mean the point in question lies. Table 1 in the Appendix gives the tail area for a given Z value. The table is entered with the Z value calculated to two decimal places (hundredths); tabular entries give areas in decimal proportion to four decimal places. A 10-step procedure for calculating the area under the normal curve was provided.

Areas are usually reported in percent. Any area taken from a table should not be reported to hundredths or even tenths of a percent but can be rounded to the nearest whole percent and preceded by the word *about*. A conservative approach to reporting simply recognizes the uncertainty in estimating the mean and standard deviation and in assuming the characteristic of normality.

Other tables are available that provide areas under different portions of the normal curve; it's a simple matter to determine the area for a specific portion of the curve using any table. Hand calculators are available that give areas under different portions of the standard normal curve. One shortcut was introduced for approximating areas under the standard normal curve.

16.14 Putting It into Practice

1. Before working on the problems, be sure that you know how to read a table of areas under the normal curve. Answer the following questions first:

   (a) What left-tail area corresponds to a Z value of -0.75?

   (b) What is the area to the left of the Z value of $+1.25$?

   (c) What value of Z corresponds to a right-tail area of 5.0%?

   (d) What value of Z corresponds to a left-tail area of 2.5%?

   Draw normal curves for Problems 2 through 6.

2. Tread lengths of tires of a particular tire size, based on measuring hundreds of tires, can be assumed to be normally distributed. Recently a random sample of 60 tire tread lengths from a production run yielded a mean of 80.00 inches per tire with a standard deviation of 0.12 inches. (Draw the normal curve.)

   (a) What percentage of the total production run can be expected to be less than 79.75 inches, the lower specification limit?

   (b) Is the process acceptable?

3. Certain metal cans have a compound deposited on the inside to protect the contents, and the compound weight is critical. It was decided, based on a histogram, that the weights are normally distributed. Use a sample mean of 75.5 milligrams (mg) and a sample standard deviation of 15.0 mg. (Draw the normal curve.)

   (a) Estimate the percentage of cans whose compound weights will fall between spec limits 46.0 mg and 96.0 mg. (*Hint:* Determine areas separately in right and left tails.)

   (b) Is the process acceptable?

4. Sample weights of a certain popular candy bar resulted in a mean of 54.97 grams, a standard deviation of 1.60 grams, and a histogram that was reasonably symmetrical and reasonably bell-shaped. (Draw normal curves.) If the label weight is 51.0 grams,

   (a) Estimate the percentage of bars that will be underweight.

(b) What target (average) should be established so that about 2.5% of all the bars will be below the label weight (that is, underweight)?

5. At a local bank the length of time for transactions at tellers' windows was monitored over a two-week period for the purpose of improving service to customers who had complained of long waiting times. A histogram indicated that a normal distribution was a reasonable model, with a mean of 4.87 minutes and a standard deviation of 1.33 minutes. (Draw the normal curve.)

(a) What is the probability that a teller will be occupied with a customer for more than 7 minutes?

(b) What can be done to speed up the transaction time?

6. Some high-voltage readings were obtained on a newly designed television chassis. In a random sample of 95 chassis, beam current was measured at maximum brightness/maximum current in milliamps (ma). The histogram suggested that a normal curve is an acceptable model. (Draw the normal curve.) The sample results:
Mean = 1.730 ma;   Standard deviation = 0.183 ma.

(a) Estimate the percent of chassis that will be within specifications of 1.6 to 2.0 ma.

(b) Is the product acceptable?

Answers to Problems 1 through 6

1. (a) Area = 0.2266

   (b) Area = $1.0000 - 0.1057 = 0.8943$

   (c) $Z = +1.645$

   (d) $Z = -1.960$

2. (a) $Z_{79.75} = (79.75 - 80.00)/0.12 = -2.08$
      Area = 0.0188 = about 2%

   (b) The process is not acceptable since everything does not meet specs.[4]

3. (a) $Z_{46.0} = (46.0 - 75.5)/15.0 = -1.97$
      Left-tail area = 0.0244

---

[4] For a discussion of attitudes toward specifications, see H. Pitt, "Specifications: Laws or Guidelines?" *Quality Progress*, American Society for Quality Control, Milwaukee, July, 1981, Vol. 14, No. 7, pp. 14–18.

$Z_{96.0} = (96.0 - 75.5)/15.0 = +1.37$
Right-tail area $= 0.0853$
Area between 46.0 and 96.0 mg $= 1 - (0.0244 + 0.0853)$
$$= 1 - 0.1097 = 0.8903$$
$$= \text{about } 90\%.$$

(b) The process is not acceptable since everything does not meet specs.

4. (a) $Z_{51.0} = (51.0 - 54.97)/1.60 = -2.48$
Area $= 0.0066 =$ about 1%

(b) Target $=$ Label Wt. $+ Z_{51.0}(S) = 51.0 + 1.960 (1.60)$
$$= 54.14 \text{ grams}$$
(Alternative solution: $Z_{51.0} = (51.00 - \text{Target})/1.6 = -1.960$.
Solve equation for Target; same result.)

5. (a) $Z_7 = (7 - 4.87)/1.33 = +1.60$
Area $= 0.0548$; probability is about 5%.

(b) To start, analyze data by type of teller transaction. Elicit suggestions from tellers themselves on ways to improve service.

6. (a) $Z_{1.6} = (1.6 - 1.730)/0.183 = -0.71$
Left-tail area $= 0.2389$
$Z_{2.0} = (2.0 - 1.730)/0.183 = +1.48$
Right-tail area $= 0.0694$
Area between 1.6 and 2.0 $= 1 - (0.2389 + 0.0694)$
$$= 1 - 0.3083 = 0.6917$$
$$= \text{about } 70\%.$$

(b) Not acceptable since everything does not meet specs.

CHAPTER 17

Predicting for Attributes
with Confidence Belts

AT TRIB UTE

A common problem of prediction involves the estimation of the extent to which a particular attribute is present in a population or process. *An attribute* is a characteristic that is either present or not present. Examples of attributes include package tears or leaks, metal fatigue, discoloration, cancer, an electrical short, a poisonous substance, a level of vacuum, emission of a particular gas, a clerical error, a missing component, spoilage, contamination, a nonconformity, not meeting specifications, meeting specifications, and so on. Attributes may be desirable or undesirable. The incidence of undesirable attributes may be reported, for example, as number per area or number per length or number of service calls per region, and in manufacturing it is usually reported as fraction or proportion defective (p), percentage of product units (%), or parts per million (ppm).

A *variable* characteristic, on the other hand, is measurable on some continuous scale, such as inches of length, centimeters of depth, chemical pH, or electrical voltage. A variable characteristic can be expressed as an attribute, such as percentage of units that exceed a certain measurement.

17.1 An Example of an Undesirable Attribute

Suppose that a random sample of 100 new gasoline-powered push-type lawn mowers of the same brand, style, and model from a large production lot is tested to determine the incidence of those that will not start within two attempts. It is found that 15 mowers, or 15% of the sample, exhibit this undesirable attribute. If such mowers are called *defective*, the results can be succinctly expressed as follows:

$$n = 100$$
$$p = 0.15 \text{ proportion defective,}$$

$$(17.1)$$

where n is the sample size and p is the proportion of lawn mowers in the sample that will not start after two tries.

What can we say about the presence of this attribute in the entire lot (or population) from which the random sample of 100 mowers came? Would one dare to predict that the true proportion of nonstarting mowers in the entire lot, designated p', is also *exactly 0.15,* or 15%? No, it would be considered risky to do so.

The sample result, 15%, is only an estimate of the unknown presence of the attribute in the lot. Had we taken another random sample of 100 mowers from the same lot, the percentage not starting could very well be quite different from 15%. It is important, again, to emphasize the relationship between the sample *statistic p* and the unknown population *parameter p'*:

$$p = \text{Est. of } p'.$$

$$(17.2)$$

The sample result p is called a *point estimate* because it provides only one figure (like a point on a graph) for the estimate of p'. Although the sample proportion p is the best single estimate of p', we don't really know how close it comes to the truth. Can we make other predictive statements about p', the true proportion (or percentage) of nonstarting mowers in the lot, that take into account the sample size and the expected variability in samples?

17.2 Concept of Confidence Intervals

A very practical prediction tool is the family of confidence intervals that provide an *interval within which the true value of the parameter lies with a specified level of confidence.* The beginning and end points of the interval are called *confidence limits.*

For example, a typical confidence interval might read as follows: "We are 95 percent confident that the true percentage of defective lawn mowers in the lot is somewhere between 8 percent and 24 percent." The calculation of the confidence limits that define the confidence interval depends on four elements: the sample result, the sample size, the statistical model for the behavior of the sample statistic involved, and a probability or confidence level. Although the sample statistic is used to calculate the confidence limits that determine the interval, it should be emphasized that a confidence interval is a probability statement about a *population parameter*, not about a sample statistic.

Strictly speaking, the concept of, say, a 95% confidence interval is that, if such intervals were calculated many, many times in the same way with different samples, 95% of those intervals would contain the true value of the population parameter. In a specific study or experiment, the one confidence interval calculated from a sample result is treated as a random sample from all the possible confidence intervals.

We can determine confidence intervals for important population parameters other than the proportion p', such as the mean μ and standard deviation σ.[1] We will confine our discussion in this chapter, however, to confidence intervals for population proportion, such as percent defective.

Confidence limits for population proportion can be conveniently obtained graphically, without calculation, by the use of *confidence belts*. Graph 1 in the Appendix contains a series of confidence belts, or curves, for three levels of confidence: 90% (Graph 1A), 95% (Graph 1B), and 99% (Graph 1C).

Refer, for example, to Graph 1A, a graph with 90% confidence belts. These belts, or curves, provide confidence limits for four different sample sizes shown in the center of the graph: 50, 100, 250, and 1000 . There are two curves (belts) for each sample size. *Interpolation*, selecting other sample sizes between curves, is permitted, but it becomes more difficult to read the vertical scale accurately.

Although the determination of these belts is made from exact calculations using the appropriate statistical model, the visual accuracy in reading the curves and scales is necessarily limited. Thus the results obtained for the confidence limits, using these curves, is best described as approximate but quite adequate.

The bottom horizontal scale (the *abscissa*) is for the observed proportion of the attribute in the sample. The vertical scale on the left (the *ordinate*) is for the estimated proportion in the population or lot. Sometimes one or both of these scales in other published confidence belts are in percent rather than in decimal proportion. The steps in using the confidence belts for proportion are given in the next section.

17.3 Steps in Using Confidence Belts for Proportion in Graph 1

1. Select the graph of belts for the confidence level chosen.

2. Enter the graph on the base scale (horizontal scale at the bottom) at the observed proportion in the sample p for the attribute under study.

3. Go vertically from the sample proportion to the intersection of the *first* belt corresponding to the sample size.

---

[1] Confidence intervals for the population mean involve the t distribution, confidence intervals for the standard deviation involve the chi-squared distribution, and confidence intervals for the proportion involve the binomial distribution.

4. Read the vertical scale on the left for the *lower* confidence limit of the interval, the lower estimate of p'.

5. Continue vertically from the sample proportion to the intersection of the *second* belt corresponding to the same sample size.

6. Read the vertical scale on the left for the *upper* confidence limit of the interval, the upper estimate of p'.

7. Express the confidence interval statement as follows: *We are _____ percent confident that the true proportion (or percentage) in the lot exhibiting the attribute is somewhere between _____ and _____ .*

You must state the confidence interval completely and clearly. If you wish, the limits of the confidence interval can also be stated in percent instead of in decimal proportion. Be careful, however, in distinguishing between percent for the confidence level (a probability) and percentage for the attribute (an occurrence).

17.4 Use of the Confidence Belts in the Lawn Mower Example

Let us determine the *90% confidence interval* for the percentage of mowers in the production lot that will not start after two attempts. Refer to Graph 1A in the Appendix for the 90% confidence level. The confidence belts for a sample size of 100 are partially reproduced in Figure 17.1. The vertical scale has been changed from proportion to percent.

Following the step-by-step procedure outlined in Section 17.3 and referring to Figure 17.1, enter the base at $p = 0.15$, and go vertically to the intersection of the first curve for sample size 100. Reading the vertical scale gives us about 10%, the lower limit of the 90% confidence interval. Continue vertically at $p = 0.15$ to the intersection of the second curve for sample size 100. Reading the vertical scale gives us about 22%, the upper limit of the 90% confidence interval.

We now make a concluding statement with these results:

We are 90% confident that the true percentage of lawn mowers in the lot that will not start after two tries is somewhere between 10% and 22%.

We do not know where in the confidence interval, 10% to 22% defective, the truth lies, but we are 90% sure that it is in there somewhere. The probability that the statement is wrong is $1.00 - 0.90 = 0.10$, often designated by the Greek letter α (*alpha*). Note that the interval statement pertains to the entire lot and not to the sample.

These confidence belts are developed from the *binomial distribution*, whose full description is not attempted here. The binomial distribution applies to phenomena where only two states can exist, such as OK/not OK, yes/no, go/no go,

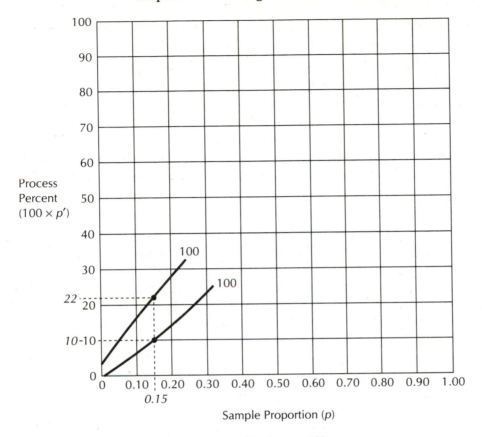

Figure 17.1. Portion of 90% confidence belts for $n = 100$.

and so on. It is particularly applicable to units of product that can be declared defective or not defective. The word *binomial* has the prefix *bi* signifying two (OK, not OK).

The confidence belts or curves are unbroken—that is, they are smooth and continuous. But sample proportions are *discrete*, meaning that they can be calculated only in separate and distinct increments. For example, for samples of 100 the increment is 0.01: 1/100 = 0.01, 2/100 = 0.02, 3/100 = 0.03, and so on. Larger sample sizes would result in smaller increments, but still separate and distinct. Thus the belts are first determined by plotting separate and distinct points on the graph, and then the points are joined with a smooth curve.

17.5 Increasing the Level of Confidence

A little scenario, not entirely far fetched, will now be presented to see where increasing the level of confidence leads. Suppose that your immediate supervisor, to whom you just reported the 90% confidence interval, asserts that he or she would like to make a predictive statement with a little bit more confidence, say, 95%, and with a smaller chance of being wrong.

Refer to Graph 1B for the 95% confidence belts. Enter the sample result, 0.15, until the two belts for sample size 100 are intersected, and read the vertical scale on the left. You should obtain about 0.08 for the lower confidence limit and about 0.24 for the upper confidence limit of the interval. Now for the concluding statement with these results:

We are 95% confident that the true percentage of lawn mowers in the lot that will not start after two tries is somewhere between 8% and 24%.

The 95% confidence interval is a little wider than the 90% confidence interval. Once again we do not know where in the confidence interval, 8% to 24%, the true value lies. The probability that the statement is wrong is $1.00 - 0.95 = 0.05$. Note again that the statement is one about the process parameter, not about the sample.

Now suppose that your immediate supervisor reports the latter result to his or her superior, perhaps a vice president, who asks, "Does this mean that there is a five percent chance that the statement is not true?" to which the supervisor replies, "Yes." The vice president, in turn, would like to make a predictive statement with even more confidence, say, 99%, and with a smaller chance of being wrong.

Refer to Graph 1C for the 99% confidence belts. Verify, with a sample proportion of 0.15 and a sample size of 100, that the 99% confidence limits are now about 0.07 and about 0.26. The concluding statement is:

We are 99% confident that the true percentage of lawn mowers in the lot that will not start after two tries is somewhere between 7% and 26%.

To continue the scenario, the vice president forwards these results to the president who asks, "Does this mean that there is a one percent chance that the statement is not true?" to which the vice president says, "Yes." Uncomfortable even with this apparent small chance of being wrong, the president wishes to make a predictive statement with 100% confidence, the ultimate level that would appear to satisfy a person of that stature.

17.6 The Ultimate Confidence Level

The task is to construct a 100% confidence interval with no chance of the accompanying statement being wrong. If you have not already searched for it, there is no Graph 1D for 100% confidence belts in the Appendix. Is a 100% confidence interval possible to construct, and can one write a 100% confidence interval statement? The answer is yes:

We are 100% confident that the true percentage of lawn mowers in the lot that will not start after two tries is somewhere between 0% and 100%.

Obviously such a statement, although true, is useless.[2]

It may seem desirable, from the examples just discussed, to make a statement with as high a level of confidence as possible. But that leads to wider and wider intervals and the confidence interval ultimately becomes useless.

What level of confidence should one choose? This is not necessarily a statistical decision. The answer lies in the risk of being wrong and in the business or economic consequences if the stated confidence interval happens to be wrong. The relationship between confidence level and risk of being wrong is clear:

$$100\% - \text{Confidence level} = \text{Risk of being wrong} = \alpha.$$

If the consequences of being wrong in the confidence interval stated are going to be very costly, such as having to purchase expensive new equipment or completely redesigning a process, then a small risk will be needed and the confidence level chosen will be relatively high.

17.7 Reducing the Width of the Confidence Interval

Another desirable objective to consider is reduction of the width of the interval so that the confidence statement apparently converges to (that is, approaches) the true value of the parameter. How can the width of the interval be made narrower? There are two ways:

1. Increase the sample size.

A close examination of the confidence belts of Graph 1, Appendix, shows that, as the sample size is increased from 50 to 100 to 250 to 1000, the corresponding pair of curves gets closer together, indicating that the width of the interval read off the vertical scale gets narrower and narrower. Thus, there is a cost to pay for a narrower confidence interval obtained by increasing the sample size: namely, increased cost of sampling.

2. Decrease the level of confidence.

If the results of the lawn mower example are summarized, we can see that, indeed, as the confidence level is reduced, the width of the interval gets nar-

---

[2] The author does not recommend reporting this result to the president or to any officer of the organization.

rower and narrower, seemingly converging to the true value of the parameter as shown in the following:

Confidence Level (Probability)	Confidence Interval for p' (Percent of defective mowers)	Risk of Being Wrong (Alpha)
100%	0% to 100%	0
99%	7% to 26%	0.01
95%	8% to 24%	0.05
90%	10% to 22%	0.10
—	—	—
—	—	—
—	—	—
0%	Zero width	1.00

Should we stop at the 90% confidence level? Not necessarily. There is nothing magical or sacrosanct about the 90% level of confidence or even the 95% or 99% levels. An interesting exercise is to reduce the confidence level even further and observe the corresponding decrease in the width of the confidence interval.

As the confidence level is reduced, the interval gets narrower and narrower, and the risk of being wrong increases. When the confidence level reaches 0%, the two confidence limits merge into a *single figure* for the population parameter, and the risk of being wrong reaches 100%.

What is the single figure for the population parameter when the confidence interval is zero width? It is the *sample proportion, p = 0.15,* suggesting that we have no confidence whatsoever that the true percent of nonstarter lawn mowers in the production lot is exactly the same as that in the sample! Thus, there is a cost to pay for a narrower confidence interval by reducing the level of confidence: namely, less confidence in the interval result and increased risk of being wrong.

The discussion in this section again supports the observation that, in statistics as well as in life's experiences, there is no Santa Claus. If better statistical results are desired, it has to be paid for in some way, either by increasing the sample size and therefore the cost, or by reducing the confidence level and increasing the risk of being wrong.

17.8 Normal Approximation to the Binomial

Under certain conditions we can calculate approximately the confidence limits easily using a relatively simple formula called the *normal approximation to the binomial*. When the sample size is large and the sample proportion is between 0.10 and 0.90, formula (17.3) can be used as a reasonably good approximation for determining the confidence interval for proportion:

Confidence limits for process proportion $= p \pm Z_{\alpha/2} \sqrt{\dfrac{p(1-p)}{n}}$ (17.3)

where

n = sample size

p = attribute proportion in the sample

Z = standardized normal variable

α = alpha = the risk of being wrong

$\alpha/2$ = area in one tail under the normal curve beyond Z.

Since the term to the right of the $\pm$ sign is to be added to and subtracted from p, formula (17.3) gives confidence limits that are *equally distant* from a 45-degree line drawn on a graph of confidence belts from the lower left corner to the upper right corner.

Examine the 99% confidence belts in Graph 1C of the Appendix to see more clearly why the restrictions in the first paragraph make sense. To help visualize the relationships, imagine a 45-degree line drawn on the graph from the lower left corner to the upper right corner.

When n is 100 or greater, the two curves for any sample size are approximately equally distant from the 45-degree line. When p is greater than 0.10 or less than 0.90, the two curves for any sample size are also approximately equally distant from the 45-degree line. When $p = 0.50$, the two curves are precisely equally distant from the 45-degree line.

Let us see how closely formula (17.3) comes to the 90% confidence limits determined from the confidence belts for the lawn mower example.

$n = 100$

$p = 0.15$

$\alpha = 0.10$ (for 90% confidence interval)

$\alpha/2 = 0.05$

$Z_{0.05} = 1.645$ (from Table 1, Appendix).

Substituting in formula (17.3), the 90% confidence interval is

$$0.15 \pm 1.645 \sqrt{\frac{0.15(1-0.15)}{100}} = 0.15 \pm 0.06 = 0.09 \text{ to } 0.21.$$

We saw in Section 17.4, using the confidence belts, that the 90% confidence interval was 0.10 to 0.22. So the normal approximation formula, Eq. (17.3), provides a reasonably comparable confidence interval, even though the sample size was not huge and the sample proportion was not close to 0.50. If the sample proportion had been considerably closer to 0.50, the match would have been much greater.

17.9 One-Sided Confidence Intervals

All of the discussion so far concerns itself with *two-sided confidence intervals*, where two confidence limits define the interval. Sometimes one-sided intervals are of interest, where only one confidence limit is needed, either an upper confidence limit for the population proportion or a lower confidence limit for the population proportion.

To find one-sided confidence limits, we can use the same confidence belts as for two-sided limits; however, the confidence *level* has to be changed. For example, if we wish to find the 95% upper confidence limit (or the 95% lower confidence limit), we use the 90% confidence belts and refer to only one of the two curves for a sample size. For the lawn mower problem, with $n = 100$ and $p = 0.15$, refer again to Graph 1A in the Appendix. The 95% *upper* confidence limit is about 0.22, and the concluding statement is as follows:

We are 95% confident that the true percentage of lawn mowers in the lot that will not start after two tries is no more than about 22%.

Similarly, if we are interested in a lower confidence limit, using the same confidence belts, the 95% *lower* confidence limit is about 0.10, and the concluding statement is as follows:

We are 95% confident that the true percentage of lawn mowers in the lot that will not start after two tries is no less than about 10%.

17.10 Confidence Belts for Small Percentages

If the sample proportion p is quite small, say, 0.05 or less, or quite large, say, 0.95 or more, the confidence belts in Graph 1 are almost unreadable at these extreme ends of the confidence belts (lower left corner and upper right corner). An excellent and very useful set of confidence belts which effectively magnify the extreme ends is contained in an article by Lloyd S. Nelson.[3]

---

[3] L. S. Nelson, "Confidence Belts for Small Percentages," *Journal of Quality Technology*, American Society for Quality Control, Milwaukee, July 1981, Vol. 13, No. 3, pp. 215-217.

These belts are reproduced as Graph 2 in the Appendix. Belts are provided for two-sided 95% and 99% confidence intervals and for sample sizes 70, 100, 200, 400, 1,000, and 5,000.

17.11 Confidence Belts for More Sample Sizes

Several publications are available that contain confidence belts for proportion for a wider array of sample sizes. Two of the best are:

1. W. J. Dixon and F. J. Massey, *Introduction to Statistical Analysis*, 3rd ed., Tables A–9a, b, c, McGraw-Hill Book Company, New York, 1969.
   Excellent set of four graphs that include 80%, 90%, 95%, and 99% confidence belts.
   Sample sizes included are 5, 10, 15, 20, 30, 50, 100, 250, and 1,000 ($n = 5$ is omitted from the 95% and 99% belts).

2. *Biometrika Tables for Statisticians*, Table 41, Vol. 1, Cambridge University Press, New York, 1954.
   Two graphs for 95% and 99% confidence belts.
   Sample sizes included are 8, 10, 12, 16, 20, 24, 30, 40, 60, 100, 200, 400, and 1,000.

17.12 Summary

This chapter deals with confidence intervals for attributes, which are characteristics that are either present or not present. The proportion of units in a sample that have the attribute (such as being defective) is designated p, while the proportion in the population, process, or lot from which the sample came is designated p'.

With p as a point estimate of p', the task at hand is to estimate (predict) p' using confidence intervals or belts within which p' lies with a certain confidence or probability. Easy-to-use graphs of confidence belts were introduced that provide the confidence limits, without calculations, for selected sample sizes and selected levels of confidence; these provide two-sided confidence intervals. One-sided confidence intervals can also be obtained from the same graphs. Samples are assumed to be random. Under some conditions a formula for the normal approximation to the binomial can be used for specific sample sizes and levels of confidence not provided by graphs. Special care is needed to state a confidence interval clearly and correctly, either in decimal proportion or in percent. The risk of a confidence interval being wrong is directly related to the level of confidence, and its consequences are a business and economic matter. It may seem desirable to reduce the width of the confidence interval by increasing the sample size or decreasing the level of confidence, but both have limiting value.

17.13 Putting It into Practice

1. What is wrong with the following confidence interval statement?

   We are 90% confident that the percentage of defective dead-bolt locks in the sample is somewhere between 9% and 14%.

2. In a random sample of 250 external computer drives from a large shipment, 175 were found with an electrical short. In a complete statement, what is the 90% confidence interval for this defect in the shipment? Do this problem two ways: by confidence belts and by the normal approximation to the binomial. How do the results compare?

3. In one day's production of canned tomatoes, a random sample of 75 cans revealed that three of them showed signs of vacuum loss. In a complete statement, what is the upper 97.5% confidence limit?

4. If your organization produces some small discrete units of product, select a sample of 100 and inspect them for visual defects. Record the number of units that have defects. What is the 99% confidence interval for these defective units in the population? Define the population. Determine if you have a problem.

Answers to Problems 1, 2, and 3

1. This is a statement about a sample. A confidence interval should be a statement about a population or process parameter.

2. $n = 250$; $p = 175/250 = 0.70$.
   By confidence belts, Graph 1 in the Appendix:
   90% confidence interval is 0.65 to 0.75.
   By normal approximation to the binomial:

$$0.70 \pm 1.645\sqrt{0.70(0.30)/250} = 0.70 \pm 0.048$$
$$= 0.652 \text{ to } 0.748.$$

   "We are 90% confident that the true percentage of computer drives in the shipment with electrical shorts is somewhere between 65% and 75%." The two methods compare very favorably.

3. $n = 75$; $p = 3/75 = 0.04$.
   By confidence belts for small percentages, Graph 2: With interpolation between curves for sample sizes 70 and 100, about 11.3%.

   "We are 95% confident that the true percentage of canned tomatoes with vacuum loss in the day's production is less than about 11.3%."

... [A] state of statistical control is not a
natural state for a manufacturing process.
It is instead an achievement, arrived at by
elimination, one by one, by determined effort,
of special causes of excessive variation.

—W. Edwards Deming*

C H A P T E R   1 8

Introduction to Shewhart Control Charts

Control charts deserve a place at the heart of SPC. They represent perhaps the most original and remarkable of the statistical tools that constitute SPC. Their apparent simplicity belies the sophistication of the theory behind them. This theory, to be discussed in the next chapter, can be easily learned and understood, and encourages the proper implementation and interpretation of control charts. The foundation concepts of control charts are introduced in this chapter.

18.1 Brief History of Control Charts

Control charts—sometimes called Shewhart control charts—go back a long way. They were developed by Dr. Walter A. Shewhart, a member of the technical staff at Bell Telephone Laboratories in New York. Although he had previously written some articles introducing control charts, it was in 1931 that his famous book was published describing the new tool. It revolutionized the industrial world and gave a new meaning to quality control from inspection after the fact to understanding the process itself.

---

* "On Some Statistical Aids toward Economic Production," *Interfaces,* Vol. 5, No. 4, p. 5, The Institute of Management Sciences, Providence, Rhode Island, August 1975.

Shewhart's classic book is called *Economic Control of Quality of Manufactured Product*.[1] He described his book as ". . . an indication of the direction in which future developments may be expected to take place." It is doubtful if he could have predicted its enormous impact. In its 1991 publications catalog, Quality Press, the publishing arm of the American Society for Quality Control (ASQC), stated, "This monumental work laid the foundation for the modern quality control discipline, and it remains as current today as ever."

World War II provided the first national and international incentive to use control charts in the United States. The need for quality armaments and munitions was apparent, and quality control at that time consisted, almost exclusively, of inspection and more inspection. It was not unusual to perform 100% inspection to find defective product, an ineffective practice sardonically called *inspecting quality into the product*.

With factories geared toward the war effort operating around the clock, seven days a week, it was evident in a number of U.S. factories that there simply were not enough personnel to accomplish adequate inspection as practiced. Control charts, which enabled their users to make decisions based on samples from a process, seemed to be a solution to this wartime dilemma. Their use began to spread in U.S. factories engaged in manufacturing for the military, and soon control charts crossed the Atlantic and entered the allied factories of England.

When World War II ended, and factories began to gear up for badly needed consumer goods, some companies began to introduce control charts into their operations. The ASQC was formed in 1947, and soon control charts were being taught in many short courses and seminars. Many U.S. companies that had heard about the new tool began to use it, but many of the control chart programs initiated after the war were either abandoned outright or suffered the ignominy of indifference.

Quality took a back seat to production in the immediate postwar era. The demand for consumer goods was so strong that quality and quality control tools, such as control charts, did not seem important. Eventually many control chart programs degenerated into mere record-keeping activities, an ineffective use of a powerful quality tool.

Several reasons can be cited for the postwar deterioration in control chart programs. Among them are the following:

1. People were intent on buying consumer goods regardless of quality, so quality control tools received only secondary priority.

---

[1] Originally published in 1931 by D. Van Nostrand Company, New York, the book has been out of print for a number of years. However, the American Society for Quality Control in Milwaukee reprinted the book in 1980, and copies can be obtained from them.

2. Control charts seemed to be too statistics-oriented and were therefore perceived as too difficult to understand.

3. Control charts were looked on as a technical tool designed for, and to be used only by, quality control personnel.

4. Management did not see control charts as a management tool and so disassociated itself from them. At the time, management did not see the quality function as a vital part of business strategy and management responsibility.

As time went on, and Japan's recovery from the war became ever more dramatic, the effect on American production—especially in automobiles and electronics—was traumatic. American market share in the United States and around the world declined, and poor quality was considered the culprit.

In 1980 a National Broadcasting Company (NBC) television program, entitled "If Japan Can, Why Can't We?", explored the problem of quality in America and the threat of Japan's perceived superior quality. In the telecast Dr. W. Edwards Deming,[2] a practicing statistician in Washington, D.C., was identified as the individual responsible for teaching statistical quality control methods to Japanese engineers and managers, beginning in 1950. For the first time, it seemed, the real impact of statistical methods on quality, especially statistical quality control methods, was dramatically revealed.

It wasn't long before Deming's statistical impetus and management philosophy were sought by major manufacturers in the United States. The demand for Deming's attention and consulting services skyrocketed. Control charts, the heart of statistical quality control that had lain essentially dormant, were given new life and respect. It is fair to say that control charts, as well as other statistical tools, were reborn in the 1980s and that Deming deserves the credit for their regeneration and new appreciation.

18.2 The Basic Concept of Control Charts

Every process exhibits variability. Some of the variation is due to basic elements that comprise the process, such as raw materials, machines, manpower, methods, measurements, environment, and management. The process is called a *constant-cause system* when it is behaving in a random fashion, is stable, and is predictable. Under these conditions the inherent variability is least, and therefore the process can be described as doing its best. The process is then said to be

---

[2] For a well-written biography and exposition of Deming's ideas, see A. Gabor, *The Man Who Discovered Quality—How W. Edwards Deming Brought the Quality Revolution to America*, Random House, New York, 1990. Also offered through ASQC Quality Press, Milwaukee.

in statistical control. The variability of such a system can be attributed to *chance, random,* or *common causes.*

Occasionally, certain aberrations in a process occur, due to factors such as defective raw materials, breakdown or wear of machines, improperly trained personnel, uncalibrated instruments, or inconsistent management policies, causing the process variability to increase beyond that attributed to chance. Such a process is said to be *out of statistical control,* and such aberrations are referred to as *assignable* or *special causes.*[3] Other special causes may result in a reduction of variability and are considered desirable—for example, a new method of treating materials or managing equipment.

Control charts enable us to determine when a process is not, or is, in statistical control; that is, whether or not a special (or assignable) cause is present. Sample statistics calculated from samples taken periodically from a process are plotted as points on the charts. The statistical behavior of the points is interpreted with regard to calculated limits and to certain patterns or configurations. The limits for sample statistics are called *control limits* and represent the *expected variablity* of the sample statistic under the hypothesis that the process is in statistical control.

Sample statistics and associated Shewhart control charts include

1. Sample mean ($\overline{X}$-chart)

2. Sample range (R-chart)

3. Sample proportion or sample fraction defective (p-chart)

4. Sample number of defectives (np-chart)

5. Sample number of defects (c-chart)

6. Sample average number of defects per unit (u-chart or $\overline{c}$-chart).

These control charts are examined in detail in the next three chapters.

18.3 The Concept of Noise and Signals

Another way of looking at control charts is by considering the components of *noise* and *signals.* If a process is behaving in a random fashion, is stable, is predictable, and is doing its best, the variation it exhibits is due to chance and can be called *noise.* When undesirable special (or assignable) causes enter the process, the overall variation tends to increase beyond that due to chance alone.

---

[3] The expressions *constant cause* and *assignable cause* are due to Shewhart. *Common cause* and *special cause* are due to Deming.

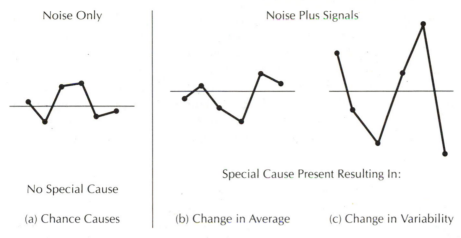

Figure 18.1. Noise, and noise plus signals.

Control charts can detect the statistical *signals* that are generated by the excessive variation.

The presence of a special cause can result in a change in the process *average* or in an increase (or even decrease) in the process *variability*, or both. In either case the total variability now has two components: *noise* and *signals*, and the job of control charts is to measure the noise component so that the signal component can be detected. All three conditions (noise, change in average, increase in variability) are depicted in Figure 18.1 as parts (a), (b), and (c), respectively.

In Figure 18.1(a), the variability is random and is the smallest that the process can exhibit; it represents noise always inherent in a process. In Figure 18.1(b), a change in process *average* increases the overall variation, including the initial noise, and should trigger a signal on a control chart. An increase in process *variation*, Figure 18.1(c), increases the overall variation and should trigger a signal on a control chart. (We will see in Chapter 20 that a decrease in variation can also trigger a signal.) Thus, control charts are designed to detect *changes*.

18.4 Analogy to a Court of Law

A courtroom analogy to process quality was suggested in Section 9.8 of Chapter 9. An interesting analogy can also be made between control charts and a court of law that may help us to understand the reasoning behind the charts. In our system of justice, a defendant is presumed innocent until proven guilty "beyond a reasonable doubt." The burden of proof is on the prosecution, at least in theory, to present evidence that contradicts the presumption of innocence.

If the contradictory evidence is convincing, a jury finds the defendant *guilty beyond reasonable doubt* of the charges, and action is taken to convict the defendant. "Reasonable doubt" is the probability or risk of the guilty verdict being wrong, hopefully very small in a court of law. Obviously, wrong decisions can be made; occasionally, innocent people will be found guilty (small risk), or guilty defendants will be found not guilty (larger risk).

If the prosecution's evidence is not convincing, the jury finds the defendant *not guilty*, which does not mean that the defendant has been proven innocent; it means that the evidence was inadequate to contradict the presumption of innocence. The defendant is then *treated* by the court as still innocent of the charges and is released.

With similar reasoning, a control chart has control limits set for the sample statistic on the presumption that the process is *in statistical control* (innocent). Evidence, in the form of sample statistics, is plotted on the chart.

If the plotted points go beyond the control limits or form a conspicuous pattern of nonrandomness (contradictory evidence), the process is declared to be *out of statistical control* (guilty), and action is taken to search for a special cause (conviction). The location of the control limits on the chart determines the probability of the declaration being wrong, usually set at about 0.001 (see Chapter 19). Wrong decisions can be made. Occasionally, a process in statistical control is declared to be out of statistical control, and a subsequent search for special causes is fruitless.

If the plotted points fall within the control limits or exhibit patterns of randomness (insufficient contradictory evidence), the process is said to be *in statistical control* (not guilty). This does not mean that the process has been proven to be in statistical control; it means that the evidence was inadequate to contradict the presumption of statistical control. The process is *treated* as if it were in statistical control (innocent), and no action is taken on the process (freedom).

18.5 Kinds of Basic Control Charts

Two broad categories of control charts are available: *variables* and *attributes*. Charts for attributes can be subdivided further into those for defectives (nonconformances) and defects (nonconformities).[4] Table 18.1 identifies the names of the basic charts, the sample statistics involved, and the parameter of the process whose change the chart is designed to detect.

The np-chart and the c-chart require fixed sample sizes (n). Variable sample sizes may be used for the other charts, because the formulas for the control limits

---

[4] The terms *defective, defective unit,* and *defect* have been used for many years, but some legal problems of understanding have arisen in their use. The American National Standards Institute (ANSI) and the American Society for Quality Control (ASQC) have jointly agreed to replace those terms with *nonconformance, noncomforming unit,* and *nonconformity,* respectively.

Table 18.1. Kinds of Basic Control Charts

Name of Chart	Sample Statistic	Detects Changes in Process
	Variables	
Average chart	$\overline{X}$	Mean
Range chart	R	Variability
	Attributes	
Defectives		
p-chart	p	Proportion or fraction defective
np-chart (fixed n)	np	Number of defectives
Defects		
c-chart (fixed n)	c	Number of defects
u- (or $\overline{c}$)-chart	u (or $\overline{c}$)	Average number of defects/unit

take the sample size into account. In practice, however, the sample sizes should be fixed for each of the charts, when possible, in order to simplify the calculations for the control limits.

Other Shewhart control charts have come to be used, including the *individuals chart* (*X*-chart) and the *standard deviation chart* (*S*-chart). More recently, a variety of control charts have been developed that reflect specialized uses or expansions of the basic Shewhart charts. They are not yet in the stable of basic control charts, but might very well be as general understanding and use increase. Included are

1. Median chart

2. Modified control limits chart

3. Adaptive control chart

4. Moving-average and range charts

5. Acceptance control chart

6. Cumulative sum (CuSum) chart

7. Zone control chart

8. Exponentially weighted moving-average (EWMA) chart.

Some of these are discussed in Chapter 22.

18.6 Uses and Misuses of Control Charts

The ultimate purpose of control charts is to aid in getting a process into statistical control. A process in statistical control exhibits its least variability; any further improvement requires special study, experimentation, and management involvement.

Getting a process into statistical control with proper use of control charts has a number of rewards. Process behavior becomes stable and predictable. Process capability of meeting requirements can be determined. The smallest variability inherent in the process has been reached. Genuine process improvement can be pursued scientifically by focusing on the common causes of the process.

The charts help to identify conditions when a special cause is present. When such evidence is present, those in charge of the process have the responsibility to search for the special cause and to remove it if it is undesirable, or retain it if it is desirable. Thus the control chart serves as the basis for conducting an investigation of a process in order to identify the special cause. If an undesirable special cause is one that can be feasibly and economically removed, then the process can be brought into statistical control.

It should be pointed out that control charts *do not control anything*. Control charts do not adjust equipment, change raw material, investigate processes, identify special causes, or supervise people. They are merely tools for providing data that can be used for managing processes and, as such, should be looked on as management decision-making tools. In this sense the term *control charts* is a misnomer.

A common misuse of control charts may occur if they are used exclusively to decide when to *adjust* a process; that is, to change the process average after a shift in average has been detected. It is a misuse because it focuses only on the symptoms and not on the causes for excessive variability. What must be remembered is that the control chart's basic function is to identify the presence of a special cause responsible for the average change that resulted in excessive variation. The special cause responsible for the shift in average should be sought first in order to take corrective action on the process.

If a process adjustment is made without searching for the special cause, the cause may still be present, and excessive variation may occur again in the process. The variation may even be aggravated by adjusting the process. Thus the real sources of excessive variation have been overlooked. *Process adjustment without a search for assignable causes does not effectively help the process.*

The control chart is an effective operations tool that helps to remove the element of subjectivity. When operators, for example, rely only on subjective criteria—such as intuition, feel, or experience—to decide how to manage the process, it is certain that the criteria will vary from operator to operator, resulting in increased overall process variability.

18.7 Control Charts as Quality Improvement Tools

Almost all quality practitioners would agree that a process is said to be improved if its *variability* can be economically reduced. In the years since control charts were introduced, they have been credited with process improvement, especially if they are properly used and interpreted. When control charts are first applied to a process, it is not uncommon for the process to be found "out of statistical control," meaning that excessive variation is present due to one or more special causes. As each undesirable special cause is identified and removed, process variation is reduced, apparently satisfying the criterion for improvement. In this sense the control chart does help to improve a process.

Bringing a process into a state of statistical control effectively reduces its variability to a point where the variability cannot be reduced further without making fundamental changes in the process. The changes usually require management's involvement and may include changing the product design, the equipment, the raw materials, the methods, the skills of the personnel, the environment, or management policies. The selection of factors involved in making changes is determined by conducting designed experiments to identify process factors that have the most impact on reducing variability. Making changes in a process challenges the process engineer and other responsible people to bring the process into statistical control again, after which changes must be introduced to improve the process further.

The cycle of continual process improvement becomes more clear. It is now widely accepted that true improvement of a process, the reduction of variability beyond that limited to its basic elements, can be achieved *after* the process is first brought into statistical control. The activity of gradually removing special causes does reduce variability, but admittedly it merely brings the process up to its inherent potential; that is, bringing it up to par, so to speak. After that, the common causes of variation must be addressed, studied, and modified to reduce variability further.

One point of view states that control charts have a limited use as tools to *monitor* a process. Monitoring a process implies passive activity and minimal impact. Control charts, however, have a more dynamic role of providing insight into understanding the behavior of a process, a prelude to improvement.

It has also been suggested that control charts cannot effect improvement at all, that improvement can be achieved only by making fundamental changes in the process, and that, in fact, control charts are the opposite of improvement. One spokesman for this point of view is Dana M. Cound, former president of

ASQC and vice president of quality for GenCorp. In a short paper entitled, "Control: The Antithesis of Improvement,"[5] he states:

> In discussions of quality there is sometimes a tendency to use "quality control" and "quality improvement" interchangeably. But the notions of "control" and "improvement" are fundamentally different. . . . By their very nature, control mechanisms prevent change. But improvement is change—specifically, change for the better. Therefore, tools of control tend to prevent improvement. . . .
>
> One of the statistical tools of control is the control chart. . . . Given evidence "beyond reasonable doubt" that the process average has changed, we expect the operator to adjust the process back where it belongs. If the variability has increased, we investigate the cause and restore the process to its former state. . . .
>
> Because the function of a control chart is to cause processes to behave predictably instead of chaotically, . . . experimentation [is] necessary to break through to a higher level of performance. . . . That job belongs to the tools of improvement.
>
> The tools of improvement that accompany the statistical tools of control are experimental designs. What is an experimental design? It is the deliberate introduction of change in order to assess its effects on product or process performance. This is the antithesis of control!

Cound's arguments are well stated and provocative. Another argument treats the enlightened use of control charts as *leading to and contributing to* improvement practices, such as experimentation, once a state of statistical control has been achieved. When control charts are properly used, the identification and removal of assignable causes will indeed cause change: the gradual reduction of variability, ultimately to the minimum variability inherent in a process that is in statistical control.

Some quality practitioners, supervisors, and manufacturing personnel confuse statistical control with meeting specifications. A process that is in statistical control may not necessarily be able to meet specifications. Such a process is said to be *not capable* of meeting specs. Conversely, a process that meets specifications may not necessarily be in statistical control and therefore not operating to its potential. If such a process is left alone, opportunities for optimizing the process are lost. The process knows nothing about specifications, which are often arbitrarily chosen, and behaves according to the unique nature of its combination of the basic elements of materials, machines, people, methods, measurements, environment, and management.

18.8 Summary

Control charts, named Shewhart charts, were developed by Dr. Walter A. Shewhart of Bell Telephone Laboratories and reported in a classic book published in

---

[5] A sidebar appearing in *Chemical and Process Industries Division News*, ASQC, Milwaukee, January 1988, p. 7.

1931. Control charts, a statistical tool, were used during World War II and there-after, but they did not achieve widespread success during the immediate post-war period for various reasons. Dr. W. Edwards Deming taught statistical methods to Japanese managers and engineers. After Deming appeared on a national television program in 1980, control charts and other statistical tools began to be widely appreciated.

Sample statistics from a process are plotted on control charts and interpreted from control limits that are calculated under the hypothesis that the process is in statistical control. A process in statistical control is behaving at random, is stable, is predictable, is doing its best, and exhibits its least inherent variability. A process is improved if its variability is reduced. After statistical control is achieved, any further improvement requires special study, experimentation, and management involvement. Statistical control is not necessarily equivalent to meeting specifications.

A process not in statistical control is affected by one or more special (or assignable) causes, which can be undesirable (the usual case) or desirable. Unde-sirable special causes, when removed, help to bring the process into statistical control; desirable ones are to be retained and made a part of the process. The ultimate purpose of control charts is to aid in getting a process into statistical control. Interpretation of control charts is analogous to decisions from a court of law. Basic variables charts include $\overline{X}$ (mean) and R (range). Basic attributes charts include p (proportion), np (number of defectives), c (number of defects), and u (or $\overline{c}$) (average number of defects per unit). A control chart used only for adjusting a process without identifying and removing undesirable special causes is an underused chart. Control charts, when properly used, can contribute to process improvement.

18.9 Putting It into Practice

1. Survey your organization to determine the history of control charts. If con-trol charts are or have ever been used, go to Problem 2. (If control charts have never been used, read Chapters 19 through 22. Then organize a committee to develop a plan for their introduction.)

2. Uncover problems, if any, associated with the use of control charts, includ-ing understanding of concepts, training, applications, or responsibility. Then organize a committee consisting of involved parties to develop a plan for correcting the problems.

*The judge of quality must be familiar
with the rules of probable inference
and rules of evidence.*

—Walter A. Shewhart*

CHAPTER 19

Why Control Charts Work:
Introduction to Variables Charts

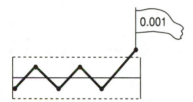

We can safely conclude that the theoretical reasons why control charts can identify conditions when a process has special (or assignable) causes present—that is, when the process is not in statistical control—are not entirely clear to many of those who use control charts regularly. One may argue that it is not necessary to understand the theory, that it is much like driving a car: You don't have to understand the engineering principles that make a car operate in order to become a good driver. But that analogy is questionable when it comes to control charts. A driver can respond to a car's performance, which is observable and generally controllable; but a quality practitioner or machine operator may not give credence to a signal that a control chart sends because there may be no direct, observable behavior of the process that relates to the signal.

The quality practitioner or machine operator using a control chart is left to depend on blind faith, on training, or on orders from superiors. Suspicion and uncertainty that may result in misunderstanding, misinterpretation, and even misrepresentation can be and must be overcome.

Let us seek a clear notion as to why a control chart can perform its miracles as advertised.

---

* *Statistical Method from the Viewpoint of Quality Control*, p. 43, Dover Publications, New York, 1986. From original works published 1939, Graduate School of Department of Agriculture, Washington, DC.

19.1 An Example in Development of a Control Chart

To serve as an example, the ideas and concepts that lie behind the $\overline{X}$ (X-bar) control chart, which is used to detect changes in the process mean μ, will be considered. Table 18.1 in the previous chapter identifies the several basic control charts.

Suppose that a manufacturing process is in statistical control; that is, it is affected only by common causes unique to the process with no special causes present. The process produces large quantities of an aluminum part used in automobiles, and we are interested in a particular linear measurement, length. Suppose that the process mean and standard deviation, respectively, of the linear measurement are as follows:

$$\mu = 50.0 \text{ cm and } \sigma = 5.0 \text{ cm.} \tag{19.1}$$

What does the actual process distribution of individual-unit measurements look like? We don't know for sure, of course, even with a histogram drawn from a large sample size. The true distribution of individual units may not appear to be even close to normal. It could be something like that shown in Figure 19.1, which is not a normal curve. For the purposes of this discussion we may not even care, as we shall soon find out.

Also shown in Figure 19.1 are the upper and lower process limits (maximum and minimum measurements), UPL and LPL, respectively, and the upper and lower specification limits, USL and LSL, respectively.

Now suppose that random samples of four individual units at a time, called *subgroups*, are taken from this process; that is,

$$n = 4. \tag{19.2}$$

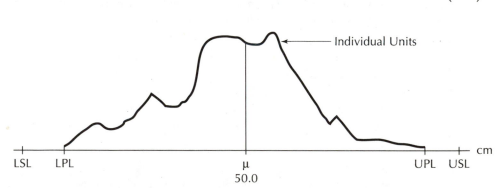

Figure 19.1. True process distribution of individual units showing process limits (LPL, UPL) and specification limits (LSL, USL).

The subgroup sample size of four is chosen for convenience. Each unit in a subgroup of four is measured, and the sample average $\overline{X}$ of the subgroup is calculated. We collect at least 25 subgroups of four for a total of at least 100 units, which will yield at least 100 observations.

At this point, before we go further, we should pause and make an adjustment in thinking. It is important to distinguish carefully between *individual units X* and *averages of sample subgroups* $\overline{X}$. The former, *X*, is what the specification limits and process limits usually apply to; the latter, $\overline{X}$, is the sample statistic whose behavior will be examined and for which a control chart will be developed.

What will these sample *averages* of random subgroups of four look like? Some of them may well look like this: 51.7, 49.2, 47.5, 52.9, 51.6, 48.8, 52.2, 53.5, 47.2, 46.7, and so on. (Each of these sample averages is, statistically, an estimate of the process mean μ.) Sample averages tend to exhibit some well-known and rather surprising statistical characteristics.

19.2 Three Characteristics of Sample Averages

Sample averages have three important characteristics:

1. The mean[1] of all the subgroup sample averages tends to approach the true process mean μ as the number of subgroups increases.

This characteristic seems intuitively correct. We express it statistically by stating that the *expected value* of all sample averages is the process mean μ. Expected value is similar to a long-term mean, and it is written algebraically as follows:

$$E(\overline{X}) = \mu. \tag{19.3}$$

In other words, in the long run the mean of all possible sample averages will reflect what the true process mean is. For our process example, the more sample averages we have, the closer their mean should come to 50.0 cm, the true process mean. The mean of a finite number of sample averages is called $\overline{\overline{X}}$ (*X-double-bar*), and it, too, is an estimate (a better one) of the process mean μ, just as each sample average is.

Now for the second characteristic of sample averages:

2. The variability of sample averages $\sigma_{\overline{x}}$ is related to the variability of individual units σ_x and to subgroup sample size *n* in a particular and unique way:

$$\sigma_{\overline{x}} = \frac{\sigma_x}{\sqrt{n}}. \tag{19.4}$$

---

[1] "Mean"and "average" can be used interchangeably, but in this context "mean" will be used for a large set of data, while "average" will be used for each subgroup.

This characteristic will not be proven mathematically. Sample averages exhibit variability as almost any set of data does; its variability, therefore, can be expressed in terms of standard deviation. In Eq. (19.4), the subscripts have meaning: $\sigma_{\bar{x}}$ is the standard deviation of *subgroup averages of size n*, while σ_x is the standard deviation of *individual units*. Equation (19.4) says that the standard deviation of sample averages will be *smaller* than the standard deviation of individuals by a factor of $1/\sqrt{n}$. This relationship encourages us to keep in mind the distinction between individuals and averages.

To illustrate the relationship expressed in Eq. (19.4): If subgroups of size $n = 4$ are taken from a process, the standard deviation of their averages should be only *one-half* that of individual units. If subgroups of size $n = 9$ are taken from a process, the standard deviation of their averages should be only *one-third* that of individual units. If subgroups of size $n = 16$ are taken from a process, the standard deviation of their averages should be only *one-fourth* that of individual units, and so on. In these examples, the sample sizes chosen are convenient perfect squares so that the square root of n appearing in the denominator of Eq. (19.4) becomes an integer.

Just as Eq. (19.4) expresses the relationship between *standard deviations*, the relationship between *variances* can also be expressed simply by squaring both sides, resulting in Eq. (19.5):

$$\sigma_{\bar{x}}^2 = \frac{\sigma_x^2}{n}.$$

(19.5)

A very profound statement will now be made:

Equations (19.4) and (19.5), relating the variability of sample averages to that of individuals, are perhaps the most important relationships in all statistical methodology.

These equations, although expressing a rather simple relationship, are used time and again in more advanced statistics involving confidence intervals for process parameters, hypothesis testing, and designed experiments. Equation (19.4) for standard deviations also forms the basis for determining the control limits for the $\bar{X}$-chart, as we shall see.

Finally, the third and perhaps the most astonishing characteristic of sample averages obtained from subgroups of the same size is as follows:

3. A histogram drawn from sample averages tends to form a normal distribution as the number of subgroups increases.

Characteristic 3 represents, indeed, a fortunate situation, because so much is known about the normal distribution as a predictive tool (see Chapter 15). This extraordinary characteristic of sample averages is generally true *regardless of the shape of the original distribution of individual units* (see examples in Section 19.4).

How closely and quickly sample averages conform to Characteristic 3 depends on the subgroup sample size and the number of subgroups. Averages from large-sample subgroups tend to converge faster to a normal curve than do averages from small-sample subgroups. In addition, more averages of samples of two, for example, are needed before the symmetrical, normal curve becomes apparent.

All three characteristics of sample averages form what is called the *central limit theorem,* the theoretical basis for control charts. In other words, the behavior of sample averages, as well as that of any sample statistic for which a control chart has been developed, is predictable when the process is in statistical control. Because sample averages have less variability than individuals do, they are more sensitive to changes in the process than individual observations are. As a consequence, the larger the subgroup sample size, the more sensitive and predictable the average.

19.3 Variability of Sample Averages Affected by Sample Size

The effects of Characteristics 2 and 3—the variability of sample averages and the normal curve—can be visualized better in Figure 19.2 for sample sizes 4, 9, and 16. All three depicted sample sizes result in normal curves for sample averages. (The peaks of the curve change in order for the total area under the curves to remain about the same.)

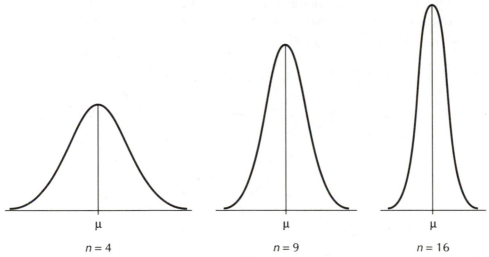

μ μ μ

$n = 4$ $n = 9$ $n = 16$

Figure 19.2. Comparison of normal curves from sample averages for $n = 4$, $n = 9$, and $n = 16$.

We can also see that, as sample size increases, the variability of sample averages is reduced as established by Eq. (19.4) for standard deviations. As the variability of sample averages is reduced, the curve of sample averages becomes more sensitive to changes in the process mean. We conclude that averages of larger sample sizes tend to respond to such changes faster than averages of smaller sample sizes.

The statistical moral of this example is that larger sample sizes are always preferred, within the constraints of cost and convenience. The reality of the principle that "there is no Santa Claus" continues to be upheld.

19.4 Extreme Examples of Sample Averages

Consider two extreme examples that dramatically demonstrate the remarkable behavior of sample averages. If the shape of the distribution of individuals is a *triangular* distribution, as in Figure 19.3, sample averages of four tend to form a normal curve. If the shape of the distribution of individuals is a *rectangular* distribution, where all values occur with equal frequency, sample averages of four also tend to form a normal curve. Two practical examples of a rectangular distribution model are (1) throws of an ordinary die and (2) occurrences of the 10 possible digits in one position of a lottery number.

The model for an infinite number of throws of a single die, assuming that all conditions of randomness and "honesty" are met, is a rectangular distribution where, in the long run, each face of the die should come up an equal number of times. If four such dice are tossed repeatedly, the calculated averages of the four faces tend to form a normal distribution as shown in Figure 19.4.

In the case of an honestly run lottery, we would expect that all 10 digits, 0, 1, 2, . . . 9, for each digital position in a lottery number, would occur with equal

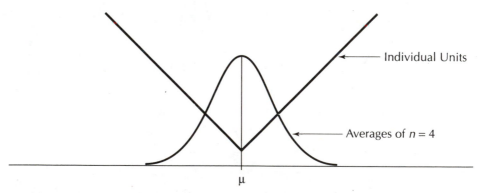

Figure 19.3. Averages of four from a triangular distribution.

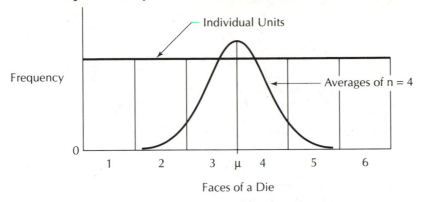

Figure 19.4. Averages of four from a rectangular distribution.

frequency in the long run.[2] Averages of four random digits tend to form a normal distribution.

The two examples just described involved symmetrical process distributions for individuals. Some industrial examples might involve a process that can be represented by a nonsymmetrical *skewed* distribution. Even here, the averages of subgroups of size four would, in the long run, form a normal curve. More subgroups of sample size less than four would be required before their averages tend to lose their initial skewness, become symmetrical, and suggest the normal curve. Averages of subgroups of more than four would tend to converge more quickly to the normal curve.

19.5 Sample Averages Applied to Aluminum Parts Example

According to the central limit theorem, sample averages of four taken from the process of aluminum parts described in Section 19.1 will exhibit the three characteristics:

1. They will be centered at the process mean of 50.0 cm.

2. Their standard deviation will be half that of individual units.

3. They will form a normal distribution.

Thus, we can superimpose a normal curve of averages of four onto the process distribution, as shown in Figure 19.5. If the standard deviation for individual

---

[2] True aficionados of lotteries actually tally these frequencies to detect anything "unusual," often not for scientific statistical curiosity but for personal gain.

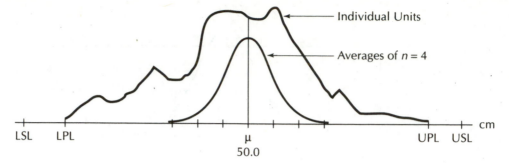

Figure 19.5. Normal curve for sample averages of four superimposed on process distribution of individual units.

units is 5.0 cm, as initially described, then the standard deviation for averages of four, determined from Eq. (19.4), will have a standard deviation of

$$\sigma_{\bar{x}} = \frac{5.0}{\sqrt{4}} = \frac{5.0}{2} = 2.5 \text{cm}, \tag{19.6}$$

which is half that of the standard deviation for individual units.

As we did for normal curves back in Chapter 15, the base scale for the normal curve of sample averages can be marked for one, two, and three standard deviations on either side of its mean. The standard deviation of sample averages of four, from Eq. (19.6), is 2.5 cm (not 5.0 cm). Thus the following readings for the base, from three standard deviations to the left of the mean to three standard deviations to the right of the mean, should be

42.5   45.0   47.5   50.0   52.5   55.0   57.5.

These figures are superimposed below the baseline in Figure 19.6.

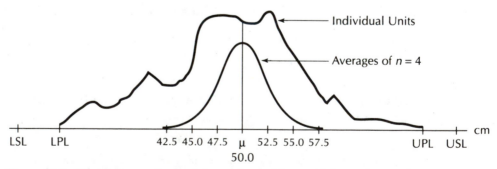

Figure 19.6. Normal curve for sample averages of four with base identified for one, two, and three standard deviations from the mean.

19.6 Predicting Sample Averages from the Process

Applying our knowledge of areas under the normal curve, it is now possible to predict the probabilities of occurrence of subgroup averages of size four taken from this process *as long as the process remains in statistical control with its mean at 50.0 cm and its standard deviation at 5.0 cm for individual units.*

We expect, therefore, that *68.26% of sample averages will fall between 47.5 and 52.5 cm;* that is, between plus-and-minus *one* standard deviation (of sample averages) from the mean. This is a powerful predictive statement.

We expect, therefore, that *95.44% of sample averages will fall between 45.0 and 55.0 cm;* that is, between plus-and-minus *two* standard deviations (of sample averages) from the mean. This is a powerful predictive statement.

We expect, therefore, that *99.73% of sample averages will fall between 42.5 and 57.5 cm;* that is, between plus-and-minus *three* standard deviations (of sample averages) from the mean. This is also a powerful predictive statement.

Finally, we expect that *about one out of a thousand sample averages (actually 0.00135) will be less than 42.5 cm, and that about one out of a thousand sample averages (actually 0.00135) will be greater than 57.5 cm;* that is, *beyond* plus-and-minus three standard deviations (of sample averages) from the mean. Again, this is a powerful predictive statement.

19.7 Choosing Decision Points: The Control Limits

Where, on the normal curve's base scale for sample averages in Figure 19.6, do we decide to take action if a sample average falls beyond it? Traditionally we choose the *plus-and-minus three standard deviation points from the mean*[3]: in the case of our example, 42.5 and 57.5 cm. If a sample average falls beyond either of these points, we conclude that a special cause is present that should be investigated, and the chance that our conclusion is wrong is only about one out of a thousand (0.00135). Very small risk indeed of being wrong.

The two points, 42.5 and 57.5 cm, are called the *control limits for sample averages* and are designated, respectively, LCL$_{\overline{X}}$ and UCL$_{\overline{X}}$, as follows:

$$\text{Upper control limit for } \overline{X} = \text{UCL}_{\overline{X}} = 57.5 \text{ cm}$$
$$\text{Lower control limit for } \overline{X} = \text{LCL}_{\overline{X}} = 42.5 \text{ cm.} \tag{19.7}$$

Note the subscript $\overline{X}$ for control limit abbreviations UCL and LCL in Eq. (19.7). Control limit abbreviations should always identify the sample statistic in a

---

[3] In England the decision points are set at plus-and-minus 3.09 standard deviations from the mean, giving a probability of almost exactly one out of a thousand (0.001) in each tail of the normal curve.

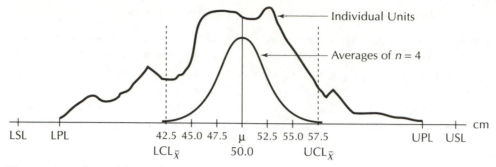

Figure 19.7. Control limits for sample averages.

subscript, because *the subscript identifies the name of the applicable control chart*. We will see more of them.

Figure 19.7 shows dashed lines drawn at the control limits.

19.8 The $\overline{X}$ Control Chart

If the superimposed figure of the normal curve with its control limits in Figure 19.7 is turned 90 degrees clockwise so that the scale of the $\overline{X}$ readings is at the left, and then inverted so that the larger values are at the top, it becomes an $\overline{X}$-chart, as shown in Figure 19.8. The normal curve shown in Figure 19.8 is not

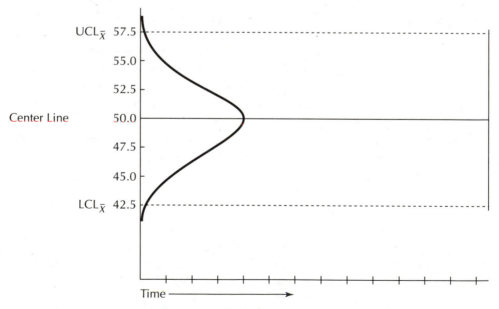

Figure 19.8. An $\overline{X}$ (*X-bar*) control chart.

part of the control chart, but is superimposed in order to emphasize the change in orientation from Figure 19.7. Note that the specification limits (LSL, USL) and process limits (LPL, UPL) are not shown on the scale of measurements and should *not* be shown on the scale of the control chart because those limits refer to *individual* measurements, while the control chart scale has to do with *averages* of subgroups. Experience has cautioned that showing individual measurements on the scale of an $\overline{X}$-chart tends to confuse the practitioner and others who read the charts.

The center line representing the process mean (or an estimate of it) is usually drawn as a solid line. The control limit lines are usually drawn as dashed or dotted lines. Note that the control limit lines are *equally distant* from the center line of an $\overline{X}$-chart, due to the symmetric nature of the normal curve model.

19.9 Model for the $\overline{X}$-Chart Control Limits

The decision points, or control limits, for the aluminum-part example, shown in Eq. (19.7), were chosen as three standard deviations[4] for sample averages on either side of the process mean. *The model for control limits of an $\overline{X}$-chart is therefore*

$$\text{Control limits for } \overline{X} = \mu \pm 3\sigma_{\overline{x}}, \tag{19.8}$$

from which

$$\text{UCL}_{\overline{X}} = \mu + 3\,\sigma_{\overline{x}} \text{ and } \text{LCL}_{\overline{X}} = \mu - 3\,\sigma_{\overline{x}}. \tag{19.9}$$

The model represented by formula (19.8) assumes four things:

1. The process is in statistical control (no special causes).

2. The process mean μ is known.

3. The standard deviation for sample averages $\sigma_{\overline{x}}$ is known.

4. The process standard deviation for individual units σ_x is known.

19.10 Trial Control Limits for the $\overline{X}$-Chart

Usually we approach a process without definitive knowledge of the two parameters, mean and standard deviation, and try to *estimate* these parameters from sample data. In our aluminum-part example we took sample subgroups of four

---

[4] More or less standard practice in the United States but keeping in mind that the probability of the area beyond the control limits (beyond three standard deviations for a normal curve) should be very small; namely 0.00135 in each tail.

and calculated the sample average $\overline{X}$ for each subgroup. We could also get a measure of variability from each sample subgroup by calculating the sample range R.

As the number of subgroups accumulates, for each of which we have calculated both a sample average and a sample range, we can get the means of these sample statistics. If we calculate the mean of all the sample averages, we obtain $\overline{\overline{X}}$ (*X-double-bar*), which is an estimate of the process mean and becomes the center line for the $\overline{X}$-chart.

If we calculate the mean of the sample ranges, we obtain $\overline{R}$ (*R-bar*). Can we get an estimate of the process standard deviation using $\overline{R}$? Recall from Chapter 13 that $\overline{R}/d_2$ is a valid estimate of the process standard deviation *if the process is in statistical control*. The factor d_2 depends on the subgroup sample size and can be obtained from Table 2 in the Appendix. A shortened version of Table 2 is reproduced here as Table 19.1. For our example with $n = 4$, $d_2 = 2.059$.

Table 19.1. Shortened Table* of Factors for $\overline{X}$-R Charts Using $\overline{R}$

| Subgroup Sample Size | Factors for | | | |
| | Sample Averages | Sample Ranges | | Process Standard Deviation |
n	A_2	D_3	D_4	d_2
2	1.880	0	3.267	1.128
3	1.023	0	2.575	1.693
4	0.729	0	2.282	2.059
5	0.577	0	2.114	2.326

Formulas for Computing Control Limits

Average Chart	Range Chart
$\text{UCL}_{\overline{X}} = \overline{\overline{X}} + A_2\overline{R}$	$\text{UCL}_R = D_4\overline{R}$
$\text{LCL}_{\overline{X}} = \overline{\overline{X}} - A_2\overline{R}$	$\text{LCL}_R = D_3\overline{R}$

Estimate of Process Standard Deviation
(Valid Only if Process Is in Statistical Control)

$$\frac{\overline{R}}{d_2} = \text{Estimate of } \sigma_x$$

*For complete table, see Table 2 of the Appendix.

When estimates of the process parameters, mean and standard deviation, are obtained from sample data and used to calculate control limits for an $\overline{X}$-chart, the control limits are called *trial control limits* and are given by the simple and well-known formula,

Trial control limits for the $\overline{X}$-chart = $\overline{\overline{X}} \pm A_2\overline{R}$,   (19.10)

where A_2 depends on the subgroup sample size and can be obtained from Table 2 in the Appendix. The plus-and-minus signs in formula (19.10) then give the separate *trial control limits:*

$$\text{Upper control limit for } \overline{X} = \text{UCL}_{\overline{X}} = \overline{\overline{X}} + A_2\overline{R}$$
$$\text{Lower control limit for } \overline{X} = \text{LCL}_{\overline{X}} = \overline{\overline{X}} - A_2\overline{R}$$

For our example with $n = 4$, Table 19.1 shows that $A_2 = 0.729$.

19.11 Derivation of Trial Control Limits for the $\overline{X}$-Chart

Formula (19.10) is widely used to calculate the trial control limits for an $\overline{X}$-chart based on sample data, but its derivation—especially the origin of the mysterious factor A_2—seems to be unknown to many, if not most, practitioners. As long as the factor A_2 is readily available from tables, the calculation of trial control limits is an easy matter, and most practitioners accept formula (19.10) on faith. It is helpful, however, to clear up any mystery about formula (19.10) because a critical point inherent in its application can enhance our understanding of control charts. Therefore, we now derive formula (19.10) in five relatively easy steps.

Step 1. Start with the *model* for an $\overline{X}$-chart control limits as shown in Eq. (19.8):

$$\mu \pm 3\sigma_{\overline{x}}.$$

Step 2. We saw in Eq. (19.4) that the standard deviation for sample averages $\sigma_{\overline{x}}$ can be expressed in terms of the standard deviation for individual units, $\sigma_x/\sqrt{n}$, based on the second characteristic of sample averages. Making the substitution in the model, we get

$$\mu \pm 3\frac{\sigma_x}{\sqrt{n}}.$$ (19.10a)

Step 3. Since $\sqrt{n}$ is a constant for any problem (for example, $n = 4$ for the aluminum-part problem), it can be placed under the other constant 3, resulting in a slight rearrangement of formula (19.10a):

$$\mu \pm \frac{3}{\sqrt{n}}\sigma_x.$$ (19.10b)

Step 4. We can estimate the process standard deviation σ_x by using $\overline{R}/d_2$, *provided we assume that the process is in statistical control.* We can also estimate the process mean μ by using the mean of the sample averages $\overline{\overline{X}}$. Making these two substitutions in formula (19.10b), we get

$$\overline{\overline{X}} \pm \frac{3\overline{R}}{\sqrt{n}\, d_2}. \tag{19.10c}$$

Step 5. Since the expression $\dfrac{3}{\sqrt{n}\, d_2}$ involves only constants, it can be represented by a single symbol or factor A_2; that is,

$$\frac{3}{\sqrt{n}\, d_2} = A_2, \tag{19.10d}$$

and substituting this expression in formula (19.10c) yields the well-known formula (19.10) for the $\overline{X}$-chart trial control limits:

$$\overline{\overline{X}} \pm A_2 \overline{R}. \tag{19.10}$$

The factor A_2 depends on the subgroup sample size, as do the factors $\sqrt{n}$ and d_2, and is obtained from Table 2 in the Appendix.

As an example of the equivalency of factor A_2 to $3/\sqrt{n}\, d_2$, consider the aluminum-part problem. Samples of size 4 were taken, making $\sqrt{n} = 2$. Then $d_2 = 2.059$ from Table 19.1. Substituting these values, $3/\sqrt{n}\,(d_2) = 3/\sqrt{4}(2.059) = 3/4.118 = 0.729$, which corresponds exactly to A_2 in Table 19.1 for $n = 4$.

The critical point to be made about formula (19.10) for the trial control limits is this: *Formula (19.10) assumes that the process is in statistical control.* This important assumption derives from the fact that the process standard deviation σ_x was estimated by $\overline{R}/d_2$, which is valid only under the assumption of statistical control. (Recall the lengthy discussion regarding this point in Chapter 13.) Therefore, the trial control limits using formula (19.10) are valid *if the process is in statistical control to start with.*

The control chart is drawn with the center line and control limits. The accumulated evidence, collected in the form of sample subgroups, is plotted on the control chart as points, and the result is judged under the assumption of statistical control.

The judgment and interpretation of the control chart results are discussed in detail in the next chapter. For now, we focus on the reasoning inherent in control charts.

If the plotted points *do not* contradict the control limits—that is, points stay within the control limits and bounce around the center line in a random fashion—then we do not have evidence that the process is out of statistical control.

Mind you, such results do not constitute proof that the process *is* in statistical control; we can simply *behave* as if the process is in statistical control.

If the plotted points *do* contradict the control limits—that is, points fall outside either control limit or exhibit a nonrandom pattern within the limits— then we have evidence, beyond a reasonable doubt, that the process is not in statistical control and that a special cause is present that should be investigated.

The statements just made reflect the same kind of reasoning that underlies the presumption of innocence for a defendant in a court of law and the presentation of evidence. It would seem to be helpful, as well as invigorating, that this important line of reasoning and logic be stressed in the teaching of SPC, because practitioners would gain a clearer insight into the proper interpretation of Shewhart control charts. At the same time, the language used to state conclusions properly could be constructively influenced (see Chapter 26).

19.12 General Model for Control Limits for any Shewhart Chart

As a guide to other Shewhart control charts that we will study, it may be helpful to see the general form or model for control limits:

$$\text{Parameter} \pm 3\times(\text{Standard deviation of sample statistic}). \qquad (19.11)$$

The use of sample data to estimate the process parameter and the standard deviation of the sample statistic leads to trial control limits. The purpose is to see if the process is in statistical control or not. If the process is not in statistical control, work must be performed to find and remove undesirable special causes. Once the process is brought into statistical control, the center line can be specified in advance, if it is not already at a satisfactory level. A predetermined value for the center line is called a *standard*.

An example would be setting a standard for the center line that is precisely the *target* for the process, assuming that the process mean can be readily changed. In our aluminum-part example, if the process is in statistical control, we might assert that the mean length of the parts should be 49.0 cm instead of 50 cm. The center line on the control chart is then drawn at the new value and the control limits determined accordingly.

19.13 The *R*-Chart (Range Chart) as a Companion to the $\overline{X}$-Chart

The purpose of the $\overline{X}$-chart is to detect changes in the process mean by noting increases in the variability of sample averages. That detection would not be possible if the process variability of individuals was also increasing, thereby confusing *signals* with *noise* (see Section 18.3 in Chapter 18). Then it would not be clear if increased variability of sample averages was due to a change in the process mean (signal) or to an increase in process variability (noise).

The ability of the $\overline{X}$-chart to detect changes in the process mean, therefore, depends on the status of the process variability—that is, to measure the amount of noise in the process. As long as the process variability is stable, then we can make a valid decision about the process mean from the $\overline{X}$-chart. The status of the process variability is determined by using a range chart, designated $\overline{R}$-chart.[5]

When subgroup samples are taken from a process, as in the example used in this chapter, we saw that both a sample range R and a sample average $\overline{X}$ can be calculated for each subgroup. As we saw in Section 19.11, the average of all the sample ranges, $\overline{R}$, is used to determine the trial control limits for the $\overline{X}$-chart. The average range $\overline{R}$ is also used to calculate the control limits for a range chart that is to be maintained together with the $\overline{X}$-chart.

The center line for an R-chart is $\overline{R}$, and the control limits are determined from the following formulas:

$$\text{Upper control limit for } R = \text{UCL}_R = D_4\overline{R},$$
$$\text{Lower control limit for } R = \text{LCL}_R = D_3\overline{R}. \tag{19.12}$$

Note the subscript R identifying the kind of control chart. Numerical values for the factors D_3 and D_4 are obtained from Table 2 in the Appendix and depend, as do the other factors discussed so far, on the subgroup sample size n. The center line $\overline{R}$ is drawn as a solid line. The control limit lines calculated from formulas (19.12) are drawn as dashed or dotted lines.

Table 2 in the Appendix shows that, when the subgroup sample size is 6 or less, there is no lower control limit for the range (essentially $D_3 = 0$). The reason is that statistically determined values for D_3 are actually negative for sample sizes of 6 or less. Since ranges cannot be negative, D_3 is shown as zero in the table. In these instances the center line $\overline{R}$ is not midway between the control limits 0 and UCL_R. When the subgroup sample size is 7 or more, there is a calculable lower control limit, and the two control limit lines are *equally distant* from the center line $\overline{R}$, just as they are in an $\overline{X}$-chart.

The two charts, appearing and working together as a pair, are designated as either $\overline{X}\&R$ chart or $\overline{X}$-R chart (*X-bar and R* chart). Figure 3.6 in Chapter 3 shows an example of the two charts.

A common mistake in introducing variables control charts into an operation or process is to use an average chart without also using a range chart. *A variability chart, such as a range chart or a standard deviation chart, should always be maintained along with an average chart,* because the center line of the variability chart is the

---

[5] In Chapter 22 we will see that another variability chart, the sample standard deviation chart, designated the S-chart, can be used under certain circumstances.

basis for determining the control limits for the average chart. In fact, the variability chart is usually interpreted first. If the variability is not in statistical control, there is no need to examine the average chart.

Another common mistake is to omit the center line of a control chart (average or range). *The center line should always be shown on a control chart*, because it plays an important part in interpreting the chart for nonrandom patterns.

More information on interpreting control charts is given in Chapter 20.

19.14 Form for the $\overline{X}$-R Chart

Many companies design their own forms for recording data and drawing control charts. A popular standard form[6] for an $\overline{X}$-R chart that is used for subgroup sample sizes of 5 or less is shown in Figure 19.9.

The top portion of the form is generally used for recording basic identifying information about the process, such as the part or item number, operation, operator, specification limits, unit of measure, coding procedure, date and time that samples were obtained, and so on. Other information that can be added includes sampling method, measurement method, work shift, line, batch number, and foreman or supervisor.

Measurement data from samples are recorded in blank spaces that may be located either at the top of the form, as they are in Figure 19.9, or at the bottom of the form. Column space is provided for 25 subgroups (of five measurements each) on a sheet, because that is the minimum number of subgroups usually needed before a determination is made as to whether or not the process is in statistical control. The author has observed many instances where fewer than 25 subgroups have been used effectively when first sampling from a process. If subgroup sample sizes greater than five are taken, either more than one column may be used for a subgroup or another form is designed specifically for the larger subgroup sample size.

There is nothing statistically sacred or magical about sample sizes of five, except that it is easy and quick to calculate the average of a group of five without using a calculator.[7] Many examples have been encountered of subgroup sample

---

[6] Similar forms, in pads of 50, can be purchased from the American Society for Quality Control, Milwaukee. They include formulas, factors for control limits, and workspace for calculating control limits.

[7] First add the readings. Instead of dividing the sum by 5, multiply the sum by 0.2. For example, for the readings 2.5, 3.6, 1.4, 2.0, 4.1, the sum is 13.6. Multiply the sum by 2, getting 27.2; then move the decimal one place to the left, obtaining 2.72 as the average. The reader can easily verify the result by dividing the sum by 5. Of course, to use this easy and quick method, it is essential that one knows how to multiply by 2. (Note that the answer has one more decimal place than the original data, consistent with the practice suggested in Chapter 10.)

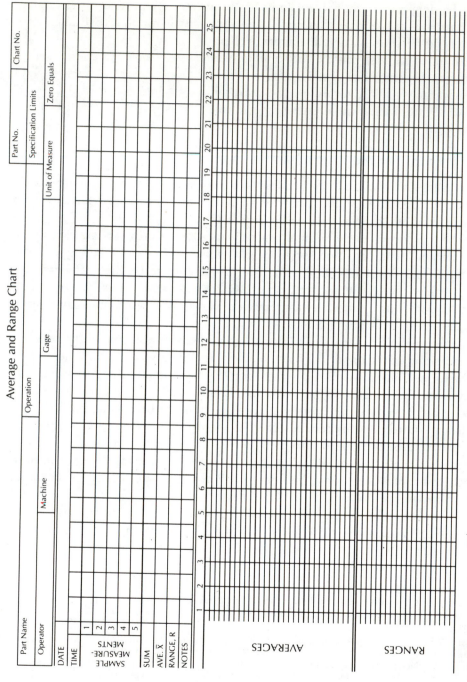

Figure 19.9. Form for $\overline{X}$-R chart.

sizes from 6 through 12 and occasionally higher, often dictated by the packaging configuration. Sample sizes of 10 are somewhat popular because it is even easier to calculate the average; more numbers, however, have to be added.

Space is provided on the form in Figure 19.9 to record the sum of the readings, the sample average $\overline{X}$, and the sample range R. Record the sample average to one more decimal place than the original data (see Chapter 10). These sample statistics are then plotted as points on the respective chart. The *points should be connected* in order to observe any nonrandom patterns (to be discussed in the next chapter). In the earlier days of control charts, connecting the points was often discouraged, especially for the range chart.

The form contains space for drawing two charts, the average and the range. The two charts are often identified as a single chart, the $\overline{X}$-R chart, to emphasize the dependence of the two sample statistics on each other. The scale for each chart should be carefully selected to cover the entire spread of measurements to be encountered. A helpful guide is to make each line marking on the *range* chart approximately twice that of the *average* chart. For example, if each line marking on the average chart is equivalent to 0.1 pound, make each line marking on the range chart equivalent to 0.2 pound. See Figure 3.6 in Chapter 3 as a good example even without all the line markings.

A useful procedure for recording data on the chart is to *code the data* (see Chapter 14). Coding does not change the configuration or the interpretation of the charts and often is necessary when data come in several digits that have to be recorded in the small boxes provided on the form.

The reverse side of the form may be used for showing pertinent formulas, factors for control limits by sample size, and tables of interest, similar to Table 2 in the Appendix. Some control chart forms include space for showing steps in performing calculations for control limits. Considerable innovation has been observed in the design of these forms.

The specification limits should never be shown on the scale for the average chart, because those limits usually refer to *individuals*, while sample *averages* are plotted on the average chart. Individual measurements and averages are two different types of data; identifying both on the same scale can result in a considerable amount of confusion. Specification limits as well as process targets should be recorded in the space provided for them in the basic identifying information section.

As a matter of developing good statistical habits, the procedures for making measurements, recording data, performing calculations, plotting points, and interpreting results should be carefully managed. Training should be adequate, thorough, evaluated, and periodically repeated (see Chapter 26). With the advent of computers and dependable SPC software, the manual task of data recording and drawing control charts is gradually being replaced by automated procedures (see Chapter 25).

19.15 Sampling Considerations and Rational Subgroups

What really determines the *sample size* of the subgroup and the *frequency of sampling?* These important decisions can be determined statistically and mathematically by taking into consideration the following:

- The past behavior of the process, especially its variability

- The cost of sampling, samples, measurements, data handling

- The cost of not detecting the presence of a special cause, including the effect on the process (yield, rework, waste, 100% inspection, downtime, labor) and on the customer (customer satisfaction, goodwill, returned product, replacement, liability)

- The cost of responding to the presence of a special cause and removing undesirable special causes.

Other costs can probably be included. To determine the sample size and frequency of sampling in their purest and theoretical sense, it would be necessary to develop a complicated mathematical model for the process. Even if it were possible to develop a model easily, other, more practical considerations enter into the picture and ultimately determine the sample size and frequency of sampling, such as:

- The ease with which samples can be obtained from the process

- The processing or manufacturing elements that determine the makeup of the samples

- The cost of the product and the samples

- The logistics involved in transporting, storing, treating, and disposing of the samples

- The work involved in measuring, recording, and plotting

- The personnel constraints of manpower availability, training, and work cycle

- Physical access to the process equipment

- The perceived business importance of the product

- The opinion and influence of the supervisor or manager.

A strategy that is frequently used in evaluating a process for the first time is simply to start with some conveniently small subgroup sample size, such as three, four, or five (rarely more), and then to sample at some rational frequency, say, once every hour or every crew change or every shift. A small subgroup sample size is preferred in order to increase the chances of detecting the presence of a special cause. At least 25 subgroups are collected (usually), for each of which a sample average and a sample range are determined. These sample statistics are summarized, trial control limits are calculated, and control charts are drawn. A determination is then made as to whether or not the process is in statistical control.

From that point on, sample size and frequency are often a matter of trial and error, dictated also by the accumulation of information about process behavior that may include some feedback from the customer or marketplace. All of this information is usually integrated, quite casually, in the minds of managers and supervisors, and results in a sample size and sampling frequency that become an official part of the SOP—standard operating procedure.

As statistical control is achieved and maintained, it is reasonable to reduce the frequency of sampling; for example, from once per hour to once every 2 hours or even less frequently. In some cases, when statistical control is sustained for relatively long periods of time, even eliminating the need for a control chart is in order. This is only one example of a payoff in savings from a process that is brought into statistical control. Other payoffs include the reduction of variability (more uniformity) and improved predictability (greater assurance of quality).

Perhaps more important than sample size and frequency of sampling is the *sampling procedure*. This is where the concept of *rational subgroups* comes into play, a key element in the successful implementation of control charts and one that was strongly stressed by Dr. Shewhart decades ago.

A rational subgroup consists of sample units that are similar; that is, units made under nearly identical conditions of materials, equipment, manufacturing method, and so on. In short, the units in any subgroup are *statistically homogeneous*. When rational subgroups are obtained, there should be little chance of a special cause affecting the variability among sample units within the subgroup. Then the variability that we observe among the units in the subgroup can be attributed to the constant causes (common causes, chance causes) of the system. When the sample units are selected under the criterion of minimum variability *within* subgroups, then the maximum opportunity exists for significant variability *between* subgroups to reflect changes in the process that will show up on the control chart as associated with a special cause.

Since the variability *within* subgroups selected in this manner reflects a constant-cause system (the natural variability of the process), it becomes the statistical yardstick for judging the magnitude of the variability *between* subgroups, expressed as the variability among sample averages on the $\overline{X}$-chart. The control limits serve that function.

One obvious and effective way to sample by rational subgroups is to take units of product in the *order of their production* and quite close together in time.

This procedure should leave little opportunity for special causes to have an effect on the variability among the sample units within the subgroup. The intrusion of a special cause will increase the variability *between* subgroups, and the control chart for averages will exhibit a point or points outside a control limit, alerting the operator or supervisor to the presence of a special cause.

In a similar manner, the control chart can be used to detect changes between machines, or between operators, or between lines, or between shifts, or between batches. For example, if one who is familiar with a process suspects that machines performing the same operation differ substantially from each other, and that person wants the control chart to detect such differences, then the subgroup should consist of sample units from a *single* machine. The points can be plotted on the same control chart, and the machine representing each point can be identified in some way on the chart.

An alternative procedure would be to have a separate control chart for each machine (or for each operator, or for each line, or for each shift, or for each batch), but this would require many control charts. It is possible to have *too many control charts*. Current wisdom suggests that control charts, at least to start, should be used with discrimination so that they have the biggest impact. Control chart programs are liable to falter if there is a plethora of control charts that hinder good management of them.

The impact of rational subgroups is important statistically, but the statistician or process engineer cannot be the only person to determine how sampling for control charts should take place. It is essential for other knowledgeable people familiar with a process, such as the machine operator or production foreman or supervisor, to play a part in deciding the makeup of the rational subgroup. The teamwork and cooperation needed to solve quality problems extend to the method for selecting sample units.

The variability exhibited within rational subgroups represents the smallest variability inherent in the system. If such variability is considered to be excessive, making it impossible for the process to meet specifications, the process is said to be *not capable* of meeting specs. The only way to reduce the inherent variability is *to change the system*, and usually management has the power and authority to provide capital that will be used to change equipment, change raw materials, or change methods.

19.16 Summary

Groups of product units sampled from a process are called *subgroups*. For each subgroup a sample average $\overline{X}$ and a sample range R can be calculated. To understand an $\overline{X}$-chart better, it is important to distinguish between individual units X and sample averages $\overline{X}$. Sample averages have three important characteristics:

1. The mean of sample averages tends to approach the true process mean μ as the number of subgroups increases. That is, the expected value of sample averages is the process mean, expressed as follows:

$$E(\overline{X}) = \mu.$$

2. The standard deviation of sample averages is related to the standard deviation of individual units and to sample size in a particular and unique way:

$$\sigma_{\overline{x}} = \frac{\sigma_x}{\sqrt{n}}.$$

3. A histogram drawn from subgroup averages tends to form a normal distribution as the number of subgroups increases.

The second characteristic says that sample averages have less variability than do individual measurements. If the subgroup sample size n is increased, the variability of sample averages decreases and the tendency to form a normal distribution is quickened. Sample averages are more sensitive than individual observations to changes in the process mean.

Because sample averages tend to form a normal distribution, we can predict the probabilities of occurrences of sample averages of size n, as long as the process mean and process standard deviation are stable. Decision points called *control limits* are chosen as plus-and-minus three standard deviations of sample averages from the process mean. The control limits are designated

$$\text{UCL}_{\overline{X}} = \text{Upper control limit for } \overline{X},$$
$$\text{LCL}_{\overline{X}} = \text{Lower control limit for } \overline{X}.$$

The subscript for UCL and LCL identifies the name of the control chart and should always be shown.

The model for the $\overline{X}$-chart control limits is

$$\text{Control limits for } \overline{X} = \mu \pm 3\,\sigma_{\overline{x}},$$

where μ and $\sigma_{\overline{x}}$ are parameters of the process. The probability of sample averages exceeding either control limit is 0.00135, the normal curve area beyond three standard deviations. The model assumes that

1. The process is in statistical control (no special causes).

2. The process mean μ is known.

3. The standard deviation for sample averages $\sigma_{\overline{x}}$ is known.

4. The process standard deviation for individual units σ_x is known.

The center line μ of the $\overline{X}$-chart is drawn as a solid line, and the control limits are drawn as dashed or dotted lines.

When values for process parameters μ and $\sigma_{\overline{x}}$ are unknown, they are estimated from sample data, and the control limits calculated from them are called *trial control limits*. The trial control limit formula is

$$\text{Trial control limits for the } \overline{X}\text{-chart} = \overline{\overline{X}} + A_2\overline{R},$$

where $\overline{\overline{X}}$ estimates the process mean μ and is obtained by averaging the sample averages; factor A_2 depends on the subgroup sample size and is obtained from Table 2 of the Appendix; and $\overline{R}$ is the average of the sample ranges. The trial control limit formula assumes that the process is in statistical control.

If $\overline{\overline{X}}$, the estimate of the process mean, is not a satisfactory target for the process, it can be changed when the process is brought into statistical control. A center line thus chosen is called a *standard*. Designating a center line presumes that the process mean can be adjusted.

A variability chart, such as an R-chart for ranges, must be used as a companion to the $\overline{X}$-chart because the ability of the $\overline{X}$-chart to detect changes in process mean depends on the status of the process variability. The center line for an R-chart is $\overline{R}$, and the control limits are determined from the following formulas:

$$\text{Upper control limit for } R = \text{UCL}_R = D_4\overline{R}$$
$$\text{Lower control limit for } R = \text{LCL}_R = D_3\overline{R}.$$

Numerical values for factors D_3 and D_4 are obtained from Table 2 in the Appendix and depend on the subgroup sample size n. The center line $\overline{R}$ is drawn as a solid line. Control limit lines are drawn as dashed or dotted lines. When subgroup sample size is 6 or less, there is no lower control limit (essentially it is zero).

The two charts appear together on the recording form and are designated $\overline{X}\&R$ chart or $\overline{X}$-R chart. Always include the center line on any control chart because it is useful in judging for nonrandom patterns.

Forms for recording data and drawing control charts are readily available; many companies design their own. *Important caution:* Never draw spec-limit lines on the $\overline{X}$-chart because confusion may result in comparing spec-limit lines for individuals and lines referring to sample averages.

Subgroup sample size and frequency of sampling depend on several cost factors, sometimes not easily determined; logistic factors usually determine those choices. The concept of *rational subgroups* is perhaps more important. Rational subgroups consist of individual units produced under very similar conditions. The probability of special causes being detected *between* rational subgroups is maximized, and the probability of special causes occurring *within* rational subgroups is minimized. A method for getting rational subgroups is to select units of product in the order of their production and close together in time. What constitutes rational subgroups is best determined by staff and line people working together.

The variability exhibited within rational subgroups represents the constant-cause system; that is, the smallest variability inherent in a system. If such variability is excessive for meeting specification limits, the process is said to be *not capable* of meeting specs. Only management involvement can reduce the variability by making critical changes in the system, possibly requiring capital expenditures.

19.17 Putting It into Practice

1. If your organization produces units of product for which samples are regularly taken for a control chart, determine if the concept of sampling by rational subgoups is being employed. If not, what is the rationale behind the sampling procedure being used? Should it be changed? If so, develop a strategy for implementing a change.

2. What is the smallest sample size one can use for an $\overline{X}$-R chart?

3. For subgroup sample size of 5, confirm that the factor A_2 used for trial control limits for the $\overline{X}$-chart is 0.577. Show all calculations.

4. Refer to Table 6.1. Each subgroup of five jars (each line of data) is a rational subgroup. Calculate the necessary sample statistics for each subgroup, and determine the center lines and trial control limits for the $\overline{X}$-R chart. Draw the control charts, and then answer the following questions:

   (a) Are any sample ranges outside of the control limits?

   (b) Are any sample averages outside the control limits?

Answers to Problems 2, 3, and 4

2. The smallest sample size for an $\overline{X}$-R chart is 2. With this sample size one can calculate a sample average $\overline{X}$ and a sample range R.

3. For subgroup size of 5, the factor $\dfrac{3}{\sqrt{n}\,d_2}$ becomes

$$\frac{3}{\sqrt{5}\,(2.326)} = \frac{3}{5.2} = 0.577 = A_2$$

4. Calculate the average $\overline{X}$ (to one decimal) and range R for each subgroup.

Subgroup No.	Readings					$\overline{X}$	R
1	21	21	19	20	24	21.0	5
2	23	20	26	21	23	22.6	6
3	21	23	17	21	19	20.2	6
4	21	22	25	24	20	22.4	5
5	17	18	20	20	20	19.0	3
6	18	15	20	21	20	18.8	6
7	23	23	23	18	22	21.8	5
8	23	20	14	21	20	19.6	9
9	25	24	24	19	19	22.2	6
10	21	21	25	15	19	20.2	10
11	15	21	19	20	21	19.2	6
12	17	15	16	20	19	17.4	5
13	13	17	17	19	17	16.6	6
14	22	20	18	21	16	19.4	6
15	17	21	18	21	21	19.6	4
16	17	20	21	19	21	19.6	4
17	19	21	22	17	20	19.8	5
18	21	18	20	23	22	20.8	5
19	19	26	20	24	28	23.4	9
20	26	26	25	26	24	25.4	2
					Sums:	409.0	113

For the R-chart:

Center line: $\overline{R} = \dfrac{113}{20} = 5.65$

Control limits for R: $\mathrm{LCL}_R = D_3\overline{R} = 0$

$\mathrm{UCL}_R = D_4\overline{R} = 2.114(5.65) = 11.9$

No ranges are outside the (upper) control limit.

For the $\overline{X}$-chart:

Center line: $\overline{\overline{X}} = \dfrac{409.0}{20} = 20.45$

Control limits for $\overline{X}$: $\overline{\overline{X}} \pm A_2\overline{R} = 20.45 \pm 0.577(5.65) = 20.45 \pm 3.26$

$\mathrm{LCL}_{\overline{X}} = 20.45 - 3.26 = 17.19$

$\mathrm{UCL}_{\overline{X}} = 20.45 + 3.26 = 23.71$

One average (subgroup No. 13) is outside the lower control limit.
One average (subgroup No. 20) is outside the upper control limit.

C H A P T E R   2 0

How to Interpret Control Charts

The interpretation of control charts has been treated as both science and art. As a science, specific control chart patterns lead to rules that identify the presence of a special cause consistent with the probabilities that the plotting on the chart implies. The patterns can number from as few as one to as many as fourteen, depending on the level of sophistication desired. As an art, dependence on a skilled eye coupled with familiarity with the process can lead to interpretations that, although possibly correct, may not be convincing or persuasive.

The use of specific patterns and accompanying rules has distinct advantages by assuring reasonable uniformity in interpretation and decision making. But rules that are too numerous to remember may make them impractical to implement, may cause unnecessary confusion, or may result in knee-jerk reactions to every wiggle on the control chart, much like the nervous owner of long-term growth stocks who checks market progress every hour. We propose a sensible compromise.

For the purposes of this chapter we shall confine our interpretations to the $\overline{X}$-R charts and assume that the interpretations also apply to the attribute charts to be introduced in Chapter 21.

20.1 Interpret the Range Chart First

The $\overline{X}$-R charts depend on the average range $\overline{R}$ to determine the respective control limits. If the R-chart appears to be in statistical control, then a valid interpretation can be made for the $\overline{X}$-chart. For example, decisions about the

---

* Quoted in D. Olive, *Business Babble*, p. 123, John Wiley & Sons, New York, 1991.

process mean based on the $\overline{X}$-chart cannot be made unless the R-chart is in statistical control.

If, however, the R-chart is not in statistical control, it means that the calculated average range $\overline{R}$ is inflated (usually) due to the presence of a special cause. This condition will spread the control limits for the $\overline{X}$-chart too far apart, making the interpretation of the $\overline{X}$-chart meaningless. Therefore, the first step in interpretation is the following:

The range (R) chart should be studied first and interpreted before the average ($\overline{X}$) chart is interpreted.

The usual order in which the two charts appear in control chart recording forms has the $\overline{X}$-chart on top and the R-chart below it, as depicted in Figure 19.9 in Chapter 19. In light of the preceding comments, it would appear that a technically better arrangement is to *reverse* the two charts,[1] placing the range chart on top to be studied first, and then calling them *R and $\overline{X}$ charts* instead of *$\overline{X}$ and R charts*.

Figure 20.1 shows the suggested new arrangement. Of course, adopting it would require us to break a habit many years in the making, but presenting the charts in the new format would place appropriate emphasis on the range chart

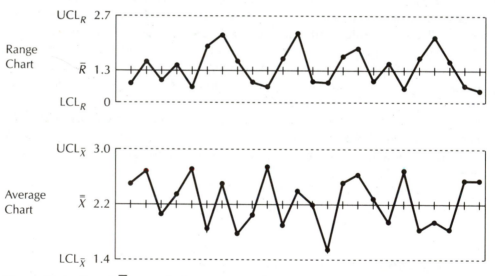

Figure 20.1. R and $\overline{X}$ control charts apparently in statistical control for package net weights in pounds. Subgroup $n = 5$ packages. (Charts presented in uncommon reverse order.)

---

[1] For the origin of this suggestion, see L. S. Nelson, "Monitoring Reduction in Variation with a Range Chart," *Journal of Quality Technology*, ASQC, Milwaukee, April 1990, Vol. 22, No. 2, p. 164.

and recognize its importance in interpreting the $\overline{X}$-chart. It would also add some assurance that the range chart has been accounted for. Too many instances have been encountered in the author's experience where the range chart is omitted entirely and only the $\overline{X}$-chart is plotted. Perhaps the new arrangement will prevent such tactical errors.

20.2 Control Charts Depicting a State of Statistical Control

The control charts in Figure 20.1 are an example of a process that appears to be in statistical control. If the sample statistic on which the control chart is based has a normal curve as its model, then the plotted points should exhibit three characteristics if the process is declared to be in statistical control:

1. Most of the points should be near the center line.

2. Only a few points should be near the control limits.

3. No points (or a rare one if many points are plotted) should be beyond the control limits.

The points on both charts appear to be bouncing around their respective center line in a random fashion. The charts suggest that the process is random, stable, predictable, doing its best, shows no evidence of the presence of a special cause, and appears to be affected only by common causes of variation. Since the range chart appears to be in statistical control, we may study and interpret the average chart.

Strictly speaking, the control charts in Figure 20.1 do not constitute *proof* of statistical control. They simply do not offer evidence that a special cause is present. In practice, however, we exercise the prerogative of *behaving* toward the process as if it were in statistical control. Therefore, we leave the process alone without searching for a special cause. The reasoning here is analogous to that associated with a defendant in a court of law, discussed in Section 18.4 in Chapter 18.

Note that 24 points are plotted on the charts. It was Shewhart who recommended that at least 25 points be plotted before a decision on statistical control can be reached.[2] Under certain circumstances, he maintained, when "economic minimum tolerances" must be attained, even 25 subgroups may not be enough to assert that a state of statistical control has been achieved. In fact, 10 times as many plotted points, giving no indication that a special cause is present, may be

---

[2] W. A. Shewhart, *Statistical Method from the Viewpoint of Quality Control*, p.37, Dover Publications, NY, 1986.

needed. He further states that "assignable causes of variation are almost always present in the early stages [of process control]. They may come and go, and the attainment of statistical control is a gradual process. A long sequence is required."[3]

Once statistical control has been achieved and is maintained, the normal curve model for sample averages suggests that one will look for a special cause, when none is actually present, once in a great while. For example, the area beyond both three-standard-deviation control limits is 0.0027 of the total. Thus we can expect about three points out of 1,000 to fall outside the control limits and present a *false signal* even when the process is actually in statistical control. The strategy pursued is that we can afford to make this infrequent error in judgment.

20.3 Evidence of a Process Not in Statistical Control

Several patterns or configurations of plotted points on a control chart exist that indicate the presence of a special cause. The patterns can generally be classified as *outside control limits, runs,* or *trends.* Each of these patterns is chosen because the probability is very small that it will occur when the process is supposed to be in statistical control. The question before us, then, is how many patterns should we look for when interpreting the control chart in order to conclude that the process is not in statistical control and therefore warrants a search for a special cause? If we choose too few patterns, we may miss opportunities to search for a special cause when one is present. If we choose too many patterns, we may overreact or become confused, responding constantly to the chart's apparent signals.

Let us examine several alternative sets of patterns or configurations proposed by various individuals and groups as criteria for the presence of a special cause. In the discussions that follow, we confine ourselves to examples on the $\overline{X}$-chart and assume that the range chart is in statistical control.

Set 1: Shewhart's Single Criterion

Shewhart essentially used only one criterion as evidence that the process was not in statistical control: a single plotted point outside either control limit, shown in Figure 20.2 as subgroup 2. The chart is taken from the example in Chapter 19 involving automotive aluminum parts where $\mu = 50.0$ cm, $\sigma_X = 5.0$ cm, and $n = 4$. Let us say that the sample average for subgroup 2 is 59.0 cm. Is it possible

---

[3] *Ibid.*

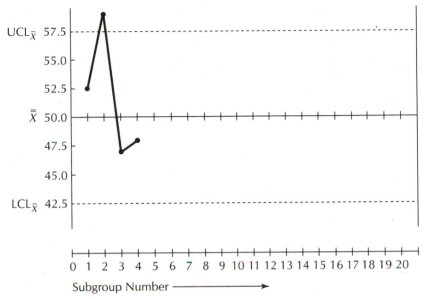

Figure 20.2. An $\overline{X}$ control chart with Shewhart's criterion: one point outside a control limit.

to get a sample average of 59.0 cm when the process is averaging 50.0 cm? The answer is *yes*. Is it probable? The answer is *no*, as long as the standard deviation for individual units is stable at 5.0 cm.

The probability that one point will exceed a control limit when the process is presumed to be in statistical control is the area under a normal curve on one side beyond three standard deviations of the mean: namely, half of 0.0027 or 0.00135. Because of the low probability, we can accept the one point outside a control limit as sufficient evidence of the existence of a special cause. We therefore declare that the process is not in statistical control and that a special cause is present. The chance that our declaration is wrong is only 0.00135, certainly a small enough risk.

Another way of looking at the $\overline{X}$-chart is to compare each plotted point with the center line to determine if there is any evidence that the process mean has shifted. As each point is plotted, we ask the question, "Is this sample average significantly different from 50.0 cm?" For three of the plotted points shown (1, 3, 4), the answer is *no*. The answer for the second point is *yes*.[4]

---

[4] Comparing a sample average with the center line is essentially performing a test of hypothesis with the center line serving as the null hypothesis. Readers interested in learning more about this statistical technique should consult an advanced statistics textbook.

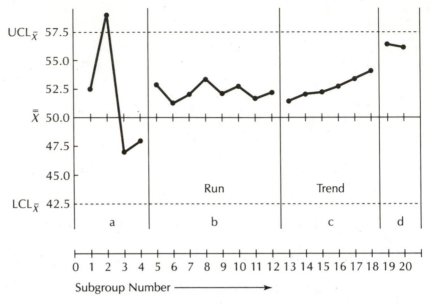

Figure 20.3. Author's four patterns that indicate the process is not in statistical control.

Set 2: The Author's Criteria of Four Patterns

Four patterns are used by the author, corresponding to a, b, c, and d in Figure 20.3, and described as follows:

a. *A single point outside either control limit* (same as Shewhart's).

b. *Eight points in a row on one side of the center line.* The probability is $(0.5)^8 = 0.0039$, and this probability is considered small enough. This pattern is called *a run*.

c. *Five or six points in a row all going in the same direction* (up or down) and all on one side of the center line. The probability is more difficult to calculate, taking into account areas under different portions of the normal curve, but it is considered small. This pattern is called a *trend*.

d. *Two points in a row just inside a control limit.* The area under a normal curve between two and three standard deviations on one side is 0.0214 (see Figure 15.8 in Chapter 15). The probability of two points in a row falling in this area is $(0.0214)^2 = 0.00046$, very small indeed.

The four patterns shown in Figure 20.3 have been selected because

1. The probability of any one of them occurring when the process is supposed to be in statistical control is very small; therefore, the pattern constitutes *strong evidence* of the existence of a special cause.

2. The patterns are very *easy to identify* on a control chart.

3. It is *easy to remember* only four patterns.

Set 3: Western Electric Rules

A widely used set of rules for judging a control chart's state of statistical control was originally published in 1956 by Western Electric Company. Known as the *Statistical Quality Control Handbook,* the 328-page hardcover book is now published and distributed (since1984) under the auspices of the American Telephone and Telegraph Company (AT&T). No changes whatsoever have been made in content.

The control chart is divided into zones corresponding to the number of standard deviations of sample statistics. The zones are created by partitioning an $\overline{X}$-chart (or any chart whose model is a normal curve) into six zones of equal width between the upper and lower control limits. There are three on each side of the center line, corresponding to one standard deviation each, and labeled A, B, C, C, B, A. Basic rules apply to each half of the control chart separately; that is, to the upper half above the center line, and to the lower half below the center line (see Figure 20.4).

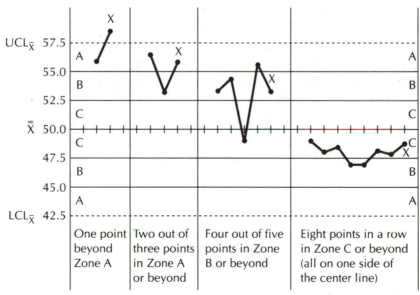

Figure 20.4. An $\overline{X}$ control chart showing zones—Western Electric rules.

Four basic patterns identify a process not in statistical control (a special cause is present), examples of which appear in Figure 20.4:

1. A *single point* outside a control limit (beyond Zone A).

2. *Two out of three points* in a row in Zone A or beyond; the odd point may be anywhere.

3. *Four out of five points* in a row in Zone B or beyond; the odd point may be anywhere.

4. *Eight points in a row* in Zone C or beyond on one side of the center line.

The last plotted point that signals the existence of a special cause has an "X" placed just above it if that point is above the center line; if the last point is below the center line, the "X" is placed just below it. Some companies using control charts prefer to draw a *circle* around the last signaling point.

Other patterns are given in the Western Electric *Handbook* that identify the presence of a special cause:

5. *Fifteen or more points in a row* all in Zone C, either above or below the center line. The points appear to hug the center line with none deviating very far from it. The pattern, although appearing to be in statistical control, is far from representing a random pattern between the control limits. It suggests *stratification*, where the sampling is done in such a way that each subgroup contains observations from two or more distributions. For example, the most common way to get this result is to sample from each operator, or from each machine, or from each line, and so on, to form the sample subgroup. The range chart under these conditions will have a large average range $\overline{R}$, spreading the control limits on the $\overline{X}$-chart and causing the points plotted on it to appear close together.

6. *Eight points in a row* on both sides of the center line but none falling in Zone C. This pattern shows a tendency to avoid the center line and suggests a *mixture*. It suggests that there are two separate distributions, from which the sample subgroups are obtained alternately, first from one distribution and then the other.

7. *Systematic or cyclical patterns,* such as high, low, high, low. Repeated patterns do not occur at random, so this condition suggests a special cause, such as variations in operator performance due to lunch periods or rest periods, worn positions in machinery, sampling in rotation from different lines, and so on.

8. *A "long" series of consecutive points* going in the same direction. This pattern identifies a *trend*. Tool wear is a common cause; change in chemical solution is another. Caution should be exercised in identifying trends because we may be fooled into thinking we see a trend where none really exists. It takes a practiced eye to identify a real trend.

Six more patterns are introduced in the *Handbook*, including "freaks," "gradual change in level," "grouping or bunching," "instability," "interaction," and "tendency of one chart to follow another." The profusion of patterns may tend to confuse the practitioner, and the authors are aware of it. They state that "it is possible to go as deeply as we wish into the interpretation of control charts." At the same time they encourage the reader to stick to the basic and simple patterns enumerated earlier.[5]

Set 4: Nelson's Eight Tests for Special Causes

Proposed by Dr. Lloyd S. Nelson and published[6] in 1984, the eight patterns are adapted from the Western Electric (now AT&T) *Statistical Quality Control Handbook* (see Figure 20.5). The eight tests (or patterns) are as follows:

1. One point beyond Zone A

2. Nine points in a row in Zone C or beyond

3. Six points in a row steadily increasing or decreasing

4. Fourteen points in a row alternating up and down

5. Two out of three points in a row in Zone A or beyond

6. Four out of five points in a row in Zone B or beyond

7. Fifteen points in a row in Zone C (above and below center line)

8. Eight points in a row on both sides of center line with none in Zone C.

Accompanying notes by Nelson in the 1984 article explain that some of the tests are used in combinations. As in the Western Electric *Handbook*, the letter "X" is placed just above (or just below) the last point signaling the existence of a

---

[5] *Statistical Quality Control Handbook*, Western Electric Company, New York, 1956, p. 31. Now distributed by American Telephone and Telegraph (AT&T) without change in content.

[6] "The Shewhart Control Chart—Tests for Special Causes," *Journal of Quality Technology*, ASQC, Milwaukee, October 1984, Vol. 16, No. 4, pp. 237–239.

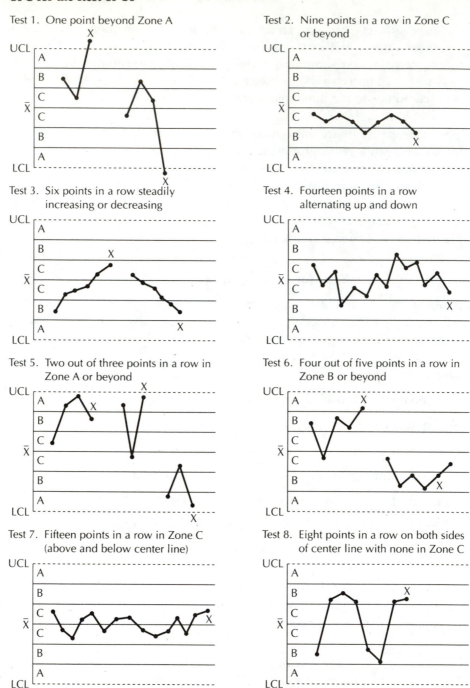

Figure 20.5. An $\overline{X}$ control chart with eight tests for special causes, by L. S. Nelson.

From *Journal of Quality Technology*, October 1984, p. 238. Reprinted with permission of ASQC, Milwaukee.

special cause. He suggests that tests 1, 2, 3, and 4 be applied by the person routinely plotting the chart; that tests 5 and 6 be added if earlier warning is desired; and that tests 7 and 8 be used for diagnostic purposes when setting up a control chart to determine if the observations within a subgroup come from more than one population (*stratification*).

In a subsequent article[7] in 1985, Nelson provides specific explanations for each of the eight tests. He cautions that the probabilities may not be accurate for a number of reasons and advises that "these tests should be viewed as simply practical rules for action rather than tests having specific probabilities associated with them." He alerts the reader to "be aware of the more common failing of imagining that something has happened when it hasn't."

Set 5: Jaehn's Zone Control Chart

In a paper[8] presented at the 41st Annual Quality Congress of ASQC in Minneapolis, Alfred H. Jaehn introduced a simplified method for determining when a variables control chart for sample statistics (that subscribe to a normal distribution, such as an $\overline{X}$-chart) signals a shift in the process and, therefore, the presence of a special cause. Using the Western Electric rules (now AT&T rules) for numbers of plotted points in runs, Jaehn assigned correspondingly weighted numerical scores to each of the zones shown in Figure 20.6. The lines bordering the zones are called *sigma limits* corresponding to the number of standard deviations for the sample statistic $\overline{X}$. The scores are assigned as follows:

Zone Location on Chart	Corresponding AT&T Zone	Score
Beyond three-sigma limit (control limit)	Beyond A	8
Between two- and three-sigma limits	A	4
Between one- and two-sigma limits	B	2
Between center line and one-sigma limit	C	1
Right on the center line		0

Instead of plotting a point precisely according to the scale used, circles are drawn in the appropriate zone with the cumulative score written inside the circle. If a data point falls on the center line, its zone score is zero. If a data point falls on one of the other zone lines, it is given the lower zone score. When the cumulative score reaches the critical number of *8 or more*, the process mean is assumed to have shifted, and "corrective action needs to be initiated to restore the process to

[7] L. S. Nelson, "Interpreting Shewhart X-bar Control Charts," *Journal of Quality Technology*, ASQC, Milwaukee, April 1985, Vol. 17, No. 2, pp. 114–116.

[8] A. H. Jaehn, "Improving QC Efficiency with Zone Control Charts," *41st ASQC Annual Quality Congress Transactions*, ASQC, Milwaukee, May 1987, pp. 558–563.

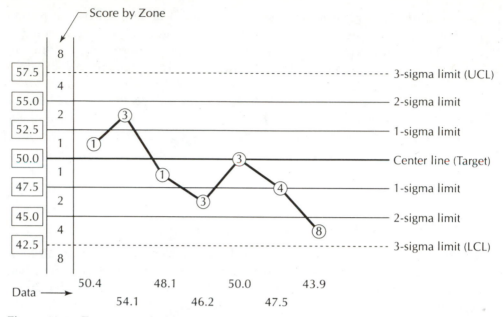

Figure 20.6. Zone control chart procedure of A. H. Jaehn showing cumulative zone scores.

its original level of performance."[9] Scoring starts over when corrective action is taken or when a point falls on the other side of the center line.

Figure 20.6 illustrates the procedure.[10] The scale shown is the same one corresponding to the $\overline{X}$-chart for the automotive aluminum parts example (Figure 20.2).

Although not discussed in the original paper, it is presumed that a variability chart, such as a range chart, is maintained and is in statistical control. The average range, of course, is needed in order to identify the sigma lines (that is, the scale) on the zone control chart. Also not discussed are the recording and retention of the original data base on which the points to be scored are based and from which additional statistical analysis can be made.

The zone control chart, according to Jaehn, is simple, fast, and easy to interpret. It has been enthusiastically received by supervisors and operators who first used it at Consolidated Papers, Inc. Operators have humorously dubbed the zone control chart the "eight-ball chart."

---

[9] *Op. cit.*, Jaehn, p. 560. Based on the paper's content, this quotation is interpreted to mean that the operator is supposed to "make a process adjustment," without trying to find the special cause responsible for the process shift in the first place. The reader's attention is directed to the discussion in Section 18.6 in Chapter 18.

[10] *Op. cit.*, Jaehn. Adapted from Figure 2 in the original paper.

Conclusion from the Several Sets of Patterns

For the purpose of keeping the number of rules few and simple, and from the author's experiences in implementation, Set 2 is recommended. It should be emphasized that none of these variables charts for sample averages should be employed without an accompanying range chart. To simplify the control chart for, say, machine operators, so that no calculations whatsoever are needed, a median chart and a range chart with special adaptation are recommended. See Chapter 22 for a description of the latter charts.

20.4 Language for Describing Control Charts: A Scenario

At the beginning of this chapter, control charts that appeared to be in statistical control were shown in Figure 20.1. The technically correct word description for these charts is "The process appears to be in statistical control."

For the subsequent charts that exhibited certain patterns of a process not in statistical control, the technically correct word description would be "The process is not in statistical control." This language, when directed toward untrained personnel not familiar with basic statistical concepts, can be very intimidating because of the word "statistical."

If a question is asked as to what is meant by "statistical control," an instructor is liable to ponder the answer to the question. He or she may realize that certain statistical concepts would have to be explained and discussed in order for the meaning of "statistical control" to be clearly understood. Some of the concepts that come to mind include random sampling, the normal curve, the central limit theorem, standard deviation, difference between population and sample, theory of control charts, and more.

Those statistical concepts are intimidating enough that one is inclined to avoid having to explain them, even to so-called technical staff. Therefore, with apologies, the instructor may correct himself or herself and declare, "I'm sorry. Forget about what I said. Let us just say that 'the process is out of control.'" The word "statistical" has disappeared—with a great sense of relief from both the instructor and the student.

In almost every book on control charts, from Shewhart to the present, and in almost all courses or seminars on the subject (except the author's), the status of a process is either "The process is in control" or "The process is out of control," with the unwritten and unstated assumption that the reader or student understands the statistical nature of such statements.

Unfortunately, taking the circuitous route of language to avoid the correct expression can result in more harm than good, because different people have different concepts of "in control" and "out of control." If one were to ask, say, a machine operator, what the stripped expressions mean, the answer undoubtedly would have to do with whether or not the process was meeting specifications, which has nothing to do with the statistical control status of the process. A process knows nothing about specifications, which are artificial constraints often unrelated to the natural behavior of a process.

The phrase "in control" implies something good about the process. The phrase "out of control" implies something bad about the process. Neither of these implications is necessarily true. A process "in control" may not be meeting specs. A process "out of control" may be meeting specs. These apparent contradictions add considerably to the confusion.

A compromise of sorts leads us out of the dilemma. Instead of using the statistically correct phrase, we can use the *center line* to describe the status of the process. Here are some examples:

- The average of the process has increased from 2.2 pounds.

- The average of the process has decreased from 50.0 cm.

- The variability of the process has increased from the average range of 12.5 concentration.

These examples should have more meaning for the student or machine operator. If, however, they result in a response such as "So what?" it would be a clue that the target or specifications or both are not understood, representing a serious management problem.

The language of statistics can very well be a study in itself.[11] See Chapter 26 for further discussion of this topic.

20.5 Responses to Control Chart Results

Responses to control charts take on two forms: (1) expressions of interpretations, conclusions, or decisions using the spoken or written word; and (2) action on the process. Let us explore the various ways each of these forms might take in order to compare them and be able to judge the most appropriate among them.

Conclusions Stated

In Figure 20.2, the $\overline{X}$-chart for automotive aluminum parts, the first two plotted points were 52.5 cm and 59.0 cm. The figure is reproduced here as Figure 20.7, together with the normal curve model for sample averages of groups of four.

---

[11] See, for example, H. Pitt, "Statistical Jargon Spoken Here!" *45th Annual Quality Congress Transactions*, ASQC, Milwaukee, May 1991, pp. 610–614.

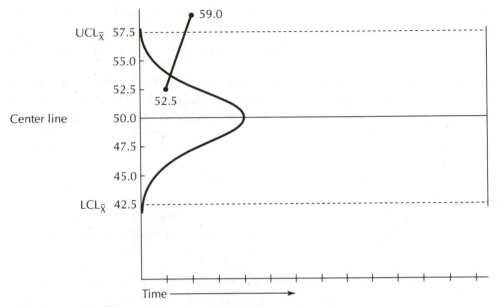

Figure 20.7. An $\overline{X}$ control chart for aluminum parts ($n = 4$).

Note where the first sample average of 52.5 cm falls in relation to the normal curve model. The sample average of 52.5 cm is not only possible but also "quite" probable from a process that averages 50.0 cm and has a standard deviation of 5.0 cm for individual units (or 2.5 cm for averages of four). *We would conclude that 52.5 cm is not significantly different from 50.0 cm and that it constitutes no evidence of a change in the process average or of the presence of a special cause.*

Now let us consider the second sample result of 59.0 cm. We have already decided in Section 20.3 that it is possible to get a sample average of 59.0 cm from a process that averages 50.0 cm, but that it is not probable as long as the standard deviation for individual units is stable at 5.0 cm. How might we state the conclusion? There may be two alternative conclusions:

1. Our tough luck! We got one of those possible but highly improbable sample results. That 59.0 could be a fluke.

2. Since the probability of such a sample result is extremely low (less than one out of a thousand), it suggests that the process mean has changed, in fact, has increased, increasing the overall process variability. The process is not in statistical control; there is a special cause present.

If you chose Alternative Conclusion 1, it means that no significance was attached to the low-probability signal.

If you chose Alternative Conclusion 2, then you chose the right one. The low probability is a signal that the process is not behaving in a random fashion. The process is no longer in statistical control, and a special cause is present that changed the mean of the process.

Note that, in order to conclude that the change occurred in the process mean and not in the process variability, the process variability must be stable, showing no increase. Therefore, a control chart for variability, such as the R-chart for sample ranges, or the S-chart for sample standard deviations, must be maintained along with the $\overline{X}$-chart.

Action Taken

Now that the decision has been reached that a change in process mean has occurred, what action should be taken? There are at least four alternative courses of action:

1. *Resample* to confirm or deny that 59.0 cm result because it could be a fluke. After all, there could be something wrong with the sample, or the measurement, or the calculation, or the recording.

2. *Adjust the process mean* down because the sample result showed that the mean has increased from 50.0 cm at which the process was supposed to be running.

3. *Look for a special cause*, such as an equipment failure or wear, a personnel factor, a change in raw material, an infraction of procedure or method, an environmental deterioration, an incorrect sampling, an error in calculation, and so on. Then correct or remove the cause.

4. *Do nothing*. It takes too much time and effort to search for the special cause. Anyway, whatever occurred will probably go away, and it won't hurt the process. We must keep the process going.

The choice of Alternative Action 1 to resample suggests that the low probability had no meaning and that a special cause is still in the process. Strange that possible reasons for the "fluke" are never proposed when the news is acceptable! See the author's article on resampling.[12]

If you chose Alternative Action 2 to adjust the process mean, be aware that this action alone does not remove the special cause that was responsible for the change in process mean. In fact, merely adjusting the process mean without investigating and doing something about the cause may actually increase the

---

[12] For a discussion of resampling and its consequences, see H. Pitt, "The Resampling Syndrome," *Quality Progress*, ASQC, Milwaukee, April 1978, Vol. 11, No. 4, pp. 27–29.

overall process variability even more. It is reasonable, prudent, and enlightened to treat the cause and not the symptom alone, which is a fundamental management philosophy reflecting the prevention of problems rather than the treatment of symptoms.

If you chose Alternative Action 4 to do nothing, an opportunity has been lost to help to improve the process. Inaction when there is clearly evidence of a special cause may suggest the existence of an attitudinal or responsibility problem or a problem about operator empowerment that would have to be addressed by management.

Alternative Action 3 is the right one. Usually the identification, correction, or removal of a special cause can be accomplished by the operator or supervisor when the cause is locally confined. After having found and removed the special cause, it would be appropriate to resample the process, allowing some time to see if the action taken had the desired effect.

Special causes may not always be identified and located. Once in a great while the special cause may be elusive, indicative of a false signal. The ability to identify the special cause also depends on the intimate familiarity of the operator and supervisor with the process. Experience of the operating staff who work with the process day after day should play a key role in identifying the special cause.

When the process is more complex, such as a sophisticated chemical or food process, technical staff may have to be called in to assist in the investigation and correction. A cooperative team effort is often needed under those circumstances to identify the real culprit known as a special cause.

20.6 Summary

Interpretation of $\overline{X}$-R charts can be considered a science or an art, but uniform rules are preferred. The R-chart should be looked at first before the $\overline{X}$-chart is studied, a procedure not always followed. If the R-chart is not in statistical control, there is no use looking at the $\overline{X}$-chart.

A process in statistical control behaves in a random fashion, is stable, predictable, doing its best, and is affected only by common causes of variation. Control charts exhibiting statistical control are not proof of statistical control; they merely offer no contradictory evidence. At least 25 points should be plotted to make a decision of statistical control, but fewer points are also practiced.

Several sets of rules or patterns are available to decide that a process is not in statistical control. They include:

1. Shewhart's single criterion of a point outside control limits.

2. The author's four patterns: single point out, run, trend, two points near a control limit.

3. Western Electric's patterns (AT&T's), described in terms of six zones. Patterns number as many as 14, but four are basic.

4. L. S. Nelson's eight tests for special causes, based on AT&T's.

5. A. H. Jaehn's zone control charts, which use numerical scores for each (AT&T) zone. The process is adjusted when the cumulative score reaches eight. The procedure is simple to use, but the R-chart may not be involved.

The correct phrases of "in statistical control" or "out of statistical control" are not often used. "In control" and "out of control" are used, implying incorrectly a connection with specs. Alternative phrases express process status in terms of the center line. Several different forms of oral and written statements of chart interpretation may be seen, as well as different actions taken; the appropriate ones are identified.

20.7 Putting It into Practice

The exercise for this chapter will consist of only one set of data, samples of moisture analysis for a chemical product. Specifications for individual analyses are 18.0% to 22.0% moisture; target is 20.0% moisture. Twenty-five subgroups of five samples each were collected. Subgroups were obtained rationally; that is, rational subgroups. Although the original data were measured to the nearest whole percent, the data recorded for the control chart were *coded*, shown on the next page. The variable of percent moisture can be considered to be normally distributed, but you may check that assumption if you need it for any part of your work.

Develop the $\overline{X}$-R control charts for this process. To work this problem methodically, provide the following information:

Sum of averages =	Sum of ranges =
X-double-bar =	R-bar =
A_2 =	D_3 =
d_2 =	D_4 =

Control Limits (show formulas)

$UCL_{\overline{X}}$ =	UCL_R =
$LCL_{\overline{X}}$ =	LCL_R =

Answer the following questions:

1. Are the ranges in statistical control?

2. Are the sample averages in statistical control?

Average and Range Chart

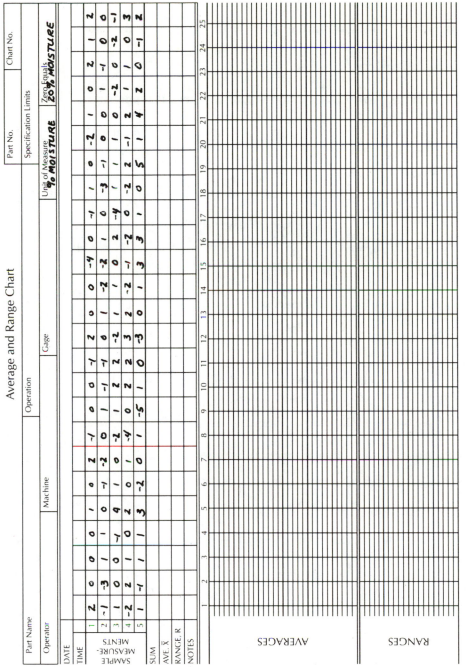

Moisture Analysis Data for Section 20.7

3. Is this a good process?

4. What can you say about the ability of this process to meet specs?

Answers to Problem

First the necessary information is provided for calculations:

Sum of averages = 5.0	Sum of ranges = 99
X-double-bar = 5.0/25 = 0.2	R-bar = 99/25 = 3.96
A_2 = 0.577	D_3 = 0
d_2 = 2.326	D_4 = 2.114

Control Limits (show formulas)

$$\text{UCL}_{\bar{X}} = \bar{\bar{X}} + A_2\bar{R} = 0.2 + 0.577(3.96)$$
$$= 0.2 + 2.28492$$
$$= 2.48$$
$$\text{LCL}_{\bar{X}} = \bar{\bar{X}} - A_2\bar{R} = 0.2 - 0.577(3.96)$$
$$= 0.2 - 2.28492$$
$$= -2.08$$

$$\text{UCL}_R = D_4\bar{R} = 2.114(3.96)$$
$$= 8.37$$
$$\text{LCL}_R = D_3\bar{R} = 0(3.96)$$
$$= 0$$

(The reader will be expected to draw the $\bar{X}$-R control charts and a histogram from the 125 individual observations.)

Answers to the following questions:

1. Are the ranges in statistical control? *Yes.*

2. Are the sample averages in statistical control? *Yes.*

3. Is this a good process?

Because both charts are in statistical control, does that make it a "good" process? *No.* The word "good" can be evaluated in terms of meeting the specifications for individual samples, 18.0% to 22.0%M. The process knows nothing about specs. A histogram drawn from the 125 observations appears reasonably symmetrical and reasonably bell-shaped, so we may draw a normal curve to represent the process. We get estimates for the process mean and process standard deviation to establish the scale for percent moisture. Then if we identify the points on the scale of percent moisture for the lower spec limit (LSL) and upper spec limit (USL), we can see how much of the process will meet specifications.

The calculated mean is the coded mean 0.2, and the decoded mean in percent moisture units is 0.2 + 20, or 20.2%M.

What do we use for standard deviation? Since the process is considered to be in statistical control, we may use $\overline{R}/d_2$ as the estimate for the process standard deviation:

$$\overline{R}/d_2 = 3.96/2.326 = 1.7024935, \text{ or } 1.7\%M.$$

(Why is no decoding required for $\overline{R}/d_2$?)

The normal curve representing the process looks like this:

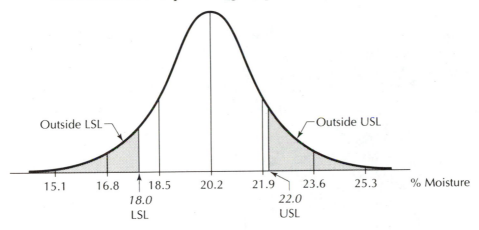

4. What can you say about the ability of this process to meet specs?

   It is obvious that a large proportion of the process will not meet the specifications 18.0% to 22.0%M. Since the process appears to be in statistical control, it is doing its best. If what we see is its best, then it is *not capable* of meeting specs.

   (Out of curiosity, if you were to calculate S, the sample standard deviation, which is another estimate of the process standard deviation obtained by using all 125 observations, how would it compare with $\overline{R}/d_2$? Try it.)

CHAPTER 21

Attributes Control Charts

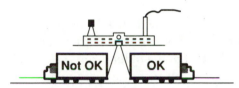

Characteristics of product that are measurable make use of variables control charts such as those discussed in Chapter 20. When characteristics are not or cannot be measured but are described in attribute terms, another class of control charts is appropriate.

An attribute is a characteristic that is either present or not present, such as meeting specifications (which, by the way, can sometimes be determined by measuring); the working of a switch; the presence of a contaminant; the proper fit in an assembly; edibility of a food product; or meeting a gauge criterion. Attributes may be desirable or undesirable.

Although an attribute may be expressed in positive terms, such as meeting specifications, it is customary to express it in negative terms. The popular word *defect* is a single attribute characteristic that is undesirable from some point of view; for example, a package tear or leak, broken weld, discoloration, or not meeting a particular specification. The popular word *defective* (technically a *defective unit* or *item* or *area*) is a unit or item or area that has at least one defect; for example, a tool that doesn't work properly, a car that does not start, a bolt of cloth with discoloration and tears, a service that the customer doesn't like, or not meeting specifications in some respect.

---

* R. Lederer, *Anguished English*, p. 81, Dell Publishing, New York, 1989.

21.1 Alternative Language: Nonconformity and Nonconforming

The words *defect* and *defective* are generally quite clear to the quality practitioner who identifies them with failure to conform to technical requirements, such as not meeting specifications. But popular meanings of these words tend to connote something more menacing, such as being unfit for use or even hazardous to life, even though such fears may be technically unfounded. The result has been some misunderstandings during litigation in liability cases in courts of law.

To avoid the confusion, the word *defect* is now generally called *nonconformity*, while the word *defective* is now generally called *nonconforming* or *nonconforming unit*.[1] While defect and defective generally are ascribed to usage requirements, *nonconformance* usually, but not always, has to do with meeting specification requirements. Sometimes, of course, specification requirements coincide with customer-usage requirements.

A quality statistic such as *proportion defective* (or fraction defective) is now generally called *proportion nonconforming* (or fraction nonconforming). Similarly, *percent defective* is now *percent nonconforming*. Note that the older terms, *defect* and *defective*, despite the attempts to keep them out of our technical vocabulary, are still widely used by many quality practitioners, manufacturing and engineering personnel, managers, legal professionals, and the general public.

To summarize the alternative language:

Defect becomes *Nonconformity*

Defective becomes *Nonconforming or Nonconforming unit*

Proportion defective becomes *Proportion nonconforming*

Fraction defective becomes *Fraction nonconforming*

Percent defective becomes *Percent nonconforming*

For the remainder of this book we will use the words *nonconformity* and *nonconforming* and occasionally add the words *defect* and *defective* to serve as reminders and to help in the understanding.

Before control charts for attributes are introduced and discussed, it is important to understand that, in any application, a nonconformity and a nonconforming unit must be thoroughly defined and described, using every medium of

---

[1] These terms were officially approved and adopted in the 1980s by the American National Standards Institute (ANSI) and the American Society for Quality Control (ASQC). Other attribute terms in use include *blemish* and *imperfection*. Additional discussion can be found in (a) ANSI/ASQC Standard A1-1987, *Definitions, Symbols, Formulas and Tables for Control Charts,* and (b) *Glossary and Tables for Statistical Quality Control,* 2nd ed., ASQC, Milwaukee, 1983.

communication available, in order to achieve a uniform and consistent recognition of the attribute. The inability to identify attributes uniformly and consistently can easily result in statistical results that may cause the wrong action to be taken on a process or a lot. How many times have you heard "Anyone can see that this product is defective," and not everyone agrees? In particular, nonconformities and nonconforming units whose detection depends on the human senses of sight, sound, feel, smell, or taste require special care in definition and description. For example, how does one describe natural blemishes on agricultural products such as potatoes, lettuce, apples, or bananas that are to be detected uniformly by packing personnel or factory process inspectors? When is a metallic crack not a metallic crack?

In addition to creating well-written descriptions, diagrams, photographs, movies, physical examples, and other visual aids, providing adequate and periodic testing and training of those who inspect is called for in order to maintain the uniformity of evaluation.

21.2 Types of Attributes Control Charts

Let us start by comparing attributes control charts with variables control charts. There is little specific information in declaring an item of product to be nonconforming or containing a nonconformity. There is more information in declaring an item to be, say, 14.5 cm long. Accordingly, we'll find that larger sample sizes are usually needed for attributes charts in order to be able to detect shifts in process levels or to detect the presence of a special cause. But attributes charts are appealing because they are simple to understand and usually require very little or no calculations; only basic counting is needed.

The attributes charts can be divided into two types: nonconforming units (defectives) and nonconformities (defects). Each of these can be divided into two variations. Thus we have four basic attributes charts:

Charts for Nonconforming Units (Defectives)

1. p-chart for proportion or fraction or percent nonconforming

2. np-chart for number of nonconforming units per sample subgroup

Charts for Nonconformities (Defects)

3. c-chart for number of nonconformities per sample subgroup

4. u-chart (or $\bar{c}$-chart) for average number of nonconformities per unit.

The names of these control charts also describe the sample statistic that is actually plotted on the respective chart. The plotted points for the p-chart and the

u-chart (or $\overline{c}$-chart) require a calculation, while those for the np-chart and the c-chart require only a count.

21.3 p-Chart for Proportion Nonconforming, Fixed Sample Size

For a p-chart, a sample of n units or items is inspected. The number of units in the sample that are nonconforming, say, r, is divided by n to obtain the *proportion nonconforming r/n* that is plotted, usually expressed as a decimal fraction. If this ratio is multiplied by 100, then $(r/n) \times 100$ is the *percent nonconforming* that would be plotted on the chart, often easier for some people to understand. Therefore, the scale used is up to the user.

The sample size n does not have to be constant from subgroup to subgroup, but the control chart is easier to manage if the sample sizes are constant. When the sample size varies from subgroup to subgroup, the statistic r/n is not comparable from one subgroup to another, technically requiring separate control limits for each sample subgroup. The next section describes how to respond to this situation.

The *standard deviation of the sample statistic p*, proportion of nonconforming units, is

$$\sqrt{\frac{p'(1 - p')}{n}}$$

where p' (*p-prime*) is the true value of the proportion of nonconforming units in the process. Since p' is usually unknown, an estimate of p' is obtained by averaging several sample proportions, resulting in $\overline{p}$ (*p-bar*). (The exact procedure for averaging a group of proportions will be illustrated by example.) Then the *trial control limits for proportion nonconforming* become

$$\text{Control limits for the } p\text{-chart: } \overline{p} \pm 3\sqrt{\frac{\overline{p}(1 - \overline{p})}{n}}. \qquad (21.1)$$

If, instead of plotting the proportion nonconforming, we wish to calculate, record, and plot the *percent* of nonconforming units because it may be easier to understand, change *1* in formula (21.1) to *100*. Then the control limits formula (21.1) for *percent nonconforming* becomes

$$\overline{p} \pm 3\sqrt{\frac{\overline{p}(100 - \overline{p})}{n}}.$$

Now let us look at some data to see how formula (21.1) is used. In a plant manufacturing a small specialty gear used in the assembly of a farm implement, an optical comparator is used to check gears sampled periodically throughout the day for compliance to a dimensional specification. A cumulative sample of exactly 100 gears is obtained daily, checked on the comparator, and the number not meeting specs is recorded. The results for 26 consecutive workdays in the month of June (one shift operating, including Saturdays; no Sundays) are shown in Table 21.1.

Table 21.1.   Daily Inspections of Gears, Constant Sample Size

Date	Day of Week	Number Inspected n	Number not Meeting Specs r	Proportion not Meeting Specs p
June 1	M	100	3	.03
2	T	100	5	.05
3	W	100	12	.12
4	Th	100	10	.10
5	F	100	6	.06
6	Sa	100	5	.05
8	M	100	7	.07
9	T	100	3	.03
10	W	100	2	.02
11	Th	100	9	.09
12	F	100	3	.03
13	Sa	100	8	.08
15	M	100	10	.10
16	T	100	8	.08
17	W	100	5	.05
18	Th	100	7	.07
19	F	100	3	.03
20	Sa	100	11	.11
22	M	100	7	.07
23	T	100	13	.13
24	W	100	7	.07
25	Th	100	6	.06
26	F	100	6	.06
27	Sa	100	8	.08
29	M	100	11	.11
30	T	100	5	.05
Totals		2,600	169	$\bar{p} = 0.065$

First we determine $\bar{p}$. Because the sample sizes each day are the same, we could simply add the last column, divide by the 26 days, and find $\bar{p}$, the mean of proportion nonconforming. If the sample sizes varied each day, however, we would not find $\bar{p}$ in this manner; instead we would have to add up the total number not meeting specs, which is 169, and divide by the total inspected, 2,600. It is a good habit, however, to find $\bar{p}$ using the latter method, even though the daily sample sizes are the same; the outcome is not changed. (Reader: You should verify this.) Thus,

$$\bar{p} = \frac{\text{Total number not meeting specs}}{\text{Total number inspected}} = \frac{169}{2,600} = 0.065.$$

Substituting this result in formula (21.1), the control limits for the p-chart are

$$0.065 \pm 3\sqrt{\frac{0.065(1 - 0.065)}{100}} = 0.065 \pm 3\sqrt{0.00060775}$$
$$= 0.065 \pm 0.073957758.$$

After adding and subtracting the last term from 0.065, rounding the answer to three decimal places, and converting to percent, we get

$$\text{UCL}_p = 0.138957758 = 13.9\%$$
$$\text{Center line} = \bar{p} = 0.065 = 6.5\%$$
$$\text{LCL}_p = -0.008957758 \text{ or } 0\%.$$

Note that the lower control limit for p calculates to a negative number. Since proportion nonconforming cannot be negative, we label the lower control limit as zero. These control limits say that, if the process is averaging 6.5% nonconforming and is in statistical control, almost all random samples of 100 gears from this process may run anywhere from 0% to 13% nonconforming. (If a sample of 100 gears had 14 nonconforming gears, the result would be outside the upper control limit.)

There seems to be quite a bit of expected variability in percent nonconforming in sample sizes of 100, even when the percent nonconforming in the process remains stable at 6.5%. The reason, mentioned earlier and worth repeating, is that there is not much information in simply declaring a unit of product as conforming or not conforming; so large sample sizes are needed to detect changes in the process, and relatively large variability in sample results is to be expected. If we had recorded the actual measurement of the dimension under study, we would deal with variables data, use $\overline{X}$-R charts, and require much smaller sample sizes. The moral is to obtain variables data whenever possible.

What does the control chart for p, the proportion of gears not meeting specs in June, look like? See Figure 21.1. Note that the vertical scale is in *percent* nonconforming instead of proportion nonconforming because most people can understand percent more readily.

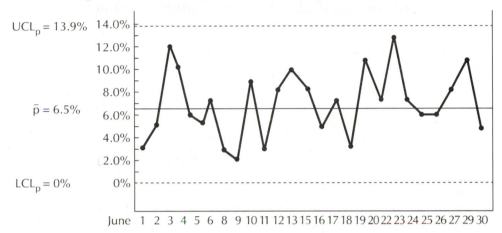

Figure 21.1. p-chart for percent nonconforming with constant sample size 100 (see Table 21.1).

The p-chart does not show any points outside the upper control limit, and there do not appear to be any identifiable runs or trends. We would have to conclude that there is *no evidence* that the process is *not* in statistical control. We will, therefore, behave toward this process of gears as if it were in statistical control; that is, devoid of special causes. Action: Do nothing, except that . . .

When management was presented with these results, the air among middle managers and department heads was charged with portentous electricity. It had been management's perception that, if product had been shipped, it met all specs. Management was not aware that six to seven percent of the gears did not meet specs. It also happened that the customer for these gears, a manufacturer of farm implements, was using the gear in a combine, an expensive and multitask piece of farm equipment used in harvesting crops. The gear was found to be responsible for some breakdowns that were very costly to the manufacturer of the combines, to say nothing about the downtime on the farms where a limited window of time for harvesting was available. Complaints were increasing.

Management demanded that the percent of gears nonconforming be reduced to zero immediately. When told by engineering, manufacturing, and quality control that the process was in statistical control and could not perform better without making some basic changes in the process, management approved expenditures for designed experiments that ultimately focused on the alloy used in the gears as the culprit. Meanwhile management compromised, "Cut the percent out of specs in half!" As an interim procedure, gears were inspected 100% to cull out those that were out of specs. Additional experiments were conducted to select the optimum alloy. The percent nonconforming was appreciably reduced, and the p-chart for the gears was implemented with a *standard* of $p' = 0.025$ that the process was capable of yielding. A select team was assigned the ongoing task of seeking further improvements in the process. Complaints decreased dramatically.

21.4 p-Chart for Proportion Nonconforming, Varying Sample Size

How is the p-chart developed when the sample sizes vary? Before management became aware of the extent to which these gears did not meet specs, a sampling system was installed that automatically deposited a small spot of fast-drying red paint on every 50th gear produced. The objective was to get sample sizes related to the amount of production, leading to a somewhat better picture of process yield, and to remove any bias in the selection of gears for inspection. The gears identified as such constituted the sample for the day. Since the number of gears produced varied from day to day, the sample size also varied daily. Inspection results for 20 production days in July are shown in Table 21.2.

Because the sample sizes vary from day to day, it would not make sense to add the last column and divide by 20 days to determine $\bar{p}$, the estimate of p'. We must, instead, add up the total number of gears not meeting specs (111) and divide by the total number inspected (1,734). Thus,

$$\bar{p} = \frac{\text{Total number not meeting specs}}{\text{Toal number inspected}} = \frac{111}{1734} = 0.06401384 = 0.0640.$$

From formula (21.1) for the p-chart control limits, we can see that the control limits are affected by the sample size n in the denominator of a fraction:

$$\bar{p} \pm 3\sqrt{\frac{\bar{p}(1 - \bar{p})}{n}}.$$

The last term in the formula, to be added to and subtracted from $\bar{p}$, will move the control limits farther apart when sample sizes are smaller (because the fraction becomes larger) and bring the control limits closer together when sample sizes are larger (because the fraction becomes smaller). From Table 21.2 we can see that daily sample sizes for July ran from a low of 60 on July 18 to a high of 109 on July 24. Thus, to be technically correct, each day's sample should require separate calculations for the control limits by substituting the actual sample size in formula (21.1).

The control limits for each day are shown in the last two columns of Table 21.3. For each day the lower control limit for p calculated as a negative number. Since p is meaningless when it is negative, the lower control limit is shown as zero, while the upper control limits vary depending on the sample

Table 21.2. Daily Inspections of Gears, Varying Sample Size

Date	Day of Week	Number Inspected n	Number not Meeting Specs r	Proportion not Meeting Specs p
July 1	W	87	6	.069
2	Th	96	9	.094
6	M	85	2	.024
7	T	101	7	.069
8	W	82	7	.085
9	Th	85	3	.035
10	F	95	9	.095
11	Sa	84	8	.095
13	M	89	6	.067
14	T	92	6	.065
15	W	73	5	.068
16	Th	97	4	.041
17	F	94	6	.064
18	Sa	60	2	.033
20	M	72	5	.069
21	T	96	6	.063
22	W	79	5	.063
23	Th	80	2	.025
24	F	109	10	.092
25	Sa	78	3	.038
	Totals	1,734	111	$\bar{p} = 0.0640$

size. For the smaller sample sizes the upper control limit is higher, and for larger sample sizes the upper control limit is lower, reflecting the important fact that the variability of p depends on the sample size. The corresponding p-chart for gears produced in July, with upper control limits varying according to sample size, is shown in Figure 21.2.

As was noted in the June control chart (Figure 21.1), the July control chart (Figure 21.2) has no points outside the various upper control limits, and no runs or trends are apparent. The process for July also appears to be in statistical control.

Table 21.3. *p*-Chart Control Limits, Varying Sample Size

Date	Day of Week	Number Inspected n	Number not Meeting Specs r	Proportion not Meeting Specs p	$\bar{p} \pm 3 \sqrt{\dfrac{\bar{p}(1-\bar{p})}{n}}$ LCL$_p$	UCL$_p$
			Daily Inspection of Gears		Control Limits	
July 1	W	87	6	.069	0	.1427
2	Th	96	9	.094	0	.1389
6	M	85	2	.024	0	.1436
7	T	101	7	.069	0	.1371
8	W	82	7	.085	0	.1451
9	Th	85	3	.035	0	.1436
10	F	95	9	.095	0	.1393
11	Sa	84	8	.095	0	.1441
13	M	89	6	.067	0	.1418
14	T	92	6	.065	0	.1406
15	W	73	5	.068	0	.1499
16	Th	97	4	.041	0	.1386
17	F	94	6	.064	0	.1397
18	Sa	60	2	.033	0	.1588
20	M	72	5	.069	0	.1505
21	T	96	6	.063	0	.1389
22	W	79	5	.063	0	.1466
23	Th	80	2	.025	0	.1461
24	F	109	10	.092	0	.1343
25	Sa	78	3	.038	0	.1471
Totals		1,734	111	$\bar{p} = 0.0640$		

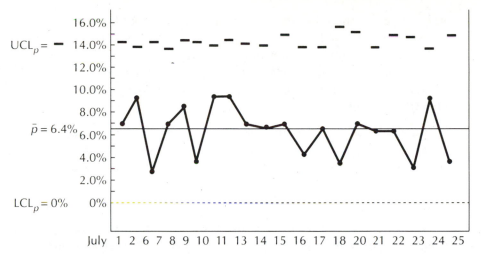

Figure 21.2. p-chart for percent nonconforming with varying sample size (see Table 21.3).

Having to calculate the upper control limit each time samples are drawn from the process seems to entail quite a bit of work.[2] In addition, the picture of the control chart seems to be a little confusing (even "unattractive" according to some authors) with different upper control limits, especially to the novice practitioner. However, several alternative procedures could be used when sample sizes vary:

1. We could calculate the *average* of the 20 sample sizes $\bar{n}$ and use that in the formula to determine common control limits for *all* samples. In the case of the July data, the average sample size $\bar{n} = 1734/20 = 86.7$ gears. Then the common control limits would be

$$\bar{p} \pm 3\sqrt{\frac{\bar{p}(1-\bar{p})}{\bar{n}}} = 0.064 \pm 3\sqrt{\frac{0.064(1-0.064)}{86.7}} = 0.064 \pm 0.079$$
$$= 0 \text{ and } 0.143$$

Fortunately, in our example, the common upper control limit of 14.3% did not change the control chart picture at all and would have been suitable for all 20 subgroups. The difficulty with this alternative, however, is that, for

---

[2] The calculation can be simplified somewhat by calculating $3\sqrt{\bar{p}(1-\bar{p})}$, which is the same figure for each day, and then dividing by $\sqrt{n}$, which varies from day to day, before adding to $\bar{p}$.

other processes and other sets of data, some points could possibly be outside the common control limit erroneously, and some points could possibly be just inside the common control limit erroneously. We could, therefore, be making some wrong decisions about the process. A rule of thumb to follow here is to *use the average sample size $\bar{n}$ if the sample sizes do not differ from each other by more than 25%.*

2. A second alternative procedure is to use the average sample size $\bar{n}$ as above, but if a point appears close to the common control limit, either outside or inside the limit, calculate the exact control limit for that point using the actual sample size.

3. A third alternative procedure is to group the sample sizes according to magnitude, calculate the midpoint (or mean or median) sample size for each group, and use that to determine control limits for samples in each group. For example, from Table 21.3 for July, we might group the sample sizes as follows and use the midpoint sample size as shown:

Sample Size Group	Midpoint Sample Size $\bar{n}$
60 to 69	64.5
70 to 79	74.5
80 to 89	84.5
90 to 99	94.5
100 to 109	104.5

We end up having to calculate five sets of control limits instead of 20. The bad news is that the control chart is likely to look like Figure 21.2 anyway with apparently different upper control limits for each sample, since the sample sizes do not occur together as we grouped them.

If an SPC computer software program is available, the exact control limits for any sample size can be calculated automatically, avoiding questionable situations that can arise by using any of these alternative methods. Another desirable feature of good computer software is its ability to alert the user to the presence of an assignable or special cause when certain nonrandom patterns appear. (See Chapter 25 for additional discussion of computer software for SPC.)

Regardless of whether one uses manual or automated methods for calculating control limits for p-charts, obtaining fixed sample sizes affords some real benefits in simplicity, ease of calculation and interpretation, as well as an uncluttered appearance of the control limits on the control chart. Even if process lot sizes do vary, fixed sample sizes provide the same level of reliable information for all process lots.

21.5 *np*-Chart for Number of Nonconforming Units

For an *np*-chart, a fixed sample size of *n* units is inspected. The total number of nonconforming units in the sample, say, *r*, is noted and counted. As long as the sample size *n* is constant, only the *number of nonconforming units r* needs to be plotted on the chart. *An np-chart requires a constant sample size.* Since no calculations for the sample statistic *r* are required, this type of chart is easy to record and maintain.

If we multiply the proportion nonconforming *p* by the sample size *n*, we get the *number of nonconforming units in the sample, np*, the basis for the *np*-chart. For example, if the sample size *n* = 50, and the proportion nonconforming is *p* = 0.06, then the number of nonconforming units in the sample is *np* = 50(0.06) = 3.

The standard deviation of the sample statistic *np* is obtained by multiplying the standard deviation for *p* by *n*, giving us

$$\sqrt{np'(1 - p')}.$$

If the true proportion nonconforming *p'* is unknown (the usual case), an estimate of *p'* comes from averaging several sample proportions to obtain $\overline{p}$, as we did for the *p*-chart. Multiplying $\overline{p}$ by *n* gives us $n\overline{p}$, the average number of nonconforming units in samples of size *n*. Then the trial control limits for the *np*-chart become

$$\text{Control limits for the } np\text{-chart: } n\overline{p} \pm 3\sqrt{n\overline{p}(1 - \overline{p})}. \qquad (21.2)$$

This formula *requires that the sample size n be constant;* otherwise the number of nonconforming units is not comparable from subgroup to subgroup. The *np*-chart does not require any calculation for each point plotted; we merely count the number of nonconforming units in the (constant) sample size *n*. Therefore, it is a very easy chart to maintain. The *np*-chart has the same appearance as the corresponding *p*-chart with constant sample size.

For example, referring to Table 21.1, showing 100 gears sampled daily in June, the middle column, *r* = *np*, shows the number of gears not meeting specs in each sample of 100 gears. If the number nonconforming were plotted on a control chart, the chart would look like Figure 21.3. One can see that Figure 21.3 for *number* nonconforming in samples of 100 gears is identical in appearance to that of Figure 21.1 for *percent* nonconforming in samples of 100 gears. In comparing the *np*-chart and the *p*-chart, the *p*-chart, especially one expressed in percent nonconforming, seems to be easier for some people to understand.

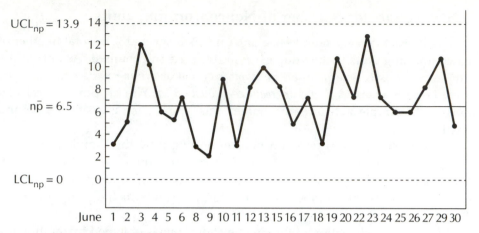

Figure 21.3. *np*-chart for number nonconforming with constant sample size 100 (see Table 21.1).

21.6 *c*-Chart for Number of Nonconformities

For a *c*-chart, a sample subgroup is inspected. The sample subgroup can consist of only one item; a group of items; or an "area of opportunity," such as a fixed glass area, integrated circuit board, a table top of fixed surface area, or a fixed weight or volume. The total number of nonconformities, *c*, found in the sample subgroup is noted and counted. As long as the sample subgroup size is constant, only the *number of nonconformities c* is plotted on the chart. *A c-chart requires a constant sample subgroup size.* Since no calculations are required for the sample statistic *c*, this type of chart is easy to record and maintain.

The standard deviation of the sample statistic *c* is the square root of the average number of nonconformities *c'* (*c-prime*) for a constant sample size of *n* units taken from the process:

$$\sqrt{c'}.$$

If *c'* is unknown (the usual case) or is not prescribed as a standard, an estimate of *c'* comes from averaging numbers of nonconformities from several samples, each of which contains the same number of units, obtaining $\overline{c}$ (*c-bar*). Then the trial control limits for the *c*-chart become

Control limits for the *c*-chart: $\overline{c} \pm 3\sqrt{\overline{c}}$.   (21.3)

Formula (21.3) *requires that the number of units in each sample n be constant*; otherwise the number of nonconformities is not comparable from sample to sample.

Of all the control charts available to us, the c-chart control limits are the easiest to calculate because of the simple formula. The constant sample size n may consist of only one item, such as one gear or one can or one sheet of film or one automobile hood; or it may consist of several items, such as four gears or a six-pack of cans or three sheets of film or two hoods, each group of which is treated as a single sample. The *total* number of nonconformities in each sample of n units is what is recorded and plotted on the chart.

Let us look at some data. Table 21.4 shows the number of nonconformities in each of 25 automobile hoods inspected.

Table 21.4. Number of Nonconformities (defects) in 25 Automobile Hoods

Hood Number	Number of Nonconformities
1	2
2	3
3	1
4	0
5	2
6	6
7	1
8	1
9	0
10	2
11	2
12	3
13	7
14	1
15	2
16	0
17	2
18	1
19	3
20	1
21	0
22	0
23	3
24	2
25	2
Total	47

These hoods are made of reinforced fiberglass, are produced in a Midwestern plant, and are carefully packed and shipped to an assembly plant in another state where they are installed in a popular American sports car. The sports car at one time enjoyed a large market share, but imports of foreign sports cars had eroded the market share.

Management was determined to recover much of the market share and made some engineering improvements in the sports car. Management was also concerned about the cosmetic appearance of the cars and decided to focus on the hood because of its high visibility to the typically upbeat driver in the cockpit.

Stringent in-process specifications were set for the hoods. Inspectors were carefully selected and specially trained to detect nonconformities. The list of nonconformities included tiny scratches, bubbled paint, unpainted spots, discoloration, streaks, holes, several other nonconformities, and a category called "miscellaneous" (a popular catchall for unexpected nonconformities). Specially lighted inspection stations were set up to provide maximum advantage to the inspectors. Hoods that passed inspection (an arbitrary number of nonconformities) were carefully packed and shipped to an assembly plant. Hoods that did not pass were either rejected and sold as scrap or they were reworked. During a period of about a year the high reject rate of the hoods, although gradually declining, represented a serious erosion in profits. Production-floor people facetiously dubbed the operation "Robbin' Hood."

Management persisted. Sometimes the trained inspectors saw nonconformities that production people did not see, and heated conversations ensued, resulting in bad feelings. Management, however, always sided with the inspectors because of the company's strong position to recapture its market share.

When the recovery program was started, a run chart without control limits was started to record the incidence of nonconformities. Beginning at an average of about 10 nonconformities per hood, the figure was gradually reduced to about 2 after the installation of new molding machines and the updating of some paint equipment. At this point management decided to set a *standard* (meaning average) of 1.5 nonconformities per hood and directed that appropriate control charts with control limits be used. Table 21.4 shows the results for 25 hoods during the visual-inspection period. Meanwhile new automated methods for detecting surface flaws by means of laser technology were being designed to replace the controversial visual inspection at a much later date.

To prepare for the c-chart, we calculate $\bar{c}$, the average number of nonconformities per hood, for the center line:

$$\bar{c} = 47/25 = 1.88 \text{ nonconformities per hood.}$$

Then the trial control limits from formula (21.3) are

$$1.88 \pm 3\sqrt{1.88} = 1.88 \pm 4.11 = (-2.23 \text{ and } 5.99) = (0 \text{ and } 5.99).$$

Since c cannot be negative, the lower control limit is set at zero. The readings for hoods 6 and 13 are above the upper control limit, suggesting that special causes were responsible. Such special causes may include differences among inspectors if more than one took part in the inspection of the 25 hoods; inconsistency of an inspector in identifying the nonconformities; an error in counting and/or recording; or a special cause that is due to the manufacturing process itself.

Recall that management had set a standard c' of 1.50 nonconformities per hood. It was assumed that this standard was achievable since the process level had already reached fewer than 2 nonconformities. It was felt that undesirable special causes were still present, and if they could be identified and removed, the level could be brought down to the standard. If it is found, however, that no more special causes were present—that the process was in statistical control—management was willing to make more changes in the process, changes to be determined by designed experiments. Accordingly, the control limits for the c-chart should be

$$1.50 \pm 3\sqrt{1.50} = 1.50 \pm 3.67 = (-2.17 \text{ and } 5.17) = (0 \text{ and } 5.17).$$

The control chart with the center line at $c' = 1.50$ is shown in Figure 21.4.

If the special cause or causes responsible for the high readings of hoods 6 and 13 could be identified and economically removed from the process, then we may exclude those two points from the c-chart in Figure 21.4 and *recalculate the center line and control limits for future process control*. The remaining 23 hoods will then

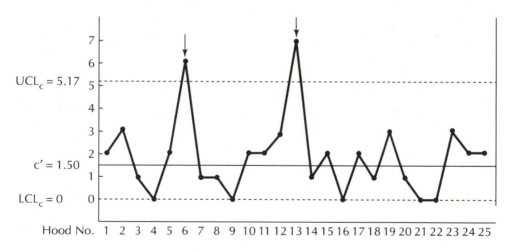

Figure 21.4. c-chart for number of nonconformities in 25 automobile hoods, standard center line (see Table 21.4).

have a total of 34 nonconformities (47 minus 13) for an average of 34/23 = 1.48 nonconformities per hood, which meets management's requirement for this process. The new upper control limit becomes 5.13. (Reader: You should verify this.) The process appears to be in statistical control.

If the special cause for hoods 6 and 13 cannot be identified, the points for those hoods and the control limits remain on the control chart, at least until further investigation identifies the special cause. Caution should be exercised in discarding data indiscriminately without a thorough engineering investigation as to their causes.

21.7 u-Chart for Average Number of Nonconformities per Unit

For a u-chart (or $\bar{c}$-chart), a sample subgroup of n items or areas of opportunity is inspected. The total number of nonconformities in the sample subgroup, c, is divided by n to obtain the *average number of nonconformities per item* $c/n = u$ that is plotted. For this reason the u-chart is sometimes called a $\bar{c}$-chart, suggesting an average, which it is. The sample size n may vary from one subgroup to another, but the sample statistic, average nonconformities per item, is comparable from one subgroup to another since the reporting unit is the same (per box, per car, per foot, per square meter, etc.). Separate control limits may need to be calculated for each sample subgroup. For example, cars can be compared on the basis of a *common reporting unit* such as breakdowns-per-mile, regardless of the number of cars in a sample or the number of miles driven for each car. If the sample subgroup size n is constant, this chart reverts to a c-chart.

The standard deviation of the sample statistic u is the square root of the overall average number of nonconformities per reporting unit in the process:

$$\sqrt{u'/n}.$$

If u' is unknown (the usual case) or is not prescribed as a standard, an estimate of u' comes from adding all the nonconformities from several samples and dividing by the total number of units, obtaining $\bar{u}$. Then the trial control limits for the u-chart become

$$\text{Control limits for the } u\text{-chart: } \bar{u} \pm 3\sqrt{\bar{u}/n}. \tag{21.4}$$

The best way to illustrate a u-chart is through example. We borrow an example from the *ASTM Manual on Quality Control of Materials*.[3]

---

[3] A publication of the American Society for Testing and Materials, 1967, Philadelphia. Adapted from an example on p. 87.

Twenty lots contain varying amounts of a complex machine. Random samples of varying numbers of machines from each lot are examined for compliance to several requirements, including dimensional, physical, and finish. A nonconformity is any requirement that is not met, and it is possible for machines to contain more than one nonconformity. All nonconformities are counted. The recording document identifies the different nonconformities for further analysis, interpretation, and corrective action. The reporting unit is a single machine. Table 21.5 shows the number of machines n sampled from each lot, the total number of nonconformities c in each sample, and the nonconformities per unit u in each sample.

Table 21.5. Number of Nonconformities per Unit in Samples from 20 Lots of Complex Machines*

Lot No.	Sample Size (Number of Machines) n	Total Nonconformities in Sample c	Nonconformities per Unit (Machine) $u = c/n$
1	20	72	3.60
2	20	38	1.90
3	40	76	1.90
4	25	35	1.40
5	25	62	2.48
6	25	81	3.24
7	40	97	2.42
8	40	78	1.95
9	40	103	2.58
10	40	56	1.40
11	25	47	1.88
12	25	55	2.20
13	25	49	1.96
14	25	62	2.48
15	25	71	2.84
16	20	47	2.35
17	20	41	2.05
18	20	52	2.60
19	40	128	3.20
20	40	84	2.10
Totals	580	1,334	$\bar{u} = 2.30$

*Adapted from *ASTM Manual on Quality Control of Materials*, Special Technical Publication 15-C, p. 87, 11th printing (September 1967); published by the American Society for Testing and Materials, Philadelphia.

In preparation for the control chart, calculate first the overall average number of nonconformities per unit $\bar{u}$ by using the column totals. This will give us the *center line* for the control chart:

$\bar{u}$ = 1334/580 = 2.30 average number of nonconformities per machine.

As for the control limits, note from Table 21.5 that three different sample sizes occur: 20, 25, and 40. We will have to determine control limits for each of the three different sample sizes, as follows.

For n = 20, the control limits are $2.30 \pm 3\sqrt{2.30/20} = 2.30 \pm 1.02$:

LCL_u = 1.28 and UCL_u = 3.32.

We can see from Table 21.5 that u for lot number 1 is above the UCL_u.

For n = 25, the control limits are $2.30 \pm 3\sqrt{2.30/25} = 2.30 \pm 0.91$;

LCL_u = 1.39 and UCL_u = 3.21.

We can see from Table 21.5 that u for lot number 6 is above the UCL_u.

For n = 40, the control limits are $2.30 \pm 3\sqrt{2.30/40} = 2.30 \pm 0.72$;

LCL_u = 1.58 and UCL_u = 3.02.

We can see from Table 21.5 that u for lot number 10 is below the LCL_u, and u for lot number 19 is above the UCL_u.

We conclude that this process is not in statistical control and that special causes are present. Let us develop the control chart that visually confirms our analysis of the data (see Figure 21.5). The center line is at 2.30. The three different sample sizes are distributed among the lots as follows:

n = 20: Lots 1, 2, 16, 17, 18

n = 25: Lots 4, 5, 6, 11, 12, 13, 14, 15

n = 40: Lots 3, 7, 8, 9, 10, 19, 20

The three different sets of control limits for the three different sample sizes can be seen in Figure 21.5. Note that the control limits for the smaller sample sizes are further apart; those for the larger sample sizes are closer together. These observations are consistent with the size of the standard deviations: the smaller the sample size, the larger the standard deviation.

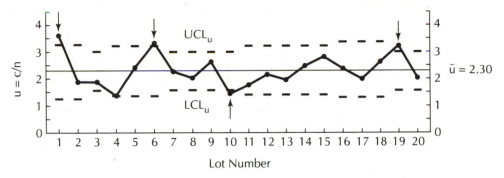

Figure 21.5. u-chart for average number of nonconformities per unit (see Table 21.5).

The four points that are outside control limits are highlighted by the arrows on the chart. Let us assume that the special causes responsible for the four points can be identified. Are we interested in trying to remove those special causes from the process? The answer is yes for the three points outside the *upper* control limit, since they represent an undesirable special cause responsible for an *increase* in nonconformities. But the special cause responsible for point number 10 outside the *lower* control limit represents a *desirable* special cause responsible for a *decrease* in nonconformities. Therefore that special cause, if it can be identified, ought to be retained in the process because it represents improvement.

We would declare that sample number 10 is evidence that the average number of nonconformities per machine has decreased from 2.30.

21.8 The Directional Aspect of Attributes and Range Charts

All of the attributes charts and the range chart have a unique feature often overlooked by quality practitioners. When a point is outside the *upper control limit*, or when a run or trend of points occurs *above the center line*, it is considered evidence of the process not being in statistical control and signals the presence of a special cause. It means that, in the case of the attributes charts, there is evidence that the incidence of nonconformances has *increased* and is therefore a sign of a *bad* situation. In the case of a range chart (or any chart that tracks variability), it means that the variability has *increased* and is therefore also a sign of a *bad* situation. The special cause should be sought out and removed from the process.

Suppose, however, that a point is outside the *lower control limit*, if there is one, or a run or trend of points occurs *below the center line*. Either of these situations is also evidence of the process not being in statistical control and signals the presence of a special cause. However, it means that, in the case of the attributes charts, there is evidence that the incidence of nonconformances has *decreased* and is therefore a sign of a *good* situation. We saw this situation occur in the example in the previous section. In the case of a range chart (or any chart that tracks variability), it means that the variability has *decreased* and is therefore also a sign of a *good* situation. However, the person responsible for the control chart may mistakenly conclude that "the process is out of control" because the patterns follow the standard rules of being "out of control."

But what about the special cause in the latter situation? The special cause responsible for an improvement in the process should be sought out and *retained as a permanent part of the process.* It could be some unexplained modification made by an operator, an accidental change in the raw material used, an unplanned adjustment in a parameter of the process, or any one of a myriad of other desirable special causes.

The inappropriate use of the phrase "out of control" automatically triggers a negative response and discourages a search for a cause that might create genuine improvement. That is why a different language response is encouraged, as mentioned earlier in this chapter.

Referring to the center line of the process helps to choose the right words when interpreting the control chart patterns. One can say such things as "The percent nonconforming has increased" (bad), or "The variability has increased" (bad), or "The number of nonconformities has decreased" (good), or "The variability has decreased" (good). The attributes and range charts uniquely describe good and bad situations in the process without having to refer to any specifications.

The directional aspect of attributes and range charts is depicted in Figure 21.6.

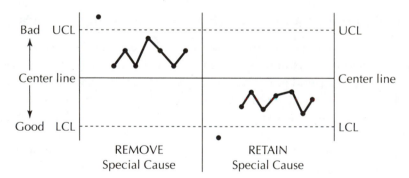

Figure 21.6. Directional aspect of attributes and range charts.

21.9 Additional Comments on Attributes Control Charts

Two statistical distributions, the *binomial* and the *Poisson*, play an important part in control chart theory, and their applications will be mentioned briefly without exploring them further.

The control limits for the two charts for nonconforming units (defectives), the p-chart and the np-chart, are based on the *binomial distribution,* which presumes that p', the true proportion of the attribute in the process, remains constant in the process as we take one sample subgroup after another. In other words, the process is considered to be large enough so that sampling does not change the true proportion p'. The binomial distribution enables us to determine the standard deviation for the sample statistics p and np. The word *binomial* has the prefix *bi* meaning two, which corresponds to the two possible attribute conditions of a unit of product: Either the attribute is present or it is not.

The binomial distribution approaches the normal distribution as the sample size n increases and as the proportion p' approaches 1/2. In practice, these constraints do not appear to be too stringent or prohibitive in using the Shewhart model formula for control limits. When either p' or $1-p'$ (or their estimates) is very small, the sample size n must be large enough so that the control limit formula is a valid "normal approximation to the binomial." A statistical guideline to use is for the product of multiplying p' (or $1-p'$) by n should be greater than or equal to 5; that is, $np' \geq 5$ or $n(1-p') \geq 5$. Some statisticians use 4 as the limit criterion effectively.

The control limits for the two charts for nonconformities (defects), the c-chart and the u-chart, are based on the *Poisson distribution*. The Poisson distribution enables us to determine the standard deviation for the sample statistics c and u (the latter with the help also of the normal distribution). The Poisson distribution is used when the areas of opportunity for nonconformities are large and the incidence of nonconformities is small. Examples include dents or scratches on a new automobile, poor solder joints on an integrated circuit board, tears or smudges on new clothing, and tipeograficle errors in a book such as this.

The degree of severity or seriousness of nonconformities (defects) can be designated by categories or classes. For example, a typical designation might include the following with definitions that are appropriate to a particular product:

Class 1: *Critical*—May cause death, severe injury, or catastrophic economic loss.

Class 2: *Major*—May cause product failure or system deterioration.

Class 3: *Minor*—May result in minor dysfunction or unfavorable cosmetic appearance.

The Critical category is sometimes further divided into *Very Serious* and *Serious* together with their appropriate definitions. A fourth class, *Incidental*, may be used for the least serious nonconformities. Separate control charts are often assigned to each class. Assigning an arbitrary numerical score to each degree of severity can lead to a quasi-objective statistical analysis of such data, especially helpful if the evaluation is subjective.

21.10 Which Control Chart Should You Use?

Now that the basic control charts have been discussed, both variables and attributes, some comparisons can be made among them. In comparing variables with attributes charts, it should be obvious that variables charts contain more information, as was noted previously. Accordingly, also noted earlier, larger sample sizes are needed for attributes charts in order to be able to detect shifts in process levels or to detect the presence of a special cause.

In comparing nonconforming charts (p and np) with nonconformity charts (c and u), the latter charts certainly have more information. When recording data for a c-chart or a u-chart, frequencies of occurrences for specific nonconformities should be recorded as a means of identifying any special causes.

Thus, among the charts discussed so far, the p-chart and the np-chart provide the *least* bit of information about a process, while the $\overline{X}$-R charts provide the *most* amount of information.

It is useful to set forth a logical selection procedure that determines which control chart should be used under various conditions. An excellent example of a selection procedure in the form of a flow chart appears in the *Fundamental Statistical Process Control Reference Manual*, a publication of the Automotive Industry Action Group (AIAG).[4] The flow chart is reproduced here as Figure 21.7.

Some variations of the basic control charts, mentioned in the flow chart, have not yet been discussed here. They include the following:

• The median chart

• The individuals chart with moving range (X and mR)

• The average and standard deviation charts ($\overline{X}$ and S)

---

[4] The flow chart, entitled "Selection Procedure for the Use of the Control Charts Described in This Manual," appears as Appendix C on page 139 of the manual. The *Reference Manual*, published in 1991, is a unique cooperative effort prepared by the quality and supplier assessment staffs at Chrysler, Ford, and General Motors, working under the auspices of the Automotive Division of the American Society for Quality Control (ASQC) Supplier Quality Requirements Task Force, in collaboration with the Automotive Industry Action Group (AIAG). Copies can be ordered from AIAG at 26200 Lahser Road, Suite 200, Southfield, Michigan 48034, or by calling (313) 358-3570.

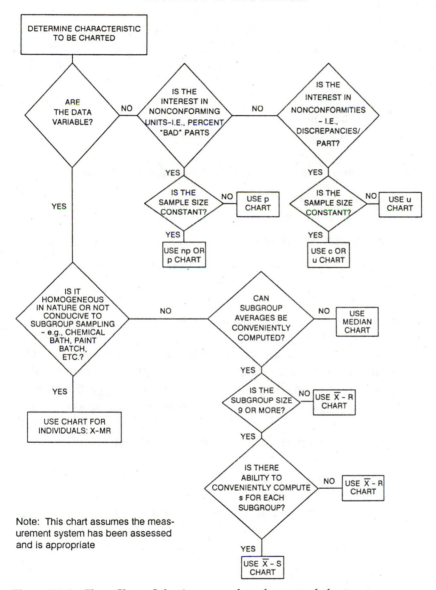

Selection Procedure for the Use of the Control Charts Described in This Manual

Note: This chart assumes the measurement system has been assessed and is appropriate

Figure 21.7. Flow Chart: Selection procedure for control charts.

Reprinted with permission, Automotive Industry Action Group (AIAG), Southfield, Michigan.

These charts, plus the moving-average and moving-range charts ($m\overline{X}$ and mR), the cumulative-sum chart ($CuSum$), and the exponentially weighted moving-average chart ($EWMA$) are discussed in Chapter 22.[5]

21.11 Summary

Attributes are characteristics, usually negative, that are either present or not present. A defect is an attribute that is undesirable from some point of view. A defective is a unit of product that has at least one defect. Officially, although not universally practiced, *nonconformity* replaces the word defect; *nonconforming unit* replaces the word defective. Attribute terms must be thoroughly defined and described, using every available medium that appeals to the human senses.

The four basic attributes charts:

1. p-chart for proportion or fraction or percent nonconforming (defective)

2. np-chart for number of nonconforming units (defectives) per sample subgroup

3. c-chart for number of nonconformities (defects) per sample subgroup

4. u-chart (or $\overline{c}$-chart) for average number of nonconformities (defects) per reporting unit.

All of these charts require counting, but the p-chart and the u-chart also require a calculation for the sample statistic. The sample statistics are p, np, c, and u. The sample size may vary for the p-chart and the u-chart, but it must be constant for the np-chart and the c-chart. The use of constant sample sizes simplifies the work of interpreting and managing control charts, particularly the p-chart. The control limits follow the model for the Shewhart charts:

Parameter $\pm 3 \times$ (Standard deviation of sample statistic).

The center lines for the control charts may be determined from actual sample data providing averages of the sample statistics; or they may be established in advance, called *standards*. The standard deviations for the p-chart and np-chart are based on the binomial distribution, while those for the c-chart and u-chart are based on the Poisson distribution. The formulas for the control limits, using sample data, are shown in Table 21.6.

---

[5] Another excellent flow chart, perhaps more elaborate and detailed than the AIAG one, appears in D. J. Wheeler, *Understanding Statistical Process Control*, 2nd ed., 1992, SPC Press, Knoxville, Tennessee.

Table 21.6. Formulas for Control Limits, Attributes Charts

Kind of Chart	Detects Changes in Process	Control Limits Formula*	Remarks
p-chart	Proportion or fraction of items or units nonconforming (defective).	$\bar{p} \pm 3\sqrt{\dfrac{\bar{p}(1-\bar{p})}{n}}$	$\bar{p}$ is the average proportion or fraction nonconforming (defective). If this is to be expressed as a percentage, replace $(1-\bar{p})$ with $(100-\bar{p})$. Sample sizes n may vary. If they vary by 25% or less, use average sample size $\bar{n}$ and recalculate for any point close to a control limit. If they vary by more than 25%, calculate control limits separately for each sample size.
np-chart	Number of nonconforming items or units (defectives) in samples of size n.	$n\bar{p} \pm 3\sqrt{n\bar{p}(1-\bar{p})}$	$n\bar{p}$ is the average number of items or units in the sample of size n that are nonconforming (defective). Sample size n must be constant from sample to sample.
c-chart	Number of nonconformities (defects) in samples of size n.	$\bar{c} \pm 3\sqrt{\bar{c}}$	$\bar{c}$ is the average number of nonconformities (defects) in the sample. Sample size n may consist of one unit, several units, or an area, but the sample size for counting nonconformities must be constant from sample to sample.
u-chart (or $\bar{c}$-chart)	Average number of nonconformities (defects) per item or unit.	$\bar{u} \pm 3\sqrt{\bar{u}/n}$	$\bar{u}$ (or $\bar{c}$) is the average number of nonconformities (defects) per item or unit. Sample size n may vary, but all samples have a common reporting unit and therefore can be compared. Control limits are usually calculated separately for each sample size.

*If lower control limit calculates to be negative, set it at zero. In order for the control limits for the p-chart and the np-chart to be valid normal approximations to the binomial, $n\bar{p}$ or $n(1-\bar{p})$ must be 4 or greater.

The attributes charts and the range chart have a unique directional aspect. When any of these control charts shows evidence of being out of statistical control on the high side, the situation is considered bad, and we are inclined, appropriately, to find the special cause responsible and to remove it from the process. But if there is evidence of being out of statistical control on the low side, the situation is considered good, and the special cause should be identified and retained, if at all possible, as a permanent part of the process. The process should not be called simply "out of control" in either case because this unfortunate phrase implies only something bad with the process. An effective way to avoid such misinterpretation is to make a statement involving the center line of the control chart: it has either increased or decreased, suggesting different courses of action.

Nonconformities sometimes can be usefully classified according to degrees of seriousness, such as critical, major, and minor. Separate control charts are usually assigned to each class.

The decision as to which control chart to use was systematically determined from a simple flow chart.

21.12 Putting It into Practice

1. There must be some attributes in your company or organization that describe characteristics of your product or service that are either desirable or undesirable. Check the descriptions, definitions, or specifications for one or more of these attributes to see if they are clear, concise, and completely understood by involved personnel. If their meaning is not entirely clear, is there any evidence of incorrect decisions resulting from it? What can (should) you do to clarify the meaning and understanding?

2. Consider the following statement:

   We wish to start a percentage control chart (p-chart), set the center line at a standard of 1.4% nonconforming units, and take constant sample sizes of 200 units so that we don't have to calculate the control limits frequently.

   Is there anything wrong with this statement?

3. A morning newspaper publishes every day except Sunday. The number of separate sections is usually four, with abbreviated versions on Saturday. Each section is headed by a different associate editor. The various sections are identified as follows:

   A—International, national, state, and local news, feature articles, and editorial page.

   B—Sports. Want ads, also contained in this section, are excluded from the study.

C—Special features, including cartoons, and radio and TV listings.

D—Business news. Stock quotations are excluded from the study.

E—Food section only on Thursdays.

In a recent 6-month period the number of letters from readers complaining about typos (typographical errors) has increased to the point where the managing editor decided to do something about it; the quality image of the newspaper was at stake. It was apparent that spell-checkers in computer software being used by reporters did not catch even simple spelling typos (for example, *planing* for *planning* and *their* for *there* were not caught). The managing editor ordered that a special study be conducted: The first galley proof for each section is to be inspected every day for a week (six days) by the editor in charge of the section, and typo data are to be recorded. Typos to be recorded include spelling, omissions, punctuation, grammar, syntax, misplaced lines, and so on. Results are shown in the following table.

Day of Week	Section	Number of Pages	Number of Typos
Monday	A	18	15
	B	16	28
	C	6	3
	D	10	12
Tuesday	A	18	14
	B	16	27
	C	6	5
	D	10	12
Wednesday	A	16	14
	B	16	16
	C	6	5
	D	12	2
Thursday	A	16	14
	B	14	19
	C	6	2
	D	12	13
	E	6	8
Friday	A	18	13
	B	16	20
	C	6	3
	D	10	8
Saturday	A	12	6
	B	8	9
	C	4	3
	D	8	6

Draw the appropriate attributes control chart that includes all sections, and answer the following five questions:

(a). Which attribute chart should be used, and why?

(b). What is the reporting unit?

(c). If the sample size varies, what do you do about control limits?

(d). Is the process in statistical control?

(e). If so, what can be done to reduce the average number of typos occurring? If not, how can one identify the special cause or causes?

Answers to Problems 2 and 3

2. The statement is flawed because a basic condition for the use of the p-chart is not satisfied: Multiplying n and p' gives $200(0.014) = 2.8$, which is less than the minimum of 4 in order for the control limits to be valid normal approximations to the binomial distribution. This means that the probabilities associated with the control limits will not be valid, and wrong decisions about the process are likely to occur. The solution here is to increase the sample size to a minimum of $n = 4/p' = 4/0.014 = 285.7$ or 286.

3. (a). *Which attribute chart should be used, and why?*
   We are dealing here, obviously, with nonconformities (typos), and this suggests either the c-chart or the u-chart. Since the sample size (number of pages) varies from sampling to sampling, the u-chart is the attributes chart to use. The control limits are, therefore, $u \pm 3\sqrt{\overline{u}/n}$.

   (b). *What is the reporting unit?*
   If we label the column "Number of Pages" as n for sample size, and "Number of Typos" as c for number of nonconformities, then another column can be added, "Typos per Page," labeled $c/n = u$. The reporting unit is "Typos per Page." See the expanded table, next page.

   (c). *If the sample size varies, what do you do about control limits?*
   The number of pages n varies from sample to sample, and theoretically we should calculate separate control limits for each sample. But let us use an average sample size $\overline{n}$, apply common control limits to all samples, and recalculate control limits only for those sample results that come close to either common control limit or that are questionable.

   To find the center line $\overline{u}$, total the columns c and n and divide the totals to obtain

Day of Week	Section	Number of Pages n	Number of Typos c	Typos per Page $c/n = u$	Actual UCL_u
Monday	A	18	15	.833	
	→B	16	28	1.750	1.707 ←
	C	6	3	.500	
	D	10	12	1.200	
Tuesday	A	18	14	.778	
	B	16	27	1.688	
	C	6	5	.833	
	D	10	12	1.200	
Wednesday	A	16	14	.875	
	B	16	16	1.357	
	C	6	5	.333	
	D	12	2	.167	
Thursday	A	16	14	.875	
	B	14	19	1.357	
	C	6	2	.333	
	D	12	13	1.083	
	E	6	8	1.333	
Friday	A	18	13	.722	
	B	16	20	1.250	
	C	6	3	.500	
	D	10	8	.800	
Saturday	A	12	6	.500	
	B	8	9	1.125	
	C	4	3	.750	
	D	8	6	.750	
	Totals	286	277	$\bar{u} = 0.969$	

$\bar{u}$ = (Total number of typos)/(Total number of pages)

= 277/286 = 0.969 average typos per page.

Accordingly, since there are 25 samplings altogether,

$\bar{n}$ = 286/25 = 11.44 average pages per sampling.

Substituting these two values in the control limit formula to get the common control limits,

$0.969 \pm 3\sqrt{0.969/11.44} = 0.969 \pm 0.873$.

$LCL_u = 0.096$ and $UCL_u = 1.842$.

From the expanded table, the value of u for Monday, section B, 1.750, seems close to the common upper control limit of 1.842, and so the exact UCL is recalculated for that sample with $n = 16$ as follows:

$$UCL = 0.969 + 3\sqrt{0.969/16} = 0.969 + 0.738 = 1.707,$$

as shown in the expanded table. Thus Monday's result for section B exceeds the upper control limit.

We next draw the control chart. The data points for the last section of one day and the first section of the next day are not connected because there is no implied continuity, making a search for runs or trends meaningless. The data points are essentially drawn by day, although all the data are combined to determine control limits.

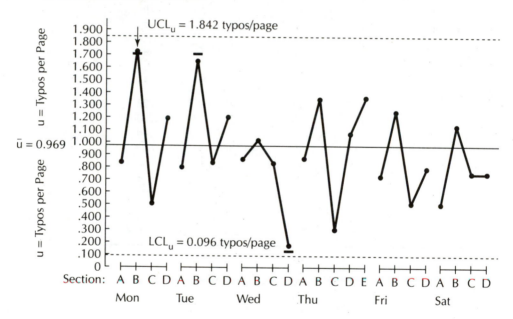

(d). *Is the process in statistical control?*
No. The calculation of the exact upper control limit for Monday, section B, shows that the reading is actually beyond it. Tuesday, section B, also seems a little high but it is not beyond the exact upper control limit, which is the same as that for Monday, section B, since both have the same sample size. Wednesday, section D, has a low reading, 0.167, close to the common lower control limit, but the exact calculation for the lower control limit is 0.117, and the point is inside it.

(e). *If so, what can be done to reduce the average number of typos occurring?
If not, how can one identify the special cause or causes?*

The first part of this question is not relevant at this time. The special cause is identified with section B, the sports department. In fact, a closer look at the original data table or the control chart shows that the sports department (section B) has consistently reported more typos per page than any other department. We can conjecture that one of the reasons why Monday's result was out of statistical control is that the reporting of sports results on Monday follows the usual heavy activity in sports during the previous weekend, and there is added pressure on the staff to get their reports in on time. But that conjecture does not explain the consistently high typos in section B for the rest of the week. Furthermore, we must remember that each section had a different "inspector" (an associate editor in charge), and we might be seeing important differences among the editors in their ability to detect typos.

(Despite these conjectures, the real epilogue to this study revealed that most of the typos in section B were attributable to one sports writer, a former professional football player. He was frequently heard in conversations and on radio and television using phrases such as "he don't . . . ," "between he and I . . . ," and "I could care less." His knowledge of sports, however, was extensive. Ultimately he was "retired" to a different assignment on the newspaper staff.

That did not solve the problem of the general level of typos. The average typos per page, exclusive of section B, was 0.790, still too high as far as the managing editor was concerned. In cooperation with a local university, he organized a program for all of his writing and editing staff to attend weekly classes over a period of several months to improve English language and writing, all on paid company time. The staff generally was positive in its response to this initiative. The managing editor continued the editing studies, of the kind described here, every eight weeks or so. The quality of the newspaper improved during that time, and the number of complaints from readers declined steadily. The following year two state awards were won for excellence in reporting.)

If you take something apart
and put it back together enough times,
eventually you will have two of them.

—Rap's Law of Inanimate Reproduction*

CHAPTER 22

Other Kinds of Charts

S ince the publication of Shewhart's classic book in 1931, several different kinds of control charts have been introduced to fit special situations or to improve on the old charts. All of them have the same objective: to improve the quality of processes, products, and services. The development and popularity of these charts have been influenced by the availability of calculators and computers, electronic tools that reduce much of the manual calculations and graphing that usually characterize control charts. Research into innovative adaptations of Shewhart charts and development of new charts are continuing processes involving academicians and quality practitioners. Some of the more familiar variations will be introduced in this chapter. They include:

1. The average and standard deviation charts ($\overline{X}$-S)

2. The individual and moving-range charts (X-mR)

3. The moving-average and moving-range charts ($m\overline{X}$-mR)

4. The median chart ($\tilde{X}$)[1]

5. A brief discussion of the cumulative-sum chart (CuSum) and the exponentially weighted moving-average chart (EWMA).

---

* A. Bloch, *Murphy's Law, Book Three*, p. 43, Price/Stern/Sloan, Los Angeles, 1982.

[1] The wiggle above the letter X is called a *tilde*.

22.1 Average and Standard Deviation Charts ($\overline{X}$-S Charts)

The standard deviation S-chart can be used in place of the range R-chart, especially when the subgroup sample size exceeds, say, 10. The sample standard deviation S, defined and discussed in Chapters 11 and 12, is actually a somewhat better measure of variability than the range R because it uses all of the data in the sample subgroup instead of just the minimum and maximum values. As sample size increases, the range becomes less reliable.

The standard deviation chart has seen little use because of the complexity of calculating the sample standard deviation S and the difficulty in understanding its concept. But the advent of calculators and computers and improvement in training methods have enhanced the popularity of the standard deviation chart. When the S-chart is used, the $\overline{X}$-chart that goes along with it has its control limits determined by the average of the subgroup standard deviations $\overline{S}$ (S-bar) instead of the average of the subgroup ranges $\overline{R}$. It is assumed that the subgroup sample size is constant. The general model for the control limits for the S-chart is the same as that for all Shewhart charts and is repeated here once more:

Parameter $\pm$ 3 x (Standard deviation of sample statistic).

The *trial control limits* for both the $\overline{X}$-chart and the S-chart, based on current or past data, are determined from a new set of constants (A_3, B_3, and B_4) as follows:

Control limits for the $\overline{X}$-chart: $\overline{\overline{X}} \pm A_3\overline{S}$
(Center Line = $\overline{\overline{X}}$) $\hspace{2cm}$ (22.1)

Control limits for the S-chart: $\mathrm{LCL}_s = B_3\overline{S}$ and $\mathrm{UCL}_s = B_4\overline{S}$
(Center Line = $\overline{S}$) $\hspace{2cm}$ (22.2)

The constants depend on the subgroup sample size and are obtained from Table 2 of the Appendix. Table 22.1 is an abbreviated version of Table 2.

The rules for interpreting the $\overline{X}$-S control charts are the same as those for interpreting the $\overline{X}$-R control charts. The S-chart, like the R-chart, should be interpreted *first* before the $\overline{X}$-chart is interpreted.

Let us develop both the $\overline{X}$-R control charts and the $\overline{X}$-S control charts from the same set of data so that the two sets of charts can be compared. We will use the data in Table 6.1, screw-cap torques in inch-pounds. The $\overline{X}$-R control charts were developed from these data in Problem 4 at the end of Chapter 19. Table 22.2 shows these same data with S calculated for each subgroup. The reader should confirm some of the S readings.

Table 22.1. Shortened Table* of Factors for $\overline{X}$-S Charts Using $\overline{S}$

Subgroup Sample Size n	Factors for			
	Sample Averages A_3	Sample Standard Deviations B_3	B_4	Process Standard Deviation c_4
2	2.659	0	3.267	0.7979
3	1.954	0	2.568	0.8862
4	1.628	0	2.266	0.9213
5	1.427	0	2.089	0.9400
6	1.287	0.030	1.970	0.9515
7	1.182	0.118	1.882	0.9594
8	1.099	0.185	1.815	0.9650
9	1.032	0.239	1.761	0.9693
10	0.975	0.284	1.716	0.9727

Formulas for Computing Control Limits

Average Chart

$$UCL_{\overline{X}} = \overline{\overline{X}} + A_3\overline{S}$$
$$LCL_{\overline{X}} = \overline{\overline{X}} - A_3\overline{S}$$

Standard Deviation Chart

$$UCL_S = B_4\overline{S}$$
$$LCL_S = B_3\overline{S}$$

Estimate of Process Standard Deviation
(Valid Only if Process is in Statistical Control)

$$\frac{\overline{S}}{c_4} = \text{Estimate of } \sigma_x$$

*For complete table, see Table 2 of the Appendix.

The answers to Problem 4 in Chapter 19 showed that the R-chart was in statistical control, but the $\overline{X}$-chart was not. The $\overline{X}$ for sample 13 was below the lower control limit (17.19), and that for sample 20 was above the upper control limit (23.71). The process represented by these data is not in statistical control.

Using the sample standard deviations S and the formulas in Table 22.1 for the $\overline{X}$-S charts, we find the following results.

For the S-chart, the center line is $\overline{S}$ = 45.8/20 = 2.29. The control limits for the S-chart are

$$LCL_s = B_3\overline{S} = 0 \text{ and } UCL_s = B_4\overline{S} = 2.089(2.29) = 4.8.$$

Table 22.2. Screw-Cap Torques in Inch-Pounds, Showing $\overline{X}$, R, and S for Each Subgroup of Five

Subgroup No.	Readings					$\overline{X}$	R	S
1	21	21	19	20	24	21.0	5	1.9
2	23	20	26	21	23	22.6	6	2.3
3	21	23	17	21	19	20.2	6	2.3
4	21	22	25	24	20	22.4	5	2.1
5	17	18	20	20	20	19.0	3	1.4
6	18	15	20	21	20	18.8	6	2.4
7	23	23	23	18	22	21.8	5	2.2
8	23	20	14	21	20	19.6	9	3.4
9	25	24	24	19	19	22.2	6	2.9
10	21	21	25	15	19	20.2	10	3.6
11	15	21	19	20	21	19.2	6	2.5
12	17	15	16	20	19	17.4	5	2.1
13	13	17	17	19	17	16.6	6	2.2
14	22	20	18	21	16	19.4	6	2.4
15	17	21	18	21	21	19.6	4	1.9
16	17	20	21	19	21	19.6	4	1.7
17	19	21	22	17	20	19.8	5	1.9
18	21	18	20	23	22	20.8	5	1.9
19	19	26	20	24	28	23.4	9	3.8
20	26	26	25	26	24	25.4	2	0.9
					Totals	409.0	113	45.8

There are no S readings outside these control limits. We conclude that the S-chart is in statistical control and may proceed to interpret the $\overline{X}$-chart.

For the $\overline{X}$-chart, the center line is $\overline{\overline{X}} = 409.0/20 = 20.45$, the same result, of course, that was obtained in Problem 4 in Chapter 19. The control limits for the $\overline{X}$-chart, using $\overline{S}$ and referring to the factors in Table 22.1, are

$$\overline{\overline{X}} \pm A_3\overline{S} = 20.45 \pm 1.427(2.29) = 20.45 \pm 3.27,$$

from which we get

$$\text{LCL}_{\overline{X}} = 20.45 - 3.27 = 17.18 \text{ (compare with 17.19 in Problem 4),}$$
$$\text{UCL}_{\overline{X}} = 20.45 + 3.27 = 23.72 \text{ (compare with 23.71 in Problem 4).}$$

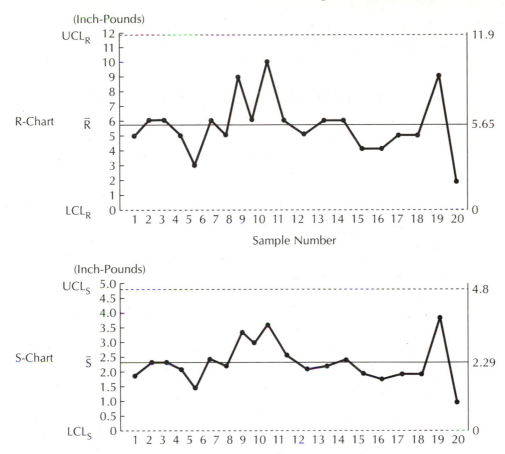

Figure 22.1. Comparison of R-chart and S-chart (see Table 22.2).

Again we find that $\overline{X} = 16.6$ for sample 13 is below the $\text{LCL}_{\overline{X}}$ and that $\overline{X} = 25.4$ for sample 20 is above the $\text{UCL}_{\overline{X}}$. Thus the results of the two sets of charts, the $\overline{X}$-R charts and the $\overline{X}$-S charts, are the same.

The physical comparison between the two sets of charts requires comparing only the R-chart and the S-chart, since the $\overline{X}$-chart will be the same for both procedures. Figure 22.1 shows the two charts. It is evident, even to the casual observer, that the two charts exhibit strikingly similar patterns.

The moral of this statistical discussion is the following:

1. The R-chart and the S-chart are quite similar in appearance and interpretation when the subgroup sample size is, say, 10 or smaller. As the sample size increases, however, the range becomes less reliable.

2. The R-chart is preferred over the S-chart for sample sizes of, say, 10 or smaller (the usual industrial sample size), because the range is easier to calculate and to understand.

22.2 Individuals and Moving-Range Charts (X-mR Charts)

Sometimes it is difficult or uneconomical to gather samples of two or more at the same time to form a rational subgroup. The sample may be very costly; or it takes considerable time for the sample to be analyzed in a laboratory; or the difficulty in getting the sample prevents us from taking more than one at a time. Under these conditions, a sample size of one may be the only alternative, and yet control charts can still be used. These are the individuals and moving-range charts, designated X-mR charts.

The individual reading X from a sample of one becomes the sample statistic. A measure of variablity, the moving range mR, is obtained by using two or more *consecutive* readings of X to form a subgroup of constant size. As each new reading is obtained, the oldest one is removed from the subgroup, and a new range is calculated. Thus each reading is used more than once in determining the range. This is what we mean by *moving range*.

Table 22.3 shows 23 consecutive daily analyses of blood glucose (blood sugar) in milligrams per deciliter (mg/dL) from a hospitalized patient. Since it is not reasonable to draw more than one drop of blood at a time for the blood-glucose analysis in order to form a subgroup, the sample size is only one. The moving range of *two* successive readings provided the measure of variability. Note that we end up with 23 individual readings but only 22 ranges and that each reading, except the first and last, is used twice in determining the ranges. The first 9 readings were obtained in the hospital while the patient was recovering from major surgery. The remaining 14 readings were obtained after the patient was discharged and recovering at her home; she went to the same hospital every day to have a blood sample drawn.[2]

The control limits for the moving-range chart use the same formulas as those for the regular range chart:

$$\text{UCL}_R = D_4\overline{R} \text{ and } \text{LCL}_R = D_3\overline{R}.$$

The control limits for the individuals chart follow the same model as that for the usual Shewhart control charts, symmetrical around the average:

Parameter $\pm$ 3 $\times$ (Standard deviation of sample statistic).

---

[2] After this study was completed, the patient was diagnosed as adult-onset diabetic. She was given a portable monitor with which she checked her blood-glucose levels at home, sometimes every few hours. She started insulin injections, using rules for adjustment of dosages prescribed by her physician.

Table 22.3. Daily Readings of Blood-Glucose with Moving Ranges for $n = 2$

Day	Blood-Glucose mg/dL	Moving Range mR
1	110	—
2	142	32
3	131	11
4	159	28
5	187	28
6	189	2
7	242	53
8	174	68
9	153	21
10	166	13
11	140	26
12	152	12
13	170	18
14	161	9
15	69	92
16	143	64
17	154	21
18	129	25
19	107	22
20	158	51
21	192	34
22	178	14
23	156	22
Totals	3,562	666

The control limits for individuals, using current or past data, are based on an estimate of the process average provided by the average of the individual readings $\overline{X}$, and on an estimate of the standard deviation for individuals provided by the average of the moving ranges $m\overline{R}$ divided by the factor d_2. (Recall Chapter 13 on estimating standard deviation from ranges, and see Table 2 of the Appendix.) Thus the control limits for individuals are

$$\overline{X} \pm 3 \times (\text{Est. of } \sigma_x \text{ using moving-range average}) \text{ or}$$
$$\overline{X} \pm 3(m\overline{R}/d_2). \tag{22.3}$$

The first moving range, 32, in Table 22.3 is determined after the second reading. Note that each reading is involved in determining *two* consecutive

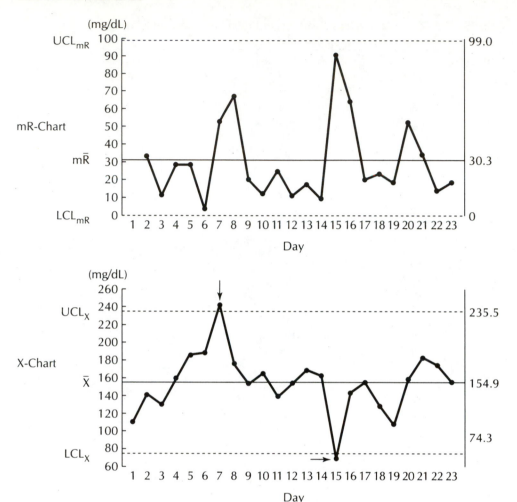

Figure 22.2. Individuals and moving-range charts (X-mR) for $n = 2$ (see Table 22.3).

ranges. This means that the ranges are not independent of each other, while in Shewhart control charts the subgroups are considered to be independent of each other. The moving ranges, therefore, will not be as variable as independent ranges, suggesting a smoothing effect.

The average of the moving ranges (center line for the mR-chart) is

$$m\overline{R} = 666/22 = 30.3 \text{ mg/dL.}$$

Control limits for the moving-range chart are

$$\text{UCL}_R = D_4 \, (m\overline{R}) = 3.267(30.3) = 99.0 \text{ and LCL}_R = 0(30.3) = 0.$$

Since none of the moving ranges is outside the control limits, we conclude that the ranges are in statistical control, and we may go ahead and interpret the individuals chart.

The average of the individual readings (center line for the X-chart) is

$$\overline{X} = 3562/23 = 154.9 \text{ mg/dL}.$$

Control limits for the individuals chart, from formula (22.3), are

$$154.9 \pm 3(30.3/1.128) = 154.9 \pm 80.6 = 74.3 \text{ and } 235.5.$$

The control charts for these data are shown in Figure 22.2. The reading for the 7th day, 242, is above the UCL, and the reading for the 15th day, 69, is below the LCL. The "process" is out of statistical control for those two days. Investigation revealed the special cause: The patient's elevated blood-glucose on the 7th day was due to a minor infection that was quickly controlled. Her low blood-glucose on the 15th day, while she was at home, was due to delays in two meals as a result of social commitments.

In order for the control limits for the X-chart to be symmetrical around the process average, the individual readings should come from a normal distribution or at least be symmetrical. This assumption is no problem when dealing with sample averages (see Chapter 19). But with individuals the assumption should be checked by constructing a frequency histogram from individual readings that are in statistical control.

22.3 Moving-Average and Moving-Range Charts ($m\overline{X}$-mR Charts)

The individuals chart introduced in the previous section is not very sensitive to changes in the process average. Furthermore, the requirement of normality for the individual readings is always in doubt. The sensitivity can be increased and the normality requirement can be more assured—when a sample size of only one is the current practice—by using *moving averages* designated $m\overline{X}$ as well as *moving ranges mR*. As an example of this procedure, we will use the blood-glucose data of Table 22.3, but this time we will use *sample sizes of three* (see Table 22.4)

The control limits for the moving-range chart use the same formulas as those for the regular range chart:

$$\text{UCL}_R = D_4\overline{R} \text{ and } \text{LCL}_R = D_3\overline{R}.$$

The control limits for the moving-average chart use the same basic formula as that for the regular average chart but use the mean of the moving ranges,

Table 22.4. Daily Readings of Blood-Glucose with Moving Averages and Moving Ranges for $n = 3$

Day	Blood Glucose mg/dL	Moving Average $m\overline{X}$	Moving Range mR
1	110	—	—
2	142	—	—
3	131	127.7	32
4	159	144.0	28
5	187	159.0	56
6	189	178.3	30
7	242	206.0	55
8	174	201.7	68
9	153	189.7	89
10	166	164.3	21
11	140	153.0	26
12	152	152.7	26
13	170	154.0	30
14	161	161.0	18
15	69	133.3	101
16	143	124.3	92
17	154	122.0	85
18	129	142.0	25
19	107	130.0	47
20	158	131.3	51
21	192	152.3	85
22	178	176.0	34
23	156	175.3	36
Totals	3,562	3,277.9	1,035

$$m\overline{\overline{X}} \pm A_2(m\overline{R}), \qquad\qquad (22.4)$$

with A_2 dependent, as usual, on subgroup sample size and obtained from Table 2 in the Appendix.

The first moving average, 127.7, and the first moving range, 32, in Table 22.4 are determined after the third reading. Note that, except for the first two readings and the last two readings, each individual reading is involved in *three* consecutive moving averages and in *three* consecutive moving ranges. This means that the moving averages are not independent of each other, nor are the moving ranges independent of each other. The moving averages are correlated (called *autocorrelation*) and exhibit a smoothing effect that takes some of the variability out of the individuals chart. The same can be said for the moving ranges. We first calculate the center line and control limits for the two charts.

The center line for the mR-chart is the average of the moving ranges:

$$m\overline{R} = 1035/21 = 49.3 \text{ mg/dL.}$$

Control limits for the mR-chart are

$$\text{UCL}_{mR} = D_4 (m\overline{R}) = 2.575(49.3) = 126.9 \text{ and LCL}_{mR} = 0(49.3) = 0.$$

Since none of the moving ranges is outside the control limits, we conclude that the ranges are in statistical control, and we may go ahead and interpret the moving-average chart.

The center line for the $m\overline{X}$-chart, as in the previous section, is the mean of the individual readings:

$$\overline{X} = 3562/23 = 154.9 \text{ mg/dL.}$$

If we were to use the mean of the moving averages instead, the result would be

$$m\overline{\overline{X}} = 3277.9/21 = 156.1 \text{ mg/dL,}$$

slightly different because all of the readings were not used an equal number of times in calculating moving averages.

Control limits for the mX-chart, from formula (22.4), are

$$154.9 \pm 1.023(49.3) = 154.9 \pm 50.4 = 104.5 \text{ and } 205.3.$$

The control charts for these data are shown in Figure 22.3. Once again, the result for the 7th day, moving average 206.0, is above the UCL and identifies a situation that is not in statistical control. But this time the result for the 15th day, moving average 133.3, did not fall below the LCL. In fact it was not even the smallest moving average. An important effect of moving averages is to smooth out fluctuations in individual readings, and this effect masked the result for the 15th day.

Compare the moving-average chart of Figure 22.3 with the individuals chart of Figure 22.2 to see the effect of smoothing.[3] The moving averages are useful for detecting trends in the process and appear to follow each other, like circus

---

[3] For an interesting discussion about moving averages, see L. S. Nelson, "The Deceptiveness of Moving Averages," *Journal of Quality Technology*, ASQC, Milwaukee, April 1983, Vol. 15, No. 2, pp. 99–100.

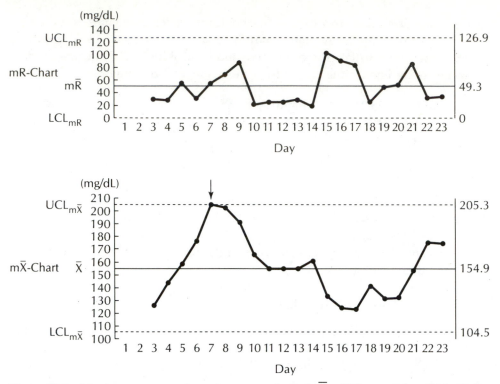

Figure 22.3. Moving-average and moving-range charts ($m\overline{X}$-mR) for $n = 3$ (see Table 22.4).

elephants, in a smooth transition from one point to the next. There appears to be less variability among the moving averages than among individual readings, a characteristic to be expected since sample averages have less variability than individual observations.

Thus we might conclude that the patient's blood-glucose level appeared to improve (was lowered) after discharge from the hospital on the 9th day and that self-monitoring at home would be a major step toward further improvement.

22.4 Median and Range Chart ($\tilde{X}$-R Chart)

Did you ever want a control chart that any machine operator, other "floor person," or administrative clerk could use and maintain with minimum training and without performing *any* calculations whatever? The median ($\tilde{X}$) chart is such a chart.

The simplicity of the chart, the retention of individual readings when plotted, and the freedom from calculating any subgroup sample statistics give this chart much appeal. The author introduced the median chart to a group of machine operators in a large machine and parts manufacturing plant in Pennsylvania. The charts were accepted with enthusiasm and continue in use several years after the author left the scene.

The median control chart is one of those underused and underpromoted statistical charts that deserve much more practical implementation than they have experienced since Shewhart control charts were first introduced. The median control chart seems to enhance the acceptance and successful implementation of control charts in general, a goal that is mostly responsible for the writing of this book.

The median is the middle value of a group of data arranged in order of magnitude (see Chapter 10). Half of the readings are larger than the median; half are smaller. Although the median of a sample subgroup is not as sensitive to changes in a process as the sample mean is, its simplicity and ease of use more than offset any minor statistical deficiency. A subgroup sample size that is odd-numbered is preferred, such as 3, 5, 7, and so on, because the middle value can be easily observed when the individual data are plotted on a chart. Medians of even-numbered sample sizes have to be calculated. We will use a sample size of three to show how the median chart is developed and used.

The concept of a median chart is shown in Figure 22.4 for subgroup sample size $n = 3$. Each individual value in the subgroup is plotted on the chart as an X, or other chosen mark, according to the measurement scale in original units on the left. The median is the middle plotted value in each subgroup, it is usually circled, and successive medians are connected. The control limits apply to the circled points—that is, to the medians—*not to the individual points* X. Individual

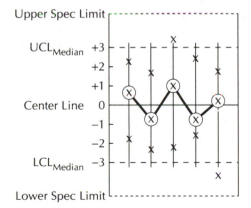

Figure 22.4. Portion of a median chart showing individual data plotted and medians connected for $n = 3$.

points that are beyond the control limits are of no concern when interpreting the chart. Since the scale applies to individual values, the specification limits may also be shown on the chart, but this practice is not recommended.

Often the center line for the median chart may be established from the overall average of past data instead of from the average of a set of medians; the difference can be considered negligible. Sometimes the center line may be a standard established for the process, such as an overall desired mean or target value.

The control limits for the median chart, like those for the $\overline{X}$-chart, are determined from a measure of variability within subgroups, such as the average range $\overline{R}$. Technically a range chart should go along with the median chart, but that implies that the range would have to be calculated for each subgroup. Our goal is to make the chart calculation-free for operators and others.

An innovative way to avoid calculating ranges has been introduced successfully by the author. Someone, perhaps in the quality assurance department, would be responsible for determining $\overline{R}$ from previous data. Control limits for the R-chart are calculated in the usual way:

$$\mathrm{UCL}_R = D_4\overline{R} \text{ and } \mathrm{LCL}_R = D_3\overline{R}.$$

If the subgroup sample size is 3 or 5, there is no lower control limit for ranges (see Table 2 of the Appendix). Then UCL_R can be represented by a *template* or *mask* with a jaw whose height is exactly the value of $D_4\overline{R}$. The template would simply be placed over the three (or five) plotted individual points in a subgroup.[4] *If a point is hidden by the template, the subgroup range exceeds the upper control limit for ranges* (see Figure 22.5).

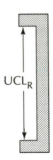
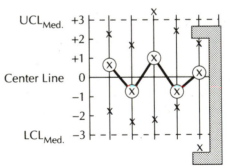

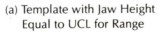

(a) Template with Jaw Height   (b) Median Chart with Range
    Equal to UCL for Range   Template Over a Subgroup

Figure 22.5. Use of template on median chart to determine ranges that exceed UCL_R.

---

[4] If the sample size exceeds six, the jaw height of the template will be $(D_4 - D_3)\overline{R}$.

As long as all three (or all five) plotted points in a subgroup are visible inside the jaw of the template, the range does not exceed its upper control limit. Of course this device cannot be used to determine if there are any runs or trends among the ranges, but its practical simplicity, ease of use, and speed far outweigh this deficiency.

The formulas for the trial control limits for the median $\tilde{X}$-chart look similar to those for the $\overline{X}$-chart, except that the factor A_6 is used:

$$\text{UCL}_{\tilde{X}} = \overline{\overline{X}} + A_6\overline{R} \text{ and } \text{LCL}_{\tilde{X}} = \overline{\overline{X}} - A_6\overline{R}, \tag{22.5}$$

and in word form,

$$\text{Control limits for medians} = \text{Center line} \pm A_6\overline{R}.$$

Values of A_6 for subgroup sample sizes 3 and 5 are as follows:

Sample Size	A_6
3	1.187
5	0.691

More complete values for A_6 are contained in Table 2 of the Appendix. The efficiency of the sample median, compared with the sample mean in estimating the process average, decreases as the sample size increases, especially for odd-numbered sample sizes.[5] It is recommended that subgroup sample sizes of 3 or 5 be used for a median chart.

Let us now look at some data. Consider a process where operators assemble a critical bolt-like part to a housing and measure the torque in foot-pounds (ft.-lbs.) needed to do the job. The data in Table 22.5 show the results from one operator measuring torques in groups of three housings at a time, four times a day for a week. The total is 20 subgroups.

Before the operator uses the median chart, a staff person in the quality assurance department has summarized the data and has determined the trial center lines and the trial control limits for both the range chart and the median chart. For the range chart,

$$\overline{R} = 31/20 = 1.6 \text{ ft.-lbs., the center line for the range chart.}$$

[5] W. J. Dixon and F. J. Massey Jr., *Introduction to Statistical Analysis*, Table A-8b(4), McGraw-Hill, New York, 1969 p. 488. For additional discussion on median control charts, see also (a) L. S. Nelson, "Control Chart for Medians," *Journal of Quality Technology*, ASQC, Milwaukee, October 1982, Vol. 14, No. 4, pp. 226–227; and (b) E. L. Grant and R. S. Leavenworth, *Statistical Quality Control*, 6th ed., McGraw-Hill, New York, 1988 pp. 312–314.

Table 22.5. Torques for Part Assembly to Housing, Showing Medians and Ranges for $n = 3$

Day of Week	Subgroup No.	Torques (ft.-lb.)			Range
			Median		
Monday	1	35	36	38	3
	2	36	37	38	2
	3	37	38	39	2
	4	36	36	37	1
Tuesday	5	36	36	37	1
	6	36	37	38	2
	7	37	38	38	1
	8	37	38	38	1
Wednesday	9	36	37	37	1
	10	36	36	37	1
	11	37	38	38	1
	12	33	36	36	3
Thursday	13	36	37	38	2
	14	37	38	38	1
	15	34	36	36	2
	16	36	36	37	1
Friday	17	36	36	37	1
	18	34	36	37	3
	19	37	38	38	1
	20	37	37	38	1
	Totals		737		31

There is no lower control limit, and the upper control limit for ranges is

$$\text{UCL}_R = D_4\overline{R} = 2.575(1.6) = 4.1 \text{ ft.-lbs.}$$

The factor D_4 comes from Table 2 of the Appendix, for $n = 3$. None of the ranges is beyond the upper control limit.

The center line for the median $\tilde{X}$-chart, using the current data, will be

$$\overline{\tilde{X}} = 737/20 = 36.9 \text{ ft.-lbs.}$$

Using formulas (22.5), the control limits for the median chart will be

Control limits = 36.9 ± 1.187(1.6) = 36.9 ± 1.9, or
LCL_{median} = 35.0 ft.-lbs, and UCL_{median} = 38.8 ft.-lbs.

We can see from Table 22.5 that none of the sample medians exceeds either control limit. Our conclusion is that the process will be treated as if it were in statistical control.

The corresponding median chart is shown in Figure 22.6, together with the template to be used for checking the ranges. The template is drawn to scale. Note that some individual readings exceed the median control limits, but it is not relevant because the control limits apply to medians, not to individual readings.

Since the ranges and the medians appear to be in statistical control, we can continue using the template for ranges and the center line and control limits for the medians for future process control.

Although the individual readings were not recorded, they can be retrieved from a median chart if one desires to draw a histogram or to perform other statistical analyses. Thus all of the basic data are essentially retained in the use of the median chart; yet no numerical data are recorded by the operator and no sample calculations are made.

It would appear that the median chart, together with the template for ranges, makes for almost an ideal application of a Shewhart control chart that anyone can learn to use quickly and easily.

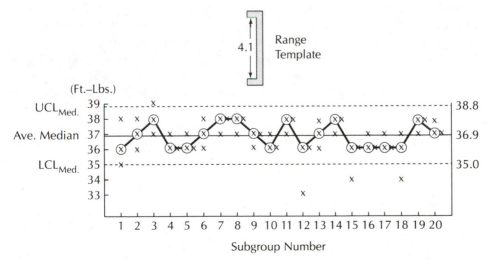

Figure 22.6. Median chart with template to check ranges for $n = 3$ (see Table 22.5).

22.5 Two More Charts

Many innovative control charts have been developed over the years to accommodate special situations that were not anticipated when the Shewhart charts were
introduced. A good source of information for newly developed charts is the
Journal of Quality Technology.[6]

In this section we discuss briefly, for awareness purposes only, the cumulative-sum (CuSum) chart and the exponentially weighted moving-average-
(EWMA) chart as examples of more sophisticated control charts.

22.5.1 Cumulative-Sum (CuSum) Chart

This chart was originally developed in England in the early 1960s and is still
in the process of refinement there as well as in the United States. The CuSum
chart is useful in detecting small but sustained shifts in process levels. Instead
of plotting the sample result, such as a sample mean $\overline{X}$, the difference between
it and some reference or target value, such as a desired process mean, is calculated. The differences from one sample to the next are added (cumulated) and
plotted.

The CuSum chart takes on a different appearance from that of an $\overline{X}$-chart. As
long as the process mean remains stable and unchanged, the accumulated
differences plot as a horizontal-like graph with random variability. If the process
mean changes, the *slope* of the CuSum plot tends to change from the horizontal
to some angle, either up or down. A device is needed to determine if the change
in slope indicates a real change in the process level. That device is a truncated
V-mask with sloped arms that serve as control limits, shown in Figure 22.7. The
V-mask can be made of transparent plastic. The point V is the vertex or point of
intersection of the two sloped arms. The point P is placed over the latest plotted
CuSum, and we look for any plotted points hidden by the mask.

Note that in Figure 22.7 the plotted CuSums are rising, suggesting an
increase in process level. When the process level has *increased,* one or more
plotted CuSums may be hidden by the *lower* arm of the V-mask, indicating that
the upper control limit has been exceeded. When the process level has *decreased,*
one or more plotted CuSums may be hidden by the *upper* arm of the V-mask,
indicating that the lower control limit has been exceeded. For example, sample 9 is hidden by the upper control limit arm, signaling that the process level

---

[6] Published quarterly by the American Society for Quality Control (ASQC), Milwaukee. Besides
numerous key articles on new control charts that appear in the *Journal,* the series of "Technical Aids"
by L. S. Nelson is a particularly valuable resource. Another source is *Technometrics,* a quarterly journal
published jointly by ASQC and the American Statistical Association (ASA).

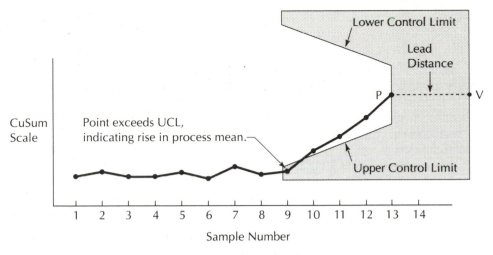

Figure 22.7. CuSum chart with typical V-mask showing point exceeding UCL.

increased at that time. The procedures require that, once the signal occurs and corrective action is taken, the CuSum is ended and started anew with the V-mask back at the baseline.

Although the CuSum chart is simple in appearance, it is the V-mask itself that requires some preliminary assumptions, some elaborate calculations, careful construction, and careful placement on the chart itself. Several characteristics must be specified before a V-mask can be constructed. These and other considerations dictate the features of the V-mask, including the angle of the arms from the horizontal and the lead distance as shown in Figure 22.7.

The CuSum chart can be used for variables or attributes, the same characteristics that identify Shewhart charts. A useful feature is that the approximate time when the process level has changed, as well as the amount of change, can be indicated by the CuSum chart; this is important because known conditions at the time of change may help to identify the special or assignable causes present.

CuSum charts are useful when samples are expensive or when sample sizes of only one are available. In comparing the CuSum chart with Shewhart charts, especially for averages, it is generally conceded that CuSum charts can detect smaller shifts in the process level. A chart for variability, such as the R-chart, must be used along with the CuSum chart to determine if variability is stable.

The complexity of the calculations necessary to construct the CuSum chart and V-mask has been somewhat of a deterrent in the growth of its popularity. Nevertheless, the chart has appealed to some of those challenged by its apparent sophistication. Some practitioners insist that the CuSum chart is more appropriate and even easier to use than Shewhart charts.[7] Computerized calculations help to make the application of CuSum charts easier.

22.5.2 Exponentially Weighted Moving-Average (EWMA) Chart

The EWMA control chart is unique in that it uses all historical data but weights them according to their "age." It is particularly useful when a process has slowly drifting means. Most weight is given to the current sample result, and progressively less weight is given to previous results as they get older. All of this information then provides a *forecast* of what the next sample result is likely to be, based on a simple mathematical formula. As each new piece of information becomes available, the formula for forecasting is adjusted to improve it. This kind of forecasting had its origin in *exponential smoothing*, which was used by economists in the 1960s for forecasting sales, inventory, and other business characteristics.

Figure 22.8, adapted from a chart by Hunter,[8] illustrates how the various charts—Shewhart (without runs), moving average, CuSum, and EWMA—weight the data from time t and before. The typical Shewhart chart gives all the weight to the latest sample result if runs are ignored. The moving-average chart divides the weight equally among several recent consecutive single samples. The CuSum chart gives equal weight to all previous historical data. The EWMA chart gives gradually less weight as historical data grow older. The EWMA chart can be given a long memory, making it analogous to a CuSum chart, or it can be given a short memory, making it analogous to a Shewhart chart without consideration of runs.

The formula in English for the EWMA predicted for the next sampling time $(t + 1)$ is as follows:

$$\text{EWMA at time } (t + 1) = (\text{Predicted value for time } t) + (\text{Weight factor}) \times (\text{Error in prediction for time } t), \tag{22.6}$$

---

[7] See, for example, a letter by D. M. Hawkins in *Quality Progress*, July 1992, pp. 6–7. For additional discussions on CuSum charts, see:
(a) E. L. Grant and R. S. Leavenworth, *Statistical Quality Control*, 6th ed., Chap. 10, McGraw-Hill, New York, 1988;
(b) H. M. Wadsworth, K. S. Stephens, and A. B. Godfrey, *Modern Methods for Quality Control and Improvement*, Chap. 8, John Wiley & Sons, New York, 1986; and
(c) G. B. Wetherill and D. W. Brown, *Statistical Process Control: Theory and Practice*, Chap. 7, Chapman and Hall, London, England, 1991.

[8] J. S. Hunter, "The Exponentially Weighted Moving Average," *Journal of Quality Technology*, ASQC, Milwaukee, October 1986, Vol. 18, No. 4, pp. 203–210.

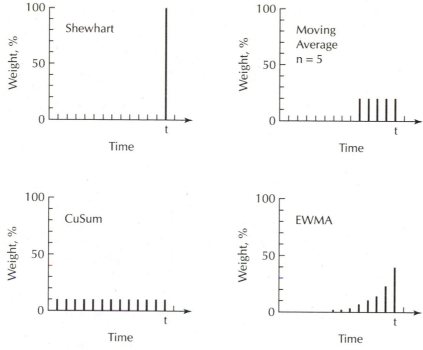

Figure 22.8. Comparing four charts with regard to weights given to data at time t and before.

which can also be written as

EWMA at time $(t + 1)$ = (Weight factor) × (Observed value at time t) +
$$(1 - \text{Weight factor}) \times \qquad (22.7)$$
(Predicted value for time t).

The last term in formula (22.6), the error term, is the difference between the observed value at time t and its predicted value, EWMA. Either Formula (22.6) or (22.7) may be conveniently used for repetitive calculations, easily programmable for computers or calculators. For example, if the following values are in effect,

50.0 = Predicted value (previous EWMA) for time t,
52.3 = Observed value at time t,
0.4 = Weight factor,

then the predicted value (new EWMA) for the next sample time $(t + 1)$, using formula (22.6), will be $50.0 + 0.4(52.3 - 50.0) = 50.92$. The reader can verify that the same result will be obtained using formula (22.7).

The weight factor is some number between 0 and 1. With a weight factor of 0.5, for example, the weights on previous observations drop 50% each time as follows:

0.50, 0.250, 0.1250, 0.0625, 0.0312, 0.0156, and so on.

With a weight factor of 0.1, the weights on previous observations decrease slowly by 10% as follows:

0.09, 0.081, 0.0729, 0.0656, 0.0590, 0.0531, and so on.

The smaller the weight factor, the greater the influence of historical data. See Hunter's article for methods by which the weight factor is chosen.

To determine the three-sigma control limits for the EWMA chart, it is necessary to get an estimate of the variability of the EWMA. A Shewhart $\overline{X}$-chart can provide such an estimate. Hunter suggests placing the averages and control limits for the Shewhart $\overline{X}$-chart and the EWMA on the same chart.

A chemical process that has a gradually changing ingredient appears to be a good application for the EWMA chart. Other sources should be consulted before implementing an EWMA control chart, including the definitive paper by A. M. Wortham and G. F. Heinrich, "Control Charts Using Exponential Smoothing Techniques," *26th ASQC Annual Technical Conference Transactions*, 1972, pp. 451–458.

22.6 Summary

This chapter looked at six other charts:

1. *Average and standard deviation ($\overline{X}$-S) charts:* The S-chart can be used in place of the R-chart when sample sizes exceed 10. For smaller sample sizes, the S-chart and the R-chart for the same set of data are similar in appearance and interpretation, but the R-chart is preferred.

2. *Individuals and moving-range (X-mR) charts:* These charts are useful when samples of one are used. The moving range mR consists of two or more consecutive samples. As each new sample is obtained, the oldest is discarded. Each sample is used more than once in calculating the moving range. Normality is assumed for the individuals and should be periodically checked with a frequency histogram.

3. *Moving-average and moving-range ($m\overline{X}$-mR) charts:* Moving averages, when samples of one are used, increase the sensitivity to process changes. Two or more consecutive samples form a subgroup for which the mean and range are calculated. As each new sample is obtained, the oldest is discarded.

Formulas for the control chart limits are the same as those for the regular $\overline{X}$-R chart. The moving average, like the moving range, has a smoothing effect on fluctuations of individual readings.

4. *Median and range ($\tilde{X}$-R) chart:* The median forms one of the most simple and easiest-to-use control charts. Each individual reading is plotted on the median chart, and the middle plotted points, the medians, are circled and connected. Odd-numbered sample sizes are preferred so that the median point can be easily observed. After the center line and control limits for both charts have been determined, no further calculations are required in plotting. No range chart is needed. Instead a template is constructed with jaws whose height corresponds to the UCL_R (previously determined). The operator places the template over the several plotted points in a subgroup; as long as all the points are visible between the jaws of the template, the UCL_R has not been exceeded.

5. *Cumulative-sum (CuSum) chart:* The CuSum chart is useful in detecting small but sustained shifts in process levels. Differences between a sample result and some target value are calculated, and these differences are added. The accumulated differences, CuSums, are plotted. As long as the process level remains stable, CuSums will plot as a generally horizontal graph. If the process level changes, the slope of the CuSum changes from the horizontal: up if the process level increases, down if the process level decreases. A V-mask placed over the last plotted CuSum is used to identify significant changes in slope. A plotted CuSum hidden by the arm of the V-mask identifies when the process level has changed. Calculations to construct the V-mask are complicated.

6. *Exponentially weighted moving-average (EWMA) chart:* The EWMA uses all historical data and weights them according to their age, providing a forecast for the next sample result. A simple formula is used to calculate the new EWMA, using a weight factor between zero and one. The smaller the weight factor, the greater the influence of past data. Choice of the weight factor can be left to the quality practitioner. EWMA control limits can be determined from the $\overline{X}$-chart control limits, but the method was not explained.

22.7 Putting It into Practice

1. Refer to Table 22.4 on blood-glucose readings.

   (a) Replace the columns for moving-average and moving-range data with those based on samples of 4.

(b) Determine the center lines and control limits for both the moving-range chart and the moving-average chart for $n = 4$.

(c) Draw the two charts and interpret.

2. Refer to Table 22.2 on screw-cap torques. The R-chart for these data, shown in Figure 22.1, shows that the ranges appear to be in statistical control.

(a) Identify the medians in Table 22.2.

(b) Determine the center line and control limits for a median chart.

(c) Draw the median chart, plotting all 100 readings, circle the medians, and connect them.

(d) Construct a template to check the ranges on the median chart.

(e) Are the medians in statistical control? Compare your results with those of Problem 4 in Chapter 19.

Answers to Problem Exercises

1. (a) *Blood-Glucose Readings with Moving Averages and Moving Ranges for $n = 4$*

Day	Blood Glucose X (mg/dL)	Moving Average m$\overline{X}$	Moving Range mR
1	110	—	—
2	142	—	—
3	131	—	—
4	159	135.5	49
5	187	154.75	56
6	189	166.5	58
7	242	194.25	83
8	174	198.0	68
9	153	189.5	89
10	166	183.75	89
11	140	158.25	34
12	152	152.75	26
13	170	157.0	30
14	161	155.75	30
15	69	138.0	101
16	143	135.75	101
17	154	131.75	92
18	129	123.75	85
19	107	133.25	47
20	158	137.0	51
21	192	146.5	85
22	178	158.75	85
23	156	171.0	36
Totals	3,562		1,295

(b) *Moving-range chart:*

Center line: $m\overline{R} = 1295/20 = 64.75$

Control limits: $LCL_{mR} = 0$

$$UCL_{mR} = D_4(m\overline{R}) = 2.282(64.75) = 147.8 \text{ (rounded)}$$

Moving-average chart:

Center line: $\overline{X} = 3562/23 = 154.9 \text{ (rounded)}$

Control limits: $\overline{X} \pm A_2(m\overline{R}) = 154.9 \pm 0.729(64.75)$

$$= 154.9 \pm 47.2$$

$UCL_{m\overline{X}} = 202.1$ and $LCL_{m\overline{X}} = 107.7$

(c)

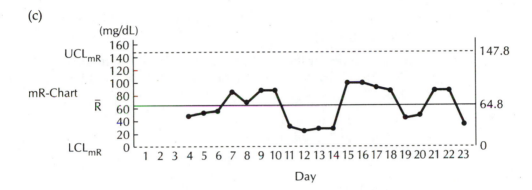

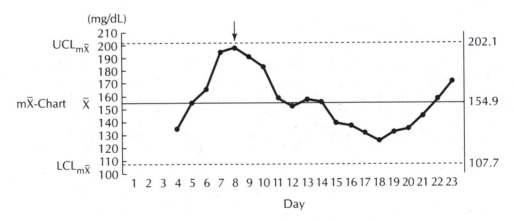

The moving-range chart appears to be in statistical control, so we may analyze the moving-average chart. Although the latter chart does not show any points outside the control limits, observe that the three consecutive moving-averages for days 7, 8, and 9 are very close to the upper control limit, suggesting the presence of a special cause.

2. (a) The medians in Table 22.2 are:

Subgroup No.	Median	Subgroup No.	Median
1	21	11	20
2	23	12	17
3	21	13	17
4	22	14	20
5	20	15	21
6	20	16	20
7	23	17	20
8	20	18	21
9	24	19	24
10	21	20	26

(b) The sum of the medians is 421. The average of the medians is 421/20 = 21.05 or 21.1 rounded.

The average range for these data had already been determined: 113/20 = 5.65. The upper control limit for ranges is $D_4\overline{R} = 2.114(5.65) = 11.9$ rounded.

Control limits for the median chart:
$$\overline{\overline{X}} \pm A_6\overline{R} = 21.1 \pm 0.691(5.65) = 21.1 \pm 3.9$$
$$\text{UCL}_{\tilde{x}} = 25.0 \text{ and } \text{LCL}_{\tilde{x}} = 17.2$$

(c) Median chart:

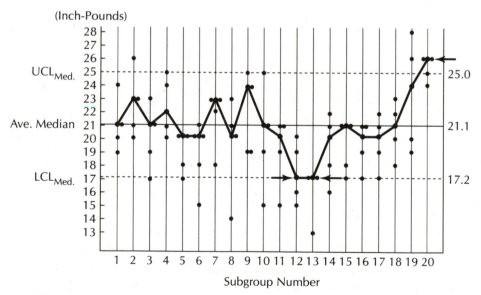

• = individual reading
• = median

(d) Range template, to scale:

(e) None of the ranges exceeds $UCL_R = 11.9$. The medians are not in statistical control. Medians 12 and 13 exceed LCL; median 20 exceeds UCL. The $\overline{X}$-chart drawn from the same data (Problem 4 in Chapter 19) shows that mean 13 exceeded LCL and mean 20 exceeded UCL. Both charts show a run of points below the center line. Both charts resulted in the same interpretation and conclusion.

Statistics is never having to say you're certain.
—American Statistical Association T-shirt

CHAPTER   23

Process Capability Studies, Strategies, and Indexes

When an organization, especially one in manufacturing, is interested in evaluating a process, the first act that is customarily taken is to determine whether or not the process is capable of meeting specifications. Interest in evaluating a process is usually preceded by some quality problem that has arisen. So the first question usually asked is: What is the status of the process as far as its ability to meet specifications is concerned?

It seems like a logical beginning. If we knew whether or not the process was capable of meeting the specifications, we could then decide on a course of action to resolve the problem that initiated the inquiry. If we find that the process is capable of meeting specifications, and yet the product does not seem to do so, there must be some operational or personnel reason that we must identify and confront. If we find that the process is not capable of meeting specifications, then we must work on the process to improve it in some significant way or consider other alternatives.

The methods that quality practitioners in industry use to conduct a process capability study vary quite a bit. This chapter addresses the basic concepts inherent in process capability studies with a view to helping the reader avoid some of the mistakes that can be made.

23.1 Definition of Capability

The definition of capability is deceptively simple:

Capability: Inherent variability, devoid of undesirable special causes.

This definition has a key word in it: *variability*. That key word reflects an old concept of process improvement: the reduction of variability, which is now considered to be a modern concept among newly enlightened people making products and performing services. It has taken decades for people in industry to recognize, accept, and understand the importance of variability in product and process control and improvement.

Variability that is *inherent* has to do with the fact that every process has natural, or built-in, variability that is unique to, and reflective of, the elements that make up a process: materials, equipment, people, methods, measurements, environment, and management (see Chapter 11). How these elements are used in combination uniquely identifies the process.

Finally, the inherent variability that we are trying to determine represents the *smallest variability* that the process is capable of exhibiting if no undesirable[1] special or assignable causes are present. Under this condition the process behaves in a random fashion and is stable, predictable, and doing its best; its behavior is said to be due to *common causes*. It's as if the several elements listed above affect the process randomly, none of them dominating at any moment. The presence of undesirable special causes tends to increase the variability above and beyond the natural, built-in, inherent variability due only to common causes.

23.2 Process Spread and Specification Spread

Since variability is a key part of the definition of capability, then a sensible measure should be the standard deviation σ or a sample estimate of it, S. The total *process spread* can be defined as six times the standard deviation (that is, plus and minus three standard deviations from the mean) to account for almost 100% of the output of a process if the normal curve is an appropriate model for the process. Let us assume that the distribution of the process measurement can be represented by the normal curve model, or at least a model that is reasonably normal and reasonably symmetrical around its mean. Then we can write

$$\text{Total process spread} = 6\sigma. \tag{23.1}$$

The concept of capability is related to the *specifications* that are required of the process and its output. Assume we are dealing with two-sided specifications; that is, an upper specification limit U and a lower specification limit L. Then the

---

[1] Recall discussion in Section 21.8 on special causes that improve a process and are therefore considered desirable.

total *specification spread*—sometimes called the *tolerance*—is defined as the difference between the two specification limits and written as

$$\text{Total specification spread} = U - L. \tag{23.2}$$

From this point on, the determination of whether or not a process is capable of meeting specifications is made simply by comparing the results of definitions (23.1) and (23.2).

23.3 Comparing Process Spread with Specification Spread

We will look at three possible situations when the process mean is somewhere near the midpoint between the specification limits U and L, and there are no undesirable special causes present. Any of the situations depicted in Figure 23.1 is likely to occur in a process capability study. The location of the process mean relative to the specification limits is not relevant in determining the *potential* capability of the process, because capability determination is simply a matter of comparing variabilities or total spreads. The question as to whether or not the process is *actually* meeting specifications is another matter that is determined by (1) its actual variability, (2) where it is centered, (3) the shape of its distribution, and (4) its stability and predictability.

Let us now examine each of the three different capability situations pictured in Figure 23.1 to discuss what each one describes, what opportunities each offers, alternatives that are open, and consequences that may arise.

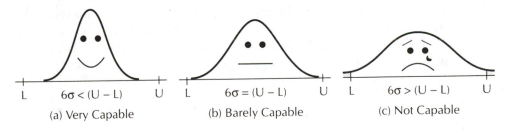

L $\quad 6\sigma < (U - L) \quad$ U	L $\quad 6\sigma = (U - L) \quad$ U	L $\quad 6\sigma > (U - L) \quad$ U
(a) Very Capable	(b) Barely Capable	(c) Not Capable

Figure 23.1. Different capability situations.

Very Capable—Figure 23.1(a)

The process spread is appreciably less than the specification spread; that is, 6σ *is less than* $(U - L)$. Algebraically, we would write this relationship $6\sigma < (U - L)$. The process is definitely very capable, potentially, of meeting specifications if its mean is properly located. This situation is obviously a happy one because everything produced will meet specifications handily as long as the mean is centrally located.

If we are so fortunate as to be faced with this happy situation, what benefits can we expect from it, and what could be done to take advantage of it? There are several alternatives:

1. *Tighten the specifications.* The advantage here is a marketing advantage, because we could assert that our product is more uniform and consistent than a competitor's. If a customer uses our output as a part, ingredient, final product, or service, that customer should experience less difficulty with it, higher yield, less scrap, less rework, less downtime, more reliability, and greater performance predictability. This advantage will translate into higher profits as long as the reduced variability and center location can be maintained.

2. *Allow the process to drift toward one of the specification limits* where there is less cost or greater savings. For example, in a filling operation, letting the process drift toward the lower specification limit is the same as reducing its mean or average fill, resulting in less material average usage. Obviously savings would accrue. It is assumed that product falling anywhere within the specification limits is perfectly satisfactory from a customer's or consumer's point of view, although that concept can be challenged. Care must be taken, however, to control the process mean and variability to minimize underweight packages if we are dealing with a consumer product such as cans or packages of a food item. This advantage will translate into lower costs and higher profits, often very substantially where high-volume products are involved. Saving an average of a tiny fraction of an ounce on a packaged product that is produced in the tens or hundreds of millions annually can result in many millions of dollars saved every year, but only if the reduced variability justifies it.

3. *Reduce inspection, sample size, frequency of sampling, or testing.* Even control charts on this process may be eliminated if there is sufficient evidence of a long-term, sustained, stable process. This advantage will also translate into lower costs and higher profits.

Barely Capable—Figure 23.1(b)

The process spread is about equal to the specification spread; that is, *6σ is about equal to (U − L).* Algebraically, we would write this relationship $6\sigma = (U - L)$. This process is capable of meeting specifications, but barely so. The situation suggests that if the process mean moves to the left or to the right, even just a little bit, some output will exceed one of the specification limits. Therefore, this is a process that should be watched carefully to detect shifts in the mean. Fortunately, we have excellent tools to detect shifts in the process mean: Shewhart control charts or one of the alternative charts described in Chapter 22. Therefore, this situation is an ideal one for the application of control charts.

Not Capable—Figure 23.1(c)

The process spread is greater than the specification spread; that is, *6σ is greater than (U − L)*. Algebraically, we would write this relationship $6\sigma > (U - L)$. This process is not capable of meeting specifications, regardless of where the mean or center of the process is located, because it has too much inherent variability. The situation is sad, indeed. It is even more sad to contemplate what could (and does) happen if the process is not capable of meeting specifications and *the responsible people are unaware of it*. Overadjustment of the process is a common consequence of lack of knowledge about process behavior, resulting in even greater variability. Bitter confrontation and condemnation are usually the outcome. The only kind of process-adjustment response that is open to, say, an operator, is to change the mean, which is usually of little benefit. There is no known piece of equipment that contains a switch for reducing the variability, which would be an ideal technological solution for a process that is not capable. Nevertheless, there are some alternatives:

1. *Change the specifications.* This alternative depends on where the specifications originated. If the specifications were influenced or directed by some governmental regulating agency, it might be difficult to change the specifications. If the specifications originated with a customer's requirement, much would depend on the working relationship with that customer and the effect on the partnership when factual evidence of the incapability of the process is presented. If the specifications originated with an organization's research and development department, a definitive study would be needed and probably requested. The effect of changing specifications on the customer's requirements is paramount.

2. *Change the process.* In this case the process would have to be carefully studied to determine not only what, specifically, can be changed, but also how much cost would be involved. If new capital equipment, material change, design change, or operational change is recommended, it is certain that top management will ask many questions about the recommendation, and evidence from studies will have to be presented to support it. Simply recommending

a change in the process, without an accompanying cost estimate, would not be persuasive.

3. *Live with the current process but sort 100%*. If neither of the first two alternatives is possible or practical, we might decide to maintain the status quo and not make any changes. Even with this decision, however, there is a change in operations to be made: Since the process will produce units outside specifications, the logical consequence should be to sort the product 100% and find and remove units outside specifications. If we are not willing to accept this consequence, because of the cost involved, and merely continue to produce and deliver units outside specifications, then in essence we have unilaterally changed the specifications.[2]

4. *Optimize (recenter) the process mean* so that the total losses outside both the upper and lower specification limits are minimized. This alternative can be considered an extension of Alternative 3. Usually the cost of exceeding the lower specification limit is somewhat different from the cost of exceeding the upper specification limit, which suggests an optimizing approach of recentering the process mean. As a simple example, a machined part cut to a specific length can be recut if it exceeds the upper specification limit; but if it exceeds the lower specification limit, it can be reintroduced as raw material or even scrapped. The costs at either end of the specifications are probably different, suggesting a level or mean of the process that would minimize the combined cost of recut, rework, and scrap.

5. *Shut down the process, stop making the product, and get out of the business.* This alternative is a very difficult one to persuade top management to accept; yet it is a legitimate alternative to consider if none of the others is acceptable. Of course, marketing considerations must be taken into account.

What is clear, when considering the several alternatives if the process is not capable, is that all of the alternatives listed involve management-level decisions. *Thus, determining the capability of a process is not simply a statistical exercise but a management tool directly affecting top-level business decisions that involve customer requirements, marketing considerations, and quality costs.*

22.4 Suggested Steps for Determining Process Capability

Many ways for conducting process capability studies have been observed. They range from merely looking at a process in motion for a few minutes to the use

---

[2] See author's article, "Specifications: Laws or Guidelines?" *Quality Progress*, ASQC, Milwaukee, July 1981, Vol. 14, No. 7, pp. 14–18.

of computerized graphics accompanied by elaborate statistical analyses. Such studies may consist of short-term determination of capability and long-term determination.

In the short-term approach, samples are taken over a relatively short period of time, such as a day or even a week, to provide a preliminary assessment of process potential. During a short-term study, all of the forces that affect a process may not be present to influence the data, but some insight can be obtained. In the long-term approach, samples are taken over a longer period of time, such as a month or several weeks, providing an opportunity for other factors to affect the process, such as changes in raw materials, wear on the equipment, different operators, environmental conditions, and so on. Regardless of the approach taken, the control chart is used as the basis for removing undesirable special causes, resulting in further reductions in process variability.

A process capability study should be looked on as a dynamic statistical tool for action on the process under the philosophy of continuous process improvement. Process capability studies beg for proper yet understandable procedures, whether for short-term or long-term analyses.

The following practical step-by-step procedures are designed primarily for processes that are measured with variables data. These procedures, applicable to either short-term or long-term determination of process capability, consist of three parts, which are (1) select and define the process, (2) determine if the specifications are now being met, and (3) determine inherent variability using an R-chart.

Part 1: Select and Define the Process

Is the process a line, machine, operator, batch of processed material, portion of manufacture, a service, or a combination of these? Is the process under study critical to the product being made or service being offered in terms of quality, performance, and cost? What are the key variables? Are they controllable? The decision as to what constitutes a "process" is important in determining how samples are to be obtained and what kind of action, if any, is to be taken.

Part 2: Determine If the Specifications Are Now Being Met

1. Collect at least 100 random observations of current data.

2. Calculate the sample mean $\overline{X}$ and the sample standard deviation S to estimate the true mean μ and standard deviation σ of the process.

3. Draw a frequency histogram. If it is reasonably bell-shaped and reasonably symmetrical, assume a normal curve model for the process. If that assumption cannot be made, see a statistician for assistance in selecting an alternative model or mathematically transforming the data.

4. If the histogram indicates that the process spread is less than the specification spread, it suggests that the process *might* be capable. If part of the histogram is outside specifications, adjustment of the mean will enable the process to meet specifications. Decide whether it might be more worthwhile to drop the study and direct resources toward another process whose questionable performance may be crying for attention.

5. If the histogram indicates that the process spread is greater than the specification spread, it suggests that the process *might not* be capable. Then proceed to Part 3 to determine the true capability. Remember that the total process spread described by the histogram includes variation from all sources: materials, equipment, people, methods, measurements, environment, and management, as well as special causes that may inflate the inherent variability. *The histogram by itself does not indicate the true capability of the process, nor does it indicate whether or not the process is in statistical control. It represents only the current performance of the process.*

Part 3: Determine Inherent Variability Using an R-chart[3]

1. Get at least 40 rational subgroups of sample size two or more at a time, preferably size four or five. Process capability studies have been observed with as few as 10 subgroups, but the results are questionable.

2. Calculate the ranges R, average range $\overline{R}$, and control limits for a range chart. Draw the range chart.

3. Discard any ranges outside the upper control limit *only* if the undesirable special cause is identifiable and can be removed from the process; otherwise, retain the excessive range or ranges.

4. Recalculate the average range $\overline{R}$ and control limits.

5. Repeat Steps 3 and 4—justifiable removal of any excessive ranges, and recalculation of control limits—until all ranges are in statistical control. No, we will not lose many ranges. See Figure 23.2 for an example of an R-chart with one excessive range.

6. Estimate process standard deviation σ from the last average range:

$$\text{Estimate of } \sigma = \overline{R}/d_2,$$

where d_2 is obtained from Table 2 in the Appendix. This estimate of σ represents the smallest variability inherent in the process with both the mean and variability in statistical control.

---

[3] An S-chart may be used, but the R-chart is preferred because of its simplicity.

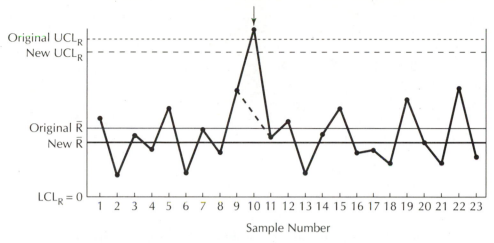

Figure 23.2. Portion of a range chart used in a capability study showing excessive range to be removed (justifiably) leaving new $\bar{R}$ and UCL_R. Sample size of six or less.

7. Using the midpoint of the specifications as the process mean, assume normality, draw a normal curve, and estimate the percentage meeting specifications. This step assumes that the mean of the process can be adjusted or recentered.

8. If the normal curve shows that the specifications *can* be met, investigate the process to determine why the specifications are not being met. Draw an $\bar{X}$-chart from the same subgroup data and interpret for clues. The problem may be merely the need to recenter the process, or it may be the presence of special causes that have increased the natural variability.

9. If the specifications *cannot* be met because of excessive inherent variability, consider the management alternatives discussed earlier: Change the specifications, change the process, live with it and sort 100%, optimize the mean, or drop the product.

10. Set up $\bar{X}$-R charts for future process improvement and control.

23.5 Coordination Strategy: Cart Before the Horse?

A common practice for decades among quality practitioners has been to distinguish between control charts and process capability studies as if they were two useful but separate and independent tools. The traditional route to process improvement tended to begin with a capability study in an attempt to answer an apparently logical first question concerning the status of the process under study: Is the process capable of meeting specifications? After the question has been answered by one technique or another, there is then an apparent follow-up effort to introduce control charts. This sequence of procedures, however, is the reverse of what it ought to be. It is like putting the proverbial cart before the horse.

If an initial process capability study shows that the specifications are being met, as described in Part 2 in the previous section, one might conclude that the process is capable, which might be true for that moment. But if the process is *not* in statistical control, the process is likely to perform differently the next day or even the next hour. In other words, if the process is not in statistical control, it is not a stable or predictable process, and any declarations about its future performance are uncertain.

The true long-term capability of a process cannot be determined until the process has been brought into statistical control first, because then the process is stable and predictable.

Some process capability studies require that no one touch the process (or machine) while sample data are being collected. An operator working on a line or on a machine, for example, is usually puzzled by this requirement while product that is obviously unsatisfactory or not meeting specifications is allowed to flow through the operation. Yet those conducting the study must be given some credit for the intuitive sense that prompted the hands-off policy. They are unconsciously simulating the requirement that the process must be in statistical control, but they are trying to eliminate only one possible special cause: the operator.

Unfortunately that policy, although commendable, does not go far enough, because special causes unrelated to the operator could still be present in the process. If the standard deviation is determined while special causes are still present, the measured process spread may be greater than that representing the true potential capability of the process. In short, the inherent variability, which is the smallest variability that the process is capable of exhibiting, will not have been correctly determined.

The only formal way in which the requirement of statistical process control can be effected is through the use of control charts. *Therefore, a proper capability study begins with an effort to get a process into statistical control first, through the use of a control chart.*

23.6 Basic Logical Sequence for Process Capability

From the previous discussion, we can now present the logical sequence that leads to effective process capability studies (see Figure 23.3). Note again that the

TO START: Let the process tell you about itself.
            Use control charts.

QUESTION 1:   Is the process in statistical control?
              (random, stable, predictable, doing its best)

CONDITION 1:   *YES, in statistical control.*

> QUESTION 2:   Is the process capable?
>
> CONDITION 1a: *YES, capable.*
> If necessary, recenter the process.
>
> CONDITION 1b: *NO, not capable.*
> Consider the management alternatives:
> change the specs; change the process; live with it (or optimize the mean); stop making the product.

CONDITION 2:   *NO, not in statistical control.*

> Work on the process to bring it into statistical control by removing undesirable special causes, one by one. Then go back to QUESTION 2 to determine process capability.

Figure 23.3.   Logical sequence for process capability.

determination of true process capability cannot be made until the process is first brought into statistical control.

The paragraph under Condition 2 in Figure 23.3, describing what has to be done when the process is not in statistical control, has a key word in it: *work*. It takes work, energy, time, and resources to bring a process into a state of statistical control. Finding the undesirable special causes challenges the experience, ingenuity, and knowledge of statistical methods of those engaged in the search. Magnanimous and in vogue as it may appear to be to empower an operator to search for special causes unassisted because the process "belongs" to the operator, that operator may need all the technical assistance available to engage in a successful search.

23.7 Flow-Chart Strategy for Process Improvement

The logical sequence of Figure 23.3 has been incorporated in a flow chart for process improvement, as shown in Figure 23.4 (the same as Figure 3.1). Note once again that, even before the question of process capability can be addressed, the process must first be brought into statistical control. Follow the flow chart carefully to reinforce the principle expressed in this section.

We briefly address the last stage in the flow chart, continuing the process improvement effort, in the last chapter of this book.

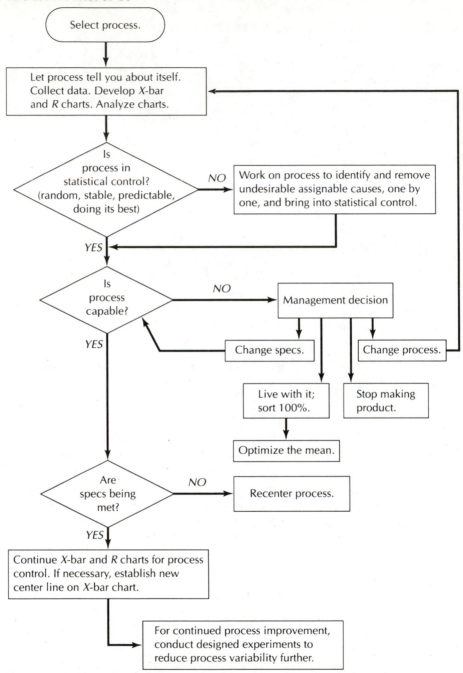

Figure 23.4. Flow chart of strategy for process improvement.

23.8 Capability Indexes

Let it be stated at the outset that various capability indexes (or, if you prefer, indices) that have been proposed, to provide a numerical score of the capability of a process to meet specifications, seem to promise more than they can deliver. Managers historically look for that elusive single figure, the one miracle number, that encompasses everything there is to know about an operation or process. Current examples include yield, quality index, supplier rating, capability index, and other numerical figures. Such scores or grades are used for making decisions about a process, comparing production lines, comparing products, comparing plants in a multiplant company, comparing past and present performance, or rating suppliers. The objective, it seems, is to avoid having to study time-consuming details that enable one to understand what is really going on.

In a special issue of the *Journal of Quality Technology*[4] devoted entirely to articles on capability indexes, Editor Peter R. Nelson warns in an introductory editorial:

> . . . [Devoting] an entire issue to the topic of capability indices . . . should not be construed as implying that *JQT* is promoting the use of capability indices. In fact, it is clear from a statistical perspective that the concept of attempting to characterize a process with a single number is fundamentally flawed. . . . [The] assumption of normality [for example] tends to be overlooked, and often computed values for capability indices are treated as if they were the actual parameter values rather than the sample estimates that they really are. . . . All capability indices depend on the process standard deviation σ, which is almost always unknown and, therefore, replaced with the sample standard deviation S.

He concludes:

> Having said all this one might wonder why we are publishing papers on capability indices at all. One answer is to give those *unfortunate enough to have to use capability indices*[5] a clear understanding of the assumptions involved and of what the indices are actually measuring. . . . [This] does not imply that *JQT* is interested in pursuing that particular topic further. Instead, authors are encouraged to work on new and novel approaches to process capability analysis.

Much like a single grade on a school report card that is supposed to evaluate achievement, attitude, and progress all wrapped up in one letter or one numerical score, capability indexes have been developed and used to characterize the performance of a process in meeting specifications and hitting targets. Capability indexes have been used by manufacturers and producers as a powerful business carrot dangled before their suppliers to initiate or sustain business relationships.

---

[4] *Journal of Quality Technology*, ASQC, Milwaukee, October 1992, Vol. 24, No. 4, p. 175.

[5] Emphasis added.

Minimum indexes are frequently required without specifying sample sizes, method of sampling, verification of the process model (such as the normal curve), or the statistical control status of the process. Suppliers, on the other hand, quickly learn to adapt, such as requesting the loosening of specifications, so that the calculation of indexes provides the desired numbers.

Development of capability indexes appears to be an ongoing activity of statistical fascination, enticing researchers to find the magical single-number index that sees all, knows all, tells all, and pleases all. A question to keep in mind: Should short-term business advantage have priority over genuine long-term process improvement that responds to the customer?

Three indexes that appear to be the most frequently discussed, C_p, C_{pk}, and C_{pm}, are introduced and explained in this section.

23.8.1. Capability Index C_p

The formula for the simplest capability index C_p is *the ratio of the specification spread to the process spread*, the latter represented by six standard deviations:

$$C_p = \frac{U - L}{6\sigma}. \tag{23.3}$$

The letters U and L are often written USL and LSL, respectively, but the single-letter nomenclature used here is intended to help the reader see the relationships in the formulas more easily. The standard deviation σ applies to individual units or items in the process; it is a process parameter. Since the units of measure are the same for both numerator and denominator, this capability index has no unit; that is, it is unitless and dimensionless, and therefore can be compared to other unitless indexes representing different processes with different units of measure.

If σ were actually known (a rarity), then C_p would be a *parameter* of the process. In practice, however, σ is estimated by the sample standard deviation S, giving us an *estimate* of the true C_p. Then the calculated C_p becomes a *sample statistic* subject to the whims of sampling variation. In addition, the 6σ spread *assumes* that a normal curve is the correct model for the process. It will be explained later that all of these assumptions and estimates can wreak havoc on the calculation of a capability index, rendering it of little practical use. Thus, treating the one calculated value for C_p as if it were the truth about the process can become an act of questionable wisdom and a dangerous practice. But let's go on.

If the inverse of the capability index C_p is multiplied by 100, one gets the *capability ratio CR*, which provides *the percentage of the specification spread that is occupied or used by the process spread*. Thus,

$$CR = \text{Capability ratio} = \frac{1}{C_p} \times 100 = \frac{6\sigma}{U - L} \times 100. \qquad (23.4)$$

The less of the specification spread used by the process, the better the capability. Figure 23.5 shows both the C_p and its inverse for various widths of the process.

In Figure 23.5(a), the specification spread $(U - L)$ and the process spread 6σ are equal. The process uses 100% of the specification spread. Its C_p is therefore 1.00, and its capability ratio is 100%.

In Figure 23.5(b), the C_p is 1.33, and its capability ratio is 1/1.33 or 75%, meaning that 75% of the specification spread is occupied by the process spread.

In Figure 23.5(c), the C_p is 1.67, and its capability ratio is 1/1.67 or 60%. *Thus, the smaller the process variability, the larger the index C_p and the better the capability.*

Index C_p can be translated directly in terms of proportion or percentage of nonconforming product outside specifications. For example, with capability index $C_p = 1.00$ [Figure 23.5(a)], we can expect 0.0027 or 0.27% of the process to be outside specifications; in other words, the area under a normal curve beyond $\pm 3\sigma$ on both sides of the mean (see Chapter 15). For $C_p = 1.33$ [Figure 23.5(b)], we can expect only 0.000064, or 0.0064%, or *64 parts per million (ppm)*, outside specifications. For $C_p = 1.67$, nothing should be outside specification limits.

What is an acceptable value for C_p? Some companies specify an initial short-term capability index C_p of at least 1.33 to their suppliers, which means that the process spread must be 75% or less of the specification spread. If the process distributional shape is a true normal curve, and if it is centered at the midpoint of the specifications, and if the true standard deviation is known, and if the process is in statistical control, then items from the supplier should contain no more than 64 ppm outside specifications. Not bad. A great burden is placed,

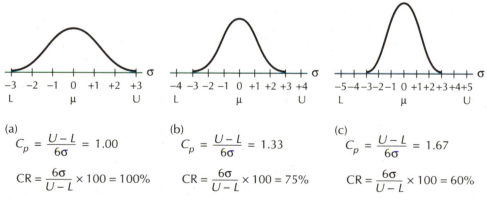

(a)
$$C_p = \frac{U - L}{6\sigma} = 1.00$$

$$CR = \frac{6\sigma}{U - L} \times 100 = 100\%$$

(b)
$$C_p = \frac{U - L}{6\sigma} = 1.33$$

$$CR = \frac{6\sigma}{U - L} \times 100 = 75\%$$

(c)
$$C_p = \frac{U - L}{6\sigma} = 1.67$$

$$CR = \frac{6\sigma}{U - L} \times 100 = 60\%$$

Figure 23.5. Some C_p values and their inverses (capability ratios) for various widths of the process distribution (scale in process standard deviation units).

therefore, on suppliers who cannot meet that criterion. Such suppliers must work very hard to reduce the inherent variability of their processes. Their management may have to authorize basic changes in the process, sometimes major changes, in order to reduce that variability.

Notice that the capability index C_p ignores the mean or target of the process. It would be possible to satisfy a criterion for C_p, such as 1.33, with the process centered at, say, the lower specification limit, but then about half of the output would be outside of the lower specification limit. Clearly, C_p is an adequate criterion for determining if the process has the *potential* to meet specifications but does not indicate if its current *performance* is adequate. Next we examine a capability index that takes the mean of the process into account.

23.8.2. Capability Index C_{pk}

If we consider where the process mean is located with respect to either of the specifications limits, U and L, then a new capability index C_{pk} can be defined as *the minimum of the two distances between the mean and the lower and upper specification limits*, as follows:

$$C_{pk} = \frac{|\mu - \text{Nearest spec limit}|}{3\sigma}. \tag{23.5}$$

The vertical lines in the numerator represent absolute values without regard to plus or minus signs, so that C_{pk} is always positive, never negative (it could be zero). Capability index C_{pk} is sometimes referred to as the *process performance index* to distinguish it from C_p, which is referred to as the *process potential index*. In other words, the actual performance of a process must also take into account where its mean is located in order to determine if it is meeting specifications. Like C_p, C_{pk} is unitless. When the process mean is precisely at the midpoint between the specification limits, the two capability indexes are equal; that is, $C_{pk} = C_p$.

Formula (23.5) is often written as the *minimum* of two values measured by the distance between the mean and the nearest specification limit:

$$C_{pk} = \text{Minimum of } \frac{U - \mu}{3\sigma} \text{ and } \frac{\mu - L}{3\sigma}. \tag{23.6}$$

The first term on the right side of formula (23.6) measures the distance between the mean and the upper specification limit; the second term measures the distance between the mean and the lower specification limit. The separate terms—

sometimes designated CPU and CPL, respectively—are never negative and are also called capability indexes.

An example may help to visualize the relationships. Suppose that we have a process that produces a steel part where a linear dimension is of interest. The specifications are

$$21.0 \text{ cm} \pm 3.0 \text{ cm; therefore } U = 24.0 \text{ cm and } L = 18.0 \text{ cm.}$$

The normal curve is the prevailing distribution, and the process is in statistical control. The standard deviation of the process is $\sigma = 0.7$ cm. What are the capability indexes C_{pk} when the process mean is at three different levels: $\mu = 21.0$ cm, $\mu = 22.0$ cm, and $\mu = 19.5$ cm.? Figure 23.6 shows the three different situations.

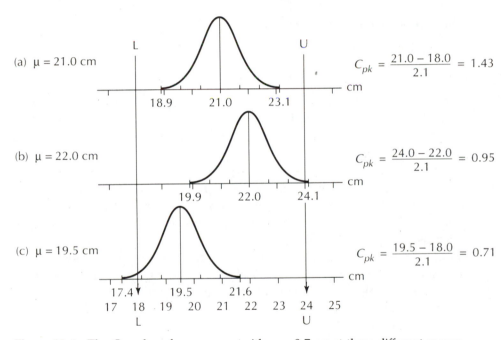

(a) $\mu = 21.0$ cm

$$C_{pk} = \frac{21.0 - 18.0}{2.1} = 1.43$$

(b) $\mu = 22.0$ cm

$$C_{pk} = \frac{24.0 - 22.0}{2.1} = 0.95$$

(c) $\mu = 19.5$ cm

$$C_{pk} = \frac{19.5 - 18.0}{2.1} = 0.71$$

Figure 23.6. The C_{pk} values for a process with $\sigma = 0.7$ cm at three different means.

The process spread $6\sigma = 4.2$ cm is obviously considerably less than the specification spread 6.0 cm, and so this process has the *potential* of being capable of meeting specifications. Its capability index C_p would be the same as its capability index C_{pk} when the mean is at the midpoint between the specification limits. Thus, $C_p = C_{pk} = 1.43$ as shown in Figure 23.6(a). Its capability ratio is $1/1.43 = 0.70$, indicating that the process spread uses about 70% of the specification spread, which is visually verifiable.

As the mean moves away from the midpoint, C_{pk} is reduced, showing that C_{pk} reflects the location of the process mean. In Figure 23.6(b) the mean is at 22.0 cm, and its $C_{pk} = 0.95$. *Since the index is less than one, a portion of the process is outside of the specification limit;* in this case, the upper specification limit. The portion beyond the upper specification limit 24.0 cm is about 0.2%, which the reader can verify by calculating the area under the normal curve (see Chapter 16).

In Figure 23.6(c), the mean is at 19.5 cm and its $C_{pk} = 0.71$. The portion beyond the lower specification limit is about 2%.

Do you find yourself accepting these results as if they are the truth for this process? Be careful. Remember the conditions and assumptions underlying these capability index calculations:
known with certainty is the specification limits, and yet in practice even these are

1. The process is in statistical control.

2. The process is normally distributed.

3. We know the true mean μ.

4. We know the true standard deviation σ.

Every one of the conditions above is *estimated* from sample data, implying that we do not know the truth about the process with certainty. The only information known with certainty is the specification limits, and yet in practice even these are sometimes loosely applied.[6]

In addition to the conditions just listed, the *sample size* used to estimate the process parameters is of great importance. Sample sizes of 30 or even 100 are hardly adequate; sample sizes of 300 or more are considered necessary because of the sensitivity of C_{pk} to sampling variability. Finally, the *method of sampling* can be critical as well, particularly the need for rational subgroups in determining the statistical control status of a process. W. Edwards Deming once stated that any process can be made to appear in statistical control merely by extending the time between samples taken within subgroups, thus allowing sources of variation other than common causes to increase the estimate of process variability, making a bad process look good.[7]

In a four-part series of enlightening articles provocatively entitled "The Use and Abuse of C_{pk}," Gunter,[8] a contributing editor of *Quality Progress*, warned that

---

[6] *Op. cit.*, "Specifications: Laws or Guidelines?", July 1981.

[7] Reported by Victor E. Kane, "Process Capability Indices," *Journal of Quality Technology*, ASQC, Milwaukee, January 1986, Vol. 18, No. 1, p. 49.

[8] Berton H. Gunter, "The Use and Abuse of C_{pk}: Parts 1–4," *Quality Progress*, January, March, May, July, 1989, ASQC, Milwaukee. See also the warnings in R. H. Kushler and P. Hurley, "Confidence Bounds for Capability Indices," *Journal of Quality Technology*, ASQC, Milwaukee, October 1992, Vol. 24, No. 4, p. 189.

the statistical issues involving the important assumptions and conditions listed earlier are unknown to many practitioners, that they are not trivial issues, and that severe problems can result when they are ignored. He states in Part 1 (January 1989):

> As a result, much of the standard usage of C_{pk} indexes is incorrect and misleading. Many professionals familiar with these issues now recommend that the use of capability indexes be severely curtailed or even abandoned because of these problems.

He observes in Part 2 (March 1989) that many, if not most, processes do not follow the beautiful symmetry and shape of the normal curve and that even subtle deviations from normality "can severely compromise the effectiveness and accuracy of C_{pk} procedures."

In Part 3 (May 1989):

> Unless a large amount of good data is taken from a stable process, C_{pk} doesn't reveal a lot about what's going on. . . .

In Part 4 (July 1989):

> The greatest abuse of C_{pk} that I have seen is that it becomes a kind of mindless effort that managers confuse with real statistical process control efforts. . . . In short, rather than fostering never-ending improvement, C_{pk} scorekeeping kills it.
>
> Simplicity [of capability indexes] is desirable when it clarifies, but it is no virtue when it promulgates bad choices.
>
> It is time to question whether it would be wiser to abandon [C_{pk}] and concentrate on promoting sound statistical practice.

In a response to a critical letter, Gunter[9] states:

> Ultimately, my biggest objection to estimated C_{pk} lies not in the statistical niceties, but in its promotion as a simple, arbitrary summary of process behavior that management can understand and apply universally. . . . This cynical application of estimated C_{pk} to all processes, stable or not, leads to disaster.
>
> Instead of the focus being on what's necessary for continuous improvement, a new version of the meet-specifications game is being played. . . . Suppliers required to meet such arbitrary criteria [as C_{pk}] will meet them, no matter what the underlying reality.
>
> Continuous improvement requires hard work and a radical change in the way we do business. . . . [C_{pk}] represents a step backward in our attempt to regain competitiveness in the world marketplace.

Exceptions to this bleak picture exist. Ford Motor Company, emphasizing quality with its popular slogan, "Quality is Job One," has led the American

---

[9] B. H. Gunter, "The Use and Abuse of C_{pk} Revisited," *Quality Progress*, pp. 90–94, January 1991, ASQC, Milwaukee.

automotive industry in implementing statistical methods within its own manufacturing facilities and those of its many suppliers. Ford specifies C_{pk} to its suppliers and requires a minimum of 1.33 for short-term capability.

Two outstanding Ford publications have been landmark examples of good statistical writing as well as recognizing the need to satisfy the assumptions underlying proper use of statistical methods.[10] A key point throughout these publications is the emphasis on a process being in statistical control before its capability can be determined, a condition often violated elsewhere.

The use of control charts to assess the status of processes during capability studies, and to achieve continuous process improvement through reduced variability, is central to Ford's successful application of statistical process control. Ford Motor Company deserves a great deal of credit for advancing the proper use of statistical methods.

23.8.3. Capability Index C_{pm}

The index C_p is considered the first generation of capability indexes. The index C_{pk} just discussed and the index C_{pm} to be briefly discussed are considered second-generation indexes.

Since C_p considers only the process spread compared with the specification spread, it identifies capability *potential*. In addition to the process spread, C_{pk} also considers the proximity of the process mean to the specification limits and therefore reflects capability *performance* in terms of *yield*; that is, in terms of percentage meeting specifications. Both of these indexes focus on reducing variability as the road to process improvement.

Now we have another capability index[11] called C_{pm} that goes one step further: It considers the proximity of the process mean μ to *a designated target T*. Referred to as the Taguchi capability index by Boyles,[12] C_{pm} is defined as

$$C_{pm} = \frac{U - L}{6\sqrt{\sigma^2 + (\mu - T)^2}} . \qquad (23.7)$$

---

[10] Publications from Ford Motor Company, Dearborn, Michigan: (a) "Continuing Process Control and Process Capability Improvement," December 1984, Statistical Methods Office; (b) "Q-101, Quality System Standard," 1983 ed., Product Quality Office.

[11] Named and introduced by L. K. Chan, S. W. Cheng, and F. A. Spiring, "A New Measure of Process Capability: C_{pm}," *Journal of Quality Technology*, ASQC, Milwaukee, July 1988, Vol. 20, No. 3, pp. 162–175.

[12] Russell A. Boyles, "The Taguchi Capability Index," *Journal of Quality Technology*, ASQC, Milwaukee, January 1991, Vol. 23, No. 1, pp. 17–26.

As is the case with the other capability indexes, C_{pm} is unitless and assumes that the process is normally distributed, that the process is in statistical control, and that C_{pm} is estimated by using sample statistics $\overline{X}$ and S for μ and σ, respectively.

The relationship among the three capability indexes is revealing. When the process mean μ is on target T, wherever that may be, then the difference $\mu - T = 0$, and formula (23.7) for index C_{pm} becomes the first index C_p shown in formula (23.3). When target T is the midpoint between specification limits, and the process mean μ is on target, then all three capability indexes are equal: $C_{pm} = C_{pk} = C_p$. We can see, therefore, that indexes C_{pm} and C_{pk} are really extensions of C_p.

One-sided specifications can be handled by these indexes when a target T is specified. Target T does not have to be the midpoint between the specification limits. Hence, capability index C_{pm} may have more general appeal, especially in applications involving component assembly such as stacking of parts.

The importance of meeting a target T, quietly recognized by quality professionals for decades, has been highlighted by Genichi Taguchi, the famed Japanese engineer, who asserted that any departure from target represents a cost (and therefore a monetary loss) to the customer or society. For example, components used in a complex assembly may have capability potential if their respective variabilities are appropriately small; but if their means are not on target, the assembly probably won't function, and the customer or consumer ends up with a defective product and attendant costs.

The Taguchi philosophy stressing the importance of centering the process has great appeal in the aerospace, automotive, and other industries. Boyles observes (p. 17):

> The appeal of expected loss is that it expresses process capability in monetary units, and therefore enters naturally into management decision-making processes. On the other hand, it may be extremely difficult to reach consensus on an appropriate set of "monetary losses to the customer or society" to include in the definition of the loss function. So the monetary basis of expected loss is both an asset and a liability.

Academicians and quality practitioners continue to work on developing more elegant capability indexes than those presented here, presumably attracted by the *magic-number syndrome* and the statistical challenge. Third-generation indexes have already been proposed.[13] But as the sophistication of indexes grows, conditions, assumptions, and statistical characteristics become more

---

[13] *Op. cit., Journal of Quality Technology*, October 1992.

complicated, and it becomes necessary to rely on more than one index to describe process performance. The dangers of focusing on a single-number second-hand representation of a process can be overcome simply by expending resources on improving the process itself. The better route lies in properly applying sound statistical methods, such as histograms, control charts, and designed experiments that reveal much of process performance.

As for process capability of *attributes data*, the control chart is the key tool and not the capability indexes introduced in this chapter. The selected attributes chart should first show statistical control (see Chapter 21). Then the *mean* of the sample statistic, $\bar{p}$, $n\bar{p}$, $\bar{c}$, or $\bar{u}$, represents the estimate of process capability, denoted by the center line of the control chart. If the calculated mean of the attribute is unsatisfactorily high, even for a process in statistical control, changes in the process itself will have to be explored in order to reduce the level.

23.9 Summary

Process capability is defined as its inherent variability, devoid of undesirable special causes. The potential capability is determined by comparing the process spread, 6σ, with the specification spread, $(U - L)$. If $6\sigma < (U - L)$, the process is very capable and will meet specifications if the mean is near the midpoint of the specification limits. Several things can be done to take advantage of this desirable situation. If $6\sigma = (U - L)$, the process is barely capable and should be watched with a control chart. If $6\sigma > (U - L)$, the process is not capable, leaving several management-level alternatives. A key principle is that process capability cannot be determined until the process is stable and predictable; that is, until it is brought into statistical control using control charts.

Three capability indexes were presented that take process variability into account: C_p, which measures the ratio of specification spread to process spread without regard to the location of the process mean; C_{pk}, which measures also the proximity of the process mean to the closest specification limit; and C_{pm}, which measures the proximity of the process mean to a designated target T. When the target is midway between specification limits, and the process mean is on target, all three capability indexes are equal. Indexes of 1.00 are considered minimal; values higher are usually specified. All indexes assume that the process is in statistical control, that the process is normally distributed, and that the true process mean and the true process standard deviation are known. In reality none of these is usually known for certain, and the calculated index is a sample statistic whose characteristics are complicated. In practice, calculated indexes are improperly used as if they were the true parameter value. Because it is not considered possible to represent total process behavior by one numerical score, the use of capability indexes is seriously challenged. Capability indexes tend to focus on achieving the specified score instead of on improving the process using proven statistical methods. Nevertheless, interest in indexes continues.

23.10 Putting It into Practice

Capability studies on four machines making the same part were conducted. The part specifications are 1.500″ ± 0.005″. Control charts on all machines showed that they were in statistical control. Histograms suggested that normal curves were appropriate models for all machines.

The studies yielded the following information:

Machine	Sample Size (n)	Mean (X̄)	Process Spread (6S)
1	315	1.495″	0.004″
2	255	1.502″	0.006″
3	330	1.500″	0.012″
4	365	1.498″	0.012″

(a). Draw distributions, one above each other, using the same baseline scale for each machine with specification limits in the same location so that the distributions can be easily compared with each other. Estimate capability indexes C_p and C_{pk} for each machine. Then answer the following questions.

(b). If the mean can be readily shifted by adjustment to the machine, which machine is the best to use?

(c). If the mean cannot be readily shifted by adjustment to the machine, and the least amount of rework or repair is permitted, which machine is the best to use?

(d). What action, if any, do you consider appropriate for each machine?

Answers to Problem

Upper specification limit U = 1.500″ + 0.005″ = 1.505″
Lower specification limit L = 1.500″ − 0.005″ = 1.495″
Specification spread $U - L$ = 1.505″ − 1.495″ = 0.010″

(a). Calculation estimates of capability indexes C_p and C_{pk}; distributions:

Est of $C_p = (U - L)/6S$.
Est of C_{pk} = Minimum of $(U - \bar{X})/3S$ and $(\bar{X} - L)/3S$.

Machine	6S	Est of C_p	Est of C_{pk}
1	0.004"	0.010/0.004 = 2.50	(1.495 - 1.495)/0.002 = 0
2	0.006"	0.010/0.006 = 1.67	(1.505 - 1.502)/0.003 = 1.00
3	0.012"	0.010/0.012 = 0.83	(1.500 - 1.495)/0.006 = 0.83
4	0.012"	0.010/0.012 = 0.83	(1.498 - 1.495)/0.006 = 0.50

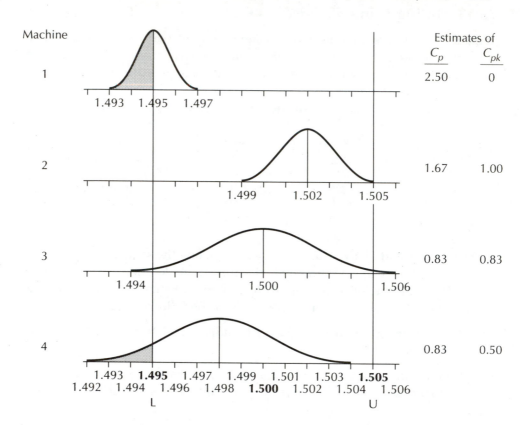

Note that the estimate of C_p for Machine 1 is very high, although about half of the output is outside specifications. The reason is that C_p is influenced only by the variability and not by the location of the mean. Also note that the estimates of C_p and C_{pk} for Machine 3 are the same because the machine is centered at the midpoint between the specification limits.

(b). If the mean can be readily shifted by adjustment to the machine, the best machine to use is 1. It has the least variability.

(c). If the mean cannot be readily shifted by adjustment to the machine, and the least amount of rework or repair is permitted, the best machine to use is 2. Note that some units can be expected to exceed the upper specification limit of 1.505", the amount beyond three standard deviations on one side of a normal curve. Answer: 0.00135 or about one out of a thousand.

(d). Since all of the machines are set up to produce the same part, and Machines 1 and 2 have substantially less variability than Machines 3 and 4, the first two machines should be examined and tested to see where they differ from Machines 3 and 4. Or could operators play a part? Or some other factor? There must be a detectable difference in the first two machines that would be worth investigating to see if the last two machines could be modified.

PART FOUR

Implementing SPC

*We are in a decade where
customer service is the battle cry.*

—Pamela Stull, vice president,
Newspaper Association of America

C H A P T E R 2 4

Implementing a System of SPC

EXCELLENCE!

SPC can be treated as a system in the overall scheme of delivering a quality product or service. SPC is a tool kit of skills, methods, and techniques, most of which are statistical in nature, but this collection does not wander around an organization looking for opportunities where the tools can be used. The reverse is the preferred approach: When an opportunity arises, usually in the form of a problem or a crisis, SPC should be available as one of many tools—in fact, a principal tool—to bring the problem or crisis into objective focus as an important first step toward the ultimate solution of *preventing* the problem from occurring again. Doctors do not roam the hospital corridors searching for patients on whom to administer the medicines in the doctors' medicine bags. Doctors and nurses in charge of hospital patients search for medicines and devices that are appropriate to the ailment.

The objectivity that characterizes SPC converts information into some form of impartial data from which emotion and preconceived notions have been culled. Anyone walking into a staff meeting with tabulated data, a histogram, or control charts lends considerable credence to problem definition and recommended solutions, devoid of hysteria, conjectures, and pet theories that may be expressed by others.

SPC can go further. SPC can be integrated into the general organization as a function just as important as cost information. Statistical information can be generated and travel along the flow chart of operations in the same way that products, components, or services are generated. At key points relevant data can accompany the process stage. Samples can be taken; means and standard deviations can be calculated; histograms can be drawn; control charts can be generated and analyzed; and other SPC tools applied. SPC can be a vital part of information flow that is needed to make dependable decisions along the way.

24.1 Part of Total Quality

As each organization modernizes itself to embrace the total quality concept, SPC can be looked on as a vital partner. The total quality concept goes beyond the quality of produced product. *Every activity* of an organization, whether it engages in batch processes, discrete items of manufacture, or various services, is subject to objective quality assessment and quality improvement.

Such activities include marketing, research and development, planning, design engineering, sales, quality assurance, training, purchasing, supplier assessment, operations, maintenance, packaging, order taking, shipping, trucking, billing, janitorial services, secretarial pools, retirement plans, data processing, software management, human resources, and all the other functions of the organization or company. Each of them consists of objectives and operations that are quality-oriented and subject to statistical assessment and continuous quality improvement. Each can depend on SPC-type of data information and analysis to help it achieve those objectives and improve the operations.

24.2 Action Items Needed to Implement SPC

Let us first look at some SPC problems that might be present in companies and organizations. The following list, labeled "The Pitfalls to Successful SPC," was prepared by Reid[1]:

- Lack of top management support

- Lack of middle management support

- Commitment in only one department

- Short-term commitment—failure to stay on course

- Haphazard approach—a little of this and that with no meaningful change in the system

- Failure to acquire the services of a competent statistician or to provide statistical training for employees

---

[1]Robert P. Reid, Jr., "America's Quality Revolution," *Quality*, August 1985, Hitchcock Publishing Company, Carol Stream, Illinois, pp. Q3–Q4.

- Measure success and guide program on the basis of short-term profits

- Failure to solicit worker input

- Overdependence on computerized quality control

- Funding failure—lack of funds to make meaningful changes in the system (for example, new machinery, training, improved raw materials)

- No market research; not knowing what the requirements are

- No testing of incoming materials—garbage in, garbage out

- Overselling hourly workers—expecting instant pudding

- Adversarial management (management by fear).

You might possibly recognize some of the pitfalls in your own organization. If there is to be a groundswell of movement to improve the quality of products and processes and to implement SPC, the initiative to overcome these pitfalls must start somewhere. Why not with you?

The suggested action items that follow are not necessarily to be achieved in the order shown. Each company or organization is different: different markets, different customers, different infrastructures. Yet many items are universal and may apply to your environment.

1. *Start SPC in a small way as a pilot program.* Develop SPC in one department or one process or one stage of a process that is critical. Choose a site where the person in charge (foreman, supervisor, manager) is amenable to trying new methods, and select only a few characteristics where meaningful data are easy to obtain. If SPC is successful here and results in a controlled and predictable process, together with reduced variability, reduced waste, higher quality, and a happier customer (internal or external), the news will spread. When possible, convert results to dollars, but do not make this the primary goal of the SPC project. Have the cost information available and let management make the inference.

2. *Educate managers in the philosophy of SPC.* Top management and plant managers must be willing participants because they own the program and are key to the success of SPC. Some statistical tools of SPC will have to be introduced, and managers tend to be receptive to new techniques and can learn statistical skills readily (of course, there are exceptions). Some success stories will have to be presented that show the effect on customers, costs, and long-term profits.

3. *Develop a long-range plan for implementing SPC.* Success is not achieved overnight, and all employees must be made aware of that fact. Be sure to involve the hourly workers in the planning.

4. *Determine customer wants and needs, and convert them to specifications, if at all possible.* Work with the customer. You probably have done so already, but everything depends on defining customer needs as precisely as possible. Establishing rapport with the customer requires effort and some cost. Let the customer visit your facility; visit the customer's facility. Develop a relationship that is akin to a partnership so that information is more freely shared between the two parties. Sometimes the customer is not quite sure what is needed. Become familiar with the end use of the product being supplied so that you are in a position to help in a more intelligent way. Then convert the customer's needs to specifications (targets and limits), drawings, physical samples, and instructions that are meaningful.

5. *Train managers and hourly workers in basic SPC.* Proceed slowly; remember that many people have been out of school for many years. Basic arithmetic may have to be reviewed. The sequence in which SPC material is introduced is critical (see Chapter 26). Teaching statistical methods effectively requires a high order of skill, so get the best teacher you can afford. This is where problem-solving skills can begin.

6. *Empower people to take corrective action that is statistically justified.* Every operator, for example, can be made to feel that the process is his or hers, but decisions to take corrective action must be based on the statistical tools learned, particularly control charts. Identifying special causes may not always be possible for operators involved with complex processes, so requests for assistance from technical staff should be encouraged and honored.

7. *Set up project teams with diversified membership.* Teams can focus on key problems. If various disciplines are represented on the teams, the interdependence of the departments will become evident and should foster improved cooperation among them. Statistics can become the common language, and problem-solving the common skill.

8. *Review measurement methods.* Replace go/no go methods with measuring equipment that will yield useful numerical data.

9. *Establish rapport with suppliers.* You have a dual role as both supplier and customer. Consider the supplier as an extension of your own facility and be willing to share information, knowledge, and skills. Visit the supplier facility; have the supplier visit your facility.

10. *Consider automatic data collection and processing equipment.* Manual recording of data will be a thing of the past as on-line recording and data-processing equipment become more available and affordable. Computers and SPC software are readily available (see Chapter 25). The objectives are accuracy, speed, and flexibility.

11. *Close the loop with continuous process improvement.* Integrate each improvement of the process into the entire system, and provide for continuous process improvement.

24.3 The Role of Management

Of course, SPC implementation is rather academic if the management of the organization does not buy into the statistical approach of doing business or running an organization. It is almost a truism to say that nothing takes place without management's approval and support. It is management that must create the right atmosphere, attitude, and aura of acceptance, commitment, learning, and implementation. However, those levels of achievements will not be reached with any effectiveness unless management goes beyond mere tacit approval and support: Management must get involved and participate.

Some managers traditionally picture themselves as cheerleaders, exhorting their subordinates to pitch in and work hard. Cheerleading might be necessary, but it's not sufficient. Managers can shift from cheerleaders to leaders, creating visions for their areas of responsibility and setting examples of involved behavior that demonstrate those visions. In the context of those visions and their demonstration by their managers, people become motivated, their objectives become more clear, and they become innovative and cooperative as they realize that their objectives are commonly shared with fellow employees.

If the powers of SPC are to be effectively realized, managers can set an example by showing that they, too, can use such powerful tools. SPC is not to be confined to the production floor, to the laboratory, or to the office. To do so limits its strengths and wide applications. In addition to all of the character traits that are supposed to epitomize a successful manager, the ingredient needed to raise SPC to a lofty level of successful implementation is that of *courage*, the courage to show a willingness to learn and to put that learning into practice that is visible.

In an entertaining and insightful description of how a hypothetical top executive struggles on his journey to quality, Cound writes[2]:

> This year we must institute the use of statistical tools at the top of our organization. Unless managers and executives are using these tools to manage and

---

[2] Dana M. Cound, *A Leader's Journey to Quality*, p. 171, ASQC Quality Press, Milwaukee, 1992.

improve their process, we can't expect them to be used by the rank and file. When managers get used to using them and develop an appreciation for their value, they will begin to think statistically. Only then will they begin to ask statistical kinds of questions of their people. Until that happens statistical process control will remain an aberration; something off to the side to please the old man in his dotage. SPC is the key to consistency. We must not only improve quality and reduce cost, but we must improve consistency of all our processes.

In a keynote address at the 1992 Fall Technical Conference of the Chemical and Process Industries Division of ASQC, Dr. Harold Porosoff of American Cyanamid discussed quality in R & D and the conversion of ideas to implementation:

> Perhaps it takes a long time to change from pleasing your boss to pleasing your customers, to change from "If it ain't broke, don't fix it" to continuous improvement, to change from trying to inspect-in quality at the end to controlling the process, to change from blaming an individual to blaming the system in which they work, and, finally, to make widespread use of statistical thinking rather than gut feel.

The prestigious Malcolm Baldrige National Quality Award (MBNQA), signed into law in 1987 by an Act of Congress, recognizes U.S. companies that have exhibited extraordinary achievements in quality and quality management. MBQNA is managed by the U.S. Department of Commerce and the National Institute of Standards and Technology (NIST), and is administered by the American Society for Quality Control (ASQC). The award program provides guidelines to companies to improve the quality of their products, processes, and services, and also contributes to the self-evaluation that many companies began to practice.[3] Candidate organizations are evaluated in the following seven key categories with the indicated weights in percentages of the total score:

1.   9.5% Leadership

2.   7.5% Information and analysis

3.   6.0% Strategic quality planning

4.   15.0% Human resource development and management

5.   14.0% Management of process quality

6.   18.0% Quality and operational results

7.   <u>30.0%</u> Customer focus and satisfaction

    100.0% Of Total Score.

---

[3] For an excellent progress report of the Baldrige Award, see Chester Placek, "Baldrige Award as a Quality Model," *Quality,* February 1992, Hitchcock Publishing Company, Carol Stream, Illinois, pp. 17–20.

The first awards were given in 1988. In 1992, for the first time, five companies received awards.

24.4 Flattening of the Hierarchy

Trends in organizational charts are beginning to show a flattening of the hierarchy. The deep economic recession of the 1980s that extended into the early 1990s forced many companies to reduce their staff and to take a fresh look at their structural organization as they prepared for the euphemistic "downsizing." Those adversely affected by downsizing took no pleasure in the cleverness of the person who facetiously observed that "unemployment isn't working." Basic questions of functional contribution were asked, activities and responsibilities were analyzed, and courageous attempts at restructuring were started. Perhaps there were things that could be done even with a reduced staff that would make people more productive without hurting the quality of goods or services.

Downsizing will usually have an effect on the quality of goods and services and on the company's objectives and policies. Here are some results of a survey[4] of 1,200 companies from 24 industries that were involved in downsizing:

- No company of any size is immune from downsizing.

- Explore alternatives to downsizing, such as a hiring freeze, restricting overtime, retraining, job sharing.

- Plan downsizing strategy in advance. Too often individuals essential to successful reorganization were not involved.

- Develop a comprehensive communications plan. One-third of those surveyed reported that employees were told about layoffs less than a week before implementation.

- Define the new company. Management should know what its new goals are, where emphasis will be placed, and the staff needed.

- Nurture the survivors of the reorganization. Remaining employees are usually confused about their future. Seventy-two percent of those surveyed said the new company was not a better place to work.

- Consider outplacement assistance.

Many companies found that they could eliminate middle management positions and shift the quality and decision-making responsiblities downward, conveniently labeled *empowerment*. Empowerment succeeds in altering the

---

[4] Reported by Wayne B. Clark in a featured news article, *Milwaukee Sentinel*, January 11, 1993.

operational structure of organizations, giving line people a new sense of partici-pation and a new sense of identification with the company's objectives. This change is reflected in the flattening of the organizational charts, a trend that is likely to continue as companies brace themselves for the "lean and mean" look triggered by the recession.

But empowerment without objective nonpartisan tools, such as SPC, for measuring, monitoring, and analyzing process behavior could paralyze consci-entious attempts to make improvements. When in-process teams are formed to study quality problems, their statistical tools become the common language that helps the team members and overseeing managers gauge the effectiveness of their studies, conclusions, recommendations, and implementations.

The advent of cross-functional teams in the auto industry, teams in which key disciplines represent the work force, is not really new, but it has taken on a new importance inspired by customer focus and the need to integrate functions and disciplines. The result seems to be a breaking down of the barriers between management and other workers. As barriers began to fall, a Ford area manager observed that "management will become invisible." Going one step further on a national scale, the three major automakers have jointly prepared an SPC reference manual (1991) in which the statistical tools for their suppliers are to be

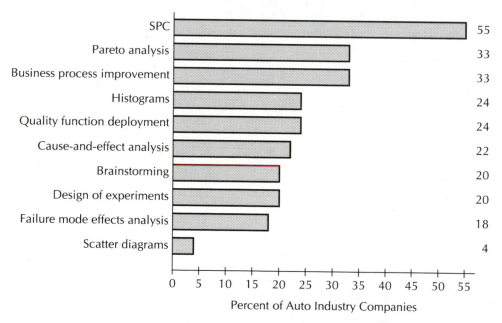

Figure 24.1. Importance of quality tools in U.S. auto industry.

Adapted from J. Wolak, "Auto Industry Quality: What Are They Doing?" *Quality,* January 1993, p. 17.

uniformly used. This unique cooperative venture was prepared by the Automotive Division of ASQC in collaboration with the Automotive Industry Action Group (AIAG), the latter headquartered in Southfield, Michigan.

A survey among U.S. companies in the auto industry showed that SPC is the most frequently used quality tool.[5] Fifty-five percent of companies polled said that SPC is used, far ahead of the 33% second-place tools, Pareto analysis and business process improvement (see Figure 24.1).

24.5 The Customer, Customer, Customer

One of the dramatic changes that seem to be taking place in American industry is the rather startling focus on three entities as the ultimate determiner of what a company should be, what it should be making, and what it should be marketing: the customer, the customer, the customer. American industry is gradually becoming customer-driven. It is no longer adequately chic to declare that mere customer satisfaction is the company's goal. After all, some managers' definition of satisfaction is to replace defective product or to refund money. Now one strives to make the customer *delighted* as well, so that the customer becomes an enthusiastic and ardent unsolicited supporter of the producer's products and services.

AT&T's Universal Card Services (UCS), which won a Baldrige Award in 1992 in the service category, has defined customer satisfaction to a higher level: "Quality is important, productivity is important, but if the customer is in trouble, drop everything and help." The policy of UCS has resulted in phenomenal growth in just three years, from its inception consisting of 35 members to a profitable billion-dollar company employing 2,500 people—and it is still growing. Customer delight extends even to card members who are delinquent. The motto of the collections group is "Make 'em happy and make 'em pay." Every day more than 100 quality measurements of various parts of the business are accessible throughout the company on TV monitors. And every month 4,000 among the more than 12,000,000 domestic customers are queried about UCS quality service in eight key areas. The result: UCS turned a profit well ahead of schedule, and 96% of employees (known as associates) felt that the company demonstrates its commitment to quality daily, almost double the U.S. norm.[6]

As National Quality Month continues to be celebrated in October each year in the United States, the customer continues to rise above the rhetoric as a

---

[5] Survey conducted jointly by Ernst & Young/American Quality Foundation and reported by Jerry Wolak, "Auto Industry Quality: What Are They Doing?" *Quality*, January 1993, Hitchcock Publishing Company, Carol Stream, Illinois, pp. 16–22.

[6] John J. Kendrick, "Five Baldrige Awards in Year Five," *Quality*, January 1993, Hitchcock Publishing Company, Carol Stream, Illinois, pp. 27–28.

dominant driving force. Note in Section 24.3 that "Customer focus and satisfaction" accounts for the largest single percentage—30%—of the total Baldrige Award score, while "Leadership" heads the first category in the scoring.

The term *customer* is relative. Customers can be external to an organization, the usual perception, or internal within an organization, the newer perception. The traditional departmentalization of companies makes any department both a supplier to the next department and a customer of a previous department. The responsibilities associated with the dual roles need to be recognized in order for the relationships to be clear and dynamic.

Any subassembly operation, for example, depends on at least one other department to provide the components, while the next department in the flow accepts the completed subassembly for further steps in the process. The dual roles force the subassembly operation to place certain quality demands on the suppliers of components and also conform to the quality needs of the next department. The political climate within organizations, however, makes the dual role unspecific so that quality demands are not as strong as they could be, and quality responsibilities to the needs of the next department are not as binding. Everyone involved, after all, is part of the same family, and one tends to be forgiving and lenient to family members. All of this is changing, however, as the total quality concept becomes more firmly entrenched.

A janitor (or sanitary engineer, if you will), for example, has quality objectives of keeping the place clean, providing continuous supplies, and maintaining equipment in operating condition. We know who the janitor's customers are. The janitor's suppliers are those who provide the disposable supplies and capital equipment. The dual roles of any operation need to be better defined.

Formal procedures, such as *quality function deployment* (QFD), stress the focus of every company and organizational function on the customer and the customer's needs and desires. Included are specifications, operating procedures, administration, training efforts, and almost every act that an organization performs.

Schools are beginning to restructure themselves according to the needs of the true customer, the student. Hospitals are managing their skills and services in an organized way around the patient's needs and care, some providing, for example, a home-like atmosphere in a recovery room after a baby is born and held by the new mother. Some medical laboratories are using control charts to maintain control over reference samples. Professional organizations, such as ASQC, identify the typical member as the customer around whom the entire Society revolves, for whom all department structures have been recreated, and to whom all staff members are focused and dedicated. The result has been some striking improvements in service quality in all of these areas.

24.6 SPC in the Service Industries

James Welch, senior vice president of American Express, observed, "Applying statistical process control (SPC) to service is still like venturing into uncharted territory."[7] Quality practitioners recognize that there is a difference between manufacturing and service organizations and that it is not immediately clear how SPC tools can be used in service or nonmanufacturing environments.

In manufacturing organizations formal specification limits are clear and well defined. Numbers are specific. Quality characteristics assigned to meet those specifications are clearly described and usually measurable. Everyone knows what length is, or weight, or hardness, or electrical resistance. Equipment is available to measure these characteristics in units that are familiar: centimeters, pounds, Rockwell units, ohms. Both variables and attributes data, we have already seen, are amenable to the methods of SPC.

But in nonmanufacturing environments the quality characteristics are more uncertain, vague, and nebulous. Specifications tend to be not too precise. Answers to the following questions tend to be "It all depends" and "As soon as possible," neither of which is very helpful:

- How soon must a package be delivered?

- How must a customer complaint be resolved, and how soon?

- How soon must a bill be sent or a refund delivered?

- What sales technique pleases a customer?

- How should a bank teller greet a waiting customer, and how long should a transaction take?

- How should a telephone call or inquiry be treated?

- What kind of after-sales service is appropriate, and how do you measure it?

- What are the kinds of service important to a hospital patient, and how do you measure them?

- Which teacher-pupil relationships are important to a student?

These and many more examples identify the challenges that face the service industries. At the same time, however, the opportunities for quantifying service

---

[7] James F. Welch, "Service Quality Measurement at American Express Traveler's Cheque Group," *The Quality Management Forum*, Winter 1992, pp. 8–11, newsletter of the Quality Management Division of ASQC. Article originally appeared in *National Productivity Review*, Autumn 1992.

characteristics and applying useful SPC tools are surprisingly endless. ASQC's Service Industries Division, chartered in 1991, enrolled more than 3,500 members in less than two years. A partial listing of the kinds of service organizations represented includes the following:

Accountants	Health care
Airlines	Hospitals
Banks	Hotels
Car and truck rentals	Insurance
Chambers of commerce	Investments
Communications	Legal profession
Consultants	Overnight mailings
Credit cards	Social services
Dental societies	Transportation
Engineering	Utilities
Government services	

Three quality characteristics appear to be universally identified with service objectives. Despite their small number, these characteristics give quality practitioners an unusual opportunity to use innovation and imagination in applying SPC tools. They are (1) timeliness, (2) accuracy, and (3) quality of responsiveness.

1. *Timeliness—The amount of time it takes to perform the service task:* Timeliness is almost always an important criterion of the service environment. It is easily measured in time units of seconds, minutes, hours, days, and so on. Specification limits are usually related to *maximum* time, such as "No more than 24 hours to start filling an order." "We guarantee delivery absolutely, positively the next day." "We shoot for no more than two rings of the telephone before it is answered." Since time is a measurable phenomenon, it is amenable to statistical calculations such as mean and standard deviation, to histograms and models, and to control chart applications.

2. *Accuracy—The service performed must be accurate:* An order must be filled correctly. The hospital patient must receive the right dosage. The customer's bank balance must be correct and up to date. The car repair must be done to the customer's satisfaction.

   The characteristic usually used to measure accuracy (or lack of accuracy) is *errors* of nonconformance or nonconformity and thus is an attribute amenable to all of the attributes control charts that detect trends, good or bad. Targets or standards are usually specified for this characteristic, usually reflecting customer satisfaction levels.

3. *Quality of responsiveness—The human side of business:* This area is, perhaps, the most difficult to quantify but the easiest to describe. It reflects the human contact with a customer: how a telephone call is answered; how a complaint is handled; how a returned product is expedited; how a salesperson greets and assists a potential buyer; and so on.

Quality of responsiveness to service is a quantifiable characteristic as long as efforts are made to obtain customer response using properly designed survey techniques, and the resulting data are properly summarized and analyzed. It is a procedure in many companies to send a postcard of inquiry to the customer after a service has been performed, asking for the customer's reaction, and using the returned information to correct deficiencies and to improve the service even more. Summarization of data and charting techniques can play a huge part in this area in measuring success of the business and in detecting trends.

Before the Saturn automobile was introduced into the marketplace in 1991, General Motors took a new look at the business of producing and servicing automobiles and introduced some innovative ways of improvement that were aimed directly at the car-buying public. First, the public was surveyed as to what features of car and service were desired. Second, these features were introduced into the car design and into the showroom and dealer operation.

As an example of how far GM-Saturn is going to please the customer, respondents to surveys indicated that insignia, stickers, logos, and emblems advertising the name of the dealer were not very popular. They were omitted in the car's design, except for the city location of the dealer: "Saturn of . . ." Eliminating the dealer's name contributed to a clean, unadorned look for the car. Availability of the service garage to accommodate working patterns of buyers was another service feature of importance, and so Saturn dealers are open at least two nights a week and also on Saturday mornings. At least one Saturn dealer independently provides a free car wash at any time to owners of the new subcompact.[8]

All Saturn-dealer employees tour the only Saturn plant, in Tennessee, and participate in team-building exercises there in order to appreciate firsthand the focus on quality and customer service. In that plant machine-tool operators use user-friendly coordinate measuring machines (CMMs) instead of hard gauges for SPC data in process control and for "feeling the pulse of the operation." Sales are reported to be brisk, and 1993 is expected to be a year in which Saturn operations will break even, quite remarkable for only the third model year.[9]

---

[8] Saturn of Milwaukee and Saturn of Waukesha, Wisconsin, operated by the Boucher Group.

[9] News item in the *Milwaukee Sentinel*, January 8, 1993.

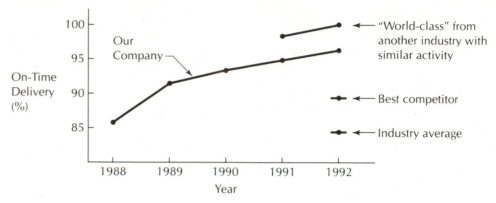

Figure 24.2. On-time delivery, last five years. MBNQA-suggested graph for a service company.

The common base for all service operations is the customer or the ultimate consumer. Once the decision is made to improve a service-oriented business, the customer and the ultimate consumer surface as the central focus of all planning, operations, and implementation. In this respect, manufacturing businesses have something important to learn from the nonmanufacturing and service businesses where, of necessity, life is customer-oriented. That concept must be realized, and operations must be designed to implement that concept, in order to be successful.

The Malcolm Baldrige National Quality Award recognizes service companies as one of three eligibility categories. The other categories are manufacturing companies and small businesses. In 1992, for the first time since the awards were issued, two service companies won the award: AT&T Universal Card Services and the Ritz-Carlton Hotel Company. MBNQA, in its award criteria and guidelines, suggests that statistical data for service achievements should be presented in a graphic format, such as that shown in Figure 24.2, which provides for a comparison with other standards or benchmarks, such as world-class companies from another industry, the best competitor in the resident industry, and an industry average.[10]

24.7 Summary

SPC can be treated as a system providing key statistical information that is generated along with product. The total quality concept embraces every organization's activity, and SPC can be a vital partner. Action items for implementing

---

[10] Adapted from *1993 Award Criteria* booklet, Malcolm Baldrige National Quality Award, NIST, Gaithersburg, Maryland, p. 14.

SPC were proposed. Management's role is to change from cheerleader to leader, from supporter to active participant in the implementation of SPC methods. The Malcolm Baldrige National Quality Award (MBNQA) recognizes management achievements in quality and serves as a self-evaluation guide as well. The recession of the 1980s and 1990s has resulted in a flattening of the hierarchy as companies laid off employees; as a result, decision-making, or empowerment, moved lower in the organization. The customer has become the driving force for organizations striving to improve their quality. Any department is both customer and supplier. The nonmanufacturing industries, including service and administration, are seeing new applications of SPC in three areas: timeliness, accuracy, and quality of responsiveness.

24.8 Putting It into Practice

Select two service or administrative functions in your organization.

1. Determine their quality objectives and how they are organized to serve those objectives, if at all.

2. Identify the customer and supplier roles in these functions.

3. If written specifications are available, determine where SPC can help in measuring progress and contributing to quality improvement.

4. Recommend specific management roles in SPC implementation.

C H A P T E R 2 5

Calculators and Computers for SPC

It should be evident so far that implementing SPC entails calculations as each sample subgroup of data enters the quality monitoring and control system. Questions arise as to who is to do the calculations and how the calculations are to be performed.

Until a few years ago, SPC sample data were recorded manually and calculations performed mentally by quality control inspectors who also selected the samples. In some cases these inspectors made adjustments to the process or else ordered the operator in charge to make the adjustments. That has changed dramatically. Manual calculations are giving way to electronic calculators, portable data-entry devices, or personal computers available at hand for immediate results. Operators may be empowered to take the sample, make the measurements, do the calculations, plot on a control chart, make a decision, and assume responsibility for adjusting the process. Even those functions are being automated in some industries.

Let's explore the marvelous hand calculator and the omnipresent computer and their impact on SPC data handling and calculations.

25.1 Calculators for SPC

This little, lightweight, portable, AC-operated device achieved a price breakthrough in the 1960s when it was sold for under $100 (that is, $99.95). Many of us stood in line to buy one—and all it could do was add, subtract, multiply, and

---

* From *The New Yorker*, October 28, 1991, p. 84, with the comment, "Don't worry, we will!"

divide. Today electronic calculators are even more compact in size, come battery-operated or solar-powered, perform dozens of arithmetic and scientific operations, have multiple memories, and have graphic capabilities, all for a fraction of the cost years ago. It is safe to say that calculators today are one of the greatest bargains in the world.

Every popular brand has a prolific variety of models serving almost every need in business, science, engineering, and education. Those operated with lithium batteries have a remarkably long shelf life. Many models are solar-powered, extending their usefulness as long as moderate lighting is available, and some solar-powered calculators have battery backups.

Calculators useful for SPC work are called statistical calculators or scientific calculators with statistical functions. Many keys serve dual functions or even triple functions. In the statistical mode these calculators, at a minimum, can store a set of data in memory and determine the sample size (number of entries), the sum, the sum of squares, the mean, and two forms of standard deviation.

Determining the correct standard deviation is of particular importance. Recall that the population standard deviation σ has a different formula from that of the sample standard S. Most statistical calculators will differentiate between the two by some symbolic notation. For example, Sharp calculators identify them as σ and S, respectively. Casio and Texas Instruments calculators identify them as σ_n and σ_{n-1}, respectively.

If a calculator does not distinguish between the population and sample standard deviation, you have the responsibility of determining which one the calculator provides. The calculator manual usually contains the explanation. The author's 1–2–3 test will serve that purpose quickly and simply (see Chapter 11, Section 11.18).

Perhaps one of the most outstanding SPC features that one can find, not available in all statistical calculators, is the ability to find the area under the normal curve, useful for estimating the percentage inside or outside specifications. The Z value corresponding to any point under study is entered, such as a specification limit, and the calculator has three keys that provide the area under different parts of the normal curve. One key gives the area from the point in question to *minus infinity;* another key gives the area from the point in question to the *mean;* and a third key gives the area from the point in question to *plus infinity* (see Figure 25.1). Furthermore, the area is given to six decimal places, more than in most popular tables for normal curve areas.

Many of these calculators also generate random numbers, which are useful for obtaining random samples from a lot (or for selecting losing lottery numbers). There are, of course, other useful features of these remarkable little calculating tools. Be sure to get one.

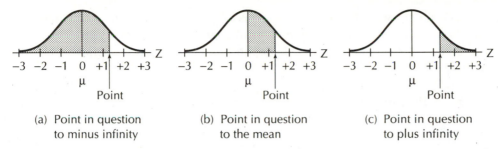

(a) Point in question
to minus infinity

(b) Point in question
to the mean

(c) Point in question
to plus infinity

Figure 25.1. Three areas under the standard normal curve provided by some statistical calculators.

25.2 Computers for SPC

The personal computer, or microcomputer, has had a major influence on how we manage data and other information. Its application to SPC is appealing and increasing as we tend to move away from manual calculations toward speedy, more accurate, more flexible, and even more automated data-processing and data-entry arrangements.

Manually recording data and graphing control charts, however, still hold an important place in SPC work. It is a myth to assume that, because we have computers, more charts are better or that perfect-looking charts must be right or that the computer becomes the instant SPC expert. Computers cannot replace people on whom we rely for judgment, even intuitive judgment. A technological bandaid is not the solution to SPC implementation.

Despite the attraction of computer technology for SPC work, a danger lies in complete reliance on such equipment. Computers are only as good as the software that runs the computer programs. The popular metaphor, "Garbage in, garbage out" is in danger of being replaced by "Garbage in, gospel out." Error-free software is still a goal, not an achievement. Even in the sophisticated, high-technology world of space science and the National Aeronautics and Space Administration (NASA), glitches in software occasionally occur that prevent space projects from being successfully completed.

25.3 SPC Software Programs

The availability of SPC software programs has exploded since the mid-1980s with the widespread use of the personal computer. The proliferation of software has made the selection of the right program a challenging exercise as competing manufacturers praise their products for being the best, fastest, most comprehensive, greatest value, and most popular.

Certain software features can be considered minimal as far as SPC requirements are concerned, primarily in control charts and their analysis. Other features can be considered optional, depending on the advanced stage of SPC activity.

Minimum Requirements (not in order of importance)

1. Descriptive statistics
     Sample size (number of data entries)
     Mean, median, and mode
     Minimum and maximum
     Range
     Standard deviations (S and σ)
     Variance (for future analysis)
     Sums, sums of squares

2. Bar chart and pie chart

3. Cause-and-effect diagram

4. Control charts
     Center line and control limits
     Average $\overline{X}$
     Median
     Range R
     Standard deviation S
     Individuals X
     Moving average $m\overline{X}$
     Moving range mR
     Proportion nonconforming p
     Number nonconforming np
     Number of nonconformities c
     Average number of nonconformities per unit u
     Analysis for presence of special causes

5. Flow chart

6. Gauge repeatability and reproducibility (GR&R)
     Statistical analysis of the measurement system

7. Histogram
     With normal curve overlay
     Optional cell widths
     Grouped and ungrouped data

8. Normal curve
   Areas under the curve to six decimal places
   Up to at least $Z = 4.90$
   Test for normality
   Test for skewness, kurtosis
   Percentage outside specs

9. Pareto chart
   Plot by frequency and cumulative percentage

10. Process capability analysis
    Capability indexes C_p and C_{pk} (if you must use them)
    Capability ratio CR

11. Random numbers
    Four-digit or five-digit
    Standard normal deviates (Z)
    At least 1000

12. Scatter diagram

13. Spreadsheet with statistical functions

Optional Features

1. Distributions (tables and graphs)
   Binomial
   Chi-square
   Poisson
   Student's t, uncorrelated; correlated (paired) data
   Variance ratio F

2. Contingency tables
   2×2, 2×3, 3×3, 3×4, 4×4
   Expected frequencies

3. Hypothesis tests
   Single population; two populations
   Mean (Z, t)
   Variance (chi-square)
   Proportion (Z)

4. Confidence intervals
   Mean
   Variance
   Proportion

5. Regression and correlation
   Line of best fit
   Correlation coefficient
   Confidence interval
   Test of hypothesis
   Regression equation
   Fitting second and third order, exponential, logarithm

6. Classic analysis of variance (ANOVA)
   Full factorial
   Fractional factorial
   One-way, two-way
   Up to five factors
   Up to four levels
   With or without replication
   Main effects and interaction
   ANOVA table
   Sums of squares, degrees of freedom, mean square, F ratio

7. Taguchi "method"
   Loss function
   Signal-to-noise ratio
   Orthogonal arrays
   Statistical analysis

We ask for little in requiring that the software programs be menu-driven and user-friendly. With the move toward real-time operations, the program should be able to access data from any work stations and interface with gauges, sensors, indicators, calipers, process controllers, bar-code readers, and other specialty machines for data acquisition. Many programs are prepared for integrated applications including data base, spread sheet, and word processing.

An important software caution for SPC is the same one that applies to calculators. Is the reported standard deviation one for a population σ or for a sample estimate S? How is the computer program treating the data? Unless the computer software specifically identifies which standard deviation it is that is being reported, the user has the responsibility to make the determination. Once again, the simple 1–2–3 test referred to in Section 25.1 and described in Chapter 11 can be used to make the proper labeling. One should also be on the watch for programs that use $\bar{R}/d_2$ indiscriminately as the estimate for the process standard deviation without ascertaining first that the process is in statistical control.

Finally, the many decimal places that software programs easily provide in a calculation do not represent more accuracy in the answer. The rules for rounding the final answer that is to be *reported* were discussed in Chapter 10 and are still recommended.

25.4 Software Suppliers

Two major quality magazines have provided periodic listings of software suppliers since the 1980s:

1. *Quality Progress,* ASQC's magazine, has published an annual QA/QC Software Directory every March since 1984. The directory comes in two parts: One part is an alphabetical listing of suppliers and a description of their specific software programs, including price. The second part is a matrix listing software suppliers alphabetically and identifies the specific software with regard to certain applications, listed as calibration, capability studies, data acquisition, design of experiments, gauge repeatability and reproducibility, inspection, management, measurement, problem solving, quality assurance for software development, quality costs, reliability, sampling, simulation, statistical methods, statistical process control, supplier quality assurance, Taguchi techniques, and training. The directory listing of March 1993 identified 235 suppliers of quality-related software products, up 45 from the previous year.

2. *Quality* magazine, published by Hitchcock Publishing Company, Carol Stream, Illinois, has published an SPC Software Listing twice a year, in June and December, since 1985. The listing is in the form of a matrix. Suppliers are listed alphabetically in a column, together with their specific software products. Across the top of the page are the various SPC applications that include histogram/normal probability plot, data transfer with external sources, real-time data chart, X-bar & R, X-bar & S, moving X & R, attributes, and run charts, as well as computer capability and cost. The intersecting cells are marked that apply. The listing of December 1992 identified 168 suppliers of 340 SPC software products.

The need for quality in software development, not only for SPC, was recognized when the Software Division of ASQC was established in 1989. Division members are concerned with software quality engineering, testing methods, preventing virus infection, networking, and sharing ideas through meetings, conferences, and publications.[1]

---

[1] See *Software Quality,* the magazine of the Software Division of ASQC, Milwaukee.

25.5 Summary

Manual calculations of SPC data are being replaced by calculators and computers. Calculators have evolved into inexpensive, compact devices with mathematical and statistical functions. Most statistical calculators distinguish between population and sample standard deviations, but caution should still be exercised to know the difference. Some calculators provide areas under the normal curve, a valuable feature. Computers are increasingly used for SPC work, although they do not yet replace human judgment. Software quality is a growing field. Some requirements were listed for software in SPC applications. Lists of software suppliers and products for SPC work are periodically reported in *Quality Progress* and *Quality* magazines.

For every person wishing to teach,
there are thirty not wanting to be taught.

—Anon.

CHAPTER 26

Training for SPC and Learning to Speak Statistics

There is no doubt that the proper and effective use of SPC requires that people learn the proper and effective use of statistics. It can be a frustrating, even a dangerous and costly experience, to use SPC methods incorrectly. For example, irrational subgrouping, confusion between parameter and sample standard deviations, or misinterpretation of a control chart can result in a wrong decision and consequent wrong action.

The responsibility for SPC training can be assumed by any one of several organizational departments. Included are quality assurance, training, engineering, operations, and human resources. Whoever assumes the responsibility faces the fact that statistics is not the most popular subject for learning. But the statistical concepts behind the tools of SPC are not beyond ordinary people's ability to comprehend them. An effective instructor is the first requirement.

This chapter contains some suggestions for conducting courses on SPC. Levels of instruction are usually customized in content and length for executive management, department heads and first-line supervisors, and hourly employees. The logistics depends on the availability of participants and the operations schedule of the organization.

26.1 Some Useful Principles of Learning and Teaching

It is very important to accept the fact that many learners in the world, the industrial world in particular, are people who may have been out of school for a number of years. Such bad news is worsened when statistical process control topics—read that as "sadistical"—may be viewed as intimidating and approached with apprehension. The good news is that effective teaching of SPC, viewed from the learner's perspective, is similar to the teaching of any other subject matter. When coupled with patience and long-term objectives, the teaching of SPC can help users make substantial contributions to quality improvement. Listed here are some learning and teaching principles, including some that may appear to be mundane and self-evident:

1. Plan the Course Carefully

Outline the topics in the sequence that is logical. Collect real-life examples, data, and exercises. Fit the course topics to the audience. Start with top management, and move down the ladder of hierarchy (the reverse, unfortunately, is a common route). State specific objectives for specific groups. For example, for first-line supervisors and operators: "If given a set of subgroups of five readings each, calculate and plot averages and ranges, plot the control charts, determine the control limits, and interpret the results."

Devise an objective way to measure the success of the course so that it can be continually improved; the measurement method can be left up to the instructor. Determine the physical needs of course site, supplies, equipment, breaks and refreshments, and restroom facilities. Check out the site personally to see that lighting, seating, visibility, and sound transmission are adequate, all of which can affect the learning process.

2. The Instructor Must be Thoroughly Familiar with SPC

This principle does not require that an instructor must have a Ph.D. in statistics, but it does require more than merely a passing acquaintance with SPC. Perhaps the best prerequisite is a combination of formal training and real-world experience, involving both technical knowledge and presentation skills.[1]

3. Use Real-Life Data and Graphics Generously

Any examples and exercises should involve data derived from the products, processes, or services with which the learner is acquainted. The concepts will become more meaningful, and the learning process will be enhanced, when the data used are relevant to the participant's world.

Real-life data, properly generated, not only provide the means to exercise the learned skills, they enhance the principle that decisions to be made should be based on objective evidence (data) and not on personal, preconceived assumptions. A desired side effect of the generous use of data is the strengthening of appreciation for variability, the heart of statistics. In addition, statistical thinking

---

[1] For some useful suggestions in developing competent instructors, see Robert D. Zaclewski, "Instructional Process Control," *Quality Progress*, ASQC, Milwaukee, January 1993, pp. 61–64.

is encouraged. The use of graphics is the quickest way to present concepts and results that, in general, have the same communication effect on everyone.

4. The Instructor Should Have Some Knowledge of the Learner's Work

Introduce the instructor to the learner's work environment in some way so that the products, processes, and language become part of the course. Plant tours for the instructor are very helpful for acquiring firsthand familiarity.

In many so-called public or open courses on SPC, where the class participants come from a wide variety of industrial backgrounds involving many different kinds of processes, it becomes a challenge for the instructor to relate the concepts specifically to the learner's experiences. There is no doubt that participants with some common backgrounds are preferred.

5. The Building-Block Approach Enhances the Learning Process

The logical progression of previously learned concepts is an important way of introducing each new concept. If this principle is violated, the participant's learning process may be interrupted and slowed, perhaps even stopped entirely. For example:

- *Distinction between process and sample precedes standard deviation* because nomenclature chosen and wording used in stating conclusions depend on distinguishing between process parameter and sample statistic.

- *Standard deviation precedes the normal curve* because areas under the curve are determined in terms of the number of standard deviations from the mean.

- *The normal curve precedes control charts* because the basic model for the charts is the normal curve from which decisions, based on area-under-the-curve probabilities, are made.

- *Control charts precede process capability* because the process must be in statistical control (determined from control charts) before capability can be ascertained.

The building-block approach, when carefully pursued, provides the necessary logic that almost all people inherently perceive and appreciate.

6. Provide Opportunities for Application in Order to Develop Skills

The usual route is to provide exercises for the participant to work on in class. Organizing the class into teams with specific problem assignments brings into play group dynamics that teach resourcefulness, cooperation, common goals, and leadership.

In addition to class exercises, another effective approach is to incorporate in the course program a time away from the formal class for the participant to apply some of the principles and skills learned, especially under supervision, in the real-world environment of the organization, company, or plant.

The development of skills is one of the most important objectives of any course. A measure of self-confidence is derived from enhanced skills that tend to be satisfying and to increase the probability of application of those skills, the supreme objective of training. Repetition to strengthen those skills is a valid teaching tool.

7. The Instructor Should Speak Clearly and Loudly

An inhibitor of good learning is the missing of key words and phrases that are critical to the explanation of concepts. The participant who does not clearly hear key words or phrases wastes time trying to identify them and make mental connections, thereby missing the concepts; such participants fall behind immediately. Speaking distinctly with moderate speed and adequate volume requires a conscious effort on the part of the instructor. Too many instructors speak and mistakenly assume that, having spoken, they are heard.

8. Let Participants Make Class Presentations

Most participants learning SPC tools will face the challenge of having to explain their SPC findings and problem-solving efforts to others, often as a group, usually an intimidating experience. By giving them the opportunity to make presentations in class to their peers (still intimidating but easier with the instructor's direction), they will develop presentation skills rarely taught in formal statistics classes.

9. Consciously Provide for Constant Feedback

Are you sure that your ideas are being understood? There are subtle ways to get answers without formal written testing. One way is to observe the participants visually during the teaching process. Eye contact, body language, attentiveness, and vocal participation are good clues. Another method is to ask questions periodically or to initiate class discussions (which usually start with a question). Instructors who instruct and hear only themselves are not genuine teachers. What about feedback for the participants? They also need to know where to improve. Class exercises and class presentations are the answers.

10. Provide Free Statistical Calculators to All Participants

Provide the same model for everyone, and have the sponsoring organization or company pay for the calculators. This little investment is a handy statistical tool, now affordable to practically everyone, pays big dividends. First, participants relish owning their own calculators. Second, since everyone gets the same model, the instructor can easily teach the basic mechanics of its use. Third, the participant develops an admired skill that can continue on long after the course is completed.

11. Award a Certificate to Participants

There is something gratifying in receiving a written and signed certificate of course completion. The participant's pride is an important psychological appeal that should not be ignored. When the certificate is signed and presented by a person of stature in the organization, the pride is enhanced and the participant recognizes the importance that top management attaches to his or her participation in the course.

26.2 Example of a Basic Course Outline

All personnel must be encouraged to undergo some level of SPC training, but course outlines have to be designed for different levels of personnel. It is advisable, even necessary, to conduct courses on SPC first for top management, then move down the hierarchy to middle managers and supervisors, then to technical staff and first-line supervisors, and finally to hourly people. Courses for top management are traditionally shorter in length, with emphasis placed on philosophy, responsibility, and relationship to the business enterprise. Courses for hourly people can be cost-effective if left in the hands of qualified in-house personnel who are available for teaching 1 or 2 hours at a time per class session stretched over a number of weeks or even months. Training the in-house trainers can be a separate course specifically designed for the purpose.

Figure 26.1 is an outline of a popular basic course on SPC taught by the author and usually conducted for technical staff and middle managers. Outlines for other homogeneous groups of people are developed specifically for them. Important features of this outline include

1. The logical sequence of the topics and skills taught

2. The use of real data from the organization or company for which the course is conducted

3. The organization of the class into teams

4. The overnight assignment of separate problems and data sets for each team

5. Presentations by teams the next morning followed by discussion.

STATISTICAL TOOLS FOR PROCESS CONTROL
Course Outline and Schedule

FIRST DAY—Foundations for Statistics

- Welcome and opening remarks by.................
- Distribution and use of hand calculators.
- Defining the process and the customer/consumer.
- What is statistical process control (SPC)?
- Role of statistical tools in process, product, and profit improvement.
- What can a graphic summary of process data tell us?
- Some basic rules of probability.
- Distinction between process and sample; nomenclature.
- Collecting data from a defined process.
- Measures of central tendency: mean, median, mode.
- Measures of variability: range, standard deviation.
- Understanding standard deviation clearly; use of calculators.
- Coding and decoding data for computing.
- Team assignments.

SECOND DAY—The Normal Curve; Control Charts

- Team presentations and discussions.
- The normal curve to predict variables; use of tables and calculator.
- How to judge "normality."
- Confidence belts to predict attributes.
- Control charts for SPC; historical background.
- Variables charts for average (X-bar), range (R), and standard deviation (S).
- Why they work as decision-making tools; a little theory.
- How to interpret control charts; decision rules.
- Use of correct language.
- Use of "assignable-cause log" on control chart worksheets.
- The dual purpose of charts: uniform decision-making and problem-solving.
- Identifying common (random) causes vs. special (assignable) causes.
- Attribute charts for defectives (p, np) and defects (c, u).
- Directional aspect of some control charts.
- Other kinds of charts to consider (median, CuSum).
- Proper planning to implement control charts.
- Team assignments.

THIRD DAY—Process Capability; Flow Chart Strategy; Plant Problems; Summary

- Team presentations and discussions.
- Process and machine capability studies; capability indexes (Cp, Cpk).
- Flow chart strategy to coordinate charts and capability studies.
- Principle of continuous process improvement.
- Open discussion on use of charts and other process controls; questions and answers.
- Course wrap-up and summary.
- Awarding course certificates and final remarks by ....

NOTE: There will be class exercises during the course.

SCHEDULE: 8:30–4:30 (12:00 on last day). Lunch 12:00–1:00.
  Breaks in morning and afternoon.

Figure 26.1. Suggested basic course outline.

The outline shown in Figure 26.1, designed for a 2¹/₂-day course, does not include acceptance sampling plans. If that topic is to be included in the outline, add another half day so that the course lasts for three full days. The logistics of whether or not the course is to be conducted on consecutive full days, the usual arrangement, or spread over a period of weeks depends on the availability of participants.

Course titles vary somewhat, reflecting the emphasis or objectives of the sponsoring organization and the appeal to potential participants. In the author's experience, sponsoring organizations assume all responsibility for selecting the course site and providing for audiovisual needs, supplies, refreshments, and hotel accommodations for the instructor. Also, organization or plant tours are provided for the instructor. A planning sheet is given to the sponsoring organization containing details of arrangements so that nothing is missed. Attention to detail in the planning stage is a key to a course's success.

Since the personnel situation in any organization is a dynamic one, with changes taking place regularly, provision should be made to offer SPC training to new hires regularly. In addition, under the philosophy that training is an ongoing enterprise and the responsibility of management, personnel who have taken a basic course should be offered refresher courses or updated courses or upgraded courses to take advantage of new SPC tools or refinement of existing tools that may become available. The accepted philosophy that processes are to undergo continuous improvement can certainly be extended to people and their training as well.

26.3 Preparing for the Future: SPC Training in Schools

(The informative material in this section was generously provided by Ray Wach-niak of Brookfield, Wisconsin, retired corporate quality director of the Firestone Tire & Rubber Company of Akron, Ohio. He is a charter member of the curriculum design committee of VICA, subject of this section.)

The focus thus far is on upgrading the SPC knowledge and skills of existing personnel actively involved in the manufacture of products and in service to customers. In a sense this is a costly endeavor because developing SPC skills among current employees is after the fact, much like playing catch-up ball. What about young students who are not yet actively employed? Is anything being done to prepare them for what lies ahead?

A group of people of vision have prepared a Total Quality Management curriculum designed for the nation's public high schools, vocational-technical centers, area vocational schools, and community colleges. Their purpose is to develop the competencies and basic skills of future employees that will nurture the drive for world-quality leadership. Their aim is long term: Prepare today's secondary and postsecondary students to become the work force for quality in the next century.

The group is called the Vocational Industrial Clubs of America (VICA), headquartered in Leesburg, Virginia. It is a professional organization for trade, industrial, technical, and health occupation students and instructors, made up of more than 250,000 members organized into 14,000 local chapters. VICA is recognized by state and federal departments of education as an integral part of the vocational-technical curriculum.[2]

VICA's mission statement, in part, is "to enhance VICA's *Quality of Work* movement by preparing students for the world of work through the addition of a Total Quality Management curriculum in the classroom environment." VICA is "dedicated to developing well-rounded students and future employees. It provides leadership, citizenship and character development programs as well as job skill training. VICA builds and reinforces self-confidence, positive work attitudes and good communications skills through its programs."

The long-term goals of VICA are unequivocal: Secondary and postsecondary students are expected to develop competencies and foundation skills to "enjoy a productive, full and satisfying life." Furthermore, the high-performance qualities "that characterize most competitive companies must become the standard for all employers." Finally, the nation's schools must be "transformed into high-performance organizations."

A curriculum design committee, consisting of representatives from industry and academia, prepared a curriculum consisting of 22 modules grouped into four sections. The comprehensive curriculum follows the guidelines of the U.S. Department of Labor Secretary's Commission on Achieving Necessary Skills (SCANS): *What Work Requires of Schools—A SCANS Report for America 2000*. The modules of the present curriculum, still under study and subject to revision, are as follows:

Section I: Total Quality Management (TQM) Overview

1. History of U.S. Quality

2. Definition of Quality

3. Who is the Customer?

4. Change

5. Quality Gurus

---

[2] A brochure containing details of VICA's total quality curriculum and a preview module can be obtained from National VICA, P.O. Box 3000, Leesburg, Virginia 22075, Attention, Department TQC.

6. TQM Definition

7. Deming's 14 Points

8. Teams

9. Benefits

Section II: Quality Tools

10. Idea Generation

11. Reaching Consensus

12. Decision-Making

13. Flow Charts

14. Cause-and-Effect Diagrams

15. Pareto Diagrams

16. Histograms

17. Scatter Diagrams

18. Trend and Control Charts

Section III: The TQM Improvement Process

19. TQM Improvement: Understand

20. TQM Improvement: Analyze

21. TQM Improvement: Improve

Section IV: TQM in the Work Environment—The SCANS Report

22. Workplace Know-How, Competencies, Foundation, Conclusions.

These modules are not necessarily sequential. They are being offered as packages of one or more modules together with teacher guides that can be taught independently of other modules. Each module represents a typical 45-minute class period.

The curriculum is undergoing an extensive pilot test. Faculty from 75 schools in 35 states took part in initial training in July 1992 in Louisville, Kentucky. The curriculum is being tested in classrooms during the academic year September 1992 to June 1993. Feedback response to the curriculum design committee at the time of this writing is "generally favorable," and adjustments to some modules may be made to fit in the 45-minute class time.

Some 8,000 community colleges in the United States are just becoming aware of the opportunity to review and discuss the proposed curriculum and its effect at the local level. There is no doubt that the interest is high and the goals lofty. After completing the curriculum, participants are expected to meet a number of quality objectives, some of which include the following:

- Define quality as meeting customer requirements.

- Differentiate between internal and external customers.

- Work effectively in teams and identify the benefits of TQM.

- Apply group consensus techniques to team situations.

- Interpret various histograms.

- Construct trend charts and control charts.

- Match quality tools to the correct phases of TQM.

26.4 Learning to Speak Statistics

Back in Chapter 20, Section 20.4, we discussed the language used in describing control chart results and deplored the commonly used phrases "The process is in control" and "The process is not in control." Such phrases, it was pointed out, can be meaningless and misdirected. The correct phrase includes the word "statistical" preceding the word "control." Then, for those who are uncomfortable mentioning that frightening word "statistical," some alternative expressions were offered that were less intimidating, but still technically valid to those who are inclined to be squeamish at the mere sight or sound of that word.

This phenomenon, both interesting and unfortunate, should alert you to the fact that the language of statistics is as important as its methodology. It is interesting because of the contradictions in meaning to which it may lead. Incorrect expressions such as those just cited have a tendency to shoot themselves in the foot. They often do not describe the real world. It is unfortunate because the correct use of statistical language is far from becoming a major topic of discussion or part of the curriculum in formal statistics courses, a situation that can be easily remedied if the world of statisticians was more aware.

Because of the widespread and long-time use of such unfortunate phrases, it becomes very difficult to change one's habits of expression. After all, some of the most prestigious writers have used those phrases, although their use implies that the reader or practitioner knows what is actually meant in the statistical sense. Not so. Many quality practitioners are unaware that they misstate statistical conclusions. A few more examples of inappropriate language will be discussed.

Example 1. "The sample of 50 shows that the true average is 107.4 milligrams."

This statement appears innocent enough, but it really reflects some confusion between a population parameter and a sample statistic. Sample statistics, such as a sample average, have the annoying habit of being variable. Had we obtained another (random) sample of 50 items, the sample result would likely be different from 107.4 milligrams. Therefore, to declare that the sample result at hand *is* the *true* average for the entire population is ludicrous, absurd, and ridiculous. We do not know what the true population mean is; we sample in order to get some idea of what it is—that is, an estimate.

The statistically correct statement should read, simply and honestly, "The sample average is 107.4 milligrams." Alternatively, we might say that "The sample average of 107.4 milligrams is our *estimate* of the population average," recognizing that it is, probably, not the truth. To make the relationship between sample statistic and population parameter more clear, it is recommended that the result be written

$$\overline{X} = 107.4 \text{ mg} = \text{Est. of } \mu. \tag{26.1}$$

Equation (26.1) tells it like it is.

Example 2. "This histogram is a normal curve."

Once again, there is confusion between a sample and a population. The normal curve is a mathematical model that exhibits perfect symmetry, a bell-shaped appearance, and perfect smoothness. The histogram, obtained from sample data, can never exhibit all of those characteristics, no matter how small the interval of measurement is.

The statistically correct statement should read, simply and honestly, "It appears that a normal curve might be a suitable model for the process." Nothing more, nothing less.

Example 3. "The table of areas under the normal curve shows that 10.38% will exceed specifications."

You learned in Chapter 16 how to estimate the area under a normal curve. You calculated a sample statistic called Z, which is the number of standard deviations that the point in question is away from the mean. You used the sample mean and sample standard deviation to estimate Z. Then you referred that value of Z to a table of areas under the standard normal curve and picked off the tabular value to four decimal places, which you converted to percent.

Because you *estimated* two parameters (the mean and the standard deviation) from sample data, and because you *assumed* that the true model for the process was a normal curve, there is no way that you can determine the percentage exceeding specifications (the area under the curve) to the nearest one-hundredth of one percent. Therefore you were urged to round your answer and to use the uncertain but properly guarded word "about."

The statistically correct statement should read, simply and honestly, "About 10 percent will exceed specifications." The same decision about the process will be made, whatever it is, with this correctly guarded statement as that you would have made with the tongue-in-cheek, fingers-crossed statement of percent area carried to two decimal places.

26.5 Summary

Learning SPC requires the learning of statistics. Any one of several organizational departments can assume responsibility for SPC training, but the content and level of training should be geared to different levels of employees. Because of the general perception of statistics as a dull and difficult subject, competent instructors must be used. A number of principles of learning and teaching were presented. A basic course outline was suggested that featured the logical sequence of concepts, the use of real data, the team approach, overnight assignments, and team presentations. SPC training in the secondary and post-secondary schools is being pursued by VICA, an organization of students and instructors, that has prepared a TQM curriculum being tested in an extensive pilot study. Learning to state statistical conclusions meaningfully, generally neglected in formal statistics courses, is an important part of SPC training. Several examples of incorrectly worded statements were given together with their correct phrasing.

We are faced with insurmountable opportunities.
When you come to the fork in the road, take it.

—Yogi Berra

CHAPTER 27

Where Do We Go from Here?

Your goal is now twofold: to use the techniques learned in this book so that you can improve your processes continually and to be inspired to pursue your statistical education further.

Invariably processes that are studied for the first time do not appear to be in statistical control because of the presence of special causes. The SPC tools presented in this book are designed to differentiate between the common causes and the special causes so that the latter can be identified and removed if they are undesirable.

To bring a process into statistical control is no small task. It is a proud accomplishment, a team effort that brings into play the knowledge and experience of those familiar with the process. Detection of special causes often starts with hunches based on experience—and there is nothing wrong with human beings using their mental powers of absorbing thousands of signals called experiences, integrating them in their minds, and sorting them out logically into a reasonable solution called a hunch. If the hunch is on target, the process usually can be brought into statistical control.

If the hunch does not turn out to be the elusive special cause, it usually means that the process is more complex than was originally thought. The process may be a chemically dependent one where there is an unknown relationship between and among the recognized variables that affect the process, further adding to the complexity of the process. Such relationships are called interactions, and sometimes they are difficult to identify and measure without conducting special studies called *designed experiments.*

On the other hand, the process may be affected by many heretofore unknown variables, and the hunch as to which one is the culprit becomes a very wild guess. The search for the special cause, in this case, becomes a detective story whose solution might elude the logical powers of a Sherlock Holmes. What would you do if you were no more talented than, say, Dr. Watson, and Mr. Holmes was not available? Well, once again we might resort to conducting designed experiments.

Let us suppose that we have, indeed, been able to identify the special- cause culprit and have removed it from our process and brought the process into statistical control. Is our work done then? Should we be satisfied with a pleasant reduction in variability, which we learned is identified with improvement? Let us be curious. Since the process is in statistical control, we can next determine its capability for meeting specifications.

What happens if we find that the process is not capable, that its inherent variability is too great to be able to meet specifications? Recall from Chapter 23 that we had some alternatives when the process is not capable. Suppose that the only reasonable alternative open to us is to change the process. Whatever factor or characteristic is changed, the change must result in reduced variability in the process. What should be changed? Everyone involved is likely to offer some suggestions as to which factor to choose. Whose suggestion prevails? You know who that is: the one with the highest rank!

But that's not fair. Other suggestions can be just as good, perhaps even better. The resolution of this minor disagreement and possible confrontation is to put the several suggestions to bed by conducting, once again, designed experiments. Through designed experiments the several factors can be tested in a methodical and orderly way to determine which, if any, will improve the process.

If we determine that changing one or more factors can improve the process, then management will have to step in and exercise authority to approve the change in the process. The change could be costly, such as replacing a piece of capital equipment, or changing the raw material and supplier, or altering the entire configuration of the production line, or retraining all of the involved personnel. It is obvious that making a change in the process that alters the basic process will involve some costs. *It is imperative, therefore, that when it comes to changing the process to improve it, management must be involved.*

It should be apparent by now that there is a collection of powerful tools that go beyond SPC called *designed experimentation,* or *design of experiments (DOE).* These tools, considered advanced to many, are based on statistical principles of sampling, variability, modeling, and analysis. DOE is beyond the scope of this book, but you are encouraged to explore that topic.

Some people insist that real process improvement comes only when the process is basically modified in some way, not simply by removing nasty special causes that don't belong there in the first place. A process brought into statistical control, it is asserted, does not represent genuine improvement. There is some validity to this assertion. But events are relative, and our perceptions are what are real and genuine to us. Our perceptions direct our lives. Processes brought into statistical control exhibit reduced variability; that's the signature of improvement.

Keep two critical points in mind. One is that attempts at process improvement are most effective when the process is brought into statistical control. The second point is that improvement in a process should be a many splendored thing, involving all people and going on all the time as a way of life, whether the life is in manufacturing, in the service industry, or in administration. Continuous quality improvement, directed toward customer delight, will result in higher productivity and lower costs. These are the stepping stones to world-class quality.

This book closes with a Calvin and Hobbes cartoon, the author's favorite series. Calvin has caught the essence of statistics and designed experimentation (see Figure 27.1).

Calvin and Hobbes   by Bill Watterson

Figure 27.1. Calvin and Hobbes.

Some Useful Tables and Graphs

Table 1A. Areas Under the Standard Normal Curve (Z = 0.00 to 3.89. *Areas to four decimal places*)

Enter table with Z value (positive or negative) to two decimal places (hundredths). First decimal-place figure (tenths) is in the first column. Second decimal-place figure (hundredths) is in a column heading. For Z *positive*, tabular area is in the *right tail*. For Z *negative*, tabular area is in the *left tail*.

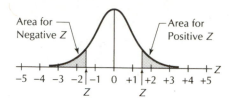

Z (tenths)	.00	.01	.02	.03	.04	.05	.06	.07	.08	.09
					TAIL AREA					
0.0	.5000	.4960	.4920	.4880	.4840	.4801	.4761	.4721	.4681	.4641
0.1	.4602	.4562	.4522	.4483	.4443	.4404	.4364	.4325	.4286	.4247
0.2	.4207	.4168	.4129	.4090	.4052	.4013	.3974	.3936	.3897	.3859
0.3	.3821	.3783	.3745	.3707	.3669	.3632	.3594	.3557	.3520	.3483
0.4	.3446	.3409	.3372	.3336	.3300	.3264	.3228	.3192	.3156	.3121
0.5	.3085	.3050	.3015	.2981	.2946	.2912	.2877	.2843	.2810	.2776
0.6	.2743	.2709	.2676	.2643	.2611	.2578	.2546	.2514	.2483	.2451
0.7	.2420	.2389	.2358	.2327	.2297	.2266	.2236	.2207	.2177	.2148
0.8	.2119	.2090	.2061	.2033	.2005	.1977	.1949	.1922	.1894	.1867
0.9	.1841	.1814	.1788	.1762	.1736	.1711	.1685	.1660	.1635	.1611
1.0	.1587	.1562	.1539	.1515	.1492	.1469	.1446	.1423	.1401	.1379
1.1	.1357	.1335	.1314	.1292	.1271	.1251	.1230	.1210	.1190	.1170
1.2	.1151	.1131	.1112	.1093	.1075	.1057	.1038	.1020	.1003	.0985
1.3	.0968	.0951	.0934	.0918	.0901	.0885	.0869	.0853	.0838	.0823
1.4	.0808	.0793	.0778	.0764	.0749	.0735	.0721	.0708	.0694	.0681
1.5	.0668	.0655	.0643	.0630	.0618	.0606	.0594	.0582	.0571	.0559
1.6	.0548	.0537	.0526	.0516	.0505	.0495	.0485	.0475	.0465	.0455
1.7	.0446	.0436	.0427	.0418	.0409	.0401	.0392	.0384	.0375	.0367
1.8	.0359	.0351	.0344	.0336	.0329	.0322	.0314	.0307	.0301	.0294
1.9	.0287	.0281	.0274	.0268	.0262	.0256	.0250	.0244	.0239	.0233
2.0	.0228	.0222	.0217	.0212	.0207	.0202	.0197	.0192	.0188	.0183
2.1	.0179	.0174	.0170	.0166	.0162	.0158	.0154	.0150	.0146	.0143
2.2	.0139	.0136	.0132	.0129	.0125	.0122	.0119	.0116	.0113	.0110
2.3	.0107	.0104	.0102	.0099	.0096	.0094	.0091	.0089	.0087	.0084
2.4	.0082	.0080	.0078	.0075	.0073	.0071	.0069	.0068	.0066	.0064
2.5	.0062	.0060	.0059	.0057	.0055	.0054	.0052	.0051	.0049	.0048
2.6	.0047	.0045	.0044	.0043	.0041	.0040	.0039	.0038	.0037	.0036
2.7	.0035	.0034	.0033	.0032	.0031	.0030	.0029	.0028	.0027	.0026
2.8	.0026	.0025	.0024	.0023	.0023	.0022	.0021	.0021	.0020	.0019
2.9	.0019	.0018	.0017	.0017	.0016	.0016	.0015	.0015	.0014	.0014
3.0	.0014	.0013	.0013	.0012	.0012	.0011	.0011	.0011	.0010	.0010
3.1	.0010	.0009	.0009	.0009	.0008	.0008	.0008	.0008	.0007	.0007
3.2	.0007	.0007	.0006	.0006	.0006	.0006	.0006	.0005	.0005	.0005
3.3	.0005	.0005	.0005	.0004	.0004	.0004	.0004	.0004	.0004	.0004
3.4	.0003	.0003	.0003	.0003	.0003	.0003	.0003	.0003	.0003	.0002

3.50 to 3.61: **Area = .0002.**
3.62 to 3.89: **Area = .0001.**

(Table continues on next page)

Example: If Z = -1.96, area in *left* tail = .0250.

Table 1B. Areas Under the Standard Normal Curve (Z = 3.90 to 4.90. Areas to six decimal places)

Z (tenths)	.00	.01	.02	.03	.04	.05	.06	.07	.08	.09
					TAIL AREA					
3.9	.000048	.000046	.000044	.000043	.000041	.000039	.000038	.000036	.000035	.000033
4.0	.000032	.000030	.000029	.000028	.000027	.000026	.000025	.000024	.000023	.000022
4.1	.000021	.000020	.000019	.000018	.000017	.000017	.000016	.000015	.000015	.000014
4.2	.000013	.000013	.000012	.000012	.000011	.000011	.000010	.000010	.000009	.000009
4.3	.000009	.000008	.000008	.000008	.000007	.000007	.000007	.000006	.000006	.000006
4.4	.000005	.000005	.000005	.000005	.000005	.000004	.000004	.000004	.000004	.000004
4.5	.000003	.000003	.000003	.000003	.000003	.000003	.000003	.000002	.000002	.000002
4.6	.000002	.000002	.000002	.000002	.000002	.000002	.000002	.000002	.000001	.000001
4.7	.000001	.000001	.000001	.000001	.000001	.000001	.000001	.000001	.000001	.000001
4.8	.000001	.000001	.000001	.000001	.000001	.000001	.000001	.000001	.000001	.000001
4.9	ZERO									

Commonly Used Tail Areas
and Their Corresponding Values of Z

Area	Z (+ or −)
.1000	1.282
.0500	1.645
.0250	1.960
.0100	2.327
.0050	2.576
.0010	3.090

Note: The Z value for any point X on the base scale is the number of standard deviations that the point is away from the mean. In formula form,

Z value for any Point = (Point − Mean)/Standard deviation

or

$$Z_x = \frac{X - \mu}{\sigma_x}$$

If X is to the left of the mean, its corresponding Z value is negative.

If X is to the right of the mean, its corresponding Z value is positive.

Table 2. Factors for Variables Control Charts

Subgroup Sample Size n	$\overline{X}$ (Average) Chart		$\tilde{X}$ (Median) Chart	R (Range) Chart		S (Std. Dev.) Chart		Factors for Estimating Process σ_x	
	Using $\overline{R}$	Using $\overline{S}$	Using $\overline{R}$	Using $\overline{R}$		Using $\overline{S}$		Using $\overline{R}$	Using $\overline{S}$
	A_2	A_3	A_6	D_3	D_4	B_3	B_4	d_2	c_4
2	1.880	2.659		0	3.267	0	3.267	1.128	.7979
3	1.023	1.954	1.187	0	2.575	0	2.568	1.693	.8862
4	.729	1.628		0	2.282	0	2.266	2.059	.9213
5	.577	1.427	.691	0	2.114	0	2.089	2.326	.9400
6	.483	1.287		0	2.004	.030	1.970	2.534	.9515
7	.419	1.182	.509	.076	1.924	.118	1.882	2.704	.9594
8	.373	1.099		.136	1.864	.185	1.815	2.847	.9650
9	.337	1.032	.412	.184	1.816	.239	1.761	2.970	.9693
10	.308	.975		.223	1.777	.284	1.716	3.078	.9727
11	.285	.927	.350	.256	1.744	.321	1.679	3.173	.9754
12	.266	.886		.283	1.717	.354	1.646	3.258	.9776
13	.249	.850		.307	1.693	.382	1.618	3.336	.9794
14	.235	.817		.328	1.672	.406	1.594	3.407	.9810
15	.223	.789		.347	1.653	.428	1.572	3.472	.9823
16	.212	.763		.363	1.637	.448	1.552	3.532	.9835
17	.203	.739		.378	1.622	.466	1.534	3.588	.9845
18	.194	.718		.391	1.609	.482	1.518	3.640	.9854
19	.187	.698		.404	1.596	.497	1.503	3.689	.9862
20	.180	.680		.415	1.585	.510	1.490	3.735	.9869

Formulas in Which Factors Are Used

	$\overline{X}$ (Average) Chart		$\tilde{X}$ (Median) Chart	R (Range) Chart	S (Std. Dev.) Chart	Estimating σ_x	
UCL:	$\overline{\overline{X}} + A_2\overline{R}$	$\overline{\overline{X}} + A_3\overline{S}$	$\tilde{\overline{X}} + A_6\overline{R}$	$D_4\overline{R}$	$B_4\overline{S}$	$\dfrac{\overline{R}}{d_2}$	$\dfrac{\overline{S}}{c_4}$
LCL:	$\overline{\overline{X}} - A_2\overline{R}$	$\overline{\overline{X}} - A_3\overline{S}$	$\tilde{\overline{X}} - A_6\overline{R}$	$D_3\overline{R}$	$B_3\overline{S}$		

All values, except A_6, from ASTM Manual #7, *Manual on Presentation of Data and Control Chart Analysis: 6th Edition*, Table 49, p. 91, 1992, by kind permission of the American Society for Testing and Materials, Philadelphia. Factor A_6 from L. S. Nelson, "Control Charts for Medians," *Journal of Quality Technology*, October 1982, p. 226.

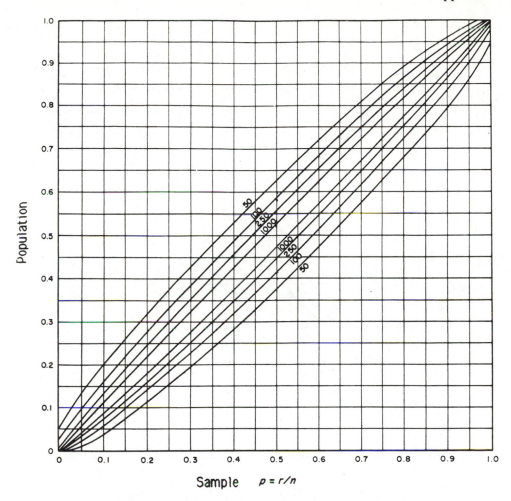

Graph 1A. Two-sided 90% confidence belts for proportions.

Reproduced from M. G. Natrella, *Experimental Statistics, Handbook 91*, National Bureau of Standards, U.S. Department of Commerce, U.S. Government Printing Office, August 1963, pp. T-45–T-47.

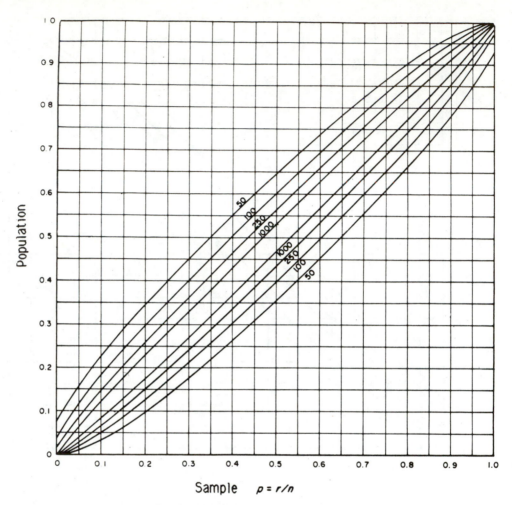

Graph 1B. Two-sided 95% confidence belts for proportions.

Reproduced from M. G. Natrella, *Experimental Statistics, Handbook 91*, National Bureau of Standards, U.S. Department of Commerce, U.S. Government Printing Office, August 1963, pp. T-45–T-47.

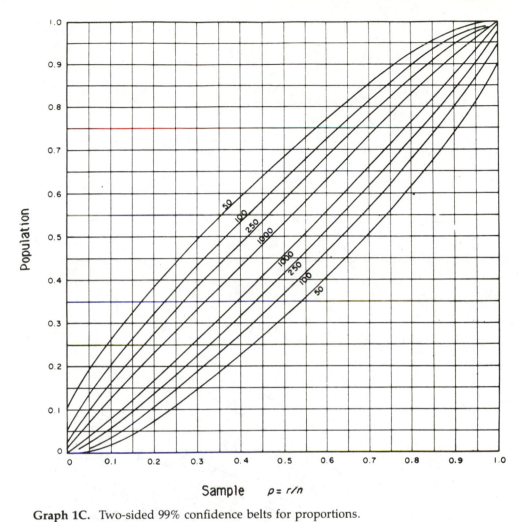

Graph 1C. Two-sided 99% confidence belts for proportions.

Reproduced from M. G. Natrella, *Experimental Statistics, Handbook 91*, National Bureau of Standards, U.S. Dept. of Commerce, U.S. Government Printing Office, August 1963, pp. T-45–T-47.

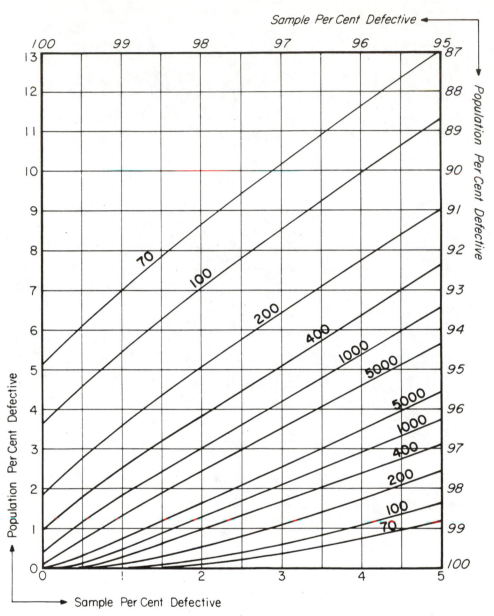

Graph 2A. Two-sided 95% confidence belts for small percentages.

From L. S. Nelson, "Confidence Belts for Small Percentages," *Journal of Quality Technology,* American Society for Quality Control, Milwaukee, Vol 13, No. 3, July 1981, pp. 216–217. Reprinted with kind permission.

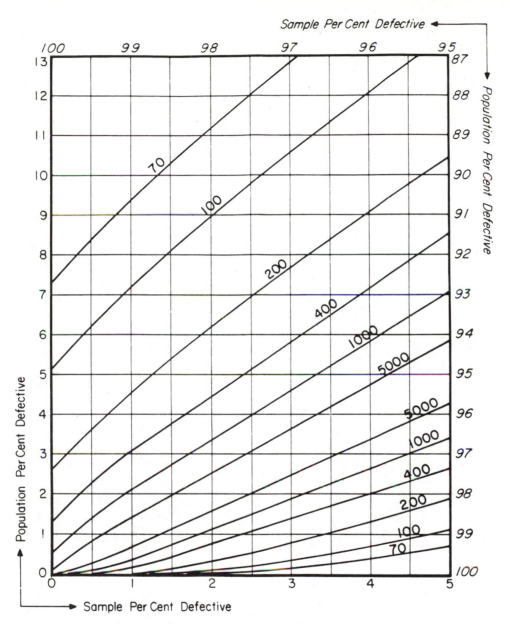

Graph 2B. Two-sided 99% confidence belts for small percentages.

From L. S. Nelson, "Confidence Belts for Small Percentages," *Journal of Quality Technology*, American Society for Quality Control, Milwaukee, July 1981, Vol. 13, No. 3, pp. 216–217. Reprinted with kind permission.

Acceptable quality level (AQL) – Designated value of percent defective (or defects per hundred units) that will be accepted most of the time by the acceptance sampling plan to be used. Also, considered satisfactory as a process average. The AQL alone does not describe the protection afforded by the plan; protection is described by the operating characteristic (OC) curve.

Acceptance sampling plan – Specific plan for sampling and making a decision about a lot or series of lots. The plan includes the sample size and the criteria for making a decision of acceptance or nonacceptance.

Alpha risk – Risk or probability of rejecting good lots. Also, probability of saying process is not in statistical control when it is. Designated by the Greek letter *alpha*.

ANSI – American National Standards Institute.

ASQC – American Society for Quality Control.

Assignable cause – Factor in a process that causes the process to behave in a nonrandom fashion. Also called a *special cause* or *nonrandom cause*.

Attribute – Characteristic that a unit or sample of product either has or does not have, such as OK or not OK. Not variable data.

Average – Commonly used to designate the arithmetic mean.

Average outgoing quality (AOQ) – Average, or overall, percent defective (nonconforming) of lots consisting of those lots that have been accepted by the acceptance sampling plan plus those lots that have not been accepted by the sampling plan and have been sorted 100% to remove or replace all defective (nonconforming) units.

Average outgoing quality limit (AOQL) – Maximum or limit of average outgoing quality. *Caution:* Individual lots may be accepted that exceed the AOQL percent defective.

Beta risk – Risk or probability of accepting bad lots. Also, probability of not rejecting an alternate hypotheses. Designated by the Greek letter *beta*.

Binomial distribution – Probability distribution used to describe the chance distribution of attribute data, such as defectives, where the quality state is one of two possible ones: OK or not OK, yes or no, go or no-go. The calculation of probabilities for large sample sizes is difficult and often requires the use of extensive tables or computers.

c-chart – Number of defects (nonconformities) control chart. Simple count of nonconformities in a constant sample size.

Capability index – One of several statistical measures that identify the ability of a process to meet prevailing specifications. Popular indexes include C_p, C_{pk}, and C_{pm}.

Capability ratio (CR) – Percentage of the specification spread occupied by the process spread. Inverse of the capability index C_p multiplied by 100.

Cause-and-effect diagram – Diagram used to help identify possible causes of a condition or symptom. It relates main causes and secondary causes. Usually developed from a brainstorming session. Sometimes referred to as the Ishikawa diagram, after its developer Dr. Kaoru Ishikawa, or the Fishbone diagram, after its skeletal appearance.

Center line – Center line on a control chart. It may be determined from the actual data (called the *average*) or it may be set arbitrarily (called a *standard*).

Class interval – Grouping of data so that the frequency distribution, usually in the form of a histogram, can adequately describe the pattern of variation. Class intervals in a distribution are usually of equal length. From 6 to 20 intervals are generally adequate, depending on how much data there are; more data justify more intervals.

Coding – Method of simplifying original data so that calculations may be performed more easily and quickly. An effective method for coding is to subtract a constant (perhaps the mode) and then divide by the size of the class interval; this reduces the original data to signed integers, the simplest data format. The coding formula should be written down in order for decoding to be performed correctly, especially for the mean and standard deviation of the original data.

Common causes – Causes of variability that are inherent to a process and that affect all aspects of the process. Process variability can be reduced by action that has an impact on the common causes.

Conforming – Act of unit, item, or product that meets specifications.

Consumer – Ultimate user of a product or service.

Consumer's risk – Probability that lots of bad quality, such as *rejectable quality level (RQL)*, will be accepted by an acceptance sampling plan. Designated the *beta risk*.

Continuous improvement – Ongoing improvement of a product, process, or service through steady reduction of inherent variability.

Control charts – Graphical method for recording sample data from a process to determine if an assignable cause is present or if the standard (center line) has changed. Usually refer to Shewhart control charts. Charts for variables data include average, range, and standard deviation. Charts for attributes data include percent defective (nonconforming), number of defectives (nonconformances), and number of defects (nonconformities). Other types of charts are available.

Control limits – Decision lines on a control chart, which, if exceeded by the sample statistic, indicate the presence of an assignable (special) cause, or the process is not operating in statistical control, or the process is not operating at the level indicated by the center line on the control chart.

Customer – Recipient of a product or service. Either internal (within a company) or external.

Customer delight – Happy state of a customer whose expectations for quality are far exceeded. Better than mere customer satisfaction, customer delight results in enthusiastic acclaim for a supplier's product or service.

Customer satisfaction – Satisfied state of a customer whose expectations have generally or merely been met. Not nearly as good as customer delight.

CuSum chart – Cumulative-sum control chart. Plotted value is the cumulated sum of the deviations of consecutive samples from some target value. Usually designated CuSum. Useful in detecting small but sustained shifts in process levels, depicted as changes in the slope of plotted points. A *V*-mask is used to detect significant changes in slope.

Data – Collection of numerical information that constitutes statistical evidence. The word *data* is plural and takes a plural verb and modifier. The singular form of data is *datum*.

Decoding – Method for converting coded data back to their original form. The decoding formulas should be written down, especially those for finding the mean and standard deviation of the original data.

Defect – Characteristic of a product that is considered undesirable from some point of view. Officially called *nonconformity* by ANSI. Defects may be classified by degree of seriousness as critical, major, minor, and incidental.

Defective – Short for *defective unit*. Unit of product that has one or more defects. Officially called *nonconformance* or *nonconforming unit* by ANSI.

Designed experiment – Formal procedure for conducting an experiment that includes certain important statistical principles of identifying factors, levels, and responses, sampling procedures, randomization, replication, data summarization, data analysis, and interpretation. A necessary activity for improving a process beyond statistical control. Sometimes designated D/E, or DOE for design of experiments.

EWMA chart – Exponentially weighted moving-average control chart. Uses all previous historical chart data, weights them according to their "age," then uses this information to forecast the next sample result using a mathematical formula. Useful for detecting slowly drifting means.

Fishbone diagram – *See* Cause-and-effect diagram.

Flow chart – Diagram that shows the progress of work or flow of materials or information through a sequence of step-by-step operations.

Frequency – Number of times that a particular reading, measurement, or observation occurs. A *frequency distribution* gives a graphic picture of the pattern of variation of a set of data.

Go/no go – Two-state condition of an attribute characteristic. Type of gauge that distinguishes between a unit meeting specifications (go) and not meeting specifications (no go). Also referred to as OK/not OK and yes/no.

Histogram – Graphic summary of a frequency distribution by class intervals. Series of vertically drawn rectangles whose widths correspond to the size of the class intervals and whose heights are proportional to frequencies occurring in each interval.

In control – Reference to an industrial process. Technically it means *in statistical control* or behaving in a random fashion, devoid of assignable causes, stable, predictable, doing its best, as determined by a control chart. Often misused or misunderstood to imply that the process is operating within specification limits, whereas specification limits have nothing to do with whether or not a process is in statistical control.

In statistical control – Correct expression to use.

Ishikawa diagram – *See* Cause-and-effect diagram. Named for its developer, Dr. Kaoru Ishikawa.

Lot tolerance percent defective (LTPD) – Designated value of percent defective (or defects per hundred units) in a lot that is considered bad and that a sampling plan should reject most of the time. Also called *rejectable quality level (RQL)* and *unacceptable quality level (UQL)*.

Lower control limit (LCL) – Lower limit on a control chart. Subscript identifies the type of control chart or sample statistic, such as $LCL_{\overline{X}}$, LCL_R, LCL_p, etc.

mR-chart – Moving-range control chart. Two or more consecutive single samples form a subgroup.

$m\overline{X}$-chart – Moving-average control chart. Two or more consecutive single samples form a subgroup.

Mean – Arithmetic mean, obtained by adding up all of the observations and dividing by the number of observations. Also called simply the *average*.

Median – Middle value in a set of data first arranged in order of magnitude. If there is an odd number of observations, the median is the unique middle one. If there is an even number of observations, the median is the average of the two middle ones.

Midpoint – Usually refers to the value that represents each class interval in a histogram. Determined by calculating the average of the interval limits (beginning and ending points).

Mode – Observation that occurs most frequently in a set of data. There may be more than one mode in a frequency distribution (*bimodal*, for example).

np-chart – Number-of-defectives control chart. Simple count of nonconforming units in a constant sample size.

Nonconformance, nonconforming, nonconformity – State of defectiveness, a defective unit, or a defect, respectively.

Nonrandom cause – *See* Assignable cause.

Normal curve – Particular mathematical distribution that is often used as a model to depict chance phenomena in nature, industry, and science, particularly for measurable or variable data. Also called the *bell curve* because of its shape, or the *Gaussian distribution* after the mathematician who discovered it. Total area under the normal curve represents 100% of the process or population. Areas under the normal curve between two points represent the proportion of product in the process or observations in a population that fall between the two points. Tables, calculators, and computers are available for this calculation.

Operating characteristic (OC) curve – Probability curve that describes how a sampling plan behaves for various levels of quality. Gives the probability that the plan will accept lots of specified quality levels. The OC curve must be known if one wishes to evaluate the effectiveness of a sampling plan.

Out of control – Reference to an industrial process. Technically it means *out of statistical control* or not behaving in a random fashion, not stable, not predictable, not doing its best, as determined by a control chart. Often misused or misunderstood to imply that the process is operating outside of specification limits, whereas specification limits have nothing to do with whether or not a process is out of statistical control.

Out of statistical control – Correct expression to use.

p-**chart** – Proportion or fraction defective control chart. Subgroup sample sizes may vary.

Parameter – In quality control work, a characteristic of a process or population, such as the mean, standard deviation, or percent defective. A constant value for the defined process or population, often unknown and usually estimated from sample data. Usually designated by a Greek letter.

Pareto principle – States that most effects come from relatively few causes. Named by J. M. Juran after Vilfredo Pareto, Italian economist. A *Pareto chart* arranges effects in order of magnitude so that the *vital few* causes can be isolated from the *trivial many*. Provides a strategy for selecting problems on which to work.

Poisson distribution – Probability distribution used to describe the chance distribution of defects. Also used to estimate the binomial distribution under certain conditions. Used in calculating probability of acceptance for acceptance sampling plans.

Population – Collection of similar items or units of product about which we wish to make a decision. Usually described in terms of space (physical location) and time. Also called lot, batch, process, shipment, pallet load, universe. Must be defined first in any problem-solving effort.

Process – *See* Population.

Process capability – Status of the ability of a process to meet prevailing specifications, measured in terms of its inherent variability devoid of assignable causes. Determined only after a process is brought into statistical control.

Process capability study is a statistical procedure to determine if a process that is in statistical control is capable of meeting the prevailing specification limits.

Producer's risk – Probability that lots of good quality, such as *acceptable quality level (AQL),* will be rejected by a sampling plan. Designated as the *alpha risk.*

Quality – (1) Conforming to customer requirements. (2) Fulfilling stated or implied needs. (3) Free of defects. (4) Characteristics that describe good performance of every function or operation in an organization. (5) Subjective. In the eyes of the beholder.

Quality assurance (QA) – That collection of activities and functions that are needed to assure that the quality of produced goods meets the company's and customers' standards for acceptance.

Quality control (QC) – That collection of activities and functions that are needed to assure that the quality of produced goods meets the company's and customers' standards for acceptance. Some people define *quality control* in a very limited sense to mean those procedures that are used to control or monitor quality only during manufacturing operations. Others assume a more comprehensive interpretation, from design engineering, to raw materials control, to in-process controls, to finished goods, through field service.

Quality function deployment – Deliberately planned activity to infuse customer requirements into every function or activity of an organization so that the "voice of the customer" is constantly heard.

R-chart – Range control chart. Analyzed first before a corresponding average chart is analyzed.

Random – Influenced by chance. A *random sample* is one in which every item in the population or process has an equal chance of being selected for the sample. A process that is in statistical control is presumed to be governed by factors behaving in a random manner. Formal procedures are available for getting random samples from a population or process; random numbers obtained from either a table or from a calculator are among the most popular. Most statistical methodology assumes that a random sample has been obtained. In real life, however, it is often difficult to obtain a true random sample; some compromises in sampling are usually practiced.

Range – Simple and popular measure of variability. Difference between the largest and smallest numbers in a set of data. In calculating the range, designated by R, the smallest number is subtracted from the largest number. The range, therefore, can never be negative, even if all of the numbers in the data set are negative. The range is very useful when the size of the data set or sample is small, usually 15 or less.

Rational subgroup – Method of sampling so that individual samples within a subgroup are produced under very similar conditions so that the probability of special causes occurring within a subgroup is minimized. This maximizes the probability of special causes occurring between subgroups and therefore their detection.

Regression and correlation – Statistical method for studying association between and among variables.

Rejectable quality level (RQL) – *See* Lot tolerance percent defective. "Bad" lots. An effective sampling plan should provide a low probability of accepting lots at the RQL. Usually expressed in percent defective or defects per hundred units.

Run – Sequence of seven or more consecutive points on a control chart, all on the same side of the center line, indicating the presence of a special cause or a shift in the process level.

Run chart – Charting of sample results, usually one sample observation at a time, in chronological sequence. Often a useful first step in a process study. Sometimes reveals unexpected process behavior.

S-chart – Standard deviation control chart. Analyzed first before a corresponding average chart is analyzed.

Sample – Portion of a population or process. The smallest sample size is one; the largest is the entire population and is called a *100% sample.*

Sample statistic – Data calculated from a sample of observations. Identifies the control chart in use.

Scatter diagram – Graphical method for depicting the relationship between two variables, between a dependent and an independent variable.

Sigma – Greek letter representing the population or process standard deviation.

Special cause – *See* Assignable cause.

Standard deviation – Measure of variability, more universal than the range. The word *deviation* refers to the distance of an observation in a set of data from the mean of the set of data. Standard deviation is a form of average deviation from the mean. Usually not clearly understood by almost all quality practitioners and has acquired, therefore, a sort of mystique; yet its logical evolution is meaningful and reflects common sense and rational thinking. Formulas for standard deviation differ between *population* and *sample*.

Statistical process control (SPC) – Set of tools, mostly statistical in nature, that are useful in helping to control a process; more particularly, to bring a process into statistical control. Often used interchangeably with *statistical quality control (SQC)*.

Subgroup – Sample consisting of two or more observations collected together for which sample statistics are determined.

Total quality management (TQM) – Management approach to improving quality performance in every function of an organization or company. Recognizes that all activities of an organization are interdependent, that quality is influenced by everything that goes on, and that quality improvement is everyone's responsibility, regardless of the task or assignment. Implemented in industry, business, government, services, schools, hospitals, etc.

Trend – Sequence of five or more consecutive points on a control chart, all going up or all going down, and all on the same side of the center line, indicating the presence of a special cause or a rise or fall, respectively, in the process level.

u-chart – Average number of defects-per-unit control chart. Also called $\bar{c}$-chart.

Unacceptable quality level (UQL) – *See* Lot tolerance percent defective.

Upper control limit (UCL) – Upper limit on a control chart. Subscript identifies the type of control chart and the sample statistic, such as $UCL_{\bar{x}}$, UCL_R, UCL_p, etc.

Variability – Characteristic of changes in measurements or observations. Sometimes called *variation*. Reducing the variability in a process is considered a sign of process improvement, the ultimate objective in product and process improvement. Causes of variability are sometimes difficult to identify conclusively. Sophisticated statistical methods are used for that purpose, such as control charts and designed experimentation.

Variable – Measure that reflects numbers on a continuous scale, such as a measuring tape of distance or a scale of weights.

Variance – Square of the standard deviation.

Vital few, trivial many – Causes that are important and not important, respectively, to explain effects or symptoms. Terms used by J. M. Juran to describe the Pareto principle.

V-mask – Device placed on a CuSum control chart to detect significant changes in the slope of consecutively plotted points. Changes in slope identify changes in process mean.

X-chart – Individuals control chart.

$\overline{X}$-chart – X-bar control chart for averages.

$\tilde{X}$-chart – Median control chart.

of SPC Symbols and Formulas

α – Lowercase Greek letter *alpha*. Designates producer's risk in an acceptance sampling plan. Risk of rejecting good lots. Probability of rejecting the null hypothesis when it is true.

A_2 – (A-sub-2) Constant used to calculate upper and lower control limits for an X-bar control chart using R-bar: $\bar{\bar{X}} \pm A_2\bar{R}$. ($X$-double bar) $\pm$ (A-sub-2) times (R-bar). Also, $A_2 = 3/d_2\sqrt{n}$.

A_3 – (A-sub-3) Constant used to calculate upper and lower control limits for an X-bar control chart using S-bar: $\bar{\bar{X}} \pm A_3\bar{S}$. ($X$-double bar) $\pm$ (A-sub-3) times (S-bar).

A_6 – (A-sub-6) Constant used to calculate upper and lower control limits for a median control chart using R-bar: $\bar{\tilde{X}} \pm A_6\bar{R}$. (Average median) $\pm$ (A-sub-6) times (R-bar).

AOQ – Average Outgoing Quality.

AOQL – Average Outgoing Quality Limit.

AQL – Acceptable Quality Level.

β – Lowercase Greek letter *beta*. Designates consumer's risk in an acceptance sampling plan. Risk of accepting bad lots. Probability of not rejecting an alternate hypothesis.

B_3 – (B-sub-3) Constant used to calculate lower control limit for an S-chart using S-bar: $\text{LCL}_S = B_3\bar{S}$. ($B$-sub-3) times ($S$-bar).

B_4 – (B-sub-4) Constant used to calculate upper control limit for an S-chart using S-bar: $\text{UCL}_S = B_4\bar{S}$. ($B$-sub-4) times ($S$-bar).

c – Number of defects (nonconformities) in a sample. Simple count of nonconformities. Also, acceptance number of defectives in an acceptance sampling plan. The lot may be accepted if there are c or fewer defectives (nonconformances) in the sample.

c_4 – (c-sub-4) Factor used to estimate process standard deviation from the average sample standard deviation S-bar. $\bar{S}/c_4 = $ Est. of σ. (S-bar over c-sub-4).

$\overline{c}$ – (c-bar) Average number of defects (nonconformities) per sample in a group of samples. Same as u. Center line for a c-chart.

$\overline{\overline{c}}$ – (c-double-bar) Average number of defects (nonconformities) per item or unit. Same as $\overline{u}$ (u-bar). Center line for a c-bar chart or u-chart.

C_p – Capability index. Ratio of specification spread to six standard deviations.

$$C_p = (\text{Spec spread})/6\sigma.$$

C_{pk} – Capability index. Ratio of positive difference between mean and nearest specification limit to three standard deviations. Considers proximity of process mean to specification limits.

$$C_{pk} = |\mu - \text{Nearest spec limit}|/3\sigma.$$

C_{pm} – Capability index. Ratio of specification spread to a measure of proximity of process mean to a designated target T. Called *Taguchi capability index*.

$$C_{pm} = (\text{Spec spread})/6\sqrt{\sigma^2 + (\mu - T)^2}.$$

d_2 – (d-sub-2) Factor used to estimate process standard deviation from the average sample range R-bar. $\overline{R}/d_2$ = Est. of σ. (R-bar) divided by (d-sub-2).

D_3 – (D-sub-3) Factor used to calculate the lower control limit for a range control chart. $\text{LCL}_R = D_3\overline{R}$. (D-sub-3) times (R-bar).

D_4 – (D-sub-4) Factor used to calculate the upper control limit for a range control chart. $\text{UCL}_R = D_4\overline{R}$. (D-sub-4) times (R-bar).

f – Frequency. Number of times a particular observation occurs in a set of data, such as in an interval.

LCL – Lower Control Limit on a control chart. Subscript identifies the kind of chart and the sample statistic plotted on the chart, such as $\text{LCL}_{\overline{X}}$, LCL_R, LCL_p, etc.

LTPD – Lot Tolerance Percent Defective.

μ – Lowercase Greek letter *mu*. Designates the mean of the population, process, or lot.

mR – Moving range. Two or more consecutive single-sample observations form a subgroup.

$m\overline{R}$ – Average of moving ranges. Center line for a moving-range control chart.

$m\overline{X}$ – Moving average. Two or more consecutive single-sample observations form a subgroup.

$m\overline{\overline{X}}$ – Average of moving averages. Center line for a moving-average control chart.

n – Number of items or observations in a sample. Sample size.

N – Number of items or observations in a population, process, or lot. Lot size.

np – Number of defective items or units (nonconformances) in a sample of size n.

$n\overline{p}$ – Average number of defective items or units (nonconformances) in a series of samples of size n. Center line for an np-chart.

np' – (n times p-prime) Expected number of defective items or units (nonconformances) in a sample of n items coming from a population or lot whose proportion or fraction defective (nonconforming) is p'.

OC – Operating Characteristic. An OC curve describes how an acceptance sampling plan behaves for lots of various levels of quality.

p – Proportion or fraction defective (nonconforming) in a sample.

$\overline{p}$ – (p-bar) Average proportion or fraction defective (nonconforming) in a group of samples. Center line for a p-chart. $\overline{p}$ = Total number of defective items/ Total sample size.

p' – (p-prime) Proportion or fraction defective (nonconforming) in a population, process, or lot.

P_a – (P-sub-a) Probability of accepting lots of a given quality level in an acceptance sampling plan.

QA – Quality assurance.

QC – Quality control.

r – Rejection number in an acceptance sampling plan. The lot may be rejected (not accepted) if there are r or more defectives in the sample. Also, sample correlation coefficient.

R – Range in a sample set of observations. Difference between the largest and smallest observations. Never negative; always positive or zero. Also, multiple correlation coefficient.

$\overline{R}$ – (R-bar) Average range of a set of ranges (all based on the same sample size). Center line for a range chart.

RQL – Rejectable Quality Level. "Bad" lots. An effective sampling plan shoul provide a low probability of accepting lots at the RQL. Usually expressed i percent defective or defects per hundred units.

Σ – Uppercase Greek letter *sigma*. Summation sign. Designates arithmetic opera tion of summing (adding) the observations.

σ – Lowercase Greek letter *sigma*. Designates standard deviation of individua items in a population, process, or lot. Also, σ_x (*sigma*-sub-x). Definitio formula:

$$\sigma = \sqrt{\frac{\Sigma(X - \mu)^2}{N}}$$

Calculation formulas (algebraically equivalent to the definition formula):

$$\sigma = \sqrt{\frac{N\Sigma X^2 - (\Sigma X)^2}{N^2}} = \sqrt{\frac{\Sigma X^2 - \frac{(\Sigma X)^2}{N}}{N}}$$

σ^2 – (*sigma*-squared) Population variance. Square of the population standard deviation. Also σ_x^2 (*sigma*-squared-sub-X). Definition formula:

$$\sigma^2 = \frac{\Sigma(X - \mu)^2}{N}$$

$\sigma_{\bar{x}}$ – (*sigma*-sub-x-bar) Population standard deviation of sample averages. Relationship between standard deviation of sample averages and standard deviation of individuals:

$$\sigma_{\bar{x}} = \frac{\sigma_x}{\sqrt{n}}$$

$\sigma_{\bar{x}}^2$ – (*sigma*-squared-sub-x-bar) Population variance of sample averages. Relationship between variance of sample averages and variance of individuals:

$$\sigma_{\bar{x}}^2 = \frac{\sigma_x^2}{n}$$

S – Sample standard deviation of individuals. Also S_x (S-sub-x). (Biased) estimate of the population standard deviation σ. S = Est. of σ. Definition formula:

$$S = \sqrt{\frac{\Sigma(X - \overline{X})^2}{n - 1}}$$

Preferred calculation formulas (algebraically equivalent to the definition formula):

$$S = \sqrt{\frac{n(\Sigma X^2) - (\Sigma X)^2}{n(n - 1)}} = \sqrt{\frac{\Sigma X^2 - \dfrac{(\Sigma X)^2}{n}}{n - 1}}.$$

S^2 – (S-squared) Sample variance of individuals. Square of the sample standard deviation. Unbiased estimate of the population variance σ^2. S^2 = Est. of σ^2.

$S_{\overline{x}}$ – (S-sub-x-bar) Sample standard deviation of sample averages. Estimate of the population standard deviation of sample averages $\sigma_{\overline{x}}$. Relationship to sample standard deviation of individuals:

$$S_{\overline{x}} = S/\sqrt{n} = \text{Est. of } \sigma_{\overline{x}}.$$

$S_{\overline{x}}^2$ – (S-squared-sub-x-bar) Sample variance of sample averages. Square of sample standard deviation of sample averages. Relationship to sample variance of individuals: $S_{\overline{x}}^2 = S^2/n$.

$\overline{S}$ – (S-bar) Average of sample standard deviations. Center line for an S-chart. Also, used to estimate process standard deviation with use of factor c_4: $\overline{S}/c_4$ = Est. of σ. (S-bar over c-sub-4).

SPC – Statistical process control.

$\sqrt{\ }$ – Square root sign. Square root of a number is another number whose square equals original number.

SQC – Statistical quality control.

u – Average number of defects (nonconformities) in a group of samples. Same as $\overline{c}$ (c-bar). Center line for a c-chart.

$\overline{u}$ – (u-bar) Average of a set of sample average numbers of defects (nonconformities). Same as $\overline{\overline{c}}$. Center line for a u-chart or c-bar chart.

UCL – Upper Control Limit on a control chart. Subscript identifies the kind of chart and the sample statistic plotted on the chart, such as $UCL_{\overline{X}}$, UCL_R, UCL_p, etc.

UQL – Unacceptable Quality Level. Same meaning as RQL and LTPD.

X – Designates collectively a set or group of data, observations, or measurements. Random variable.

$\overline{X}$ – (X-bar) Mean or average of sample data. Sample mean. Subgroup mean.

$\overline{\overline{X}}$ – (X-double-bar) Mean of a group of sample averages. Center line for an X-bar chart.

$\tilde{X}$ – Median of a set of observations. Middle value.

$\tilde{\tilde{X}}$ – Average of a set of medians. Center line for a median chart.

Z – Standardized normal variable. Number of standard deviations that a point (observation or measurement) is away from the mean. Definition formulas:

$$Z = \frac{X - \mu}{\sigma} \quad \text{(Normally distributed if } X \text{ is normally distributed.)}$$

$$Z = \frac{\overline{X} - \mu}{\sigma/\sqrt{n}} \quad \text{(Normally distributed since } \overline{X} \text{ is normally distributed.)}$$

NOTE: For a complete set of control limit formulas for control charts introduced in this book, please refer to the following sources:

Variables Charts: Table 2 of the Appendix.

Attributes Charts: Table 21.6 (Chapter 21) in the text.

BIBLIOGRAPHY

(Note: Because of the frequency with which it occurs in this bibliography, American Society for Quality Control, Milwaukee, will appear simply as ASQC.)

Basic Level Publications

Amsden, R. T., H. E. Butler, and D. M. Amsden, *SPC Simplified: Practical Steps to Quality*, UNIPUB/Kraus International, White Plains, New York, 1986.

ANSI/ASQC A1-1987, *Definitions, Symbols, Formulas, and Tables for Control Charts*, ASQC.

ANSI/ASQC B1-1985, *Guide for Quality Control Charts*, ASQC.

ANSI/ASQC B2-1985, *Control Chart Method of Analyzing Data*, ASQC.

ANSI/ASQC B3-1985, *Control Chart Method of Controlling Quality During Production*, ASQC.

ANSI/ASQC C1-1985, *Specifications of General Requirements for a Quality Program*, ASQC.

ASTM Manual No.7 on Presentation of Data and Control Chart Analysis, 6th ed., American Society for Testing and Materials, Philadelphia, 1990.

Ford Motor Company, *Q-101, Quality System Standard*, Product Quality Office, Dearborn, Michigan, 1983.

Gabor, A., *The Man Who Discovered Quality: How W. Edwards Deming Brought the Quality Revolution to America—The Stories of Ford, Xerox, and GM*, Random House, New York, 1990.

Henry, J. A., and L. A. Knowler, *Manual: Two-Day Intensive Training Course in Elementary Statistical Quality Control*, 2nd ed., Chicago Section, ASQC, Chicago, 1965.

Hollander, M., and F. Proschan, *The Statistical Exorcist: Dispelling Statistics Anxiety*, Marcel Dekker, New York, 1984.

Ishikawa, K., *Guide to Quality Control*, 2nd revised ed., Asian Productivity Organization, Tokyo, 1982. Available from UNIPUB/Kraus, White Plains, New York, 1986.

Kane, V. E., *Defect Prevention: Use of Simple Statistical Tools*, ASQC Quality Press, Milwaukee, 1989.

Kilian, C. S., *The World of W. Edwards Deming*, 2nd ed., SPC Press, Knoxville, Tennessee, 1992.

Knowler, L. A., J. M. Howell, B. K. Gold, E. P. Coleman, O. B. Moan, and W. C. Knowler, *Quality Control by Statistical Methods*, McGraw-Hill, New York, 1969.

Krishnamoorthi, K. S., *Quality Control for Operators and Foremen*, ASQC Quality Press, Milwaukee, 1989.

Kume, H., *Statistical Methods for Quality Improvement*, Association for Overseas Technical Scholarship, Tokyo, 1987.

Ott, E. R., *Process Quality Control*, McGraw-Hill, New York, 1975.

Ott, E. R., and E. G. Schilling, *Process Quality Control*, 2nd ed., McGraw-Hill, New York, 1990.

Pyzdek, T., *Pyzdek's Guide to SPC, Volume One: Fundamentals*, ASQC Quality Press, Milwaukee,1989.

Quality Control Training Manual, 2nd ed., State University of Iowa Section, ASQC, Iowa City, Iowa, 1965.

Schonberger, R. J., *World Class Manufacturing: The Lessons of Simplicity Applied*, The Free Press, New York, 1986.

Shewhart, W. A., *Economic Control of Quality of Manufactured Product*, Van Nostrand, New York, 1931. Reprinted by ASQC,1980.

———, *Statistical Method from the Viewpoint of Quality Control*, Dover Publications, Mineola, New York, 1986. Originally published 1939 by the Graduate School of the U. S. Dept. of Agriculture, Washington, D.C.

Tufte, E. R., *The Visual Display of Quantitative Information*, Graphics Press, Cheshire, Connecticut, 1983.

Western Electric Company, *Statistical Quality Control Handbook*, AT&T Technologies, Indianapolis, Indiana, 1982. Originally published 1956.

Intermediate Level Publications

AIAG, *Fundamental Statistical Process Control Reference Manual*, Automotive Industry Action Group, Southfield, Michigan, 1991.

ANSI/ASQC Z1.4-1981, *Sampling Procedures and Tables for Inspection by Attributes* (MIL-STD-105), ASQC. (Also U.S. Department of Defense, Washington, D. C.)

ANSI/ASQC Z1.9-1980, *Sampling Procedures and Tables for Inspection by Variables for Percent Nonconforming* (MIL-STD-414), ASQC.

Automotive Division, ASQC, *Statistical Process Control Manual*, ASQC Quality Press, Milwaukee, 1986. Originally published by General Motors.

Braverman, J. D., *Fundamentals of Statistical Quality Control*, Reston Publishing, Reston, Virginia, 1981.

Brush, G. G., *How to Choose the Proper Sample Size*, Vol.12, Statistics Division Basic References in Quality Control, ASQC Quality Press, Milwaukee, 1988.

Burr, I. W., *Elementary Statistical Quality Control*, Marcel Dekker, New York, 1979.

Carr, W. E., *Statistical Problem Solving*, ASQC Quality Press, Milwaukee, and Marcel Dekker, New York, 1992.

Chambers, J. M., W. S. Cleveland, B. Kleiner, and P. A. Tukey, *Graphical Methods for Data Analysis*, Bell Laboratories, Duxbury Press, Boston, 1983.

Cound, D. M., *A Leader's Journey to Quality*, ASQC Quality Press, Milwaukee, and Marcel Dekker, New York, 1992.

Deming, W. E., *Quality, Productivity, and Competitive Position*, Center for Advanced Engineering Study, MIT, Cambridge, Massachusetts, 1982.

———, *Out of the Crisis*, Center for Advanced Engineering Study, MIT, Cambridge, Massachusetts, 1986.

Dixon, W. J., and F. J. Massey, Jr., *Introduction to Statistical Analysis*, 3rd ed., McGraw-Hill, New York, 1969.

Duncan, A. J., *Quality Control and Industrial Statistics*, 5th ed., Richard D. Irwin, Homewood, Illinois, 1986.

Fellers, G., *SPC for Practitioners: Special Cases and Continuous Processes*, ASQC Quality Press, Milwaukee, 1991.

Ford Motor Company, *Continuing Process Control and Process Capability Improvement*, Statistical Methods Office, Dearborn, Michigan, December 1984.

Grant, E. L., and R. S. Leavenworth, *Statistical Quality Control*, 6th ed., McGraw-Hill, New York, 1988.

Griffith, G. K., *Statistical Process Control Methods for Long and Short Runs*, ASQC Quality Press, Milwaukee, 1989.

Hart, M. K., and R. F. Hart, *Quantitative Methods for Quality and Productivity Improvement*, ASQC Quality Press, Milwaukee, 1989.

Juran, J. M., and F. M. Gryna, editors, *Juran's Quality Control Handbook*, 4th ed., McGraw-Hill, New York, 1988.

———, *Quality Planning and Analysis*, 3rd ed., McGraw-Hill, New York, 1993.

Montgomery, D. C., *Introduction to Statistical Quality Control*, 2nd ed., John Wiley, New York, 1991.

Rand Corporation, *A Million Random Digits with 100,000 Normal Deviates*, The Free Press, Glencoe, Illinois. 1955.

Ryan, T. P., *Statistical Methods for Quality improvement*, John Wiley, New York, 1989.

Shapiro, S. S., *How to Test Normality and Other Distributional Assumptions*, Vol. 3, rev. ed., Statistics Division Basic References in Quality Control, ASQC Quality Press, Milwaukee, 1990.

Statistics Division, ASQC, *Glossary and Tables for Statistical Quality Control*, 2nd ed., ASQC Quality Press, Milwaukee, 1983.

Taguchi, G., *Introduction to Quality Engineering: Designing Quality into Products and Processes*, Asian Productivity Organization, Tokyo. Available through UNIPUB/Kraus International, White Plains, New York, 1986.

Wadsworth, H. M., K. S. Stephens, and A. B. Godfrey, *Modern Methods for Quality Control and Improvement*, John Wiley, New York, 1986.

Wetherill, G. B., and D. W. Brown, *Statistical Process Control*, Chapman and Hall, London, England, 1991.

Wheeler, D. J., *Understanding Statistical Process Control*, 2nd ed., SPC Press, Knoxville, Tennessee, 1992.

Advanced Level Publications

O'Connor, P. D. T., *Practical Reliability Engineering*, 2nd ed., ASQC Quality Press, Milwaukee, 1985.

Snedecor, G. W., and W. G. Cochran, *Statistical Methods*, 7th ed., Iowa State University Press, Ames, 1982.

Articles

Boyles, R. A., "The Taguchi Capability Index," *Journal of Quality Technology*, pp. 17–26, January 1991, ASQC.

Chan, L. K., S. W. Cheng, and F. A. Spiring, "A New Measure of Process Capability: C_{pm}," *Journal of Quality Technology*, pp. 162–175, July 1988, ASQC.

Clark, W. B., news article, *Milwaukee Sentinel*, January 11, 1993.

Cound, D. M., "Control: The Antithesis of Improvement," sidebar in *Chemical and Process Industries Division News*, p. 7, January 1988, ASQC.

Gunter, B. H., "The Use and Abuse of C_{pk}: Parts 1–4," *Quality Progress*, January, March, May, July 1989, ASQC.

———, "The Use and Abuse of C_{pk} Revisited," *Quality Progress*, pp. 90–94, January 1991, ASQC.

Heffernan, P. M., "New Measures of Spread and a Simpler Formula for the Normal Distribution," *The American Statistician*, pp. 100–102, May 1988, American Statistical Association.

Hunter, J. S., "The Exponentially Weighted Moving Average," *Journal of Quality Technology*, pp. 203–210, October 1986, ASQC.

Jaehn, A. H., "Improving QC Efficiency with Zone Control Charts," *41st Annual Quality Congress Transactions*, pp. 558–563, 1987, ASQC.

Kane, V. E., "Process Capability Indices," *Journal of Quality Technology*, p. 49, January 1986, ASQC.

Kendrick, J. J., "Five Baldrige Awards in Year Five," *Quality*, pp. 27–28, January 1993, Hitchcock Publishing Company, Carol Stream, Illinois.

Khamis, H. J., "Manual Computations—A Tool for Reinforcing Concepts and Techniques," *The American Statistician*, pp. 294–299, November 1991.

Kushler, R. H., and P. Hurley, "Confidence Bounds for Capability Indices," *Journal of Quality Technology*, pp. 188–195, October 1992, ASQC.

Nelson, L. S., "Technical Aids," in issues of the *Journal of Quality Technology* from January 1974 to date, ASQC.

Nelson, P. R., editorial, *Journal of Quality Technology*, p. 175, October 1992, ASQC.

NIST booklet, *1993 Award Criteria*, p. 14, Malcolm Baldrige National Quality Award, Gaithersburg, Maryland.

Pitt, H., "Statistical Jargon Spoken Here!" *45th Annual Quality Congress Transactions*, pp. 610–614, May 1991, ASQC.

———, "Standard Deviation, Plain and Simple," *42nd ASQC Annual Congress Transactions*, pp. 771–778, May 1988, ASQC.

———, "A Modern Strategy for Process Improvement," *Quality Progress*, pp. 22–28, May 1985, ASQC.

———, "Specifications: Laws or Guidelines?" *Quality Progress*, pp. 14–18, July 1981, ASQC.

———, "The Resampling Syndrome," *Quality Progress*, pp. 27–29, April 1978, ASQC.

———, "Pareto Revisited," *Quality Progress*, pp. 29–30, March 1974, ASQC.

Placek, C., "Baldrige Award as a Quality Model," *Quality*, pp. 17–20, February 1992, Hitchcock Publishing Company, Carol Stream, Illinois.

Reid, Jr., R. P., "America's Quality Revolution," *Quality*, pp. Q3–Q4, August 1985, Hitchcock Publishing Company, Carol Stream, Illinois.

Saturn automobile news item, *Milwaukee Sentinel*, January 8, 1993.

Shah, A. K. "A Simpler Approximation for Areas Under the Standard Normal Curve," *The American Statistician*, p. 80, February 1985, American Statistical Association.

Welch, J. F., "Service Quality Measurement at American Express Traveler's Cheque Group," *The Quality Management Forum*, pp. 8–11, Winter 1992, Newsletter of the Quality Management Division, ASQC.

Wolak, J., "Auto Industry Quality: What Are They Doing?" *Quality*, pp. 16–22, January 1993, Hitchcock Publishing Company, Carol Stream, Illinois.

Zaclewski, R. D., "Instructional Process Control," *Quality Progress*, pp. 61–64, January 1993, ASQC.

Periodicals

The American Statistician (quarterly), American Statistical Association, Alexandria, Virginia.

Annual Quality Congress Transactions, ASQC.

The Journal of Quality Technology (quarterly), ASQC.

Quality (monthly), Hitchcock Publishing Company, Carol Stream, Illinois.

Quality Progress (monthly), ASQC.

Technometrics (quarterly), ASQC, published jointly with the American Statistical Association.

INDEX

A

Absolute deviation from the mean, 106–7
Acceptance sampling plans, 26–28, 33–34
Accuracy, 360
American National Standard Institute (ANSI), 33n.2, 204n.4, 260n.1
American Society for Quality Control (ASQC), 33n.2, 164, 200, 204n.4, 260n.1, 354, 371
Arithmetic mean. *See* Mean
Assignable cause, 202, 202n.3
AT&T, 243
   Universal Card Services (UCS), 357, 362
Attribute(s)
   See also Confidence belts
   example of undesirable, 187–88
   examples of, 187
   versus variable data, 47n.5
Attributes control charts
   binomial distribution, and, 280–82
   c-charts, 204, 205, 261, 272–76
   defective/defective unit/defect, use of the terms, 204n.4, 259
   directional aspect of, 279–80
   formulas for, 285
   nonconformance/nonconforming unit/nonconformity, use of the terms, 204n.4, 260–61
   np-chart, 204, 205, 261, 271
   p-chart, 261, 262–70
   Poisson distribution and, 280–82
   types of, 204–5, 209, 261–62
   u-chart, 261, 276–79
Autocorrelation, 303
Automotive Industry Action Group (AIAG), 282, 357

B

Average
   See also Mean
   frequency histograms and, 48
Average control charts. *See* X-bar charts

Baldrige National Quality Award. *See* Malcolm Baldrige National Quality Award
Bar graph, 47n.5
Bell curve, 151
Bell-shaped curve, 151
Bimodal frequency histograms, 95
Binomial distribution, 190–91
   attributes control charts and, 280–82
   normal approximation to the, 194–96
Bloom, Benjamin S., 153n.2
Boyles, Russell A., 340, 341
Brainstorming, 21
Braverman, Jerry D., 43n.2
Brown, Don W., 312n.7
Brush, Gary G., 63n.3
Burr, Irving W., 43n.2

C

Calculators, 365–66
   normal distribution/curve and use of, 180–81
   standard deviation and use of, 111–12

P

Q